C000064334

BLASPHEMY IN THE CHRISTIAN WORLD

Blasphemy in the Christian World

A History

DAVID NASH

OXFORD

UNIVERSITY PRESS

Great Clarendon Street, Oxford OX2 6DP

Oxford University Press is a department of the University of Oxford.
It furthers the University's objective of excellence in research, scholarship,
and education by publishing worldwide in

Oxford New York

Auckland Cape Town Dar es Salaam Hong Kong Karachi
Kuala Lumpur Madrid Melbourne Mexico City Nairobi
New Delhi Shanghai Taipei Toronto

With offices in

Argentina Austria Brazil Chile Czech Republic France Greece
Guatemala Hungary Italy Japan Poland Portugal Singapore
South Korea Switzerland Thailand Turkey Ukraine Vietnam

Oxford is a registered trade mark of Oxford University Press
in the UK and in certain other countries

Published in the United States
by Oxford University Press Inc., New York

© David Nash 2007

The moral rights of the authors have been asserted
Database right Oxford University Press (maker)

First published 2007

All rights reserved. No part of this publication may be reproduced,
stored in a retrieval system, or transmitted, in any form or by any means,
without the prior permission in writing of Oxford University Press,
or as expressly permitted by law, or under terms agreed with the appropriate
reprographics rights organization. Enquiries concerning reproduction
outside the scope of the above should be sent to the Rights Department,
Oxford University Press, at the address above

You must not circulate this book in any other binding or cover
and you must impose the same condition on any acquirer

British Library Cataloguing in Publication Data

Data available

Library of Congress Cataloging in Publication Data

Data available

Typeset by Laserwords Private Limited, Chennai, India
Printed in Great Britain
on acid-free paper by
Biddles Ltd, King's Lynn, Norfolk

ISBN 978–0–19–925516–0

1 3 5 7 9 10 8 6 4 2

Acknowledgements

It is one of the paradoxes of the world of publishing that the responsibility for the authorship of books is located in one individual. Most books these days are not the product of a single lone scholar who has renounced the world for research. The reality can be more fragmented and pragmatic. Parts of this work would not have been completed without assistance in all areas of life from skilled librarianship through to trustworthy childcare.

My first debt is to my colleagues and institution. The former have all contributed in various supportive ways. I am especially indebted to Donal Lowry for extensive discussions on matters religious, doctrinal, and political. Detlef Mühlberger assisted with invaluable translations from the German. Anne-Marie Kilday provided a constant range of incisive comment and analysis and was an especially astute reader and critic of two of the most important chapters. She has also proved a continual source of encouragement, ensuring I tackle research with a questioning mind and a sense of humour. I am grateful to my institution, Oxford Brookes University, for a sabbatical semester in which the book was launched and for the award of a year-long Research Fellowship which enabled the completion of the book. This also gave me the opportunity to take up visiting professorships in Utrecht and Buffalo and a Research Fellowship at the Center for Inquiry, Amherst. I am also grateful to the British Academy for provision of a small grant which enabled the commencement of this work.

My stay in Utrecht was made comfortable and idyllic by the kindness of Bert and Ina Gassenbeek, whose wonderful converted apple store became my cosy retreat and study for nearly a month. (Aan de Gassenbeek Heel hartelijk dank voor al uw onvergeetbare gastvrijheid. Dankzij u weet ik nu wat het is om in Nederland een verjaardag te vieren!) My stay in Holland was also a fruitful source of European material, and for the wealth and breadth of this I have to thank Peter Derx, Betteke Tordoir (for her immense help in translating from the Dutch), August Hans den Boef, and Paul Cliteur.

Buffalo History Department made me especially welcome (even allowing an untried guitarist into their regular music jam!). For this and more I am indebted to Sasha-David Patrick, Pat McDevitt, Claire Schen, Erik Seeman, Markus Dubber, Lynn Mather, Tamara Thornton, Gloria Paveljack, Susan Cahn, Jim Gardner, and David Gerber.

I am also indebted for the thoughts and comments of audiences in Oxford, Nottingham, London, Reading, Rouen, Buffalo, Amsterdam, Berlin, Austin, and Canberra.

The book has involved two diligent and wise commissioning editors. Although at times they may have thought the commissioning of the book was not necessarily the product of wisdom, my response to their comments illuminated this quality in their suggestions. Ruth Parr encouraged the initial proposal and enabled it to reach the contract stage. Her enthusiasm and diligence are a deep loss to the world of publishing. Christopher Wheeler enabled it to progress and pass into print, and his perceptive suggestions have improved the finished piece immeasurably. I also have to thank skilled and patient copy-editors for their work on what must sometimes have appeared to be unpromising and/or untidy raw material.

I also owe thanks to a range of people who have all made contributions to my thoughts and progress: these include Michael and Joy Meadows, Barry Doyle, Tony Benn, Keith Porteus-Wood, Jim Herrick, Shirley Mullen, Chris Williams, Clive Emsley, Gerd Schwerhoff, Soili-Maria Eklund, Francisca Loetz, Peter Edge, Chara Bakalis, Chris Braddock, Terry Sanderson, Callum Brown, Harold Perkin, Marie Boulton, Jennifer Jeynes, Laura Schwarz, Ted Royle, Kathleen Turner, John Taylor, David Manning, Martine Spensky, David Cohen, Cassie Watson, Kees Windland, Evan Harris, Daniel Bee, Kevin Quinn, Nick Page, John Cryer, Justin Champion, Selina Rashid, Christy Davies, David Cannadine, Peter Tatchell, Elizabeth Coleman, Kingsley Baird, Geoffrey Robertson, John Mortimer, Lord Eric Avebury, Sean McEvoy, Stephen McEvoy, Robert Colls, and Ian Bryan.

My Colleagues in SOLON (Society, Order, Law, Offences, Notoriety) researching all aspects of bad behaviour have provided an enduringly catalytic environment for this work to flourish in. I am indebted to Judith Rowbotham and Kim Stevenson for the invitation to join this illustrious organization. Judith in particular has always taken an interest in the work that is indicative of a true scholar, enthusiast, and devotee of the big picture. Others from the SOLON stable who have offered assistance and encouragement include Shani D'Cruze, Lesley Abdella, Michael Salter, Bev Baker, Lorie Charlesworth, Sarah Wilson, and Paul Baker.

I am indebted for the help and constant professionalism of individuals working in the following libraries: Oxford Brookes University Library, the Bodleian Library Oxford, the Oxford University History Faculty Library, the British Library, the British Library Newspaper Collection (Colindale), the Library of the institute for Historical Research, the University Libraries of ANU, Buffalo, Utrecht, the Institute for Humanistik (Utrecht), Amsterdam Free University, the National Archives (Kew), and the Institute for Social History (Amsterdam).

My research at the Center for Inquiry, Amherst, was especially rewarding and I would like to thank Paul Kurz, Matt Cravatta, Joe Hoffman, and Tom Flynn for their hospitality. I also have much to thank the librarians and archivists of this still relatively undiscovered cornucopia of good things. Tim Binga and Leanna Jones guided me through the archives, helped in locating works, and assisted me to curate a small exhibition on the subject for the Center during my stay. Others at the Center—David Koepsel and Lauren Becker—assisted with broader research questions and offered incisive analysis that greatly aided my progress. I am also grateful to the Center for allowing me to reproduce illustrations from their extensive collection.

I am also grateful to the National Secular Society (G. W. Foote and Co.) for allowing me to reproduce pictures from the secular movement's premier newspapers, and to Avalon Productions for their permission to reproduce a still from *Jerry Springer: The Opera*.

I would like to thank all those nameless people who endured the loud typing that disturbed their moments of rest and recuperation on numerous trains, planes, and coaches as well as in cafes and airport lounges. Mercifully even I have the sense to use my voice-dictation machine only in private. Although a quasi-collective endeavour as these acknowledgements show, it is perhaps still right and proper that an individual (myself) take responsibility for all errors of fact in the forthcoming text.

Lastly I must thank both Joanne and Isabella for their patience, understanding, and their love.

For Joanne and Isabella

Contents

List of Illustrations

Reason's last step is the recognition that there are an infinite number of things that are beyond it. It is merely feeble if it does not go as far as to realize that. If natural things are beyond it, what are we to say about supernatural things?

(Blaise Pascal, *Pensées, no. 267 c.1659*)

Reason tells us that when we commit crimes, it is men, and not God, that we injure; and common sense tells us that we injure ourselves when we give way to disorderly passions.

(Denis Diderot, 'Thoughts on Religion')

I deny the right of any man, of any number of men, of any church, of any State, to put a padlock on the lips—to make the tongue a convict. I passionately deny the right of the Herod of authority to kill the children of the brain.

(Robert Green Ingersoll, Address to the Jury in the Trial of C. B. Reynolds, New Jersey, 1886)

In short, one might say, theologically, that blasphemy is entirely a question of geography; the answer to the question will depend upon the country you are in and the time you put the question.

(George William Foote, *Defence of Free Speech: Being a three hours Address to the Jury in the court of Queen's Bench Before Lord Coleridge on April 24th, 1883*)

Where were you when they crucified my Lord? Busy counting the collection and signing the latest petition in favour of easier divorce or abortion?

(Mary Whitehouse, *Quite Contrary*, 1993)

Introduction

Blasphemy—the attacking, wounding, and damaging of religious belief—has in so short a space of time suddenly returned to become an extremely combustible part of modern life. It is, once again, a living and breathing entity—one liable to grow still further with the oxygen of publicity and the highly motivated actions of both groups and individuals. This book provides a contextual history of this ill-understood subject, and offers answers to many historical conundrums about the development of the law on blasphemy and individual identity in the West. However, it also has wider ambitions. Blasphemy in its historical context illuminates changing views of the sacred and how far these have regulated societies and behaviour within them. Those who were shocked by the blasphemy they heard, or were prosecuted for a drunken misdemeanour or a profane word out of place, all left valuable clues about the importance of religion within medieval and early modern societies. Similarly, those prosecuted in the seventeenth and eighteenth centuries for advanced beliefs such as deism demonstrate one of the important mechanisms by which divine providentialism started to become less important in western society. The committed freethinkers who blasphemed in the nineteenth century also constitute an episode in the debate about full citizenship for marginal groups in the West. Likewise the later appearance of the artist as blasphemer similarly demonstrated that societies that had become less familiar with their religious pasts would spawn individuals who regarded religion as an alluring curiosity. Lastly, the pressing issues of our own age demonstrate that blasphemy is at the forefront of legal and philosophical dilemmas facing contemporary western governments. Agendas of social and cultural inclusion that protect individuals and their religious beliefs are now in conflict with the issue of freedom of expression.

Blasphemy is a concept that has undergone a number of changing definitions since its origins. This is because it has proved malleable, slippery, and stubbornly defiant of disciplinary boundaries. It is also because these changing definitions are caught up with the different religious and legal preoccupations of past societies, and more often than not actively reflect them. However, the problems do not end with defining blasphemy since its presence has also been felt in some very different spheres of social and cultural activity. Blasphemy's status as a crime asks that we consider its relationship to the rest of criminological history. Because blasphemy is also one of the richest sources historians of the West have for investigating human interaction, it also has a part to play in wider histories of manners and the 'civilizing process'. Likewise, its challenge to the sacred also means we must place blasphemy alongside other manifestations of sacred practice to fully appreciate its role as a challenge and as an affirmation of specific beliefs. Thus an introduction to blasphemy involves surveying both its changing definitions and the different areas of interpretation that are involved in writing its history.

Blasphemy was present in classical Greek and Roman societies, where it was associated with acts of treason against the state. The Bible clearly identified the offence as taking the name of the Lord in vain, and blasphemers were considered to have betrayed the covenant between God and his people by setting themselves above God. Chapter 20 of the Book of Exodus also declared that the Jews were to strictly observe the Sabbath, to have no other Gods, nor to worship 'graven images'. All this would preserve the people of Israel, since the Lord within these Commandments declared himself to be a 'jealous God'. In the Christian West the prohibition against worshipping false gods would later be translated into definitions of heresy. However, the roots of blasphemy in the West lie more readily in the misuse of the name of God and the misuse of religious images.

Attacks upon religious images represent a significant portion of blasphemy's early history. Blasphemy in the ancient and early Christian periods most frequently comes down to the historian as the written record of individual acts of outrage. During the Roman Imperial period it was the conversion of the state to Christianity that heralded the wholesale destruction of pagan religions. Yet this was not an inevitable consequence of the state's adoption of Christianity, and such action was initially frowned upon and discouraged. As late as the end of the third century the Council of Granada argued that there was no scriptural precedent for iconoclastic action against pagan idols and that perpetrators acted clearly at their own risk. This changed in the fourth century, when religious freedom was limited and orthodoxy became mandatory under an imperial decree of 379. Sacrilege and heresy then became capital crimes in the succeeding decade. After this the destruction of pagan monuments occurred on what Eberhard Sauer calls 'a massive scale', in tandem with the mature growth of Christianity during the fourth and fifth centuries.[1]

Early Christianity believed that the continued existence of pagan idols was a potential focus for evil spirits that received strength from such veneration. This worship became increasingly associated with Christianity's own pantheon of demons. Iconoclasm was eventually to have the sanction of Augustine who, in *City of God*, noted how Christianity had flourished after pagan images and objects of worship had been removed from the people's gaze. Destroying this

---

[1] Eberhard Sauer, *The Archaeology of Religious Hatred in the Roman and Early Medieval World* (Stroud, 2003), 162–4, 30, 159, 46, and 162.

link was enabling Christianity to make a new start. These assaults also contained elements of theatre and 'performativity' that some later analysts from cultural studies traditions have identified as the central component of blasphemous acts.[2]

Early iconoclasts within the Christian faith were defeated in 787 at the Council of Nicaea, giving birth to a problematic tension that has run through the issue of religious image-making ever since.[3] This not only focused the mind but provided the vital act of communication between God and man that was so essential to a pre-literate culture and society. Augustine also warned Christian society of the dangers posed by unorthodoxy in its midst and saw heresy as supplying the impetus for conformity.[4] Some parts of St Paul's message to the scattered churches of the early Christian Mediterranean had emphasized the capacity for the individual's will to be at war with God. Taming the rebelliousness of the human spirit thereafter became a central theme of medieval Christian thought.[5] Even the notorious Pauline view of women labelled the prevention of blasphemy as a central core of their domestic duties.[6] The medieval period absorbed these different streams and thus became preoccupied with the detection and punishment of heresy, and considered this a far greater threat than blasphemy. Heresy was defined as the espousal of false doctrine and apostasy from the orthodox teachings of the church; individuals guilty of this crime were to be brought back from error.[7] This offence was different from blasphemy, which was considered to show active disrespect to God and to involve the use of profane cursing or mockery of his powers.

Blasphemy began to be uncovered in the thirteenth century by the Church when it dispersed mendicant orders to preach among the people. The typical blasphemer uttered curses belittling the power of God or denying his divinity as part of impetuous outbursts. They thus were contrite, or at least appeared to be, in front of their inquisitors. Occasionally such individuals had been drunk, or as converts from Judaism had been caught inadvertently using religious practices associated with their former faith. From the end of the medieval period it is possible to see the first civic ordinances and statutes in the West aimed at eradicating and punishing public acts of blasphemy. Such acts could be isolated incidents in which otherwise religiously orthodox believers forgot conventional standards of behaviour or displayed their ignorance. For the medieval world blasphemy thus seemed more obviously a public-order problem, in which the miscreant needed primarily to be disciplined. Sometimes a charge of blasphemy also aimed at casting aspersion upon other aspects of lifestyle such as drinking, vagrancy, or gambling, a phenomenon which has a singular longevity.

---

[2] Perhaps the leading exponent of this idea is David Lawton, in *Blasphemy* (London, 1993).
[3] L. Baugh, *Imaging the Divine: Jesus and Christ-Figures in Film* (Kansas City, 1997), foreword.
[4] Augustine, *City of God*, ed. D. Knowles (Harmondsworth, 1980), 833.
[5] Peter Brown, *The Body and Society: Men, Women and Sexual Renunciation in Early Christianity* (London, 1988), 47–9.
[6] See Titus 2: 5.   [7] Brown, *The Body and Society*, 104–5.

The Reformation fundamentally altered how contemporaries viewed and consumed the sacred, and this brought changes to how the concept of blasphemy was defined. Iconoclasts distrusted the image whilst Catholicism's reforms at the Council of Trent in 1563 instituted a close Episcopal control over images. The influence of reformed liturgies (and Calvinism in particular) placed far greater emphasis upon the word and the message of the Gospels. Protestantism was also poorly disposed to depictions of the mystery of God's nature. Such depictions were castigated for showing either the omnipresent God or the physical form of Christ, thereby removing mystery from the incarnation. This new spiritual emphasis reformed religion to change the concept of blasphemy, thereby indicting many pre-reform religious practices and beliefs. With the coming of the Reformation blasphemy became equated with heretical beliefs dangerous to the polity. Henceforth the accusation began to be used against independent thinkers as well as the careless or drunks and miscreants who posed merely a nuisance. The seventeenth century saw blasphemy still defined by theologians as more closely linked than ever to the security of the state, and the wording of many statutes confirms the threat posed by blasphemers. Blasphemy legislation in England and New England aimed at combating religiously dissident groups, such as the Quakers, who considered any government other than their own to be Antichrist and thus liable to be overthrown.

In England and other parts of Europe statutory legislation against blasphemy had appeared by the end of the seventeenth century, and the English Act of 1698 reflected the belief amongst *ancien régimes* that religion and the state were mutually supportive entities. The Statute declared it blasphemy to deny the Christian religion, to deny the Trinity, or the authority of the Bible, indicating that such action eroded the power of the state. This Statute was to have less impact upon the history of blasphemy in the West than English Common Law. Whilst the Statute in England was never used successfully, the English Common Law of blasphemous libel (which evolved through the decisions of successive judges) eventually placed a tool of prosecution in the hands of English laymen and women. This was to ensure blasphemy's survival as an evolving offence into the twenty-first century.

English Common Law also had a significant effect upon the history of blasphemy and its prosecution in the United States and Australia. Both these jurisdictions would spend over a century defining their legal position around the legacy that English Common Law had bequeathed them. Whether they were bound by the wisdom of its judgements, or anxious to elude the seemingly arbitrary nature of its claims, these jurisdictions simply could not escape its influence. Within the English-speaking world English Common Law represents a common thread that plays varying roles in the development of the laws against blasphemy and blasphemous libel in the United States, Canada, Australia, New Zealand, and South Africa.

As criticism of Christianity and its churches became fused into the philosophical position of Deism, some lawyers came to recognize a distinction between the impetuous, thoughtless utterance and genuine anti-Christian dissent. The French jurist Rousseaud de La Combe argued for a distinction in France between the blasphemy caused by profane swearing and 'deliberate, premeditated comments . . . whose meaning is soberly intended'.[8] This change was to identify blasphemy with sedition and revolution. When the Society for the Suppression of Vice prosecuted the English Jacobins in the early nineteenth century, the individual court cases give a clear sense of what this society felt blasphemy entailed. In the cases against Richard Carlile's shopmen for selling copies of the *Republican* or Thomas Paine's *Age of Reason*, the witnesses were questioned by the prosecuting counsel as to what they understood by the term 'blasphemy'. The answers given by these individuals give clear insights into the popular nineteenth-century understanding of the offence of blasphemy. William Smith, testifying against an unknown individual, described blasphemy as 'Speaking against God and the scriptures. Sedition is speaking against the King and the Constitution.' Henry Baldwin Raven, testifying against James Clark in 1824, defined it as: 'Any publication which has a tendency to vilify the Bible, the Christian Religion, or our Lord Jesus Christ.' William Wilson, a Bow Street Runner testifying against Thomas Riley Perry in the same year, saw it as 'any attempt to vilify the Christian Religion, promulgated by our Saviour and his Apostles'.[9] These definitions, emanating from prosecution witnesses, saw blasphemy as a deliberate act which threatened the moral and material safety of the nation. Contemporary judges in America were prepared to reinforce this view and to construct a definition that protected the community. Justice Shaw, in the case against Abner Kneeland, described blasphemy as 'speaking evil of the Deity with an impious purpose to derogate from the divine majesty, and to alienate the minds of others from the love and reverence of God'.[10] By the late twentieth century Lord Scarman's citation of an earlier judgement carried the implication that blasphemy as a criminal offence was really about publishing opinions and the disorder they might provoke. Thus a blasphemous publication was one that 'contains any contemptuous, reviling, scurrilous or ludicrous matter relating to God, Jesus Christ, or the Bible, or the formularies of the Church of England as by law established'.[11]

Some definitions also lingered on the statute book and created surprise amongst audiences subsequently exposed to their antiquity. In the famous Mockus case in the early years of the twentieth century, the court in Maine

---

[8] Alain Cabantous, *Blasphemy: Impious Speech in the West from the Seventeenth to the Nineteenth Century* (New York, 1998), 135.

[9] 'Man', offences against the king: seditious libel, 22nd May, 1822. *The Proceedings of the Old Bailey*, Ref: t18220522–82; James Clark, offences against the king: religious offences, 3rd June, 1824, ibid., Ref: t18240603–252; Thomas Riley Perry, offences against the king: religious offences, 15th July, 1824, ibid., Ref: t18240715–151.

[10] *Commonwealth* v. *Kneeland*, 37 Mass. 206–46 (1883).

[11] *Whitehouse* v. *Lemon*, AC 658 (1979).

discovered that its relevant statute was an extensive trap for snaring most forms of religious unorthodoxy. The State of Maine was embarrassed to be prosecuting the defendant for:

using profanely insolent and reproachful language against God, or by contumaciously reproaching Him, His creation, government, final judgement of the world, Jesus Christ, the Holy Ghost, or the Holy Scriptures as contained in the canonical books of the Old and New Testament, or by exposing any of these enumerated Beings or Scriptures to contempt and ridicule.[12]

Nonetheless significant reforms, aimed at limiting state control of religious issues, discredited the power of much blasphemy legislation. Societies would more readily complain about the power of blasphemous material to enrage the sensibilities of the individual as the nineteenth century drew to a close. This introduced a growing concern about the issue of manner. In truth, this was a more refined argument about the importance of intention which had first appeared at the end of the eighteenth century. In the English-speaking world a significant change in the law's emphasis unravelled Christianity's claim to be the intrinsic law of the land. This change in English Common Law asserted that reasoned attacks upon religion were permissible, if the proprieties of debate were observed. Protecting a religiously inspired state from sedition had been superseded and the law of blasphemous libel became an adjunct to laws intended to protect public order. Although European countries would prosecute writers and artists for blasphemy, the success of such ventures was mixed, to say the least. Even successful prosecutions produced unwelcome publicity for governments and their moral agendas. As a result the defence of the sacred appeared to be in wholesale retreat from the forces of western free speech.

This particular interlude came to an end with the late twentieth-century quest to create religious equality before the law. Blasphemy in the West until this time had solely protected Christianity, yet the demands of multiculturalism required that the historic remnants of Europe's blasphemy laws be scrutinized once more. Minority religious groups, supported by human-rights agendas, sought access to the benefits of antique blasphemy laws seemingly left behind by Christianity. With their free-speech agenda, western liberals, appalled by such developments, conversely campaigned loudly for their dissolution and repeal.

Thus blasphemy has survived two millenia of religious and legal developments to become a considerably important phenomenon in the modern world. In trying to understand blasphemy, both in the past and the contemporary world, it is important to remember that it is simultaneously four things. Blasphemy is a manifestation of what people think about their God and the sacred. It is also a display of power, a crime, and a species of flawed social interaction transgressing

---

[12] 'Blasphemy. What Constitutes offense under Maine Statute', *Virginia Law Register*, NS 7: 11. pp. 835–58.

norms of manners and acceptable behaviour. These four related categorizations constitute our tools for fitting blasphemy into its adjacent areas of social and cultural history. At this stage these relationships produce questions for us to ponder within the history elaborated by this book

Issues about the sacred and the blasphemous indicate what individuals feel about the religious. It has been fashionable (a commonplace even) to suggest that religion has systematically vanished from the modern world, and sociologists have told us that it was easy enough to recognize the symptoms of this process occurring throughout history.[13] The most elementary mistake in this vision of what would happen to religion was an assumption, even a belief, that religion would suffer an ultimate extinction. In its subtler version this process was sketched alongside the West's creation of the autonomous individual. Indeed, we should note at this point that some historiographies of blasphemy amount to little more than the drawing together of these two histories.[14] When certainty of secularization's triumph fractured, it was primarily western society that had to confront the problems associated with more cautious and ambivalent ways of thinking about culture. Postmodernists, in their attack upon what they saw as 'metanarratives', argued that all-embracing belief systems should be discarded. It is a part of this book's argument that the power of religion, whether organized or not, should be systematically re-examined through the prism of blasphemy. One of the more serious lessons of the last twenty years has been to persuade all of us that religion is of enhanced and renewed importance, and has not withered away, as both modernists and postmodernists expected.

The legal history of blasphemy tends to chart the movement of the law from heresy through to modern-day laws against incitement to religious hatred. A theme which runs in counterpoint to this is the relationship of both religion and the law to conceptions of the state and its purpose in evolving modern societies. A legal history of blasphemy can thus chart legislative change, but is sometimes silent on the reasons for such change. Similarly, it can tell us about legislation and individual cases, but not always about what wider societies think about religious laws. A close relative of legal history illuminates blasphemy's part in the history of censorship and rights. Again this highlights the contextual instances of censorship as well as a history of censorship regimes and their development. The rolling back of censorship as a major task of the liberal state has, generally speaking, occurred in response to individual rights becoming a central component of the modern citizen. Clearly this philosophy also argued that with such rights came

[13] See e.g. the classic position suggested in the mid-1960s by Peter Berger in *The Sacred Canopy; Elements of a Sociological Theory of Religion* (Garden City, 1967). The classic positivist position of secularization has taken a battering in recent years, and the heightened awareness of religious conflict has strongly informed scepticism of the theory's usefulness.

[14] Hypatia Bradlaugh-Bonner, *Penalties Upon Opinion, or Some Records of the Laws of Heresy and Blasphemy* (London, 1934); Arthur Calder-Marshall, *Lewd, Blasphemous and Obscene* (London, 1972); G. W. Foote, *The Flowers of Freethought* (London, 1894).

responsibilities, whilst the struggle to maintain this balance has been a central dilemma for modern societies. Investigating fear, hate, vengeance, and historically nuanced arguments about restorative justice reconnects us with areas containing the raw emotions that the history of codified law often neglects.

Blasphemy also has a history as a form of criminal transgressive behaviour, and as a result it displays the power relationships between authority and those individuals who experienced it in the historical past. The related issues of discipline, control, power, and punishment, so central to our understanding of law, culture, and their evolution, are also informed by the history of blasphemy. Making sense of this relationship involves probing the answers offered by the chief paradigms for understanding this relationship which emanate from the work of Michel Foucault and Norbert Elias. The failure of blasphemy to vanish when faced with the modern world makes Foucault's analysis of power and control potentially intriguing for the study of this area. Blasphemy's history, and modern society's treatment of it, does not encourage the optimism that violence no longer exists for the individual nor is successfully hidden in the apparatus of the state.[15] Blasphemy's power, it should be remembered, constitutes an attack upon manners and for any society an assault upon the expectations of good behaviour within that society. Here the powerful influence of Norbert Elias and his ideas offer some further partial explanations. Elias saw human society as an agent of its own transformation, so that changes in behaviour were a deliberate choice rather than the result of pressure or coercion.[16] Certainly the state became involved more closely with blasphemy from the sixteenth century onwards, but a longer-term perspective sees this relationship as eventually fractured and dissolved. Blasphemy ultimately persisted and adapted itself to modern manners and communication media, and remained on the margins, occasionally bidden to resume a place of prominence. Thus it did not go the way of barbaric table manners or objectionable hygiene, and remained as a vibrant cultural resource with pan-class appeal.

The religious has also been central to the history of iconography in the West, and this in turn has inspired late twentieth-century artists to explore the subject-matter with new insights. Painters, sculptors, photographers, and

---

[15] Although it is possible to trace a growing leniency of punishment in the West, it is significant that the offence of blasphemy and judicial proceedings against it remain possible and are witnessing something of a revival in most European countries (notably Spain, Germany, Austria, the Netherlands, and Greece).

[16] For the influence of Elias see the contributions by James. A. Sharpe, Eva Österberg, and Pieter Spierenberg in (eds.), Eric A. Johnson and Eric H. Monkkonen *The Civilisation of Crime: Violence in Town and Country since the Middle Ages* (Urbana, Ill., 1996). The contribution of manners to a changed climate in the eighteenth century (especially in England) is valuably discussed in the opening section of Elizabeth Foyster's 'Creating a Veil of Silence? Politeness and Marital Violence in the English Household', *Transactions of the Royal Historical Society*, 12 (2002), 395–415. For an informed introduction to the ideas of Norbert Elias see Stephen Mennell, *Norbert Elias: Civilization and the Human Self Image* (Oxford, 1989).

filmmakers have all responded to the inspiration provided by religious aesthetics. However, either by accident or occasionally by design, some works have also led to widespread opprobrium. These have stimulated vocal arguments about issues of free discussion and state verses private funding for the arts, bringing blasphemy to the forefront of public consciousness. Clearly the gaze has an interesting place in blasphemy's history. It argues that religion as a subject, and religious images themselves, invoke the emotions of both the producer and the consumer. [17] Fear of what the 'gaze' might do in other genres is also evident throughout the history outlined below. The last quarter of the nineteenth century saw fear of the written blasphemous text abate somewhat, to be replaced by fear of the performance. Both theatre and film had the capacity to excite, and their powers of suggestion were frequently considered by censoring authorities to be a real social danger. The moving image, whether cinematic or theatrical, also imitated life in a way other forms of expression did not. As such societies feared its potentially didactic power, or still worse its capacity for corrupting its audience.

Following this Introduction, the initial chapter of the book demonstrates the sudden and dramatic appearance of blasphemy as a phenomenon in the modern world. In this a crime, and the sensibilities that go with it, reappeared from a remote historical past. This initial chapter, which acquaints us with the contemporary world, acts as a sharp reminder of blasphemy's contemporary immediacy as an important cultural problem in modern times. It also aims to provoke questions about the tolerance and the cultural standpoint of the reader. The shape of this chapter was significantly altered by recent developments within the United Kingdom, Australia, Austria, the Netherlands, France, and Germany, and came to reflect the troubled present that blasphemy has bequeathed to contemporary religious and ethnic relations. All too quickly theoretical speculation became contemporary history, and it became my duty to place these happenings in their wider historical context to show how the contemporary experience of blasphemy and its past are yoked together.

The subsequent two chapters provide a narrative chronological framework for how blasphemy has developed in the West since the Reformation. The first of these surveys illuminates the 300 years between 1500 and 1800, with an appreciation of developments before this date. The second half really delineates the differences (and surprising similarities) between the pre-modern and modern worlds of religious strife. This takes the reader from 1800 through the dawn of what might be termed 'the secular century' in 1900 to its chronologically premature end in 1990.

---

[17] The 'gaze' is a concept developed substantially through the works of Griselda Pollock, and is most readily identified with her. But it was also outlined in John Berger's influential introductory text *Ways of Seeing* (London, 1972).

From this survey of trends and events the book moves on to examine specific themes which demand closer attention. These demonstrate the different areas of wider social and cultural history upon which blasphemy has a significant bearing, and to which it has conclusions to offer. Blasphemy is clearly a part of the history of the sacred and of the law, yet placing it within these wider contexts involves seeing how far it fits with the existing historical models of these areas. As we shall see, the fit is far from exact, opening new questions both for the history of blasphemy as well as of law and religion.

The first theme examined is the identity of the blasphemer over the last 400 years. Chapter 4 is perhaps the first systematic attempt to analyse the phenomenon of blasphemy from a 'practitioner's' point of view. This clearly shows a significant change over time, from the unwitting blasphemer to the anti-Christian activist and artist or writer. From identifying our blasphemers, the methods of disciplining and controlling them merit substantial attention. Chapter 5 illuminates how control of blasphemous words served a number of important functions for local and central government, as well as the individual. Indeed, the rise of the individual's interest in this area provides one of the book's central themes. Blasphemy was seen to threaten most western societies in surprisingly homogenous ways. Nonetheless, approaches to controlling and eradicating it were remarkably varied and arguably inconsistent. Blasphemy's status as an offence had to be managed within the confines of the law and its wider ambitions; representing, paradoxically, a cornerstone of morality on some occasions and an anachronistic embarrassment on others.

Blasphemy and blasphemers disturbed societies in the historical past and a further neglected aspect of this history is the precise views and attitudes of blasphemy's victims. Chapter 6 addresses the issue of the damage apparent-ly caused by blasphemy and blasphemers. This involves consideration of the 'hurt' caused by the blasphemer and what (and who) precisely is damaged during the action. This again shows a distinct chronological shift from conceptions of the damaged community of believers, to the damaged social and political peace, arriving finally at the wounded feelings and convictions of modern individuals. This chapter especially emphasizes the power of the individual to use discourses about community and order from the recent and even remote historical past.

One genre in which blasphemy evolved has been singled out for extended analysis here, in Chapter 7, which considers the relationship between blasphemy and film. This topic is especially pertinent for the final sections of the book, since it locates issues around the fear of new media and their possibilities firmly within both the historical and contemporary environments. In particular this chapter highlights the difficulties faced by those who wanted to portray the essential truths of the Christian religion through the medium of film. The difficult areas of artistic licence, versus the portrayal of 'the truth', loom especially large here. A popular version of the sacred had the power to evangelize as never before, yet making the sacred intelligible risks cheapening it and diluting its message. Inevitably, the clash of 'art house' experimental filmmaking with the sincere beliefs and religious feelings of grassroots Christians is of considerable importance in the story. Perhaps more surprising is the discovery that popular and cult entertainers have found prolific mileage in lampooning and ridiculing organized religion—even if they were skilful enough to avoid major legal confrontations.

Finally, the book concludes with some speculations about what the long-term trends apparent in blasphemy's history can tell us about religion, conflict, and the laws governing the behaviour of individuals in modern society. Blasphemy's ancient origins, and the history of its shifting status, as everything from a crime to a legitimate mode of expression, make it a rich way to study the cultural history of the West. This portrays the West as by turns tolerant, persecuting, and indifferent, and its cultures responsive to the perceived needs of societies at specific historical moments. Our conclusions from this cultural history grow still more important as individuals, and states, form entrenched positions on blasphemy's past, present, and future.

1

The Past Invades the Present: Blasphemy in the Contemporary World

On a dark, stormy day in 1728 a boatman, Robert Adriaansz. Van Hoorn, cast off from a Dutch seaport. We do not know his destination, nor his cargo, nor details of the ship's complement. As all aboard were aware, sea and water travel in the eighteenth century was fraught with potential danger. Those prepared to take the risks involved, or forced to by necessity, could only place their hopeful trust in God and the competence of the professionals on board. However, what transpired on this voyage became an important matter of life and death for all on the ship. Over 250 years later it also gives vital clues to historians researching one of the West's least understood crimes. When a violent storm blew up, Van Hoorn's actions were extraordinary to say the least, and they clearly alarmed his fellow passengers. Instead of showing fear Van Hoorn engaged in bravado as he began to speak blasphemy—an act that appeared to be rapidly, and visibly, bringing adverse divine judgement upon the ship. Whilst others cowered, and probably prayed, Van Hoorn mocked the power of the almighty, commanding him to do the boatman's bidding. He declared that if God wanted to unleash the terrible storm then he should simply get on with it and let it blow. In directing and commanding the almighty he had committed the blasphemous crime of setting himself above God. Thereafter, when the wind lashed the boat violently, he was heard to scream 'go away you devil' (two insults in one). In front of his terrified audience Van Hoorn then 'tempted' the almighty still further by refusing to strike his sails, defiantly arguing he would not do so either for God or for the safety of his fellow sailors. Somehow the ship must have survived the onslaught, since when the crisis was over Van Hoorn was detained by the authorities.

There is no evidence of contrition for his actions, so it is doubtful that he had been drunk like others the United Provinces had detained for this crime. Indeed Van Hoorn remained strangely unrepentant, declaring whilst in custody, 'I am as much God as you are' ('Ik ben zoowel God als gy'). He also continued to issue further commands to the almighty, suggesting that God was thoroughly entitled to destroy him if he so wished. Thus, in a series of volatile and shocking incidents, Van Hoorn was patently guilty of the blasphemy of persistently damaging God's majesty. Van Hoorn's apparent sobriety is also suggested by the seriousness with which his actions were punished, since leniency and milder shame punishments had been customary in instances of drunken blasphemy. Despite the United Province's reputation for comparative religious tolerance, his crime was considered beyond the bounds of this principle and he was dealt with harshly by the authorities. Van Hoorn's fate was to be sentenced to the standard European punishment of boring through the tongue for an intermediate offence. But this was to be followed by a further, uncommonly harsh, sentence of death by hanging, with post-mortem exhibition of his body upon the wheel. Although the account of this incident comes down to us from a dry legal text it remains almost impossible to diminish its impact upon the reader.[1] Van Hoorn had committed the utterly unpardonable crime of blasphemy in an age that still took this issue profoundly seriously—an age that otherwise thought itself enlightened enough to have largely ceased to believe in the crime of witchcraft.

Yet how enlightened an age was it? Whilst we might excuse the fear of those on board the Dutch ship witnessing Van Hoorn's outburst, similar ideas expressed by an individual in the confines of his presumably more comfortable study are perhaps less easily dismissed. Ten years before Van Hoorn had terrified his fellow passengers a noted jurist and legal commentator, who thought rational scientific investigation a virtue, put pen to paper across the North Sea. Bulstrode Whitelocke had been writing advice to the magistrates of Middlesex and elsewhere with a degree of rational calm. He had ridiculed the idea of witchcraft offences with a cursory 'I shall not trouble with them, there being no such practice now'. But when he came to describe the heinous nature of verbal crimes against God he lost his composure almost completely. Whitelocke railed against the prevalence of blasphemy amongst certain professions (including sailors) and its potentially morbid consequences for all: 'The sin of prophane cursing and swearing is so very great, and become so general amongst the common People, the soldiery and Mariners, Hackney-Coachmen and Carmen especially, that'tis much to be feared, if there is not some stop put to it, it will draw down Veangeance from Heav'n upon us.' He also focused upon the terror blaspheming wreaked upon the universe and outlined the precise nature of the crime Van Hoorn was to commit ten years later: 'Had not God forbid this Sin, by the *Third Commandment*, the Light of Nature would have told us it were a great Crime: For Reason tells us, that Mankind should have such a *Veneration for the Divine Majesty, our Creator*, as not to use that word which forms *an Idea of God* in our minds, but on *solemn Occasions*.' But this was not enough for Whitelocke, who drove his point to its ultimate conclusion. He emphasized how even the eighteenth century still firmly believed in the wrath of God and its existence in the form of legitimate punishment: 'When the *Laws of the Land* cannot keep *down a Sin*, but it becomes *spreading*, *rampant* and *universal*, I know no *other Way*, when *human means can't prevail*, but *that God* himself should *interpose by his almighty power*; and by *pouring down Vengeance from Heaven*, try to *reclaim that people*

---

[1] M. R. Baelde, *Studiën over Godslastering* (The Hague, 1935), 137.

whom *human Laws can't reduce.*' Continuing with his liberal use of strident italics (eighteenth-century print culture's equivalent of shouting), he declared: 'No wonder that *our ships* so often miscarry when *our Mariners curse and damn* themselves *through the Sea to Hell.*'[2]

Until comparatively recently, western society's treatment of the crime of blasphemy had evolved away from the harsh justice dispensed to Van Hoorn. By the middle of the century that condemned him to his fate, subsequent blasphemers were considered victims conceivably in need of psychiatric treatment. Other, less enlightened regimes would merely imprison such victims, with or without accessory shame punishments. By the nineteenth century the twin agendas of individual rights and religious toleration had made the use of blasphemy laws, and prosecution, seem relics from the medieval past. Even the use of incarceration as a penalty was considered controversial and unpopular by the end of the twentieth century. Yet blasphemy, unlike heresy, never disappeared from the statute books of most western countries, and a minority of religious believers continued to argue that they still needed the protection of the law. Throughout almost all of the twentieth century blasphemy appeared to be a curiosity, with its days seemingly numbered. As Christianity in the West seemed to falter, and systems that enabled religious and cultural integration began to take shape, blasphemy seemed to be a mechanism with no clear function. However, at the very end of the twentieth century the viability of blasphemy in the West was rekindled by a growing interest in religion as a component of identity. Although some arguments in this vein were prevalent in areas as diverse as liberation theology, Christian fundamentalism, and post-colonial studies, the obvious catalyst for this change was the furore surrounding Salman Rushdie's novel *The Satanic Verses*. From this affair the discontent felt by religious groups beyond Christianity spread to other countries in the West.

Nearly 300 years after Van Hoorn's execution, the now tolerant culture in the Netherlands was shattered by two violent deaths in the nation's public sphere. The politician Pym Fortuyn and the filmmaker Theo Van Gogh were both victims of the first political assassinations in the Netherlands since Jesuits had murdered William the Silent during the Dutch Wars of Liberation. Both men had criticized religious/ethnic groups and the nature of their beliefs. In retaliation, desperate individuals had turned to violence, certain in their minds that these men should die for their criticism of religious identities. Blasphemy, with its verbal, visual, and written assaults upon the sacred and identity, had reappeared to become a fixture upon the West's cultural horizon.

---

[2] Bulstrode Whitelocke, *The Charge to the Grand-Jury, And other juries of the County of Middlesex at the General Quarter Session of the Peace, held, April 21ˢᵗ at Westminster Hall* (London, 1718), 12, 3–7; and *The Second Charge to the Grand-Jury, And other juries of the County of Middlesex at the General Quarter Session of the Peace, held, April 21ˢᵗ at Westminster Hall* (London, 1718), 13.

Before the fall of the Berlin Wall, the West had so often contrasted its freedoms with the Eastern bloc failure to privilege free speech and expression. Dissident writers, such as Alexander Solzhenitsyn, Andrei Sakharov, and Václav Havel had been portrayed as champions of free speech in societies that did not understand its full import. This smug view of the world, and of Europe in particular, changed dramatically with the disintegration of communism in 1989. What at first seemed an unmitigated triumph for the West spawned uncertainty, as old political alliances and positions appeared to dissolve.

Conventional political ideology began to be less important than wider conceptions of identity, often linked with ethnicity. Some, such as Francis Fukiyama, had argued that the triumph of liberal capitalism had brought history to an end.[3] Other commentators signalled the end of a different era. The philosopher Alistair McGrath argued that the fall of the Berlin Wall marked the end of a 200-year epoch which had commenced with the French Revolution. This period witnessed, as far as he was concerned, the epoch of rationalist thinking and the subsequent years had thus become 'the twilight of atheism'.[4] Another commentator, Grace Davie, noted that 1990 heralded a 'reformulation of the sacred' in which religion took its place as a species of choice within consumer society. Davie also thought these developments brought a loss of certainty about progress and the enlightenment.[5]

Whilst McGrath detected a decline in confidence and certainty about the rationalist project, this was by no means conclusive. Although mass belief and mass church attendance were in sporadic decline, it was clear that religion had scarcely vanished from public life. Indeed the 1990s ushered in a period where displays of public grief and shared experience were often framed by religious idioms and language.[6] Whilst religious attendance might have been visibly on the wane, the growth of counselling idioms as a means of 'reaching' the spiritually curious argued for a different future. Indeed the whole concept of the 'church', envisioned as an ancient building filled with homogenous believers, appeared decidedly old-fashioned. Thus the persistence of curiosity about the spiritual denied the claim that western society was wholly secular.

All this was occurring within Christianity whilst new agendas were being set by religions that arrived in the West predominantly as a manifestation of various colonial pasts. From the immediate post-war period onwards, most western countries found themselves playing host to minority communities who were

---

[3] See Frances Fukuyama, *The End of History and the Last Man* (London, 1992).
[4] Alistair McGrath, *The Twilight of Atheism* (London, 2004).
[5] Grace Davie, *Religion in Britain Since 1945* (Oxford, 1994), 39–44 and 196.
[6] Public grief and mourning have been a growing feature of Western cultural politics since the middle of the 1990s. This has embraced the commemoration of victims of terrorist attrocities as well as the untimely deaths of important figures such as Princess Diana. Grace Davie also investigated related phenomena in her consideration of religious attitudes to the Hillsborough disaster. See ibid. 88–92.

not willing to embrace the Christian heritage of the West. The Islamic, Hindu, and Sikh religions grew in both presence and visibility in the United Kingdom, France, the Netherlands, and Germany. However, popular perceptions of Islam in particular were focused for western European populations by its role in a number of geopolitical events. Whilst the oil crises of the 1970s seemed to be the political statement of forms of Arab nationalism, the events of the Iranian revolution represented a considerable sea change in how Middle Eastern politics functioned. Viewed from a western perspective, a westernized state was overthrown by a fundamentalist theocratic regime that emphatically turned its back upon the West and its culture. Religion and cultural revolt, it seemed, were capable of creating an Islamic form of liberation theology. This blueprint arguably gathered strength through the struggle of the Mujjahadin to remove Soviet influence from Afghanistan. Whilst the situations of these two revolutions were quite often light years away from the experience of communities within western nations, public opinion was sometimes shaped by these events. Similarly these communities themselves, like Catholics and Jews before them, faced cultural choices riddled with ambiguity. Whilst assimilation was possible, the option of retaining (and perhaps even enhancing) separate identity was a similarly attractive proposition.

Multiculturalism was one of the ideals of the post-war world which offered western societies the chance to integrate, and to some extent atone for various colonial past misdemeanours. One specific area where multiculturalism appeared to be gaining ground as a first principle with some effectiveness was in the law and its application. Drawing from the European Declaration of Human Rights, legal systems became compelled to treat all individuals equally within the law, and many western countries made strenuous efforts to achieve this goal. Legislation to prevent inequalities of treatment regarding race, gender, and sexual orientation moved forward in the West, albeit at varying speeds. As a result many governments and policymakers perhaps held their breath, in the hope that such a stance would address issues of economic, social, and cultural exclusion within their populations. Some commentators even suggested that multiculturalism was being exercised very much on the terms of the governing elites in western Europe. Talal Asad argued that it was an implicit assumption that multicultural agendas should not impinge upon the indigenous European populations of these countries.[7]

Even the previously robust liberal societies in the West, like the Netherlands, began to wonder how their populations might be persuaded to face up to the limits of tolerance. Growing perceptions that the immigrant community perpetrated street crime, and had similarly failed to integrate, provided somewhat unwelcome opportunities for politicians of the Right. Such criticisms were generally aimed at the complacency of the Dutch establishment and its policies, that had supposedly failed both indigenous and immigrant communities. The problem

---

[7] Talal Asad, 'Ethnography, Literature, and Politics: Some Readings and Uses of Salman Rushdie's *The Satanic Verses*,' *Cultural Athropology*, 5: 3 (Aug. 1990), 239–69, at 259.

was significant, and within the new millennium was set to get more urgent. Estimates suggested that by 2050 up to 20 percent of the Dutch population would be of non-western descent.[8] With western hysteria over immigration and asylum-seeking, the pressure had grown for all communities to integrate more successfully. Even tolerant societies were feeling potentially betrayed by minorities who had hitherto been welcomed to their shores. In the Netherlands a policy in the 1970s which had encouraged separate identity based upon the 'myth' of return migration had become, by the 1980s, a multicultural approach. This wanted to iron out the creases between cultures, by promoting emancipation for all citizens from discrimination in both their own communities and wider Dutch society. By the 1990s policies of positive discrimination to benefit individuals had become the cornerstone of an integration policy. The shocks of the early twenty-first century finally initiated the introduction of mandatory citizenship tests and attempts to persuade all in Dutch society to 'mutually adapt'. In the Netherlands a recent poll found 80 per cent of people in favour of stronger measures to get immigrants to integrate. As the *Sunday Times* argued, this was compelling evidence that 'multiculturalism is damned'.[9] More worryingly still, there seemed little encouragement for this policy from immigrants who felt 'integrated into Dutch society, but not accepted'.[10] This was followed by a flood of writings which suggested, pessimistically, that integration was an exception rather than a norm.

Importantly, some of the criticisms of assimilation policies were not so easily dismissed as simple one-dimensional right-wing racism. Many believed that well-intentioned policies had failed and looked in growing admiration at what were perceived as tougher approaches in Germany and Denmark. The election of Pym Fortuyn in Rotterdam brought this debate spectacularly to a head. Fortuyn uttered classic right-wing arguments about halting immigration and for greater levels of assimilation. Where he departed from this was in his accusation picturing Islam as a 'backward culture' which discriminated against women. This seemed to bring the Dutch (and western) ideals of equality for all squarely into conflict with the practices of minority communities. Fortuyn would eventually pay for such views with his life.

This theme of the alleged poor treatment of Islamic women struck a chord in Dutch society. The maverick film director Theo Van Gogh responded to this in a short film entitled *Submission*, which he made in collaboration with Ajaan Hirsi Ali, a Somali Muslim activist who had fled an arranged marriage. This film addressed the Islamic expectations of women and produced a damning indictment of contemporary cultural practices. Whilst this would have angered and annoyed many, Van Gogh compounded his offence by displaying sections

[8] *Sunday Times Magazine*, 27 Feb. 2005, p. 37.   [9] Ibid.
[10] Jelke Nijboer and Karen Soeters, *Death of a Filmmaker: Freedom of Expression and Tolerance under Siege* (Amsterdam, 2005).

of the Koran written on the body of a physically abused victim. Although Van Gogh was offered police protection he refused, and was assassinated in late 2004 while he cycled through an Amsterdam street.

These attitudes and these explosive events made it still harder to understand the cultural attitudes of those who had recently entered the Netherlands. Seen from the Islamic perspective, it is possible to consider how a carefully nurtured immigrant culture desired protection from a culture it misunderstood and perhaps feared. As the film director Karim Traida said, 'when Islam looks at Christian history, it's worried by what goes with liberalism. They think of the decadence of European Society.'[11] Such accusations hit hard in the Netherlands, which famously had no censorship laws beyond libel. It also had now to confront the possibility of philosophical limits upon free expression. Although jurisprudence suggested that censorship of the religiously challenging was impossible, this did not stop a Muslim group's attempt to prevent Ajaan Hirsi Ali's sequel (*Submission II*), arguing for legislation to prevent blasphemous descriptions of the Islamic faith.[12]

In the Netherlands the outcry led to calls to revive the antique law of blasphemy, which was still a part of the Dutch penal code. The justice minister, Piet Hein Donner (a descendent of the law's initiator), wanted the 1932 law against 'scornful blasphemy' to be updated to prevent attacks upon Muslims. Here, there was a direct conflict of interest within Dutch cultural traditions. The tolerance and protection offered to immigrant communities, which was still a source of great national pride, conflicted directly with the free expression of opinions and beliefs. Such freedoms had, ironically, attracted previous generations of refugees to the Netherlands. With regret, it was possible to argue that this multiculturalism had failed, and that the Netherlands should urgently undertake preparations to become a wholly secular state on the French model. The summer of 2006 witnessed something of a backlash against Ajaan Hirsi Ali, when it was revealed that she had lied about her age to gain asylum and had arguably also used a false name. The Dutch immigration minister Rita Verdonk argued for the revocation of Hirsi Ali's Dutch citizenship. Opinion was divided within Verdonk's own party (the liberal VDD), and eventually a compromise withdrew the threat of Hirsi Ali's potential deportation. What was significant was that Verdonk's own standing in liberal Holland was damaged by her uncompromising stance, arguably also ruining her chance of assuming the leadership of her party.

Those who feared the consequences of new religious and ethnic minorities in their midst pointed to the sheer scale of population movements which had made this a problem. Sometimes the same individuals, once again, attacked supra-national organizations like the European Union, blaming them for the removal of national boundaries in a context offering no adequate cultural alternative. If

---

[11] Quoted in *Sunday Times Magazine*, 27 Feb. 2005, p 39.
[12] Nijboer and Soeters, *Death of a Filmmaker*.

Muslims were increasingly identifying closely with their faith, this was placed in stark relief by the apparent decline in Christianity's hold over western European society. Such thoughts would also persuade western churches to indict the spiritual failure of the West. In the Netherlands one outspoken commentator from the Catholic church, Cardinal Adrianis Simonis of Utrecht, argued that the absence of spirituality in Dutch society had left the country liable to experience 'an Islamic cultural takeover'.[13] These attitudes, which portrayed a secular vacuum exploited by Islamic opportunism, were given still more influence by the election of a German conservative, Cardinal Reitzinger, to the papacy. From the start, Reitzinger argued, his role and mission was to combat the secular nature of modern Europe. At moments it became possible to believe that modern liberal secularism was helplessly caught in the middle between entrenched rhetorics that seemed almost unchanged from the time of the medieval crusades.

What was perhaps ironic about the new challenges of ethnicity and identity was that they were so frequently justified and encouraged by the West's own liberal agenda for rights and responsibilities. So much of this was also aided by the economic and cultural imperatives suggested by a globalized world. Recognizing the plurality of populations in the West now involved looking at more than simply the issue of ethnicity. Groups representing traditionalist and fundamentalist tendencies existed as well as those in favour of moderation, yet all asserted their right to both free expression and toleration. When the religious laws in most European and western countries were confronted by the issues in these new agendas they simply could not cope. Nations had founded religious laws for their own defence and the security of their own religious settlements. From now on they would be challenged by the pronouncements and intrusions of extra-national organizations on both sides of the argument. The agendas of international human-rights organizations increasingly saw the unfairness of religious laws, discriminating against ethnic and religious minorities that had entered western countries in the years after the Second World War.

It was thus inevitable that there would be detailed and prolonged reconsideration of religious laws, and particularly laws relating to blasphemy. Pulling blasphemy laws into the cold light of day allowed societies to question their origin, their historic credentials, and their credibility in a modern and post-colonial world. After such considerations the next logical step was to think about what other societies and jurisdictions did about the problem of blasphemy. Such scrutiny became a feature of the fifteen years after the fall of communism. Individual organizations, or groups, would occasionally investigate how blasphemy law worked in other jurisdictions, in response to attempts to rejuvenate it within their own land. Often free-speech or libertarian organizations would notice attempts by their local or national legislatures to clamp down upon blasphemy and the blasphemous.

---

[13] Ibid. 39.

This had been a growing trend in American culture and became still more overtly strident as the 1990s began. The National Endowment for the Arts would quite regularly come under attack from fundamentalist Christian thinkers, who bombarded Congress and Capitol Hill with messages protesting against the use of taxpayers' money to fund 'pornography' or 'blasphemy'. When Andres Serrano's controversial image of a crucifix suspended in human waste caused uproar it was senators such as Jesse Helms who strenuously attacked the funding of indecent or blasphemous works.[14] But such demands still rode roughshod over the First Amendment rights of individuals who wished to view such works. It also underlined the basic conception that trust and freedom were essential in allowing any endowment for the arts to operate efficiently. This became a new agenda of the religious Right, in which the arts were to be viewed with suspicion, thus wholly deserving the revival of old and inquisitorial attitudes to their practices. Moreover, it was hoped that pressure for taxpayers' funding to be devoted to wholesome and proper art would influence the 'market', placing a premium upon the orthodox and the safe. To many self-respecting artists, this made obscenity and blasphemy an apparently even more essential duty.

One aspect of 1960s counter-culture which began to have an important influence on blasphemy was the changing attitude of American youth to its own national symbols. In time this was to spawn attempts to desecrate the American flag—often interpreted as a species of blasphemy. The Supreme Court would readily resist making this an exception to the First Amendment. Nevertheless it became an incredibly emotive issue, indicating how forms of the sacred could create new forms of blasphemy. Time and again local laws would try to enact prohibitions on the misuse of the flag, only to be struck down by Supreme Court action. From the perspective of 1991, Barbara Hoffman was confident enough to suggest that: 'Today no one seriously contests the proposition that all artistic expression, written, pictorial, or performed is sufficiently imbued with elements of communication to fall within the scope of the First Amendment.'[15] Whilst the First Amendment would remain inviolable, self-appointed censors would embark on hostile action on other fronts.

This reopening of the 'culture wars' would also emerge in the unlikeliest of places. Prohibitions against textbooks in schools which discussed Halloween were hysterical forerunners of fears about a descent into Satanism. Marjorie Heins's spirited reply argued it was time libertarians went on the attack by funding and nurturing a First Amendment 'spin-doctor' who would make rights and liberties seem positive virtues again. The apparent vulnerability of First Amendment rights was self-evident proof that the atmosphere for freedom of

[14] For a full account of the Serrano affair see Ch. 3.
[15] See Barbara Hoffman, 'The Thought Police Are Out There: Reflections on First Amendment Protection of Offensive and/or Indecent Artistic Expression.' *Art Journal*, 50: 3, Censorship I (Autumn 1991), 40–4, at 40, 41, 42.

speech had changed dramatically.[16] Nonetheless local initiatives grew increasingly confident of their power and influence. This happened in New York State in 1999, when Senator Serphin Maltese, a prominent Catholic, attempted to revive the possibility of blasphemy prosecutions. This Bill (designated S2167) tried to amend the penal law and create the crime of ridiculing religious beliefs or practices. This prompted interested observers, accompanied by human-rights watchdogs such as Article 19, to embark upon ambitious surveys of the state of blasphemy in the West.

Of greater significance were the wholesale examinations of these laws undertaken by jurisdictions themselves. This occurred in Australia in 1994 and Britain in 2003. How far legal and social agendas had changed during the 1990s was very evident in the contrast between these two attempts to overhaul the law of blasphemy. The first indicated the swansong of rational liberal confidence in the law and active religious tolerance. The second indicated that doubt, ambivalence, and feelings of powerlessness could influence the legislature to redefine the limits of freedom. Almost ten years apart, the considerations of the New South Wales Law Reform Commission and those of the British House of Lords make interesting reading. The New South Wales Law Reform Commission reported very confidently in favour of the repeal of the law without replacement. Its deliberations showed a developed scepticism about the depth of religious feeling and their claims to override other considerations. More importantly, at times, it was actively prepared to criticize the nature and apparent bias of the evidence offered. Like the subsequent report, this investigation looked at the nature of the offence of blasphemous libel within its own jurisdiction, but also compared it to others. The commission noted that interest had been stirred up by the Salman Rushdie affair, but balanced this by mentioning the libertarian concerns about how it had been used to attack the fundamental right to freedom of speech. As with the later examination in Britain, four options emerged from the report: retention of the Common Law offence of blasphemous libel; modernization and codification of the offence; its replacement with public-order offences; or simple abolition.[17]

The Commission clearly suggested that blasphemy had been inherited from England only as Common Law, since the Church of England had not been established in Australia. Even then the Common Law had produced only one indigenous case, and a wholly convincing argument could be made that the offence had effectively lapsed. Nonetheless the Commission still followed the assumptions in the English Common Law of blasphemy that had formed its jurisprudence up until the late 1970s.[18] What was clear was that the Commission did not wish to admit the changes resulting from the 1978 *Gay News* case (and its

---

[16] Marjorie Heines, *Sex, Sin, and Blasphemy: A Guide to America's Censorship Wars* (New York, 1993), 182 and 188.

[17] New South Wales Law Reform Commission (hereafter NSWLRC) Report 74—Blasphemy, paras. 4.3 and 4.6.

[18] Ibid., paras. 4.8 and 4.12.

denial of intention as a mitigating factor) into New South Wales law.[19] Arguing that Australian approaches to the concept of *mens rea* (namely, the intention of the offender) had fundamentally altered, the Commission proceeded to suggest that 'manner' in publishing blasphemous material was still fundamentally important to this branch of Australian law. Using the words 'intention, knowledge and awareness', the Commission effectively excluded the impact of the *Gay News* case from its considerations.[20] By doing this it was able to demonstrate that the law looked antique and anachronistic. These suggestions, and the atmosphere they created, were reminiscent of the Commission for Racial Equality's arguments and confidence to transact repeal of the statute law in Britain in the early 1960s.

When the Commission looked at the legal position around blasphemy in other Australian territories, it illuminated what can happen to small pieces of English Common Law left on the statute book in post-colonial situations. Characteristically, there was not a uniform approach in a country that still distinguished between state and federal law. Tasmania was the only Australian territory to actively mention blasphemy by name, but again it was clear that the law resembled the pre-*Gay News* law in England with its emphasis upon the 'manner' of the religious statement made by any offender. The states of Victoria, South Australia, and the Australian Capital Territory seemed to be replicas of the situation in New South Wales. Western Australia and Queensland had abolished the offence, although objectionable literature still carried penalties in Queensland. Strangely, the situation in the Northern Territory remained unclear, turning on the ambivalent status of English Common Law within that state. Overall this patchwork looked like a legal relic and pictured a society largely untroubled by the problem of blasphemy.[21] Interestingly, however, there were more mentions of the issue in Australian federal legislation. This contained restrictions upon blasphemous films and television programmes, blasphemous books, and prohibitions upon the importation of blasphemous material without written permission from the attorney-general.[22]

Strangely, this situation looked like a reversed image of the United States. In Australia federal law nurtured and preserved blasphemy, whilst state criminal codes appeared apathetic or ignorant of the offence and its purpose. Already Australian federal legislation had witnessed the first signs of the new harassment and hatred agenda. In this, the crime of sending blasphemous materials through the post had been replaced with an offence that emphasized menace to the recipient. The new emphasis upon harassment was the occasion for the Commission to recommend the removal of references to blasphemy throughout federal legislation. The perennial problems of defining religion had also persuaded this Commission that the extension of laws about blasphemy would be an unwarranted interference with freedom of speech.

[19] For the *Gay News* case see Ch. 3.   [20] NSWLRC, para. 2.24
[21] Ibid., paras. 3.2–3.11   [22] Ibid., paras. 3.12–3.14

Meanwhile, similar changes had been occurring in Canada. The Canadian Law Reform Commission, in recodifying the criminal law, had recommended the removal of the offence of blasphemous libel. Despite this, the Canadian Criminal Code retained its link to Common Law. It was also potentially less liberal, since prosecutions could be commenced without the consent of the attorney-general.[23] The urge to modernize practice and legislation influenced the conclusion drawn by the New South Wales Law Commission. In suggesting that 'the offence may owe more to inertia in the absence of controversy', they argued that blasphemy was an amusing backwater which should now be placed out of bounds. This was enhanced by the suggestion that policing authorities more readily used other offences where blasphemy might be an issue. Such a law remained dangerous, since the Commission noted that the *Gay News* case had occurred '30 years after Lord Denning pronounced the offence "a dead letter" in England'.

When the Law Reform Commission summarized the evidence, they noted that most submissions spoke in favour of the 'absolute options' of retention of the offence intact, or of total abolition. The conclusion drawn from this was that the law was wholly symbolic in how it operated and was often actively 'imagined' by victim and by government, if not always by perpetrator. Suggestions that blasphemy directly protected morality seemed odd and scarcely altered since the seventeenth century of Robert Adriaansz. Van Hoorn. The Commission was unconvinced by this argument, strongly doubting that the laws had any deterrent value since they had been so rarely used.[24] There was also a lingering fear of creating and protecting dangerously entrenched interests. As the Commission suggested: 'religious protection is considered to be the primary aim of the offence, it is anomalous that only scurrilous attacks are penalised while well reasoned, intelligent debate is not, though such debate may be far more effective in destroying religious belief.'[25] There was no real evidence that a blasphemy law would promote religious tolerance, whilst the Commission argued that 'modern Anti-discrimination legislation is a superior vehicle to promote religious freedom and social tolerance, and to remedy conflict based on social difference'.[26] In considering the third option, the Commission noted racial hatred was covered by Division 3a of the Anti-discrimination Act of 1977 (NSW) and a recognisable equivalent existed in Article 319 of the Canadian Criminal Code.[27] Thus the Commission remained unconvinced by the arguments around extending harassment laws, as the perennial failure to define religion provoked difficulties. Finally, what they termed the 'chilling effect on free speech' became a compelling argument for ending blasphemy's tenuous existence in Australia.

Leading up to its final recommendations, the Commission began to pick away at the anomalies of the existing law of blasphemous libel. It argued that public order could be protected without such a law and that privileged

---

[23] Ibid., paras. 3.19–3.21.   [24] Ibid., para. 4.22   [25] Ibid., para. 4.17
[26] Ibid., para. 4.23   [27] Ibid., para. 4.50

protection for one set of religious convictions was indefensible. The law curtailed the right of free speech, and privileged religion over other important beliefs and lifestyles. Even if a codified offence of blasphemy were to be a solution, the Commission was adamant that this needed a very strong definition of intention and proof to be workable. Once again the constituent definition of religion was a very obvious problem; this held the inherent danger of what the commission called 'contrivance' for unsavoury groups to acquire religious status and receive protection. This was a back-door infringement of free speech that would lie dangerously in wait, and submissions supporting this suggestion did not convince the Commission. These submissions apparently failed to accept the idea of proper debate, the requirement of breach of the peace, as well as a sensible attitude to sentencing and procedure. There was also a concern that extension and codification would absorb the implications of the *Gay News* judgement, undermining the importance the Law Commission had placed upon intention.

Once again this showed a shift in emphasis which constitutes one of the major themes this book uncovers. In the liberal world which had established tolerance, those confronted by blasphemous outpouring of others had been obliged to demonstrate the scale of the hurt and offence they felt. For this jurisprudence the onus was upon an individual to use the law and seek redress. In this instance, provoked by the Law Commission's investigations, the free-speech tolerance agenda was being replaced by a more passive blasphemy. This saw the very existence of situations, writings, or images as 'a blasphemy'. This distinction, particularly amongst fundamentalist groups of many religious persuasions, was to prove extremely important in the future. Beyond Christianity, the Commission received a submission from the Islamic Council of New South Wales arguing for the extension of the law as a means of protecting multicultural society.[28] At this stage such submissions were largely subsumed and hidden amongst the more strident arguments about Christianity. These particular arguments, and the profile of those who made them, were to become stronger as the decade progressed. The Commission eventually concluded that abolition was the best course of action. In wishing to maintain the separation of church and state, it was considered unwise to limit religious debate or to be seen to be 'enforcing religious attitudes'. Free speech, at least to the Law Commission, was so important that 'the onus for justifying restrictions on freedom of speech rested heavily upon those supporting the restrictions'. Much of the Commission's findings had been based on the assumption of a world becoming overwhelmingly secular, in which laws from the early modern period had no real place.

Indeed such beliefs, for some time, acted as the cornerstone of post-war modernism and its sociological inquiry into the state of society. Interestingly, both the theory and contemporary views of the religious state of nations had been deeply challenged by both revisionist scholars, whole populations of believers,

---

[28] NSWLRC, paras. 4.41 and 4.42.

and the impact of world events. The issue of blasphemy as a law enacted against individuals and supposedly protecting society began to be overtaken by the agendas associated with what became identified as 'hate crime'. Recognition of this offence sought to prevent attacks upon minorities that lived without adequate legal protection. In many countries this led to the creation of laws against inciting types of hatred. These tried to prevent demagogues or leaflet editors from inciting attacks upon vulnerable minorities. Although in principle incitement seemed to empower and protect any social, ethnic, or cultural minority, the West extended this logic to its legal system in only a piecemeal way. However, the extension of protection brought its own problems, as difficult as the ones it sought to solve. Whilst laws against attacks on religious groups seemed inevitable, their nature proved uneven. Many of these problems were illuminated when the British government began an overhaul of religious offences. As such, this episode offers a blueprint for most western societies (and those on the current fringes of Europe) who might yet have to change their laws accordingly. What was striking about the House of Lords' deliberations is how very different they appeared from the swaggering confidence of the New South Wales Law Commission. Gone was the assumption that blasphemy was an antique relic, as was the sceptical attitude to the evidence offered by religious groups. These qualities were replaced by reticence, instinctive pragmatism, and doubt.

In 2002 the House of Lords heard evidence from a wide spectrum of religious, non-religious, and legal opinion. Some religions were by no means unanimous in their unqualified support for the status quo, others still gave it a cautious endorsement. The submission from the British-Israel World Federation argued that the concept of multiculturalism itself, as embodied in incitement legislation, was potentially anti-religious. By seeking to minimize harm to individual feelings, it was possible that the ideals of multiculturalism were setting up believers of all religions as potential offenders.

The Federation also demonstrated its Protestant isolationist agendas by invoking the sacred charge given to the monarch in the Coronation Oath. This was compounded by a list of moral concerns centred on the family and protection of the sovereign nation state. These assets, which deserved protection, were contrasted with the fear of the supra-national organizations (such as the European Union and the World Trade Organization) which threatened precious varieties of autonomy.[29] The Christian Institute was another body which saw the prevailing blasphemy law as reflecting 'the unique contribution and status of Christianity in Britain'. Linking this again with the Coronation Oath, the establishment of the Church of England and the use of a religious oath in parliament and elsewhere spoke eloquently about Christianity's imagined place in public life. The Institute

[29] Submission from The British–Israel World Federation to Select Committee on Religious Offences in England and Wales, HL Paper 95, Vol. III written evidence, p.12.

thus declared with confidence: 'the UK is not a secular state.' From this stand-point the argument against change was fearful of the implications of incitement. This potentially prevented mainstream Christianity from engaging in any form of evangelical work. As the Institute rightly pointed out, promotion of a particular religious viewpoint was some distance from 'hatred'. Such threats to the currency of belief, if left unchallenged, could undermine the moral welfare of the country, since, the Institute argued, 'beliefs govern the making of moral choices'.[30]

Representing a more obviously evangelical approach, the organization Christian Voice went beyond the constitutional importance of blasphemy, arguing that it had a precise, undiluted theological meaning. Thus the law could not be extended to protect other faiths, since their beliefs were simply 'mistaken'. Although this was a doctrinal position, it did expose the potential folly of protecting views whose revelations specifically denied the truth of other faiths.[31] This organization also targeted members of the Select Committee in person, writing to their private addresses to express equally strong opinions. The organization representing Christians within the broadcasting industry (the Centre for Justice and Liberty) saw it as essential that the blasphemy law be protected. This submission seemed to carry weight, and indicated that concerned members of the broadcasting industry might have experience of how the media regularly contained challenges to orthodox religion. The Centre saw the retention of the current law as a clear warning signal, hoping that the broadness of protection for Anglican beliefs constituted an 'umbrella' under which other faiths could shelter. This seemed preferable to legislation that would harm religious debate and hinder the expansion of the broadcasting industry into new areas.[32]

The Catholic Bishop's Conference was anxious to see the laws preventing the disruption of public worship retained. Despite this, a new incitement-to-religious-hatred law provided an elegant context for the repeal of the Common Law of blasphemous libel. Nonetheless, the Bishop's Conference was guarded in its support for incitement, wanting a clear distinction made between 'hatred' and 'merely arguing against a person's beliefs or attacking them for holding religious views'. Alongside this any new offence required a clear and coherent sense of intention in the mind of the perpetrator. Such evidence looked like the model response of a sizeable religious minority to the issue: clear on the need to offer protection for the idea of the religious, yet unconcerned by the erosion of the Anglican communion's monopoly. Incitement laws would stop violence against religious communities, but they would be rationally and sensibly defined so as not to catch religious proselytizing or the mere statement of religious beliefs.[33] At times it was clear that some religious groups betrayed their own fears about the

---

[30] Submission from The Christian Institute to Select Committee, ibid. 19.
[31] Submission from The Christian Voice to Select Committee, ibid. 23.
[32] Submission from The Centre for Justice and Liberty to Select Committee, ibid. 19.
[33] Submission from The Catholic Bishop's Conference to Select Committee, ibid. 17.

impact of religious hatred. Not surprisingly, the Jehovah's Witnesses were deeply concerned about the repeal of the Ecclesiastical Courts Jurisdiction Act that would protect the good order and conduct of their own religious meetings. This was especially pertinent since they had experienced a recent flurry of disrupted services.

Buddhist perspectives were understandably different. Whilst noting that religion had been a central object for discussion in Gorbachev's State of the World Forums, Buddhists were disappointed by the competitive stances of the Semitic monotheistic religions. Not only had the concepts of heresy and blasphemy been the means of advancing these, but siege mentalities had preserved archaic abuses of minority human rights.[34] Critical of this conflict model, they argued that religious behaviour too often bordered on the dysfunctional and that this would only be encouraged by an incitement law. Similarly, interference in religious matters was seen as beyond the concern of the state, a situation which had similarly rendered a blasphemy law redundant. Buddhists were also anxious to show that they viewed art which had elsewhere stimulated the conflict model into action (namely Monty Python's *Life of Brian*, Serrano's *Piss Christ*, and Rushdie's *Satanic Verses*) as 'intelligent but controversial explorations of belief'.[35]

When the Commission for Racial Equality (CRE) gave evidence the issue grew still more complicated. It frankly admitted the problems that had already been encountered with the incitement-to-race-hatred legislation. Prosecutions had been frustratingly few and had simply not had the intended impact. Since 1988 there had been only sixty-one prosecutions, largely because the evidential test in these cases had proved very difficult to satisfy. Material had to be shown to be obviously threatening, whilst the intention of the perpetrator to stir up hatred had also to be clearly demonstrated. In this area the CRE recommended considerable reform. Taking the Select Committee away from the dryness of the statute book, the submission of the CRE noted that race-hatred legislation had done almost nothing to prevent the circulation of racist material. Moreover, any law to stamp it out needed the co-operation of policing authorities, who laboured under problems of their own, especially when dealing with ethnic minority communities. In line with its raison d'être, the CRE was duty bound to point to the spectacular escalation of attacks upon Muslims since September 11th. It also reiterated that the case-law developed from the 1976 Race Relations Act had recognized Sikhs and Jews as racial groups, whilst such recognition was still denied Muslims and Rastafarians. If this persisted the inevitable dangerous conclusion that communities might draw from this was that some groups deserved protection more than others.[36]

The European Monitoring Centre on Racism and Xenophobia confirmed this gloomy picture still further, with evidence that anti-Muslim activity had become

---

[34] Submission from The Buddhist Society to Select Committee, ibid. 15.
[35] Submission from The Friends of the Western Buddhist Order to Select Committee, ibid. 41.
[36] Submission from The Commission for Racial Equality to Select Committee, ibid. 31–2.

a Europe-wide phenomenon in the wake of September 11th. The Centre also noted that converts to Islam were especially at risk and merited consideration as a vulnerable group in need of legislative protection. Muslims themselves confirmed the gloomy picture, presenting 'Islamaphobia' as endemic even before September 11th. Citing the report of the Runnymede Trust compiled in 1997, they outlined a sorry catalogue of fear, insecurity, and the social and economic impact upon wider British society of an ethnic group denied the implications of full citizenship.[37]

The Gay and Lesbian Humanist Association wanted the issue of incitement to be made universal, and were critical of any suggestion that religion should be singled out for particularly special treatment. From their position outside the mainstream religions, they noted that such protection for the wider concept of 'religion' would protect religious groups from criticism. This would conflict with instances where others saw the actions, or beliefs, of these groups cutting across basic human rights. From this the GALHA were concerned that any critiques of Muslim and Jewish slaughter practices, the Muslim treatment of women, and the Catholic stance on birth-control would be proscribed.[38]

Some Human Rights groups, such as 'Justice', were prepared to see an incitement law. However, they were adamant that the attorney-general should retain discretion over decisions to prosecute. This carried the latent assumption that the attorney-general would remain beyond political or religious persuasion, or indeed that religion would remain dormant as a political issue.[39] Evidence from *Searchlight*'s monitoring of the activities of both the far Right and Sikh extremists made it abundantly clear that the issue was in urgent need of attention. The British National Party had publicized that mosques were secret arms depots, and Sikh extremists (masquerading as Muslims) had engaged in letter campaigns against Hindus and fellow Sikhs. Although Jews had been recognized by the law as an ethnic group, evidence suggested that there were still problems since anonymous acts related to hatred (graffiti and other acts of vandalism) could not be covered under incitement. The Libertarian Alliance argued that its sympathizers would potentially engage in civil disobedience and asked perceptively whether an incitement law would sanction or prevent the fatwa against Salman Rushdie.[40]

After much deliberation the House of Lords Select Committee's Report concluded that there was no clear way forward. In opening the Select Committee's final conclusions, it was made obvious within a few pages that they viewed legislation against blasphemy as potentially archaic. Drawing a distinction

---

[37] Submission from The Islamic Society to Select Committee, ibid. 48–9.

[38] Submission from The Gay and Lesbian Humanist Association to Select Committee, ibid. 41–3.

[39] Submission from Justice to Select Committee, ibid. 51–2.

[40] Submission from The Libertarian Alliance and the Libertarian International to Select Committee, ibid. 31–2.

between a blasphemy law and the concept of incitement, the Report stated that 'blasphemy concerns sacred entities or beliefs, incitement relates to people or groups'. This seemed to suggest that blasphemy was about the inanimate sacred, and was thus less relevant than incitement, which was about living and breathing human beings. Quoting from what it had heard at a seminar in Cambridge, convened by Sir David Williams QC, the Report noted that tolerant attitudes needed to become proactive. The logic of this thinking seemed to propel the Committee to consider that religious incitement should have the same legal status as racial incitement. Such a decision was not being made in isolation but followed the clear lead offered by the European Union Council Framework Decision on combating racism and xenophobia, which compelled action in any case. The report demonstrated that over 3 per cent of Britain's population was Muslim, yet did not enjoy the definition of being a 'racial group'.

Having listened hard to the evidence offered by members of the Anglican Church, the Catholic clergy, and other minority Christian groups, the Committee took seriously the fears around repeal of the Ecclesiastical Courts Jurisdiction Act of 1860. After a century-and-a-half concerned with texts and works of art, the battleground of blasphemy or iconoclasm seemed to be moving towards images, premises, and buildings invested with the idea of the sacred. This response in a new millennium looked surprisingly medieval, and took the sacred some distance from negotiable postmodern Christianity that the 'Sea of Faith' organization had offered to Anglicanism in the 1980s and 1990s.

The Committee noted that the Christian groups they had encountered saw a blasphemy law as having a genuine purpose, as an expression of the fabric of life and society. This idea surfaced so regularly during the evidence that it was impossible for the Committee to ignore it. Such an ideal also served as a warning not to engage in modernization for its own sake. Noting some fears that placing all on an equal footing would constitute 'negative equalisation', the Select Committee fell some distance from recommending this. The final Report then discussed the options open to the government. It was clear that 'repeal without replacement' ran counter to the tide of evidence which argued that blasphemy law still had a symbolic and practical purpose. The difficulties of maintaining this position, however, were laid bare when simple extension of the blasphemy law to other faiths was dismissed. An option to bring in the possibility of a 'broader based blasphemy act', drawing upon a minority faction within the Law Commission's considerations, was suggested as a means of modernization. This would bring the law's 'purpose' into consideration where it had controversially been absent. The law would also be aimed at publications rather than public utterances (so often the concern of human-rights lawyers). Such action to alter legislation would also allow control of the offence, since power would reside with the Public Prosecution Service.

Interestingly, the Select Committee also noted that the spirit and protection offered by the Ecclesiastical Courts Jurisdiction Act should continue in some form, and considered them far from obsolete. Perhaps acknowledging the problems of protecting the individual person, the Committee was more committed to the protection of buildings and artefacts as outlined in both the Indian and Fijian Criminal Codes. Such protection

> would recognise, most importantly, that religious ceremonies are hallowed, the source of spiritual sustenance and emblems of community coherence. The buildings, artefacts and surroundings are imbued with a similar significance. These are aspects of the freedom of thought, conscience and religion which, in their own right, deserve protection by law against desecration and mindless, or mindful, abuse.[41]

Problems regarding incitement legislation's relationship with the threat it was supposed to counter were high on the Committee's agenda. Amusingly, legislation to counter the effects of the French Revolution was quarried as a precedent. Citing the Incitement to Mutiny Act of 1797, a temporary solution to the naval mutinies at Spithead and the Nore, the Committee noted that legislation intended to be temporary was still in force. Such reactive legislation was too readily viewed as political in nature, and the few cases tried under it merely served to confirm this. Writing in *Socialist Outlook* in 2004, Piers Mostyn expressed concern about what he argued was a creeping tide of anti-libertarian legislation. Citing both the Anti-Social Behaviour Act, the 2003 Criminal Justice Act, and the Civil Contingencies Bill, Mostyn argued that a far-reaching system of summary justice was being consciously created. His Marxist-inspired conclusions suggested that such a change was necessary as a means of handling the transition between middle and neo-liberal late capitalism.[42] It was thus by no means impossible for opponents to place the incitement-to-racial- and religious-hatred laws into their wider legislative and political context.

To make its recommendations workable the Committee defined the difference between fair criticism, and the opinions and expressions that would fall foul of either blasphemy law or any attempt to create an incitement law. It chose to use the word 'vilification' to describe the action, whilst the nature of the unacceptable criticism was anything aimed at what it termed the 'Foundations of Faith.' This conclusion was diluted by an admission that the dividing-line between acceptable and unacceptable had yet to be defined by any British court.[43] Tantalizingly, the Select Committee also suggested that any further incitement legislation would potentially open the door for the construction of a wider offence. Such an extension would probably prevent attacks upon all other minorities, with the logic of this next step proving hard to resist. The final conclusions nonetheless asserted that Britain was not secular and that religion 'continues to be a significant

---

[41] Submission from The Libertarian Alliance and the Libertarian International to Select Committee, ch. 5: The Ecclesiastical Courts Jurisdiction Act, 1860, para. 65.

[42] Piers Mostyn, 'Preparing for the "Strong State"?', *Socialist Outlook*, issue 3 (Spring 2004).

[43] Select Committee on Religious Offences in England and Wales, HL Paper 95, Vol. I Report, pp. 23–7.

component, or even determinant, of social values, and plays a major role in the lives of a large number of the population'.[44]

The Select Committee acknowledged that it had come under significant pressure to alter the scope and power of the existing blasphemy law and the protection it offered. Christian Voice was noted as arguing for a much wider scope for the law. Focusing upon the legal protection of the Church of England as an institution, the Select Committee's definition strongly emphasized the constitutional dimensions of a law that looked theoretical and remote. Christian Voice argued conversely that the law was more proactive and capable of use against any 'contemptuous, reviling, scurrilous or ludicrous matter' aimed at God, Jesus, or the Established Church. This 'definition war' was partly expressing the creeping devolution of religious power back to grassroots believers. But it was also empowering aspects of evangelicalism, that had regularly argued the Church of England had scarcely done much to defend the sacred nature of belief.

Problems were also associated with the freedoms guaranteed under the European Convention through the 1998 Human Rights Act. The situation was filled with some messy contradictions. Article 9 guaranteed freedom of thought, conscience, and religion, aided by Article 10 which enshrined freedom of expression. Yet the potential for Article 14, which prohibited sexual, racial, or other discrimination against minorities, to conflict with Articles 9 and 10 was seemingly endemic. But the Select Committee also noted the paradox that a blasphemy law was itself also potentially in breach of Article 14. Of still greater importance was the declaration that the European Convention gave equal status to Articles 9 and 10 in stark contrast to the United States, where freedom of expression was given precedence.[45]

The Select Committee, like the organisation Article 19 before it, spent some considerable time investigating what other jurisdictions did about the problem of religious offences. Whilst it noted that wholesale transplantion would be problematic, it hoped lessons could be learnt from this exercise. What this seemed to produce was an unhelpful realization that the situation in England was arguably unique. In Ireland the offence had disappeared with the disestablishment of the Church of Ireland. Whilst Article 40.6 of the Irish constitution appeared to be capable of punishing blasphemy, it was noted that a landmark decision by the Irish Supreme Court was unable to determine the nature of the offence from previous case-law. The mixed success of an incitement law in Northern Ireland was similarly less than encouraging, with a noted failure to prosecute sectarian cases. The Committee also accepted the views of a number of lawyers who suggested the law of blasphemy was likely to be effectively dead in Scotland. However the Scottish parliament had arguably been forward-thinking in creating a category of offences aggravated by religious prejudice. This again emphasized

[44] Ibid. 38.   [45] Ibid. 48.

the public-order dimension, since another offence was necessary before the idea of religious prejudice was considered by any court. France and Germany had, by now, quite strong incitement laws, whilst the Italian penal code had provisions preventing offence to religion. The Netherlands, before the Van Gogh incident, had maintained a dormant criminal offence of blasphemy but restricted it only to references concerning God and required an extremely strict test of intention.[46]

An example investigated from Britain's own legislative doorstep was a revisiting of the Indian Criminal Code of 1860, a measure which had produced an uneasy legal equality amongst India's primary religious groups.[47] By the time the final report was published the Select Committee's enthusiasm for the Indian Criminal Code solution had wavered. Whilst much of this was due to some of the standard criticisms offered about laws embracing all religious positions, perhaps the most damning evidence came from Indian commentators. The Committee's introduction finished with an impassioned plea from the Indian attorney-general, Soli Sorabjee, who outlined important experience of using the Indian Criminal Code solution in practice. Increasingly, given the nature of Indian politics, it had been impossible to tell the difference between political and religious criticism and hate. Sorabjee took the view that laws against hate speech provoked intolerant attitudes and conflict models of religious interaction, and that this had now afflicted Indian society. The Select Committee was moved to print his concluding remarks, which argued: 'We need not more repressive laws but more free speech to combat bigotry and to promote tolerance.'[48] The distinguished commentary offered by Chief Justice Hidayatullah in a 1952 Supreme Court Judgement on the Indian Criminal Code noted that it was overbearingly paternalist and threatened to hamstring the morals of a whole society. Emphasizing that draconian legislation depressed human cultural achievement, he declared: 'standards must be so framed that we are not reduced to a land where the protection of the least capable and the most depraved amongst us must determine what the morally healthy cannot view or read.'[49]

Just as two similar re-evaluations of the law ten years apart demonstrated how agendas and thinking had changed, so it was that two similar attempts to rejuvenate blasphemy as a legal and cultural concept also demonstrated this. The Salman Rushdie affair had persuaded the British government to—if only briefly—evaluate the utility of laws that covered the issue of blasphemy. Anxious

---

[46] Select Committee on Religious Offences in England and Wales, 58.

[47] See Ibid., Minutes of Evidence, 18 July 2002, and Supplementary Memo of the National Secular Society. The Code had been constructed by the distinguished judge and legal commentator James FitzJames Stephen, who was later to be vocal opponent of the Common Law of blasphemous libel in England. The two particular sections of the Code (according to the 1860 edition) relevant to this discussion are 295a and 298: '295a. DELIBERATE AND MALICIOUS ACTS INTENDED TO OUTRAGE RELIGIOUS FEELINGS OF ANY CLASS BY INSULTING ITS RELIGION OR RELIGIOUS BELIEFS', and '298. UTTERING WORDS, ETC., WITH DELIBERATE INTENT TO WOUND RELIGIOUS FEELINGS.'

[48] Ibid. 18.   [49] Ibid. 60.

to close down any extension of the law, the Home Office, through John Patten and the *ex-parte Choudoury* case, blocked the extension of the blasphemy law.[50] The complaints that had been advanced by Muslims had focused upon specific beliefs and figures of faith that Rushdie had vilified.

Coincidentally, ten years later Michel Houellebecq, the author of a similar religiously inspired novel, found himself in court. Houellebecq had been interviewed by a French literary magazine *Lire* about his novel *Platform*, which had explored religious ideas. During the course of this interview Houellebecq had expressed considerable contempt for the Muslim faith and was prosecuted for inciting racial hatred. The case was brought by the mosques of France's significant cities, as well as the National Federation of French Muslims and the World Islamic League. Houellebecq drew a distinction between faith and its adherents, with a message suggesting he was prepared to tolerate the sinner whilst hating the sin. During a discussion of the literary merits of the West's holy books, Houellebecq dismissed the Koran as less worthy than the Bible. The charges against him equated these views with Islamophobia, a view supported by France's Human Rights League. The case provoked considerable discussion in France and beyond. Some lawyers, and figures from the literary establishment, expressed deep concern that the West's most obviously secular country was allowing its laws to be shaped and used in this way. Some of these commentators were especially concerned that if the prosecution were successful it would re-establish a blasphemy law, or the very least reintroduce it as a legal category of offence. Although Houellebecq was acquitted, it was by no means clear that such prosecutions would not occur elsewhere. The activation of the law in this instance seemed to show how such laws of incitement might be used if not properly framed or regulated. If individuals or groups construed criticism as hatred, then legal systems and whole societies were going to have to embrace tighter restrictions upon freedom of expression.

One academic who advanced influential opinions on this was David Lawton, the author of *Blasphemy*, which had been one informed response to the Salman Rushdie affair. Lawton was interviewed on American public radio about the Houellebecq affair, and suggested that it seemed to be symptomatic of how the real world felt obliged to invade the creative world of novelists. Speculating on whether Houellebecq would ever write again, Lawton declared: '. . . there's a space. Its the space Rushdie talked about, the space for fiction. In a sense, that space doesn't exist any more.' It also emerged from the discussion that draconian laws of this nature might function as a specific incitement to artistic endeavour. The interviewer (Stephen Crittenden) paraphrased some of Lawton's arguments that blasphemy potentially 'becomes a necessary tool in the struggle against

---

[50] The home secretary's decision in this instance closed the door to the use of the law of blasphemous libel to protect Muslim beliefs, on the grounds that its intention and construction applied merely to the established church.

fundamentalism'. Lawton replied that laws intended to protect minorities would curtail freedom in the name of multiculturalism.[51]

If this were in fact the case, then the future appeared bleak indeed. Offensiveness, aggravated in the mind of the believer, would steadfastly be faced in the future with a tougher, less compromising species of libertarianism. This also had implications for the traditional political alignment of Right and Left. The Right had the opportunity to become more mainstream and sophisticated, as its dialogues about the failure of multiculturalism and integration brought supposedly 'more primitive' cultures into conflict with the West. Such arguments could be laced with liberalism's traditional concerns about the rights of minority groups, within what it saw as suspiciously closed societies. This had essentially been the message of Pim Fortuyn, and it could not be as readily dismissed as the one-dimensional hostility of Jean-Marie Le Penn and others. As the Right arguably drew confidence from this, the Left seemed more anxious about how its empowerment of minorities had impacted upon basic freedoms. Political correctness appeared to be incoherent and in danger of satisfying neither the religious, who saw it as a dilution, nor the philosophically liberal rationalists, who saw it as a sell-out.

Whilst it may have been the case that legislative authorities in the West were anxiously considering blasphemy to be an anachronism, nobody had told populations at large. After a period of considerable slumber, British culture and public order were rocked by two incidents which occurred within a few months of one another. Emphatically, they demonstrated that the agenda associated with laws to prevent blasphemy was being pulled down two divergent paths. The first of these demonstrated that protection for Christianity alone seemed more anachronistic than ever. The other path led precisely in the opposite direction, suggesting that Christianity was still important, that it should not be diluted by pandering to other faiths, and thus deserved privileged protection.

The first of these incidents involved the production of a play about the Sikh community staged in Birmingham. In December 2004 the Birmingham Repertory Theatre staged a play entitled *Behzti* ('dishonour' in Punjabi), written by the Sikh actress turned playwright Gurpreet Kaur Bhatti. Before it was staged it was very clear that the play would be challenging. Although it was an exposé of brutality towards women within the Sikh community, there was an extent to which the play's action owed much to more traditional 'theatre of cruelty'. Of particular concern was a scene in which episodes describing the rape of a number of young Sikh women by one of the elderly male characters are described to the audience. These are depicted as occurring specifically within a Sikh temple. Elders and spokesmen for the Sikh community protested, and were further aggrieved when their alternative suggestion that the play should be set in a Sikh community centre was rejected out of hand. Such reactions were at odds with the opinions

---

[51] Interview, ABC Radio, 23 Oct. 2002.

of western theatre critics, who were keen to see new material portray otherwise closed communities. Writing in the *Independent*, Helen Cross suggested that the play was 'offensive, and furious and bloodthirsty and angry in all the right places'.[52]

Matters came to a head on the night of Saturday, 18 December 2004, when the situation erupted explosively. A demonstration of over a thousand people from the Sikh community gathered outside the theatre protesting against the play, claiming its intent was sacrilegious and insulted the Sikh religion. The building was besieged and demonstrators managed to storm the stage, halting the performance. This was the first time violent protest around the issue of religion had halted a theatrical production in Britain. The theatre itself could not guarantee the safety of its workers, nor of the audience, and concluded it had no option but to terminate *Behzti*'s run at the theatre. The police had sustained several injuries in attempting to quell the disturbances, making several arrests on public-order charges. Certainly, some within the theatre, and within the wider theatrical world, felt that they had been let down by authority. Whilst the police had argued they would prevent trouble, they could not guarantee the safety of individuals performing in or viewing the play. Moreover, one senior officer had felt duty-bound to point out the resources that would have been tied up in protecting those involved in the play during the remainder of its run.

The British theatrical establishment reacted with horror to this incident. A letter of protest, published in the *Guardian* on 23 December 2004, argued: 'it is a legitimate function of art to provoke debate and sometimes to express controversial ideas. A genuinely free pluralist society would celebrate this aspect of our culture.' This letter was signed by the director and actors involved in *Behzti*, alongside David Edgar, Michael Frayn, Howard Brenton, Willie Russell, Andrew Motion, and others. The reaction of some members of the Sikh community was more measured. One cynical correspondent to the *Guardian* saw the production as providing 'instant fame and fortune for a virtually unknown playwright'. This fame and fortune would be substantially at the expense of the Sikh community's good reputation in Britain. Others expressed real concern that the protests, and their apparent success, would rebound upon the Sikh community, which would now be considered insular and difficult.

In the days that followed artists and libertarian campaigners saw the incident as an opportunity to argue that the blasphemy law should be repealed. The *Behzti* episode seemed to provide evidence of what might happen if an incitement-to-religious-hatred law were to be hurriedly put upon the statute book. Three weeks after the incident, the *Guardian* carried an article showcasing the arguments of Trevor Philips, the chairman of the Commission for Racial Equality, who urged that the law should be repealed, in order to give society confidence that the issue of incitement would be dealt with for the right reasons. The lessons of the *Behzti*

---

[52] *Independent*, Tuesday, 21 Dec. 2004.

incident were important and ought to have informed wider thinking, as the complacency which had surrounded the law in Britain was drawing to a close. No longer could secularized western and Christian values be seen as the only ones blasphemy was prepared to protect. Moreover, the comfortable assumption that nobody who was religious really cared about blasphemy against their beliefs was shown to be increasingly outdated. The *Behzti* incident proved that religion and identity were once again firmly rooted in specific parts of the community in western societies. A secular world had not rendered blasphemy obsolete—the logic (if not the spirit) of multiculturalism had once more made it an attractive option. Occurring between the House of Lords Select Committee considering the issue, and parliament pushing forward legislation, the *Behzti* incident was timely. It appeared to be a working example of both good and bad practice if incitement to religious hatred was to be society's legislative future.

The outcome of the *Behzti* incident appeared to be pulling the laws of blasphemy towards offering protection for all religious minorities. If blasphemy law remained viable, it was only going to be credible through being extended to cover beliefs and faiths other than Christianity. However, the logic of this was overturned by the controversy that emerged around a musical shown on BBC 2 within a month of the *Behzti* affair. Stemming from a comparatively obscure theatre workshop production, which had its origins in the Battersea Arts Centre three years previously, *Jerry Springer: The Opera* suddenly exploded into national and international prominence. It had quickly become a cult classic through its use of the purgative confessional chat-show style of Jerry Springer's television programmes. Fictionalizing this situation allowed the production to explore risky territory, amidst eyecatching spectacle and instantly memorable songs. Many reports and audience reactions remembered the tap-dancing Ku Klux Klan members and the tortuous lives of the emotionally scarred inadequates who usually formed the core of any Jerry Springer programme. What brought the show real opposition was its depiction of Jesus, God, and Satan as three such guests seeking a 'closure' of the battle which had scarred the universe for the past 2,000 years. Christ, suggesting he was 'actually a little bit gay', was berated by Springer and by his mother Mary, who chastized him for having abandoned her through his death on the cross. God was portrayed as occasionally doubtful and possibly in need of the sort of therapy Springer traditionally peddled on his show. Many Christians, but especially the group Christian Voice, saw this last aspect as particularly offensive. It seemed clearly to suggest that Springer had been elevated to sit at the right hand of God. This seemed to be confirmed, if you had no sense of the ironic, in the operatic chorus singing 'Jerry Eleison' rather than 'Kyrie Eleison'. Christian Voice seemed especially determined to make the matter not one of religious blasphemy, but specifically of blasphemy against Christianity. The organization called upon Christianity's historic right to privilege and argued for its recolonization of public space. Indicating how Christianity had let itself become fair game, Christian Voice

Fig. 1. *Jerry Springer: The Opera* reawoke Christian sensibilities about blasphemy in England.

suggested: 'of course if this show portrayed Muhammed, as ridiculous, deviant or homosexual, it would never have seen the light of day.'[53] Yet *Springer*, for all its profanities, obscenities, and larger-than-life grotesques, deserves to be considered as more subtle than opponents allowed. Just as Monty Python's *Life of Brian* had damaged the credibility of the medieval and Christian epic, so *Springer* dealt a paralysing blow to the ersatz camp neo-melodrama of Andrew Lloyd Webber's musicals.[54] The opera also satirised the quest for instant salvation and its achievement through the ministrations of Jerry Springer, who often repeated he was only a facilitator of the spectacle of confession. The opera's conclusion that there was 'No Good, No Bad', which Christian Voice took to be symptom of amorality, further indicated the vacuousness of postmodern obsessions with spectacle.

The *Jerry Springer* furore escalated when BBC television decided to screen a live telecast of the West End production. Broadcast on a Saturday evening, the

[53] Christian Voice leaflet, Feb. 2005 and repr. Apr. 2006.
[54] Python's *Life of Brian* is discussed in Ch. 8.

show attracted a monumental reaction when over 45,000 people complained about swearing and the nature of religious themes in the programme. A number of threats were made to members of the BBC management in the aftermath of the screening. For a time stories circulated that a number of them were in hiding and had received communications sent directly to their homes expressing disgust at the Springer programme and their part in it. The BBC website contained quite a cross-section of opinions from both sides of the argument. One correspondent argued that the show would enable 'future generations to be able to judge what kind of society existed in Britain. That obscene and blasphemous programmes were shown would prove how much British society has fallen over the past 50 years.' Others offered the, by now, familiar argument that viewing the television was scarcely compulsory and that the religious had been warned about the content. Put in these terms, such an argument suggested *Springer* was close to a piece of minority programming which was arguably part of the BBC's mission. Some would go further: 'if the God squad can force the BBC to put *Songs of Praise* on BBC 1 at prime-time every week, I am sure they can put up with a minority audience watching a one-off on BBC 2. I pay my licence fee too, and I object to Christians forcing their agenda down my throat.'

The BBC offered a robust defence of its decision to screen the *Springer* opera. The director-general, Mark Thompson, argued: 'there is nothing in this which I believe to be blasphemous.' The matter was dealt with more formally by the committee which subsequently convened to investigate the vast number of complaints received about the programme. This committee noted that many of these had been received by the BBC before the show had even been transmitted. Viewed in a certain way, the corporation chose to see this as a form of 'prior restraint' in which individuals with certain beliefs were seeking to police the viewing habits and enjoyment of others. Where it was noted that there were approximately 8,000 swear-words in *Jerry Springer: The Opera*, the suggestion was made to appear ludicrously overstated. The more literal-minded opponents of *Springer* had claimed the massed heavenly choir chanting expletives constituted separate and individual instances of blasphemy.

In their deliberations the committee saw it as supremely important that the BBC Producer's Guidelines on offensive material had not been breached. These noted that material was most likely to cause offence when it took audiences by surprise. The committee was clear that *Jerry Springer: The Opera* had been preceded by a very significant barrage of warnings about its content and potential capacity to offend. It was also noted that the portrayal of God and Christ occurred in Springer's own nightmare vision rather than constituting a portrayal of reality. The committee concluded: 'the very fact that the programme was broadcast at all would have caused offence to a significant number of people.' Answering the concerns that *Springer* had been chosen whereas other West End shows had been ignored, the committee argued the range of awards heaped upon *Springer* demonstrated that it was clearly of importance. Flexing its muscles about the issue of free speech, the committee argued that the BBC had an obvious mission to extend and innovate. It also noted the conflicts in the European Convention on Human Rights between those covering the right to freedom of religion, and those covering the rights to freedom of expression. The committee then concluded that complaints against *Jerry Springer: The Opera* should not be upheld. The sole dissident, Angela Sarkis, interestingly agreed that *Springer* had been well signposted, yet could not see sufficient artistic quality in it to outweigh the offence it had caused.

Jerry Springer: The Opera certainly demonstrated that there were new ways in which the religious could inspire. When traditional religious figures were combined with characteristics of modern sensationalist television, it was clear that controversy would result. If religion was the last taboo, then productions like *Springer* could only be expected. However, campaigns to stop such productions really argued that the sacred should remain inviolable. In the case of *Jerry Springer*, they also argued that Christians should not be driven out of public space if they sought to protect their own beliefs. The opposition to *Jerry Springer: The Opera*, however, also demonstrated some interesting changes in strategy and tactics. Christian Voice, fresh from its success in having a student production removed from the stage at St Andrew's University, actively galvanized itself to attack *Springer*. Using the full power of the internet and email messages that could be cascaded down through the membership, the organization was able to bring a mass presence to bear in its complaints against *Springer*. It had also adopted some of the tactics similar pressure-groups had used with success in the United States. Frustrated by attempts to use the law, Christian Voice pressurized a cancer charity, Maggies Centres, to refuse a donation from the production of *Jerry Springer: The Opera*. This prompted the show's leading actor, David Soul, to suggest that 'cancer was not just a Christian problem'. In mid-2005 plans for the show to go on a nationwide tour after leaving the West End ran into some problems. Arts Council funding was not as forthcoming as the show's producers had expected. This looked, despite denials, like a result of the sort of pressure brought to bear on the National Endowment for the Humanities in the United States. The show's producer eventually managed to gather together a consortium of regional theatres to bankroll the production, albeit with a reduced cast and budget.

Fundamentalist forms of religion had thus made their presence felt in the public spheres of the West and had finally made governments, broadcasters, and the liberal establishment take notice of their demands. Thus, it was scarcely a surprise when some advocates of the 'sanctity' of free speech chose to fight back. This occurred in September 2005, when the Danish newspaper *Jyllands-Posten* published twelve cartoons which associating Muhammad with Islamic terrorism. When Muslim community leaders complained, the Danish prime minister refused to intervene. Just how global an issue blasphemy had become was demonstrated by the rapidity with which opposition was mobilized. Danish goods were boycotted, embassies closed in sensitive countries, and Europeans were declared to be under threat of kidnap in the Palestinian West Bank. The offices of the European Union were seized and occupied by gunmen in the West Bank city of Gaza. However, the world of publishing responded with equal rapidity, with newspapers in a number of European countries publishing the cartoons in solidarity with the stance taken by *Jyllands-Posten*. Versions of the cartoons were published in Norway, Germany, Spain, Italy, the United States, and the Netherlands. In Germany, *Die Welt* argued that Muslims had no right to be 'shielded from satire in the West'. In France, the editor of *France-Soir* was dismissed by the paper's Franco-Egyptian proprietor, who promptly offered an apology to the country's Muslim population. However, the power of publishing was itself turned upon its head when it was discovered that a number of Danish imams had distributed cartoons which had never been published by *Jyllands-Posten*. The imams subsequently claimed that such images had been sent anonymously to Muslims in Denmark and constituted evidence of violent anti-Muslim feeling.[55]

The battle to introduce sweeping legislation against religious incitement also unexpectedly fell foul of the free-speech backlash. At the end of January 2006 Britain's Labour government was embarrassingly defeated in the Commons over its Racial and Religious Hatred Bill. This had contained sweeping limitations upon free expression which stunned the House of Lords into recasting the Bill in a more acceptable form. When this returned to the Commons, government attempts to introduce amendments were defeated by a rainbow coalition of opposition and disaffected MPs from the governing party.

Thus free speech and religious fundamentalism appeared locked in combat once again, after perhaps a century of uneasy peace. The rights of the religious side of the argument appeared to win the day with the final approval in the British parliament of laws against incitement to religious hatred. Those on the free-speech and free-expression side of the argument were left to consider the condition of the freedoms the West still offered and the presumption of religion to control this again. As E. L. Doctorow had suggested during the Salman Rushdie affair:

Who can say that God didn't intend for some of us to serve him in this way? Who can say the writer does not prostrate himself before God each and every day he rises to his work? Or else we all commit sacrilege, the basic sacrilege of intending to write when the sacred text of the Word of God is already written. The poet of rhapsody and celebrant of God's glory, the pious scholar, the exegete who combs the sacred text, is no less hellbound than

---

[55] *Daily Telegraph*, 3 Feb. 2006, p. 20.

the satirist, the ironist, and the skeptic. All our books should be destroyed, and all of us go into hiding.[56]

So, from where had the offence of blasphemy returned to wreak its havoc upon a world that the West thought had become religiously tolerant? The following chapters will uncover this history and highlight the stubborn endurance of this offence and how it has coloured human interactions through the centuries.

---

[56] 'Statements by Writers at Public Forum Organised by American P.E.N.', *Cardozo Studies in Law and Literature*, 2:1 (Spring 1990), 69–75, at 70.

2

Blasphemy in Words and Pictures: Part I, 1500–1800

Christianity has historically coped with substantial differences of belief within its own community, yet these have also been fundamental to its history. The great church councils of the early Christian era were a response to these differences and tried to enforce religious orthodoxy. Portrayals of Christ, in particular, have always constituted a tension between human personality and divinity, but have also reflected the changing theological emphases of Christianity itself. Images of Christ in the medieval era reflected the assertion of his divinity that had been confirmed by the thinking of the Council of Nicaea. In this iconography Christ generally appeared larger than surrounding figures, as clearly an incarnation of the divine, further emphasized by the presence of angels and dramatic visual effects. The emphasis upon the incarnation was also of much interest and concern to the early church fathers, since Augustine recognized the considerable importance of the use of signs and signifiers.

Although attempts to enforce orthodoxy were popular with secular rulers, they were never wholly successful. Despite the early church's willingness to move against groups of heretics, the phenomenon was not as important an issue as it was to become later. During the Dark Ages Christianity was significantly preoccupied in fighting for its very survival against the influx of barbarian migrants. Indeed, it is possible to overestimate the uniformity and to antedate the success of Christianity in the West. Some estimates suggest that paganism was still an important religious force in parts of Germany as late as the eleventh century.[1] This perhaps further explains early Christianity's penchant for iconoclasm. Typical of these initial Christian iconoclasts was the early seventh-century itinerant monk Columbanus who, in the company of the future St Gallus, destroyed a pagan temple at Tuggen (near Zurich), confining the pagan idols to the nearby lake. This was followed by a more obviously calculated performance in front of the assembled villagers. St Gallus berated the locals for their idolatry and promptly smashed the nearby icons and again threw

[1] Floyd Seyward Lear, 'Blasphemy in the Lex Romana Curiensis', *Speculum*, 6:3 (July 1931), 445–59, at 447.

these into the lake.[2] In a related development, the Christian theologian Origen of Alexandria tentatively constructed a notion of free will and introduced a typography of temptation. In this individual Christians found themselves the potential prey of demons, who would turn the human mind to unfortunate thoughts. Ambrose, bishop of Milan, in the fourth century further defined the importance of religious orthodoxy, making it a central part of loyalty to the state.[3]

Augustine was also importantly involved in identifying the gravity of the sin against the Holy Ghost. This helped to define heretics as those unwilling to submit to religious orthodoxy.[4] In combating heresy there was an emphasis upon the need for recantation of the erroneous opinions. The early heresies that did deviate from orthodox Christian worship, notably in France, Italy, and Germany, were generally isolated incidents associated with an excess of piety. These did not appear to spring from wholesale 'movements', like those characterizing the phenomenon's later history. What began to make heresy much more of an issue was the growing sophistication of the church and local forms of government, both symptoms of the changing nature of urban life in eleventh-century Europe.

One historian of heresy, Malcolm Lambert, suggests that our search for modern communities of belief and their impact begins in this period. Alongside social and political changes, the spread of literacy and the startlingly widespread availability of the printed word also had an important impact.[5] Self-sustaining communities who shared their interpretation of religious texts posed significant challenges to orthodoxy and authority. However, the twelfth century also saw a developing sense of the self, in which the idea of belonging stimulated different religious 'callings'.[6] Whilst these earlier heretics who sought self-exclusion could be more safely ignored, the later iconoclastic and reforming heresies of the twelfth century were of much more danger to the established church of the period. The emulation of Christ's poverty could be constructed by adherents or derided by opponents alike, as a penetrating attack upon forms of authority and spiritual focus. People, images, and buildings could all be attacked by those intent upon proving that orthodoxy was perversion or idolatry under another name.

[2] Eberhard Sauer, *The Archaeology of Religious Hatred in the Roman and Early Medieval World* (Stroud, 2003), 144, 47–52, and 10–12.
[3] Peter Brown, *The Body and Society: Men, Women and Sexual Renunciation in Early Christianity* (London, 1988), 166–7. For Ambrose see p. 347.
[4] Baird Tipton, 'A Dark Side of Seventeenth-Century English Protestantism: The Sin Against the Holy Ghost', *Harvard Theological Review*, 77:3/4 (July–Oct. 1984), 301–30, at 307.
[5] M. Lambert, *Medieval Heresy: Popular Movements from the Gregorian Reform to the Reformation* (Oxford, 1992), 26–30. This spread was uneven and probably reached Italy a century later. See also John N. Stephens, 'Heresy in Medieval and Renaissance Florence', *Past & Present*, 54 (1972), 25–60.
[6] C. W. Bynum. 'Did the Twelfth Century Discover the Individual?', *Journal of Ecclesiastical History*, 31:1 (1980), 1–17.

In the early 1130s Peter of Bruis, for example, took an especially ascetic line in condemning church buildings, the Old Testament, and even the symbol of the Cross itself.[7] He argued that church premises should be demolished because they focused upon place as the centre of worship rather than the spirituality of the individual.[8] This attitude and numerous unrecorded acts of iconoclasm represent an important series of episodes in blasphemy's early history. The desire for a purer way to God (which inspired the Bogomils, Cathars, Waldensians, and latterly the Lollards) also created the group identity of heretics. This again distinguishes them obviously from blasphemy and blasphemers, whose behaviour emerges from the early written record as individualistic and isolated.

Heretics very quickly began to acquire some of the poor reputation that would later afflict many blasphemers. The trial of Basil the Monk, the Bogomil leader in Constantinople at the end of the eleventh century, gives us a sense of an individual potentially setting himself up in imitation of God. Basil was accused of conducting his work surrounded by twelve disciples and 'women of depraved and evil character'. Such accusations persisted into the fourteenth century, when Béguin heretics were accused of inducing women to lie with them on the grounds that such instances constituted 'good works'.[9] Heresy from the twelfth century onwards was considered in almost pathological terms, with proposed remedies resembling modern methods of combating illness and disease. In some instances heretics could be described as consciously poisoning society. An early twelfth-century sermon preached against the Bogomil heretics described them as mixing poison with honey, which they dispensed whilst they 'blaspheme openly, revealing the doctrines and dogmas of the devil'.[10] Interestingly, some historians have rather borne out the fears evident in this sermon, citing the spread of the Bogomil heresy as important in introducing dualism to the West.[11] Others gained a reputation for austerity and asceticism, such as Arnold of Brescia, whose mortification of the flesh and fasting were the source of his power amongst well-placed Italian nobility.[12]

From the early twelfth century onwards these policing imperatives became almost a philosophy, as church figures began to argue that heresy needed to be controlled rather than tolerated. Gratian's *Decretum* of 1140 required the secular authorities to assist in suppressing heresy, and this view was considered orthodox

---

[7] Yuri Stoyanov, *The Hidden Tradition in Europe: The Secret History of Medieval Christian Heresy* (Harmondsworth, 1994), 155.

[8] Dawn Marie Hayes, *Body and Sacred Place in Medieval Europe, 1100–1398* (London, 2003), 11.

[9] 'A Sermon Against the Bogomils for the Sunday of all Saints (*c*.1107)', in Janet Hamilton and Bernard Hamilton (eds.), *Christian Dualist Heresies in the Byzantine World c650–1450* (Manchester, 1998), 175. For the Béguins see James Given, 'The Béguins in Bernard Gui's *Liber Sententiarum*', in Caterina Bruschi and Peter Biller (eds.), *Texts and the Repression of Medieval Heresy* (York, 2003), 147–61, 158.

[10] 'A Sermon Against the Bogomils', 211.   [11] Stoyanov, *Hidden Tradition*, 157–8.

[12] Andrew P. Roache, *The Devil's World: Heresy and Society 1100–1300* (Harlow, 2005), 73.

by 1200.[13] Many European bishops established their own inquisitions to check the spread of dangerous doctrines, aided by the commitment of successive popes towards the end of the twelfth century. It was in 1179 that the Lateran Council committed itself to the suppression of heresy, confirmed by the papal bull *Ad abolendam* issued by Lucius III five years later.[14] Twenty years after this, Innocent III's decretal *Vergentis* ordered banishment for heresy as well as confiscation of property and exclusion from inheritance, office-holding, and the benefits of the law.[15] In the early years of the thirteenth century Pope Gregory IX moved to establish an organization with sole responsibility for seeking out and destroying heresy. Thus the Papal Inquisition, with wide-reaching powers, came into being in the 1230s. This arrival of professional systematic inquiry into the hearts and minds of western Christendom was an enormous innovation. Through the act of questioning, inquisitors were involved in what one historian has termed 'the production of power'.[16] Nonetheless, for the Inquisition to prove effective within any locality it needed at least mute support from the population. Gerd Schwerhoff, the historian of Germany's medieval practice of blasphemy and its legal connotations, saw its initial appearance as a result of the thirteenth-century church's desire to minister more directly to the pastoral needs of the laity. This contact produced a growing clerical awareness of indiscipline, so that the religious mendicant orders became interested in the detection of heresy and other religious lapses. Schwerhoff sees this phenomenon as evidence of a more intensive Christianity bent on salvation and reconciling error, rather than discipline merely for its own sake.[17] In their travels mendicant friars clearly encountered everything from mute bewilderment to their arch-opponent, outright heresy.

The Inquisition's ranks throughout Europe were filled almost entirely by Dominicans, members of an order that had vowed to counteract heresy with determination and efficiency. The rise and development of groups like the Dominicans and Franciscans also gave an ideological edge to Catholic Christendom's relationship with the dissidents in its midst. In many respects some of the individual Inquisitors' reputations for high-handedness stemmed from their early training in theology rather than law.[18] From a policy of comparative indifference, Dominican theology gave a much-enhanced priority to the promotion of the

[13] Peter D. Diehl, 'Overcoming Reluctance to Prosecute Heresy in Thirteenth Century Italy', in Scott L. Waugh and Peter D. Diehl (eds.), *Christendom and its Discontents: Exclusion, Persecution and Rebellion 1000–1500* (Cambridge, 1996), 47–66, at 48–9.

[14] R. I. Moore, 'Popular Violence and Popular Heresy in Western Europe c. 1000–1179', in *Persecution and Toleration: Studies, in Church History*, Vol. 21, ed. W. J. Shiels, (Oxford, 1984), 43–50, 44. See also Stoyanov, *Hidden Tradition*, 161.

[15] Diehl, *Overcoming Reluctance*, 53.   [16] See Given, 'The Béguins', 148.

[17] Gerd Schwerhoff, *Zungen wie Schwerter: Blasphemie in alteuropäischen Gesellschaften 1200–1650* (Konstanz, 2005), 300.

[18] This is suggested by Henry Ansgar Kelly in 'Inquisition and the Prosecution of Heresy: Misconceptions and Abuses', in *Inquisitions and Other Trials in the Medieval West* (Aldershot, 2001), 439–51, at 451.

faith and a more urgent insistence upon orthodoxy. It also gave priority to the conversion of Jews and Muslims, through the exposure of flaws in their own sacred writings. The attitude to the Jews would also come to fluctuate wildly, with some religious opinions actively indulging the popular attacks upon them for their inherited guilt associated with the crucifixion. Still others were more lenient, seeing the Jews as keepers of the Old Testament covenant, and hoping for their conversion in the last days. Within this polarity of attitudes there was nonetheless widespread agreement about the need to restrict the influence of Jews in the secular Christian community at large. Fines, deprivation of property, and most notably the denial of various civil rights mark the first modern-looking use of this last penalty for those guilty of forms of religious deviance.

Periodically Jews would also be associated with blasphemous opinions, since their own faith mocked the Christian order. Such attitudes informed the numerous attacks in Spain upon the *conversos* (Jews who had converted to Christianity), as urban populations came to doubt the sincerity of such conversions, and resented the appearance of former Jews in public life.[19] However, individuals were also the victims of prying neighbours, and evidence of the pressures to conform become evident. John Edwards found that some accusations of blasphemous behaviour stemmed from misconstruing the religious practices of others. In Spain, many *conversos* maintained habits, gestures, and practices from their previous faith that survived to cause offence to onlookers. Unorthodox methods of prayer and contemplation, and a failure to conform precisely in communal acts of worship, were all seen as evidence of *converso* ambivalence about their new faith.[20] Nonetheless, the association of the Jews with outright blasphemy persisted. As late as the first years of the seventeenth century a number were executed in Italian Mantua for the blasphemous nature of their religious practices.[21] From this there is strong evidence that blasphemy, as the sin of dishonouring God, drew upon contemporary attitudes to the Jews and in particular their violation of the Second Commandment. This suggests that the Jews constituted perhaps the earliest blasphemous archetype in the Christian West.[22]

The origin of medieval Europe's coherent blasphemy laws can be pinpointed to the thirteenth century, when blasphemy was quickly envisaged as a crime with secular repercussions. The challenge to God's authority was theorized as an attack upon all secular authority that also derived legitimacy from a supreme creator. Blasphemy appeared as a sin in the work of Peter Lombard and Thomas Aquinas,

---

[19] For more on the history of the *conversos* in the Iberian Peninsular see Michael Alpert, *Crypto-Judaism and the Spanish Inquisition* (New York, 2001). See also Alain Cabantous, *Blasphemy: Impious Speech in the West from the Seventeenth to the Nineteenth Century* (New York, 2002), 18.

[20] John Edwards 'Religious Faith and Doubt in Late Medieval Spain: Soria circa 1450–1500', *Past & Present*, (1988), 120, 3–25, at 9.

[21] C. Fabre-Vassas, *The Singular Beast: Jews, Christians and the Pig* (New York, 1997), 145.

[22] Schwerhoff, *Zungen wie Schwerter*, 301.

who made much of the church's right to discipline its adherents. Aquinas had begun to take the potential evil perpetrated by blasphemy and blasphemers more seriously than had previous generations of theologians. He argued that blasphemers should suffer the ultimate penalty because they followed a false faith and actively intended to do harm to God's honour. In practice, most medieval blasphemers did not fit the model that Aquinas proposed, since blasphemy was more readily apparent in brief lapses of discipline. This perspective is confirmed through the testimony of frightened individuals before the courts of the various Inquisitions.

Some legal innovations also saw municipalities develop laws against blasphemy, which were a means of asserting forms of urban governance. Such municipal laws are present in Italy as early as the 1260s, where the civic courts of Orvieto were dispensing heavy fines and mutilation, generally catching the poor and socially marginal in the process. The earliest French statutes come from this particular period and were reiterated within a decade. For urban government, blasphemous utterances also represented a misuse of the oath which the new commerce had come to rely upon increasingly.[23] Whilst a distinction between blasphemy and heresy emerges in this last suggestion, other traces of blasphemers and their crimes remain hard to find.

Religious reformers and charismatics expressed a wish to save the church from its own errors. Within their doctrines there are important precursors of anti-trinitarianism, dualism, and latent iconoclasm. Alongside these characteristics were challenges to orthodoxy in the dismissal of miracles, of Purgatory, and the power of indulgence. The pre-eminent heretical doctrine of all was denial of the divinity of Christ. Close scrutiny of the accounts of heresy for the Middle Ages shows blasphemy to be an intrinsic component of these deeper and more heinous crimes. The campaigns of the religious and secular authorities against the Bogomils, Cathars, the Waldensians, and the doctrine of the Free Spirit sometimes involved an accusation that individual parts of these beliefs were blasphemous. Yet we also get a sense that anticlericalism was born in some of the thoughts such heretics entertained about the orthodox church of their age. One Cathar in the early fourteenth century rejected the practice of placing a blessed candle in the mouths of the deceased by suggesting that it would be as usefully inserted into the deceased's anus. He also saw the chants of priests and their prayers as merely a pretext for exacting money from the deluded.[24]

Many historians note that convicting heretics on the basis of belief alone was difficult, and sometimes religious practices which marked individuals out, such

---

[23] Carol Lansing, *Power and Purity: Cathar Heresy in Medieval Italy* (Oxford, 1998), 166–7. See also John Marshall, *John Locke, Toleration and Early Enlightenment Culture* (Cambridge, 2006), 231–2, for both later Catholic and Zwinglian opinion upon the importance of oaths and their destruction by heresy in a later period.

[24] René Weis, *The Yellow Cross: The Story of the Last Cathars* (Harmondsworth, 2000), 265.

as abstention from meat or dairy products, would be used against them.[25] Part of this problem was the fluid and shifting nature of some of these doctrines, primarily those of the Free Spirit. This antinomianism (the rejection of external authority, in favour of the spirit within) was bred by the search for holiness, simple piety, and a denunciation of the church for abandoning these principles. Sometimes, as was the case with Catharism, there was a determined attempt to establish a counterpart to the orthodox religious hierarchy. Frequently, those steeped in such piety asserted that their actions, no matter how divergent or deviant, were proof positive of their holiness. These people were considered dangerous and threatened the 'bonds of religious authority within society, and finally of the religious creed itself'.[26] Schwerhoff argues that the distinction between blasphemy and heresy was recognized within such heresies, although complementary accusations of both crimes could live side by side. Blasphemy was also sometimes substituted when a charge of heresy could not be wholly sustained.

Despite its only occasional appearance, most historians agree that blasphemy in the medieval period was overshadowed by heresy. If the late medieval period was an age of managed piety, some influential cultural historians have characterized its successor as an age of anxiety. This view, interestingly, can paint the Reformation as the culmination of this process rather than its immediate cause.[27] Peter Brown's influential work suggested that the process of constructing the notion of the overriding capacity for guilt within Christianity had been accomplished by the onset of the high medieval period. The medieval cults of saints were attempts to relate to perfected human bodies as a psychological refuge of the sinfully frail.[28] Jean Delumeau has argued that a later period is arguably more significant, suggesting: 'No civilisation had ever attached as much importance to guilt and shame as did the Western world from the thirteenth to the eighteenth centuries.'[29] Delumeau advocates that guilt was not a species of passive powerlessness but was just as likely to be a spur to forms of creativity. The conscience made individuals strive to deserve their place in the universe and to have a greater sense of their own culpability before God.[30] For these versions of history, Protestantism became the heir to a society that had already replaced piety with a species of guilt. This needed ways of coping with guilt but also ways of detecting and policing the perceived guilt of others. Those in authority had

---

[25] Lansing, *Power and Purity*, 141. See also Stoyanov, *Hidden Tradition*, 155, and Peter Biller, 'Why no Food? Waldensian Followers in Bernard Gui's *practica inquisitionis and culpe*', in Caterina Bruschi and Peter Biller (eds.), *Texts and the Repression of Medieval Heresy* (York, 2003), 127–46.

[26] Alexander Patchovsky, 'Heresy and Society: On the Political Function of Heresy in the Medieval World', in ibid. 23–41, at 26.

[27] Jean Delumeau, *Sin and Fear: The Emergence of a Western Guilt Culture 13th–18th Centuries* (New York, 1990).

[28] Brown, The *Body and Society*, 434 and 444–5.   [29] Ibid. 3.

[30] See John Bossy, *Christianity in the West, 1400–1700* (Oxford, 1985), 35. Bossy reiterates that sin was conceptualized as a challenge to the whole community.

a particular sense of duty in this area, which insisted upon their diligent action against miscreants.

This interpretation allows us to see the late medieval indulgence as a product of this sense of guilt, spreading its tentacles of popularity amongst western Christendom before the Reformation. This also argues that a heightened sense of sin was an important catalyst in Reformation Protestantism's eventual rejuvenation of the concept of blasphemy. Man was no longer the pious, if deluded, seeker after truth, but potentially a criminal in mind and spirit. Thus a greater sense of the conscious mind discovered more opportunities for it to stray and misbehave. Yet this may also have focused attention on some sins rather than others. John Bossy notes that the sixteenth-century shift towards the Ten Commandments as the West's moral exemplar was 'nothing short of revolutionary'. This in turn may have highlighted the issues of duty and honour to God, which eclipsed the earlier focus upon individual conduct.[31]

This particular theme of human culpability has been emphasized by historians of medieval speech, as well as those more directly concerned with the issue of blasphemy. Maureen Flynn's analysis of Renaissance Spanish evidence uncovered that blasphemy became a particularly serious matter because members of the Inquisition argued that its appearance in speech should be taken at face value. Without the benefits of later philosophy concerning the workings of the human mind, the official handbook of the Inquisition argued for the close scrutiny of speech. This was the clear expression of real inner feelings, so that verbal insults to God and the sacred were obviously intended by those who spoke them.[32]

This suggests that blasphemy was theorized in the medieval and early Renaissance world as a passive entity. Words and utterances were not blasphemous but rather 'a blasphemy'. The crucial distinction was that the offended need not have encountered the blasphemy themselves or had personal beliefs attacked. The affront to order and the community came from knowledge that such an event had occurred, without any need to witness or experience it. Victims in this model could remain 'passive' in the knowledge that religious or secular authority would take action to restore order and tranquillity. This is a conception we may recognize from the ancient world, and has a relationship to medieval conceptions of heresy—hence the Inquisition's attempts to actively investigate and find it, rather than letting it come to them.

The mechanism for identifying and detecting error had been dramatically popularized, whilst religious devotion could be more readily measured against the ideals offered by scripture and catechism. Both sides of the Reformation, as many have commented, eventually used their confessional divide to introduce

---

[31] Ibid. 38.
[32] Maureen Flynn, 'Blasphemy and the Play of Anger in Sixteenth Century Spain.' *Past & Present*, 149 (1995), 29–56, at 35–6.

heightened levels of knowledge about the nature of orthodoxy and unorthodoxy.[33] Luther in particular denounced Catholic religious practices, including the mass and veneration of the saints, as blasphemous. He was equally outspoken about the religious practices of Jews and Muslims, and conceivably gave renewed impetus to the scrutiny of Jews in particular. John Calvin similarly enhanced the status of blasphemy as a religious crime, and saw 'denying, defying, or denouncing God' as specific and heinous crimes within the wider offence of dishonouring God. Blasphemy's importance was also enhanced alongside other forms of poor behaviour, since Calvin regularly stressed that mankind was permanently on the edge of sin.[34]

Catholicism's response recognized Protestant criticisms and tried to suggest less idolatrous reasons for persisting with religious images. The Council of Trent suggested that they provided example and a focus for devotion rather than objects of outright worship. Moreover, the provisions of the Council also charged bishops with responsibility for policing the use of existing images and the establishment of new ones:

Furthermore, in the invocation of the saints, the veneration of relics, and the sacred use of images, all superstition shall be removed, all filthy quest for gain eliminated, and all lasciviousness avoided, so that images shall not be painted and adorned with a seductive charm, or the celebration of saints and the visitation of relics be perverted by the people into boisterous festivities and drunkenness, as if the festivals in honor of the saints are to be celebrated with revelry and with no sense of decency.[35]

Nonetheless, it would still be a mistake to assume an informed piety amongst European populations as a result of these changes. As late as the 1580s clerical visitors to outlying areas of Saxony were still depressed by the levels of religious ignorance and lax morality they encountered.[36] Whilst Catholicism had already developed a language and conception of heresy, Protestantism carved itself a similar liturgical space by finding new definitions of religious error. The adoption of blasphemy by Lutherans as a label to describe unwelcome religious change or to distance themselves from opponents was an innovation. But it would be a mistake to assume there was uniform and decisive change. Schwerhoff and Loetz have both argued from German and Swiss evidence that Reformation ideas about blasphemy were able to draw on some medieval precedents.

[33] In his denial of the possibility of atheism in the Renaissance, Lucien Febvre strongly asserted the desire of sixteenth-century Europe to make everything a reflection of the divine. See Lucien Febvre, *The Problem of Unbelief in the Sixteenth Century: The Religion of Rabelais*, tr. Beatrice Gottlieb (Cambridge, 1982), 455–64.

[34] Tipton, 'A Dark Side of Seventeenth-Century English Protestantism', 311, 315, and Leonard Levy, *Blasphemy, Verbal Offence Against the Sacred from Moses to Salman Rushdie* (New York, 1993), 60–2.

[35] Proceedings of the Council of Trent, Twenty Fifth Session, December 3 and 4, 1563, in *Canons and Decrees of the Council of Trent*, tr. H. J. Schroeder (London, 1941).

[36] Susan C. Karant-Nunn, 'Neoclericalism and Anticlericalism in Saxony 1555–1675', *Journal of Interdisciplinary History*, 24:4 (Spring 1994), 615–37, at 619.

The reactions of both Luther and Calvin shed light upon the redefinition of blasphemy as a thoroughly Renaissance offence. In this it related man to the text, or word of God, and wrote a blueprint for the nature of worldly power and secular rule. This dispersal of religious power, and the new role of secular authorities in Protestant states, made such issues of faith the concern of the Renaissance prince. Issues of governance and obedience were preoccupying both laity and theologians themselves. Luther had been deeply shocked by the implications of the Anabaptist episodes, the Peasant's Revolt, and the so-called 'Knights War'. By 1526 he appears to have accepted that religious toleration needed severe restriction when the potential danger of sedition existed.[37] In Geneva blasphemy was more strictly codified, with the facets of the offence listed in ascending order of seriousness. These commenced with the profane swearing by the name of Christ and progressed to misusing the name of the almighty to sanction trivial oaths. The higher-level offences included participating in impious chants or invocations and concluded with the most serious offence, which was dishonouring God. This list demonstrates that there was an important attempt to instil discipline at the heart of the Reformation. One study of a locale in Switzerland provides evidence of how this process developed. Swiss Valangin established a consistory court to investigate moral transgressions in 1538, which began to meet with greater frequency to try cases of blasphemy. This seems related, in this instance, to the creation of a new regime of discipline, since the initial years of the court's operation tried significantly more cases than it did after 1570.[38] The religious offences were clearly issues related to disrespect, levity, and a lack of seriousness in dealing with sacred words. The crime of speaking false doctrine was interestingly included as a component of the last and most serious offence.[39] Further east the Elector August of Saxony's attempts to instil discipline in his subjects led his court official, Melchior von Osse, to compile a written manual describing such actions.[40]

Occasionally older laws and pronouncements against blasphemy could be updated to reflect the new doctrinal emphasis. In the north Netherlands, for example, the laws of Charles V were maintained under the subsequent Calvinist republic and began to be extended. In 1518 a law was passed to prevent swearing and blasphemy, and was followed in 1531 by a subsequent police edict. The first law of 1518 declared: 'As a cure against blasphemers we forbid blasphemy against the holy names of God, the Virgin and the Saints. It is also forbidden to deny scorn or belittle them.' The penalty for

---

[37] N. M. Sutherland, 'Persecution and Toleration in Reformation Europe', in W. J. Shiels, *Persecution and Toleration: Studies in Church History*, Vol. 21 (Oxford, 1984), 153–62.

[38] Jeffrey R. Watt, 'The Reception of the Reformation in Valangin, Switzerland, 1547–1588', *Sixteenth Century Journal*, 20:1 (Spring 1989), 89–104.

[39] See David J. Nicholls, 'The Nature of Popular Heresy in France, 1520–1542', *Historical Journal*, 26:2 (June 1983), 261–75', and Levy *Blasphemy: Verbal Offense Against the Sacred*, 60–2.

[40] Karant-Nunn, *Neoclericalism and Anticlericalism in Saxony* 617.

this offence was imprisonment for a month with bread and water, but if vehement intent could be proved then boring through the tongue would ensue. The influence of reformed practices can be seen in the latter edict's removal of the saints from the proscribed list of targets, to be replaced with Holy Scripture.[41]

Much of the impetus behind this push for theological control over behaviour was inspired by Calvin's own views on the matter. In suggesting the role of the state was to protect the true religion, Calvin identified the punishment and vengeance it might wreak as emanating directly from God himself. From this point onwards Protestant theologians increasingly dismissed the beliefs of Catholics and also of Jews through using the description 'blasphemy'. This became distinct from the Catholic use of the term 'heresy', and avoided uncomfortable comparisons with earlier use of this same term against Protestant martyrs. But this growing distance also began to reflect significant doctrinal changes. Catholicism and Judaism, through their respective beliefs and liturgies, showed detachment and distance from the Protestant emphasis upon the word and the scriptures. Thus what could be termed idolatory, and denial of the incarnation, became attacks upon Protestant beliefs. Both Luther and Calvin were responsible for promoting such ideas, and Calvin's own godly state, which made a point of executing the anti-trinitarian reformer Servetus, embraced the growing conception of a godly commonwealth.[42] Princes, as never before, interested themselves in religious conformity and came to see the security of the state as dependent upon ending religious deviance. Particular jurisdictions, such as the English Star Chamber, became central to legislative attempts to control religious beliefs, and significantly could upstage the ecclesiastical authorities when they were so inclined. A number of German principalities also followed suit, as religious conformity became an important matter of state throughout Europe.

The reform of Christianity may have been accomplished amongst the educated, but the history of blasphemy in this period provides important evidence of occasions where new and old thinking could collide. In 1526 a roof-tiler from Warmond in the Netherlands got into an argument over a meal with his employer that was to prove costly. The tiler's employer began to speak animatedly of the recent religious events in Germany. In particular, he was angered by the actions of the religious reformers who had abused the host and wine by treading it underfoot. Taken aback by this, the roof-tiler dissented from this opinion, declaring: 'What is it more than bread? The very bread we eat at this table is the same.' Not content with this, he eloquently quoted Matthew 24: 23, 24 and Acts 17: 24, 25 which were quite inflammatory texts, especially in this context. Whilst he may have known his Bible, he was also showing

---

[41] M. R. Baelde, *Studiën over Godslastering* (The Hague, 1935), 111–12.
[42] Diarmaid MacCulloch, *Reformation: Europe's House Divided 1490–1700* (London, 2003), 188.

the disrespect for a social superior inherent in the wider population's 'use' of religious texts.[43]

But it was not simply princes and the theologically competent who wanted to identify blasphemy as an offence against the state. There is ample evidence throughout Europe that the impact of blasphemy was felt profoundly at a more local level. One such species of authority was represented in the increasingly assertive forms of urban governance that began to appear in Germany in the 1490s. Schwerhoff suggests that displays of this authority were a response to unruly and transient urban populations. Blasphemous utterances attacked the power and sanctity of the oath. Increasingly, the pressure to safeguard and restore municipal credibility loomed larger than the desire to exact retribution from the blasphemer. This latter motive for punishment only emerged recognisably in the fifteenth century.[44] Such an analysis tends to justify Delumeau's argument for a pre-Reformation Europe-wide assertion of guilt and a growing premium upon religious discipline.

If the post-Reformation crime of blasphemy seems to have been imposed by clerical and secular elites, then we need to know more about what communities at large thought of such a crime. Evidence from Germany, the Netherlands, Switzerland, and France indicates that European populations from the fifteenth century onwards were well accustomed to the sight and experience of blasphemers being disciplined and punished. What is important here is not to distinguish between Catholic and Protestant or reformed practice in punishing blasphemy, but to note how seriously individual states, towns, and jurisdictions considered the crime at specific moments in time. This often reflected pressing fears about governance and the safety of the community that spanned the confessional divide. Some of the earliest studies from a free-speech perspective saw action against heretics and blasphemers as a demonstration of authoritarian rule intended to expunge the beliefs of the previous regime.[45]

Blasphemous crimes naturally enough involved both criminals and victims, whilst reporting them also brought the agents of authority into play. However, theologians and lawyers were increasingly convinced that the crime harmed the community at large. This fear that blasphemy might contaminate the community has not received the consideration from historians that it deserves. It is easier to encounter blasphemy through trials and through the stern didactic literature that warned potential blasphemers of the dire consequences awaiting them. Precious

---

[43] Baelde, *Godslastering*, 110. The text from the King James Bible has Matt. 24: 23, 24 as: 'Then if any man shall say unto you, Lo, here is Christ, or there; believe it not. For there shall arise false Christs, and false prophets, and shall shew great signs and wonders; insomuch that, if it were possible, they shall deceive the very elect.' Acts 17: 24, 25 is rendered as: 'God that made the world and all things therein, seeing that he is Lord of heaven and earth, dwelleth not in temples made with hands. Neither is worshipped with men's hands, as though he needed anything, seeing he giveth to all life, and breath, and all things.'

[44] Schwerhoff, *Zungen wie Schwerter*, 303.

[45] Hypatia Bradlaugh-Bonner, *Penalties Upon Opinion* (London, 1934), 13–14.

little survives of what individuals in the pre-modern community thought of the blasphemer. Nonetheless, Gerd Schwerhoff has attempted to chart the way in which the 'missing people' of blasphemy's history might be re-created. Schwerhoff suggested that previous historiography had concentrated too closely upon the religious context without proper consideration of the secular community.[46] The balance and status of both the sacred and the secular in any situation could govern how an audience for blasphemy might react. Thus a blasphemous utterance could equally be viewed as a joke, as inconsequential, as a verbal insult, as a precursor to assaults of other kinds, or even as a fundamental attack upon belief.

In an age that scarcely had even the most rudimentary conception of the subconscious, observers and audiences were encouraged to believe and treat seriously what they saw or heard. This was because early modern thought regarded the crime as unique, since it was divorced from the bodily appetites. It obviously appeared to engage the mind and intellect and thus it appeared symbolic. As Maureen Flynn has commented, speech in the medieval world was very obviously the mouthpiece of the soul and was the means by which wishes and desires were made known. Inquisitors were further convinced of this reasoning by the directions they received. Their leading handbook of instruction, the *Directorium Inquisitorum*, compiled by the Roman inquisitor Nicolás Eymerich, argued that spoken contradictions of the orthodox faith were to be considered seriously. This served to link blasphemy, at least in a procedural way, with heresy. As Flynn suggests, 'speech guaranteed the reality of thought, illuminating the dark and mysterious caverns of consciousness'.[47]

Nonetheless, it was unclear from this advice how tribunals should proceed in practice when faced with supposed blasphemers. When defendants were subsequently examined, their genuine intention to do harm was hard to establish. This particular phenomenon has plagued legal practice around blasphemy until this day, and remains substantially unresolved. Individuals in Spain, for example, regularly pleaded that they had indulged in throwaway remarks, such as the individual Juan Gutierrez from Avila in 1516, who had uttered the words 'God is nothing'. Others protested innocence or naivety, claiming they had spoken words which they did not intend. It became difficult to blame such people, especially when it seemed unbidden thoughts had tripped them up. A brush with authority would instill proper behaviour, and their plea of naivety would inevitably result in an order for further supervision and instruction. Some churchmen also veered away from ascribing full responsibility for chance utterances. In doing so they had no less a guide than Aquinas, who suggested that blasphemy was not as regular an occurrence as some suggested. He concluded that language and speech were often engaged in action before the mind was conscious of this. Flynn has argued that later church practice was still more malleable. The Inquisition was

---

[46] Schwerhoff, *Zungen wie Schwerte*, 304.
[47] See Flynn, 'Blasphemy and the Play of Anger in Sixteenth Century Spain', 34–5 and 39.

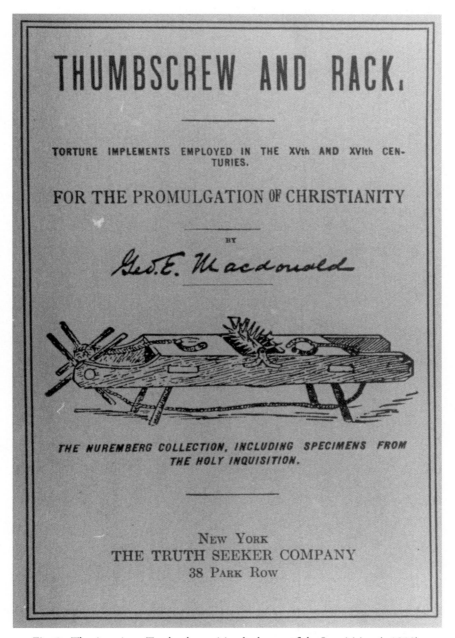

Fig. 2. The American *Truthseeker* revisits the legacy of the Inquisition (*c.*1910).

well aware that blasphemy could be the product of outbursts of anger, and on occasions could be surprisingly indulgent to this phenomenon. Some devotional works went as far as merely recommending prayer as the remedy against sudden provocation.[48]

When it came to contemplating punishment, blasphemers were considered to be individuals adrift from the society that provided protection and prosperity for them. Many punishments, especially for a first offence, reflected this element and gave an opportunity for the community to observe the blasphemer marked out as a figure to be laughed at, spurned, and ridiculed. This was in answer to the way this individual had treated God and the beliefs of the community. Pius V, in *Cum primum apostolatus*, codified early church law around blasphemy, insisting upon monetary fines or the practice of standing before the church door with hands tied behind the back. This would be followed by flogging, exile, and piercing for subsequent offences.[49]

Although occurrences of people being reported for speech or actions within their own home or private sphere do exist, blasphemy generally came to the attention of the populace at large as a result of some public incident. The overwhelming location for this was in the tavern or the street. A number of examples exist of early modern Europeans cursing, swearing, and blaspheming after bouts of heavy drinking. The impression we get of such incidents is of only moderately serious misdemeanours for which the guilty party was more or less contrite. It was obvious that such incidents were clear breaches of the public peace, and their nature suggests that blasphemous language was a significant taboo, broken only when normal social constraints were relaxed by drink. The intention to clear the streets of such nuisances is evident in a 1526 French ordinance which empowered the provost of Paris to seize vagabonds, beggars, and blasphemers. A little later, in the 1530s, similar ordinances clearly identified drink as a major cause of blasphemy, as well as of idleness and physical assault leading to death. [50] But drink was not the sole cause of tavern and street incidents of blasphemy. The tavern was the location of many disputes that turned around the issue of honour. Chance words or even deliberate slighting could easily escalate into challenges to reputation. Such reputations were cherished and guarded, providing social currency within public spaces like the tavern.

Whilst drunken individuals often regretted their actions, other profane activities excited even more interest and concern amongst religious and secular authorities. In particular the location of blasphemy amongst gamblers was a consistent worry and concern to early modern European authority. Evidence

---

[48] For Gutierrez see ibid. 41–2, 44, and 46, and Maureen Flynn, 'Taming Anger's Daughters: New Treatment for Emotional Problems in Renaissance Spain', *Renaissance Quarterly*, 51:3 (1998), 864–86, at 878, 881.

[49] 'Taming Anger's Daughter', 870.

[50] Thomas Brennan, *Public Drinking and Popular Culture in Eighteenth-Century Paris* (Princeton, 1988), 74.

from early modern Germany, Spain, France, and Mexico indicate that the world of gambling and its consequences profoundly troubled all these societies, as contemporaries realized the phenomenon would not disappear overnight. German sources contain a significant number of illustrative woodcuts that show the perils of gambling, with suggestions that it naturally led to violence or was habitually overseen by the devil. In southern Europe, but especially Spain and the Spanish colonial territories, gambling was also a perennial source of concern. In New Spain (Mexico) and Cuba the governing authorities attempted to prohibit the circulation of dice and to limit the availability of playing-cards. This latter decision was double-edged, since it also ironically enforced a state monopoly upon the supply of gambling paraphernalia. Attempts to instill discipline within these colonies were not assisted by the fact that leading conquistadors were themselves significant culprits. Hernán Cortés was fined for organizing card games at which blasphemy occurred, and he was also known to turn a blind eye to the practice amongst his soldiers.[51]

Reasons for this affinity between blasphemy and gambling are scarcely hard to find. The gaming-room, or back parlour, of the average early modern tavern was, after all, an obviously gendered male world in which displays of bravado would have been second nature to those present. This isolated world provided the opportunity to step out of constraints and to adopt new modes of behaviour frequently hidden from the public gaze. Contemporaries even thought that the opportunity to blaspheme in the gaming-room was itself an attraction. Gambling also sometimes brought together individuals from disparate parts of the community who had to demonstrate or boast about their status. The blasphemous expression allowed the aristocrat to emphasize his lofty status, whilst the vagabond could use it to show contempt for all authority. Within gambling circles the desperate individual sometimes craved fortune by appealing to the better nature, or the omnipotent power, of the almighty. Yet attempts to invoke such help were seen by many theologians as a clear instance of blasphemy. This was considered tantamount to 'tempting' God and a clear trivialization of his divine purpose. Somewhat more common was the exasperated outburst against bad luck and the failure of God's own favour.[52]

Early modern attempts to control the world of bravado, quarrel, offence, and punishment revolved around communal desires for safety. This involved policing a slippery phenomenon that could appear in many guises, from drunken horse-play to dangerous antagonism of a God who regularly intervened in human affairs. Such perceptions began to change during the seventeenth century, and

[51] Javier Villa-Flores, 'On Divine Persecution: Blasphemy and Gambling in New Spain', in Susan Schroeder and Stafford Poole (eds.), *Religion and Society in Colonial Mexico* (New Mexico, forthcoming), 133–4.

[52] This is evident in incidents recorded throughout both northern and southern Europe as well as the Americas. See also Jonathan Walker,' 'Gambling and Venetian noblemen c1500–1700', *Past & Present*, 162 (1999), 28–69.

from this point we begin to notice blasphemy conceived of as a potential danger to the power, majesty, and security of central government. As the seventeenth century progresses it is possible to see the pace and range of Europe-wide legislation quickening. This seems to have been part of a European imposition of varieties of discipline upon unruly populations as an essential by-product of centralizing the state. This built significantly upon the rudimentary attempts made in the sixteenth century to control the problem. The culture of European courts involved the development and reiteration of species of discipline which were passed on and replicated in circles far beyond the court.[53] Courtiers became adept at observing the behaviour of others, but especially the behaviour of themselves. This was increasingly internalized as passions were governed and gestures controlled as an essential mode of preserving status and precarious position.[54] The competition of court life ensured elements of control but also inspired the calculation of behavioural choices, use of etiquette, and the choice of words instead of weapons as the means of settling conflict.[55] All these were profound antidotes to behaviour that displayed uncouthness and lack of restraint, such as the blasphemous outburst. Such areas of supposed rationality were also capable of influencing enlightenment ideologues such as Voltaire.[56] Yet seeing this as a part of Norbert Elias's 'Civilising Process', whereby unruly behaviour was eradicated by the growth of individual mechanisms of psychological restraint, is by no means the whole story. Such an analysis fails to reflect the importance of religion and in particular the far-reaching significance of the Renaissance. Jeroen Duindam noted how ideas and beliefs, as much as structures and behavioural codes, equally shaped behaviour when he observed that 'a study that focuses on restraint of "affects" cannot ignore the role of piety and the church'.[57]

In seventeenth-century England the Interregnum had unleashed a multitude of different and often opposing religious opinions. Those whose beliefs were an especial challenge to authority became a particular concern of commentators who had earlier made the entire issue of authority one of intense debate. Once again access to the vernacular text of the scriptures was a decisive factor in creating religious sects who took authority for and upon themselves. The political end of this phenomenon was represented by the Putney Debates, but the nature of religious authority in many societies collided with this ideology in important places. Puritans had always been quite active in proposing legislation which empowered the English state to control and regulate individual vices. Such policing of morality was one of the few unifying features of early Jacobean parliaments.[58]

[53] Robert van Krieken, *Norbert Elias* (London, 1988), 97.
[54] Norbert Elias, *The Court Society* (Oxford, 1983), 105.
[55] Ibid. 111 and 240.   [56] Ibid. 113.
[57] Jeroen Duindam, *Myths of Power* (Amsterdam, 1995), 164.
[58] Stephen Foster, *The Long Argument* (Williamsburg, 1991), 116.

As we saw, Calvin's Geneva had, for some time, exercised a legally coherent conception of blasphemy. Similarly, the city state of Venice possessed the *Escutori*, a unique and specific jurisdiction designed to prosecute and punish only blasphemy.[59] The situation for blasphemy in France in some respects reflects that country's turbulent religious history during this period, with a plethora of modifications and restatements of the law. Local areas had produced edicts in the 1560s that controlled blasphemy in print and the theatre. The Sorbonne had published an index of prohibited books as early as 1543, but by the 1560s the monarchy was seeking to gain regulatory control over printing and publishing for itself.[60] This dawning of a centralizing imperative was an innovation suggesting evidence of struggles for power and control over jurisdiction, as well as the ineffectiveness of many local measures.[61] This explains the later statutes against blasphemy of 1594, 1617, 1631, 1651, and 1681. The last of these confirmed mutilation and capital punishment as sentences handed down by royal decree, demonstrating that the divine right of the monarch as God's representative on earth cast him as the instrument of divine rule and punishment.[62] Similar edicts were passed against blasphemy in the Austrian empire in 1656, 1675, 1707, and 1768. This last piece of legislation established the offence as the most serious of the Theresian penal code. For a first offence the limb instrumental in the commission of blasphemy was forcibly removed, and for subsequent offences the tongue was removed and the body of the blasphemer burned alive.[63]

Effectively this type of legislation did not so much replace ecclesiastical authority with secular authority, but rather allowed both to go forward within a fruitful partnership. In some instances such states demonstrated a fear that criticism of religion could produce a conviction amongst the population that all authority was based upon falsehood. The provisions of the Massachusetts 1646 statute against blasphemy perhaps demonstrates the seventeenth century's imperative of linking church and state through statutory defence. Section 19 declared: 'common reason requireth every state and society of men to be more careful of preventing the dishonour and contempt of the most high God, (in

---

[59] See Elizabeth Horodwich, 'Civic Identity and the Control of Blasphemy in Sixteenth-Century Venice', *Past & Present*, 181 (2003), 3–33. See also Cabantous, *Blasphemy*, 51–4. But note that Loetz saw the town council of Zurich as dragging its feet in the face of the Reformed church's desire to innovate: *Mit Gott handeln*, 534–5.

[60] John Bossy notes that this coincides with the royal edict of 1560 which suppressed municipal brothels. See Bossy, *Christianity in the West*, 41.

[61] Alfred Soman, 'Press, Pulpit and Censorship in France before Richelieu', *Proceedings of the American Philosophical Society*, 120:6 (Dec. 1976), 439–63, at 441, 454.

[62] Cabantous, *Blasphemy*, 67, 78–9. See also Bettina Lindorfer, '*Peccatum Linguae* and the Punishment of Speech Violations in the Middle Ages and Early Modern Times', in Jean E. Godsall-Myers (ed.), *Speaking in the Medieval World* (Leiden, 2003), 32. Lindorfer argues that this was the first time that speech violations were seriously scrutinized in France. Spain witnessed a flurry of similar legislation in the first couple of decades of the sixteenth century and analogous provisions were also made in the territories of the Holy Roman Empire.

[63] Baelde, *Godslastering*, 188.

whom we all consist) than of any mortal princes, or magistrates: it is therefore ordered, and decreed by this court for the honor of the eternal God, who only we worship.' Within this statute witting blasphemy was a serious crime, but the effect upon others and society at large was conveyed in the suggestion that such reproaches treated religion 'as if it were a public device to keep ignorant men in awe'.[64]

The work of England's common lawyers eventually produced probably the most cogent statement that outlined the principle behind church and state in partnership. Lord Chief Justice Sir Matthew Hale, in passing sentence upon John Taylor in 1675, argued that religion and the laws of England were one, and that attacks upon religion were attacks upon the law. The law thus had a right to defend itself and the moral underpinning religion offered. This principle was enshrined within the English monarchy's attempt to re-establish religious discipline at the end of the seventeenth century, following other European models. The relevant statute (9 & 10 William III c.32) resembles some of the French statutes pronouncing against anti-trinitarian views, denying the truth of the Christian religion or of the scriptures. Its preamble saw blasphemous opinions as 'tending to the dishonour of Almighty God' and potentially 'destructive to the peace and welfare of this kingdom'.[65] Across the Atlantic, many individual New England states took their own flexible and pragmatic approaches to law. Some of this colonial American legislation, as we have seen, bears comparison with contemporary European statutes. Although blasphemy was the most serious of crimes that threatened the community and the state, there was nonetheless recognition of lesser misdemeanours. This was evident in provisions to police and punish such offences as profanity, swearing of false oaths, and the misuse of God's name.[66]

Much of this legislation was aimed at ideas that were supposedly damaging and seditious. This became a fear of forms of unorthodox piety fuelled by blasphemy's growing association with ideas that were testing the credulity of listening and reading publics. Yet this legislation and its provisions also caught the unorthodox anti-trinitarians such as Anabaptists, Socinians, Unitarians, Quakers, and Rosicrucians, who regularly excited both popular and official hostility. In short, the power of individuals with unorthodox views was no longer being treated solely as a species of public-order problem, especially since these ideas were now capable of coherent transmission. Concern had been expressed about the power of print to influence the populace as early as the start of the sixteenth

---

[64] Andrew Dunlap, *A Speech delivered before the Municipal Court of the City of Boston in defence of Abner Kneeland on an Indictment for Blasphemy January Term 1834* (Boston, 1834), 59.

[65] 9 William III c. 32 (Statutes, Revised).

[66] Foster, *The Long Argument* 172 and n. Foster notes that the Massachusetts 1646 blasphemy statute was 'carelessly worded' and contained attacks upon heterodox opinion and upon 'scoffing and irreligion'. Foster is more impressed with the subsequent 1652 heresy statute and the 1656 enactment against Quakers, which he sees as an altogether more effective piece of legislation.

century, whilst limitations upon the power to print and publish became a feature of legislation and control in France and England.[67]

The situation in the Netherlands gives us useful evidence of how even a comparatively tolerant authority found it necessary to proceed in this area. Despite a considerable measure of religious toleration, some notable fringe-groups were scarcely immune from blasphemy accusations. In the 1620s the Dutch authorities were especially suspicious of Rosicrucians, and the municipal authorities in Haarlem found one of their number, Johannes Torrentius, guilty of blasphemy. Although there were calls for him to be burnt, he was finally sentenced to twenty years imprisonment. He was eventually pardoned by the Stadtholder and exiled himself at the court of Charles I in England. The works of Socinian authors were also considered specifically dangerous, and were banned from Holland and West Friesland by a law of 1674.[68] This type of action began to catch Unitarian writings, works of biblical criticism, as well as some quasi-political works, such as Hobbes's *Leviathan*. A few years later the ideas of Spinoza came under concerted, if posthumous, attack and his latter-day disciples also suffered. For example, Fredericus Van Leenhof's book *Heaven on Earth*, one of the earliest works of the Natural Religion tradition, was declared to be in conflict with Christianity. The nervous reaction of the Dutch authorities to the spread of dangerous opinions can be gauged by the proclamation of 1678, which stridently asserted the powers of the almighty. In a manner reminiscent of the 1646 Massachusetts statute, the Dutch proclamation outlined its enemies in a manner sufficiently hysterical to encourage them. It argued strongly that 'God had used wonders to demonstrate his power and had fortified belief in the process'. This was followed by dire warnings against those who explained the mysteries of the universe through, supposedly, rational means.

By the mid-seventeenth century the Dutch authorities considered the spread of blasphemous publishing to be manifestly out of control. They thus proceeded against printers and publishers, burning many editions of dangerous works. In Amsterdam in 1698 a lawyer and doctor of medicine, Adrianus Koerbach, was fined 4,000 guilders by the authorities and banished for ten years for publishing a blasphemous dictionary. Soon afterwards the bookseller Aert Wolsgryn was condemned to the bridewell for eight years followed by twenty-five years banishment and a fine of 3,000 guilders for publishing an irreverent and satirical *Life of Philopater*. Voltaire's works would later be proscribed, which allowed the story to circulate that error and poisonous ideas had been a French import which the authorities had a duty to keep out of Dutch society.[69] A similar course of events occurred when, in 1652, the Socinian-inspired Racovian Catechism,

---

[67] For additional insights see Alfred Soman, 'Press, Pulpit and Censorship', 442. For campaigns against the Quakers see Marshall, *John Locke*, 94–102.

[68] John Marshall suggests, perhaps optimistically, that the Netherlands were notably tolerant of Socinian views. See 138–40 and 149–69.

[69] Baelde, *Godslastering*, 128–34.

translated by John Biddle, arrived in England. This had first appeared in Poland in 1609 and its suppression involved burning by the public hangman under orders of parliament.[70]

Certainly all of this seems evidence that authoritarian fear of the merely casual blasphemer had lessened as a result of these legislative processes. Evidence from the *Parlement* of Paris during the eighteenth century suggests that blasphemy had become merely an aggravating factor in other offences. Sometimes it was brought in alongside crimes such as sacrilege, assault, and defamation in indictments. Of those accused between 1700 and 1790, where blasphemy was a contributory factor, roughly two-thirds of those convicted could expect a capital sentence, enslavement in the galleys, or banishment. Crimes of blasphemy alone began to receive more lenient treatment. One of these, concerning an individual called Gibassier, significantly involved lengthy consideration of the defendant's own sanity.[71]

However, more seismic changes were to alter the prevalence of blasphemy in eighteenth-century society. Providentialism may have exercised the minds of seventeenth-century man, but the eighteenth century witnessed a period in which this relationship began to be profoundly questioned. The seventeenth century in England had, for the first time, brought issues of religious tolerance to the forefront of discussions about religion. Nonetheless, tolerance as an issue led government to act against Christians on both sides of the spectrum. Zealous Tories, such as Sir Henry Sacheverell, disturbed the good order of the kingdom by inspiring riotous action against religious Dissenters. Sacheverell's argument had been that Dissenters disrupted and endangered the kingdom in a manner as blatant and damaging as any blasphemer could achieve.[72] Government chose to be even-handed in its treatment of such nuisances. Only seven years earlier Daniel Defoe had suffered extreme penalties for an eloquent, if ill-advised, defence of Dissenters' rights. For this he was imprisoned and made to stand in the pillory, although the latter sentence resulted in a considerable display of public sympathy.[73]

Advocates of the church-and-state relationship and Dissenters were joined in the equation by a third party who came to reject the value of religious creeds

---

[70] Theodore Schroeder, *Constitutional Free Speech Defined and Defended in an Unfinished argument in a case of Blasphemy. Free Speech league* (New York, Free Speech League 1919; De Capo Press edn. 1970), 279. For more on Arian, Socinian, and Unitarian doctrines and differences see Frank Schulman, *'Blasphemous and Wicked' The Unitarian Struggle for Equality 1813–1844*. (Oxford, 1997), 19–24. For an exposition of contemporary fears regarding the Socinians see J. Gailhard, *The Blasphemous Socinian Heresie Disproved and Confuted* (London, 1697).

[71] See Françoise Hildesheim, 'La Répression du blasphème au XVIIIe siècle', in J. Delumeau (ed.), *Injures et blasphèmes; Mentalités*, ii (Paris, 1989), 63–82, at 70–4.

[72] See Geoffrey Holmes, 'The Sacheverell Riots: The Crowd and the Church in Early Eighteenth-century London', *Past & Present*, 72 (1976), 55–85, and Brian William Cowan, 'Mr. Spectator and the Coffeehouse Public Sphere', *Eighteenth-Century Studies*, 37:3 (Spring 2004), 345–66.

[73] Schroeder, *Constitutional Free Speech Defined*, 316.

and hierarchies altogether. The rise of what became known as Natural Religion had its roots amongst the writings of philosophers like Spinoza, but it was also represented by a host of more minor figures that published and publicized religious explanations of the universe. Men like John Toland in England and Voltaire in France were significant figures in the spread of deism, an alternative to a divinely inspired and operated creation. This denied the divine hand of providence at work in the universe, and preferred to see it as a self-adjusting and self-regulating mechanism. Whilst there was still room for a creator, this Supreme Being had stepped back from creation and allowed it to regulate its own course. Deism, with its rationality and coherence achieved through philosophical justification and observation, was effectively the antinomianism of its age.[74] Whilst the latter had placed the sovereign light of the spirit in the individual, deism instead emphasized that the sovereign light of reason should be the individual's guide through a material universe. Although criticism of religious authority and its pretensions was often polite, it had an appeal beyond aristocratic circles. Even those who wished to keep such an idea from the servants cannot have reckoned with the skill and devotion of its enthusiastic publicists.

In France the so-called *libertines érudits* of the early seventeenth-century court circles, such as Guy Patin and Petrus Gassendi, were the staging-post in sceptical thought between Montaigne and Voltaire. Certainly some later commentators saw them as credible libertines and associated them with the views of the notorious Theophile de Viau.[75] The Jesuit François Garasse embarked on a crusade against libertinism in most of its forms. In doing so he enthusiastically categorized the varieties of unbelief and scepticism which he encountered. This provides a useful list that demonstrates that unbelief could sometimes be observed precisely as an attitude or disposition of the unbeliever concerned. Garasse saw 'furious and enraged atheism', 'atheism of libertinage and corruption of manners', 'atheism of profanation', 'wavering or unbelieving atheism', and 'brutal, lazy melancholy atheism'. What is significant in this list is how it constitutes a catalogue of unbelief's effects upon populations at large. Atheism of the mind and perhaps even of the dotage is clearly contrasted with atheism of confrontation and of public denial. This suggests just how slippery the slope from atheist utterance to outright blasphemy could be in the minds of society's moral and cultural policemen.[76]

One especial virtue of the 'deist' position was its capacity to show religious enthusiasm as stemming from sources of personal instrumentality. The writings of the third Earl of Shaftesbury attracted the French deists because they suggested that

[74] For a hostile contemporary view of the deists see John Leland, *A View of Principal Deistical Writers that have appeared in the Last and Present Century and some account of the answers that have been published against them* (London, 1754; 1837 ed.).

[75] Richard Popkin, *The History of Scepticism from Erasmus to Descartes* (Assen, 1964), 89–91.

[76] Ibid. 114–15.

fanaticism was a retreat from social interaction and that ecclesiastical authority could, in any case, exist wholly independently of the state. Between them Voltaire and Shaftesbury advanced the art of biblical criticism and equated Christian miracles with species of superstition. Certainly, most natural opponents of Christianity and established churches would commence their dissidence through mastering biblical criticism. This became effectively a full-time publishing industry for freethought in the nineteenth century, only falling out of favour in the first years of the twentieth century. Even so, a fear of evangelicalism and the need for affirmation of atheism at deathbeds would sometimes send freethinkers searching for the critical texts of the previous generation.[77] Deists who wrote critiques of established religion often had to adopt ingenious methods of spreading their ideas whilst escaping attack and censure. Disguising their arguments in footnotes was a favoured method, as were other rhetorical devices employed by openly critical blasphemers in the subsequent century. Diderot peppered his footnotes with ironic assertions about the unimpeachable virtue of the clergy. Elsewhere he would attack the behaviour of religion's representatives in the rest of Europe, thereby implying criticism of the French clergy.

In England an attachment to Spinoza's methodological approach landed deists in trouble. John Toland's work *Christianity not Mysterious* had claimed, in a quasi-anthropological way, that Christianity had subsumed many pagan rituals. In September 1697 the Irish parliament voted to have the book burned by the common hangman, with some members advocating the burning of Toland himself. Thomas Woolston's work between 1720 and 1729 embraced this philosophy so wholeheartedly that he was instrumental in the further development of modern biblical criticism. Woolston vigorously applied to the scriptures Spinoza's precept that all that contravened reason and nature should be rejected. His main targets were Christ's miracles, which he labelled 'absurdities, improbabilities and incredibilities'. Although some suggest that Woolston's allegorical alternative interpretation made him ahead of his time and an anticipator of the radical german theologian D. F. Strauss, he looks more readily a victim of the preoccupations of his own period. His writings resulted in his expulsion from a Cambridge fellowship, accusations that he was insane, and finally imprisonment until his death in 1731. Denying the miraculous squarely undermined the divinity of Christ and threatened to open the door for toleration of Socinian and Unitarian views. Moreover, even his clerical opponents admitted that Woolston had exposed the unwelcome power miracles exerted over the popular mind. His conviction and imprisonment were not universally popular, yet more importantly these alerted the reading public to the arguments showcased in the trial. To

---

[77] See David Nash, ' "Look in her face and Lose thy dread of dying": The Ideological Importance of Death to the Secularist Community in Nineteenth Century Britain', *Journal of Religious History*, 19:2 (Dec. 1995), 158–80.

many this looked like reasoned argument pitched squarely against shabby superstition.[78]

Jacob Ilive in 1756 found himself prosecuted for writing *Modest remarks upon the Bishop of London's several Discourses preached in the Temple Church*. The indictment showed that Ilive had portrayed the almighty as 'an imposter' and had denied the truth of the scriptures, calling them 'a gross piece of forgery'. He was sentenced to three years imprisonment with hard labour, exhibition in the Charing Cross pillory, and sureties were demanded for his good behaviour. Perhaps the most important deistical writer to suffer in England was Peter Annet who was tried in 1763 for his publication the *Free Inquirer*. This discredited the scriptures, and saw God as an imposter and the Pentateuch as an invention, echoing some of Ilive's conclusions. Leniency was granted to Annet because he was 70 years of age, although he was still sentenced to one year's hard labour, a month at Newgate, and to stand twice in the pillory with the label 'Blasphemer' around his neck. Theodore Schroeder was later to suggest that 'Annet's writings are of some interest as forming a connecting link between the deism of the early part of the eighteenth century and the more aggressive and outspoken deism of Paine and the revolutionary period'.[79]

Voltaire drew much from his association with Woolston, Toland, Ilive, and Annet—indeed, their influence led him to actively seek a public audience for his philosophical position. From the principles of deism Voltaire advanced an argument for a species of religious toleration. This was founded upon a universal belief in the relativity of customs and behaviour. From this standpoint it became obvious that the oppression the Catholic church in France exacted upon its 'enemies' was indefensible. In a wider philosophical sense, intolerant established churches were betraying any sense of virtue which they otherwise preached. But French rationalists also had good reason to fear authority's enforcement of orthodoxy as well as the climate that provoked it. The early eighteenth century witnessed religious hysteria around relics such as those of abbé Pâris. These were augmented by piecemeal attacks upon the Catholic church's opponents. Sometimes these included accusations of blasphemous iconoclasm and disrespect. In 1766 the Chevalier de la Barre was executed for having mutilated two crucifixes in the town of Abbeville and for showing disrespect during a religious feast to commemorate the Holy Sacrament.[80] The sentence was confirmed by the *parlement* of Paris as an example to the clergy and to reaffirm formal systems of politeness and discipline. This episode uncomfortably demonstrated how blasphemy could still function as a political accusation, whilst it could still

[78] For additional material see James A Herrick, 'The Rhetorical Career of Thomas Woolston: A Radical Challenges the Rules of Discourse', *Quarterly Journal of Speech*, 78 (1992), 296–316.

[79] Schroeder, *Constitutional Free Speech Defined*, 313, 339, and 341.

[80] Dorothy B. Schlegel, *Shaftesbury and the French Deists* (Chapel Hill, Nebr., 1956), 2. Michael Burleigh, *Earthly Powers: Religion and Politics from the French Revolution to the Great War* (London, 2005), 30.

provoke government action to exact the ultimate punishment. Nonetheless, this event ran against the tide of most intellectual and philosophical developments around the issue of religious toleration, which the third earl of Shaftesbury had centred around issues of politeness. The ideological lineage that was to lead to Thomas Paine was clearly visible in the construction of humanitarianism as a viable eighteenth-century philosophy. Both Voltaire and Shaftesbury demanded an enhanced respect for all human kind. Thomas Paine would eventually publicize this as an acquisition of rights and later as justification for systems of benevolent welfare.

Paul Thyry, better known to posterity as the Baron d'Holbach, emerged as even more strident in his criticism of the Christian religion than Diderot or Voltaire had been. His argument is pertinent to our history of blasphemy, since his attacks similarly indicted the secular as well as the religious authorities for the power they wielded. This was a recognition of how often these twin authorities had operated in tandem and been used to buttress each-other's power. Such views reflected the determinist outlook that the voluntary actions of humans were determined by the apparent good and that wrongdoing was the pursuit of evil or a reflection of ignorance. Secular rulers were culpable in their disregard for their citizens, and D'Holbach also dismissed the power of priests as dependent upon superstition and the incoherence of vague prophecy. Similarly, he identified the Bible with savagery and dwelt especially upon the supposedly primitive nature of Jewish society and custom.[81] These staple arguments were to become central to anticlerical culture in France, and would regularly resurface. The criticism of both church and king also set the ideological tone for *philosophe* criticism which culminated in the French Revolution's simultaneous attacks upon both.

Providence and providential views also had kindred enemies, and these were individuals who sought to demonstrate rationality within the universe. Determinism had been as old as Plato and it had found echoes in Aquinas, although he had in the end shrunk from the proposition that God's knowledge of events predetermined their inevitability. In some respects the association of gambling with providence actively provoked these musings. Cardano, and particularly Pascal, approached the problem of uncertainty through theorizing around gambling and chance. From Pascal's thought sprang probability theory, which saw risk and chance as no longer phenomena in themselves, but rather as factors within life that could be regulated and calculated.[82] Probability could only move forward with the invention of the average by Pascal. This was the enlightenment's answer to the irrational darkness that providential attitudes to gambling provoked. Such students and scholars sought to minimize the capacity or writ of divine intervention within the world. Probability was an attempt to make gambling rational and to remove providence from the mind of mankind.

[81] Schlegel, *Shaftesbury and the French Deists*, 88–93.
[82] Gerda Reith, *The Age of Chance: Gambling in Western Culture* (London, 1999), pp. xiv and 24.

Thus gambling became a place where scientific rather than sacred dramas were played out.[83] For the enlightenment, chance was reconstituted as a lack of knowledge about the universe or specific events. Such lacunae would eventually be filled though experiment and observation. Eventually this would lead to the science of statistics.

The arguments of the *philosophes* sought proof of the utility of institutions, while criticism of the church might well be constructed and offered in a rational and polite manner. This was some distance from the attacks upon religious doctrine which blasphemy had constituted. At this point we might detect a significant difference between those who argued philosophically against revealed Christianity and those who defiled it. It is easy to see this solely as a class divide, with polite and philosophical deism tolerated behind closed doors, whilst rude and popular anticlericalism found itself the subject of judicial attack. Although there was a grain of truth in this assessment—Voltaire did not want religious unorthodoxy discussed in front of the populace—an image of a cultural divide that made doubt elegant and profanity rude is too simplistic. In France especially, fear of the rise of the libertine and the moral carnage (s)he could wreak was an essential ingredient in considerations about blasphemy during these years. Libertines disdained the moral order and were popularly believed to indulge their animal instinct at the expense of society and the community.[84] Many philosophical developments had acted as catalysts for the high-profile rise of libertines and, invariably, their philosophy. The first of these was the growing interest in Epicureanism and the rise of the philosophically empowered sensual materialist.[85] Although almost always aristocratic, the ripples associated with this lifestyle and those who encountered it left a lasting impression. These were conveyed further when libertines justified their experiences for an audience that grew surprisingly avid.

Materialist ideas also filtered down through the work of clandestine treatise writers and copyists flowing from 'the current of spinozism slowly penetrating French consciousness during the closing years of the seventeenth century'. Most of these works were familiar to later eithteenth-century critics of church and state, notably Voltaire, Diderot, and D'Holbach.[86] However, it is also revealing how many potentially blasphemous works in French provincial libraries of the period emanated from English deists. Ira Wade found works by Woolston and Toland scattered amidst a number of abridgements and paraphrased editions of Spinozist and other materialist thought. Some sought to justify faith by reason, whilst others were prepared to go beyond the deist's conceptions of God to

---

[83] Ibid. 29

[84] It is worth noting that contemporaries distinguished between intellectual libertine critiques of Christianity and the indulgent sensual and sexual libertinism. See Marshall, *John Locke*, 713–15.

[85] This is more fully discussed in Ch. 4.

[86] Ira Wade, *The Clandestine Organisation and Diffusion of Philosophic Ideas in France from 1700 to 1750* (Princeton, 1938), 269, 277–321.

reject the idea of reason moulding the universe.[87] Robert Darnton has also traced the later circulation of these ideas, suggesting they were clearly an important component of the literary underground of *ancien régime* France.

A law of 1757 prescribed the death penalty for the publication of irreligious opinions in France, but it was never enforced, whilst its sponsor, Malherbes, became a convert to the free trade in printed works.[88] Many of such works in circulation wielded considerable influence upon attitudes to the sacred and its place. Darnton's analysis of the books traded by a late eighteenth-century provincial book-dealer suggested that roughly a third of anti-religious works were abstract treatises, recognizably the work of *philosophes*. The most popular of these authors were Helvétius, La Mettrie, and D'Holbach, with an especially steady demand for the last of these. Cheap printing had made these works enormously accessible, and they could be consumed readily, almost as they appeared.[89] This suggested a taste for 'rank atheism of the sort that horrified Voltaire himself' amongst consumers of, admittedly, clandestine works. The rest of this dealer's circulation of quasi-religious material was largely of a popular anticlerical nature that attacked the papacy and the religious orders.

Although demand for these works was eclipsed by political libels, Darnton nonetheless asserts that there was, even in the backwater of eighteenth-century Troyes, 'a considerable demand for works of the extreme, Holbachean Enlightenment'. Darnton's calculation of the underground bestsellers of pre-revolutionary France, ordered from the Société Typographique de Neuchâtel, noted works by Voltaire and D'Holbach in the 'top twenty', selling a total of 3,331 books. In other calculations by Daunton these were also the two most popular authors, whose works were ordered by the reading public, adding up to a total of 4,202 copies, approximating to one quarter of the overall total. They were also prominent in the lists of works confiscated by Parisian customs.[90] Many *ancien régime* societies attempted to limit the distribution of such works through the publication of an index banning their circulation (Austria's index of 1765 listed over 3,000 volumes). Others increased the resources devoted to the routine censorship of questionable material, with the number of censors operating in France more than doubling between 1745 and 1789.[91] Much of this was to no avail, and the

[87] Ira Wade, *The Clandestine Organisation and Diffusion of Philosophic Ideas in France from 1700 to 1750* (Princeton, 1938), 269, 256–62.

[88] Robert R. Palmer, *Catholics and Unbelievers in Eighteenth Century France* (Princeton, 1939), 17. But see also Marshall, *John Locke*, 517–21, for an assertion that circles of 'conversation' were equally important in the early spread of enlightenment ideas.

[89] Nigel Aston, *Religion and Revolution in France 1780–1804* (Basingstoke, 2000), 84.

[90] Robert Darnton, 'Trade in the Taboo: The Life of a Clandestine Book Dealer in Pre-Revolutionary France', in Paul J. Korshin (ed.), *The Widening Circle: Essays on the Circulation of Literature in Eighteenth-Century Europe* (Philadelphia, 1976), 13–83, at 50–2, and Darnton, *The Corpus of Clandestine Literature in France 1769–1789* (New York, 1995), 194–202.

[91] See Robert Justin Goldstein, *Political Censorship of the Arts and the Press in Nineteenth-Century Europe* (Basingstoke, 1989), 35.

spread of anticlerical and seditious literature had become a flood by the eve of the Revolution. As one of the most recent commentators on French religious life of this period has suggested, 'the doubts of the philosophes about revelation, originally confined to the salons and polite society, had put down deep roots and become common intellectual property'.[92]

It was deism of this sort that inspired Thomas Paine to rail against the evils of established religion and to give birth to a tradition in England and America that would enshrine the mentality of questioning. Moreover, his own anticlerical writings, most obviously *The Age of Reason*, were to inspire shopmen, printers, and publishers in the age of enlightenment radicalism. For authority faced with this ideology, the central issue was to contain the spread of such ideas and to limit their constituency. This was not always easy, especially since some of these ideas permeated the senior echelons of the French clergy, who sometimes downplayed the superstitious elements of Christian faith whilst combating anti-scientific prejudices. During the Revolutionary period some bishops adopted a liberal stance as a bulwark against the more extreme views of people like Voltaire. This was in the hope that the French people would accept that the *philosophes* offered them 'religion for the people' and that the secular tendencies unleashed by the Revolution might yet be reversed.[93]

Nonetheless, we should be wary of seeing an easy and linear transition between the street culture that spawned blasphemous incidents and this world of reasoned literary dissent. Pre-Revolutionary France still saw the taverns as sites of unruly behaviour and debauchery. The jurist Edme de la Poix de Fréminville, in his catalogue of contemporary police procedure, cited an ordinance of Dijon which listed the infinite excesses individuals commit in taverns to the ruination of their families. Amongst these he listed 'offensive discourse' and suggested that blasphemy was endemic in such places.[94] This was more than a cautionary fear, since the police believed divine retribution could still be visited upon those who threatened the moral safety of the community. What also lay behind the considerable attention the police paid to taverns was a fear that such places were homes to precisely those subcultures that would invert the moral order. Occasional outbursts of impiety and the tension this generated regularly provided potent evidence that such subcultures existed and were active amongst the impressionable.

Thus, on the eve of the French Revolution, we have a confluence of factors influencing the course of blasphemy's history. Libertinism, deism, and the messages of anticlerical literature discredited spiritual authority just as secular authority was under fire. This occurred as regimes that linked church with state

---

[92] Aston, *Religion and Revolution in France*, 350.

[93] Ruth Graham, 'The Revolutionary Bishops and the Philosophes', *Eighteenth Century Studies*, 16:2 (Winter, 1982–3), 117–140, at 122, 140.

[94] Quoted in Thomas Brennan, *Public Drinking and Popular Culture in Eighteenth-Century Paris* (Princeton, 1988), 23.

Fig. 3. The cover of Thomas Paine's *Age of Reason*. Probably the single most popular and widely read work to be accused of blasphemy. This is an early twentieth-century American edition.

were coming to be questioned. By the eve of the Revolution there was significantly widespread opinion and practice which suggested that state-supported churches had no mandate to coerce their citizens. The makeup of those who blasphemed against such churches had also altered. Blasphemers had ceased to be confused and occasionally wilful outcasts, and had now become rational, ideologically committed individuals. No longer did they merely want the sovereignty of their own opinion, but they wanted civilization to change as well. Laws against blasphemy had also altered by this point, to reflect its status as a political offence. All these factors were to be pulled into the whirlpool of the French Revolution. The century that followed had no choice but to engage with the consequences for religious belief and the law.

3

Blasphemy in Words and Pictures: Part II, 1800–2000

The French Revolution undoubtedly provided the first conspicuous focus in the West for secular and anticlerical world-views. These ideas, as we shall see in later chapters, began to redefine radically both blasphemy and the blasphemer. The latter part of the eighteenth century in France had increasingly conceded that blasphemy had become an expression of individual feeling and conscience. Likewise, the Revolution's assault upon the monarchy was a popular means of undoing the reverence previously offered to sacred objects.[1] The Revolution quickly proclaimed religious tolerance through its Declaration of the Rights of Man, and placed this within a definition of community and public order. Article 18 suggested this right be protected if such beliefs did not infringe upon the peace of others. This emphasis upon public peace was to retain importance throughout the nineteenth century, and gradually framed the toleration debate within modern cultures. We discovered at the end of the last chapter how the circulation of cheap and seditious literature had helped to spread the ideas that influenced the French Revolution. Henceforth, for the first fifty years of the nineteenth century, most blasphemers who graced the courtrooms of the West could generally trace their motivation back to this seismic event.[2] These individuals, either alone or with compatriots, worked to expose a religion that they believed to be both corrupt and corrupting. Moreover, their opinions were available to populations that had become overwhelmingly literate by the end of the nineteenth century. The freedom to express opinions had also by this time become a cherished enlightenment ideal, whilst the culture of reason created ripples in Europe and beyond to the English-speaking lands. In the former the legacy is best traced through the history of law and jurisprudence; in the latter, firmer evidence exists in the campaigns of the Revolution's enthusiasts.

[1] Alain Cabantous, *Blasphemy: Impious Speech in the West from the Seventeenth to the Nineteenth Century* (New York, 2002), 19 and 154.
[2] B. Clifford, *Blasphemous Reason: The 1797 Trial of Tom Paine's Age of Reason* (Hampton, 1993); James Epstein, *Radical Expression: Political Language, Ritual, and Symbol in England, 1790–1850* (Oxford, 1994); Joel Wiener, *Radicalism and Freethought in Nineteenth-Century Britain: The Life of Richard Carlile* (Westport, Com., 1983); David Nash, *Blasphemy in Modern Britain* (Aldershot, 1999); id., *Secularism, Art and Freedom* (London, 1992); Edward Royle, *Victorian Infidels* (Manchester, 1974).

The political changes wrought by the French Revolution and its aftermath had a series of significant impacts upon the history of blasphemy as an offence in Europe. Certainly, the Revolution imposed and encouraged legal changes that only fully unravelled by the end of the nineteenth century. In some instances the influence of the Revolution rendered blasphemy an obsolete offence, and in these jurisdictions the crime became impossible. In others the Revolution's ripples produced merely a liberalization, where penalties were downgraded. In these states a more rational view of divine providence reduced blasphemy to a simple public-order issue. Some territories were caught between these positions, and opted to protect church rites and property against the onslaught of blasphemers, who were now occasionally seen as subjects for psychiatric observation or treatment. Once again this position saw the protection of public order as the paramount consideration. The great German jurist Willhelm von Humboldt, whose ideas appeared in his treatise *The Sphere and Duties of Government*, argued that religion was clearly beyond the concern of the modern state.[3] Only when the rights of others were transgressed did the state have a responsibility to intervene. The Bavarian legal reformer Paul Anselm von Feurbach echoed Humboldt's ideas, noting that the concept of damage or hurt could only be proved against religious objects and not religious ideas.

Feurbach's own career was infused with a desire to remove the subjective and arbitrary nature of legal procedure and punishment. These particular principles eventually appeared within legislative thinking about blasphemy under the various German jurisdictions. The process had begun as early as 1783, when the penal code of Saxony saw blasphemy not as a sin but as a phenomenon undermining civil society. Although clearly punishable, there were obvious moves within these provisions to decriminalize the treatment of offenders and to label them instead as insane. Further east, the Prussian General Law of 1794 reflected the importance of the public-order dimension of blasphemy. In the section on 'Beleidigungen der Religiongesellschaften' (insults against religious societies) the provision's Paragraph 217 noted that: 'Whoever by public utterances of vehement blasphemies gives public annoyance will be given 2–6 months imprisonment and taught the seriousness of his crime.' Beyond this, Paragraph 219 required the prisoner's pastor to confront him with the grievousness of his crime in the presence of the whole church council, where he would be expected to crave forgiveness. The principle of graduated punishment was retained, with a second offence incurring a double-length prison sentence. New aspects of this law demonstrated a public dimension of punishment, the urge to protect religious feelings, and the prevention of attacks upon religious associations.[4]

The approach adopted by the Napoleonic Code was reflected in the legal mechanisms of several European countries. The code frequently rationalized

[3] This appeared in 1851 as *Ideen zu einem Versuch, die Granzen der Wirksamkeit des Staats zu bestimmen*.

[4] E. J. de Roo, *Godslastering* (Deventer, 1970), 17, 20, 21.

legal systems and punishment regimes, yet also reflected contemporary views of the source of peace and order within communities. Napoleon himself continually viewed religion as a politically useful social cement, justifying forms of authority and providing a vocabulary which promoted a form of conditional obedience. Paradoxically, such a stance placed Napoleon closer to England's own religious conservatives than either might have been prepared to admit. Yet Napoleon himself was periodically alerted to the danger of social ferment, and the legal systems of several European countries betray the influence of this thinking. His police-chief Joseph Fouché warned of the potential dangers inherent in 'the previously unknown pressures of public opinion'.[5]

The Antwerp law of 1804 governing the use of corporal punishments is representative of a jurisdiction influenced by the Napoleonic Code. It still had a clear section on denying God and blasphemy, relatively undiluted from some earlier statements of religious doctrine. Article 31 saw blasphemy as purposely denying the existence and power of a supreme being, with distributing this denial as the specific offence of blasphemy. The subsequent article made it an offence to make fun of, speak evil of, or slander Almighty God. Article 33 meanwhile specified these types of offence to be verbal or written, whilst Article 34 noted that these crimes weakened society and broke the bonds which held society together. The subsequent article stipulated the punishment for the crime to be imprisonment followed by permanent banishment. Likewise, the criminal law of the Kingdom of Holland in 1809 still demonstrated that God needed protection from deist ideas. Article 86 also stated that individuals could not joke about the almighty or spread such malicious ideas in public.

Further east, the modernized Bavarian penal code of 1813, constructed by von Feuerbach, did not mention a workable legal concept of blasphemy. Nonetheless' there was an article entitled 'Disturbing the Religious Peace' aimed at protecting church buildings, services, the mistreatment of priests, and insulting church associations. Oldenburg absorbed this code in 1814, but added a regulation specifically against disturbing the religious peace and blasphemy. The emphasis here upon public order also fitted in with the professionalization of policing techniques and bureaucracy of censorship which arrived in German states after the Carlsbad Decrees of 1819. There was also a contemporary movement away from public shame punishments to incarceration in both Prussia and the other German states. It has been suggested that this shift also represented a progression from an eighteenth-century society of orders, where the maintenance of honour was compromised by public shame punishments. In its place came a 'class society' which found the removal of criminal types more effective.[6] In this light it is worth considering how the nineteenth century really gave birth to the accusation that

---

[5] Quoted in Robert Justin Goldstein, *Political Censorship of the Art and the Press in Nineteenth Century Europe* (Basingstoke, 1989), 9.
[6] Richard Evans, *Tales From the German Underworld* (New Haven, 1998), 2.

blasphemy was a class-specific offence that would punish the poor and ignore the rich. Where restrictions upon the freedom of the press were concerned, these ebbed away only episodically in nineteenth-century Europe. Although England removed censorship by way of prior restraint in the 1690s, it disappeared in some countries as a result of the end of the Napoleonic Wars (in France, the Netherlands, Norway, and Sweden), and in some others as a result of the 1848 Revolutions (Prussia, Switzerland, Italy), with a number following later in the 1860s (Austria, Hungary, Romania, Russia).

Blasphemy law was also a tool of regimes seeking to re-establish credibility. Imposing doctrinal conformity to protect secular authority was a cornerstone of the reintroduction of the monarchy in France. The socially and religiously conservative regime of Charles X reinstituted a sacrilege law in 1825 that prescribed graduated punishments from mutilation to execution, on the grounds that respect for the sacred was essential. This restoration of religion as a cornerstone of society proved unpopular and focused opposition to the regime. Nonetheless, the Revolution of 1830 still brought with it only a different approach to censorship. In particular, there was recognition of the power of the 'gaze' that made visual depictions more seditious than written ones. The relevant article of censorship legislation declared that the power of pictures to 'speak to the eyes' represented 'more than the expression of an opinion'.[7]

After the 1830 Revolution religio-legal matters also changed in Switzerland, where more liberal concessions were made alongside the reconstruction of the Swiss Confederation. After this date the penal codes of Freiburg, Neuchâtel, Aargau, Zurich, Geneva, and seven other cantons contained no blasphemy law, although violating religious objects and services remained punishable. By 1850 the situation throughout Europe still showed only piecemeal and sporadic change. Blasphemy was still punishable in Altenburg in 1841, Brunswick in 1840, Prussia in 1851, Austria in 1852, and Saxony in 1855. The concept of God and religion as central to the laws of the land was explicitly expressed within these jurisdictions in the manner of the Hale judgement.[8]

In some European countries there were individuals prepared to dispute this assertion and to go further by claiming God was no longer central at all. Moreover, the French Revolution's advocacy of change in the name of the people was similarly important. In the English-speaking world the writings of Thomas Paine primed a popular desire to unravel the connection between church and state. The American lawyer and commentator Theodore Schroeder noted the influence of Paine, whose works 'were having a great effect in promoting the cause of those who disbelieved in the divine right of bishops'.[9] It is the response

---

[7] Quoted in Goldstein, *Political Censorship of the Arts*, 73.
[8] For more on these laws see de Roo, *Godslastering*, 18–20.
[9] Theodore Schroeder, *Constitutional Free Speech Defined and Defended in an Unfinished argument in a case of Blasphemy* (New York, Free Speech League 1919; De Capo Press edn. 1970), 354.

to these writings which really gives us a clear picture of where blasphemy became an important instrument of modern articulate religious criticism.

Nonetheless, some of these individuals were sometimes capable of obstruction, cantankerous behaviour, and obcurantism. Chief among these was a man whom we shall meet again in a later chapter, the political and religious radical Richard Carlile, who demonstrated all these credentials by reading the entire text of Paine's *Age of Reason* to an exasperated courtroom. Although this was the dubious highlight of legal proceedings against him, it did draw attention to the issue of legal rights. The lasting impact of his actions was to portray authoritarian interruption of his oratory as an attack upon the popular notion of a 'fair' trial, and likewise the admissibility of a 'fair' defence. Similarly, attempts to prevent the repetition of blasphemy in the courtroom exposed Christianity as an idea apparently above even reasoned criticism. Nonetheless, reading *Age of Reason* aloud did allow Carlile to demonstrate his confidence in the morality of the work. Here Carlile strongly argued that the issue of intention was important, and strongly asserted that his own motives, and those of Paine in writing the work, were above reproach.[10] Moreover, for a modern audience Carlile exposed the limits of religious toleration and how this very idea was by definition a threat to an authoritarian state church. If previously heterodox views were now to be tolerated (the recent Toleration Act had relaxed disabilities upon Unitarians), then this nullified the established church's claims to universality. Such arguments also fuelled the discussions that occurred in nineteenth-century France. Of course, any relaxation of religious control meant that full toleration was possible, leading deists and atheists to contest the lingering privileges of any established church.[11]

During this period such arguments were regularly answered by suggestions that religion, as Napoleon had suggested, was an instrumental source of consolation to the poor. The rich might discuss such issues, but ultimately were not driven by desperation to undertake an immoral orgy of rapine and despoliation. The confrontational approach to religion offered by Carlile and others suggested the infidel denial of religion's universal values promoted a 'kind of moral anomie' which would dissolve respect and responsibility. Contemporary works fearful of the impact of French ideas showed the 'mob' despoiling the scriptures.[12] It was clear that dangerous ideas were to be limited and circumscribed, and organizations to suppress vice took avidly to this task. Carlile's prosecution was followed by a determined campaign against those who rose up to take his place as journalist, publisher, and hawker of the blasphemous and the seditious.

---

[10] *The Report of the Proceedings of the Court of King's Bench, in the Guildhall, London, on the 12th, 13th, 14th and 15th days of October; Being the Mock trials of Richard Carlile for Alleged Blasphemous Libels* (London, 1822), 25 and 37–8, 79

[11] Hypatia Bradlaugh-Bonner, *Penalties Upon Opinion* (London, 1934), 48.

[12] C. Hole, *Pulpits,Politics and Public Order in England 1760–1832* (Cambridge, 1989), 210. See also Eileen Groth Lyon, *Politicians in the Pulpit: Christian Radicalism from the Fall of the Bastille to the Disintegration of Chartism* (Aldershot, 1999), 57.

Fig. 4. Richard Carlile, the archetype enlightenment agitator.

Eventually these moralistic campaigns ran out of steam and even began to prove counter-productive. Carlile's sworn enemy, the Society for the Suppression of Vice, was not always efficient, and the accusation that it targeted the poor and defenceless was not easily refuted. As early as 1809 Sydney Smith had described it as 'a society for suppressing the vices of persons whose incomes do not exceed £500 per annum'.[13]

Religious authority was also challenged across the Atlantic in the early years of the nineteenth century. Deism became an important influence in educational institutions, and Elihu Palmer lectured prolifically across the eastern United States, leaving deistical societies in his wake.[14] Yet in America it would ultimately be the legal profession which would lead the push for the recognition of

---

[13] Quoted in Peter Coleman, *Obscenity, Blasphemy Sedition* (Brisbane, 1966), 14.
[14] For more on American deism see Kerry S. Walters, *Rational Infidels: The American Deists* (Durango, Colo., 1992), 10–12.

individual rights. Writing a century after these events, the lawyer Theodore Schroeder noted that disturbance of the civil peace had played a significant part in the early legislative history of American blasphemy laws. The understanding of the law implied that 'to endanger the eternal soul of others' was the justification for defending religious orthodoxy.[15] Although blasphemers were indicted for their challenges to public morals, the issues became somewhat different when the matter was actually prosecuted. These courtroom battles of the first half of the nineteenth century focused upon different interpretations of the US Constitution. On one side the rights of state and municipal courts to regulate morals on their own doorstep was contrasted with the Constitution's desire for equality before the law. However, another dimension of these controversies was the struggle between the law's regulation of moral violations and the rights of free expression guaranteed by the Constitution.

Sometimes these battles also involved some important legal questions about how far America had 'inherited' English Common Law. Once again, such arguments had two distinct sides, with some seeing the Common Law as a venerable collection of robust and reliable judgements, while others saw the shadow it cast over American legal standards as oppressive and as the unacceptable remnant of colonial misrule. These two positions joined battle in the New York Supreme Court's case against an individual called Ruggles. This individual had spoken blasphemy to a shocked multitude in 1811, declaring 'Jesus Christ to be a bastard and his mother must be a whore'. There is little more known about this case beyond the verdict and the sentence, but the judgement and arguments that were derived from it were of lasting significance. When Ruggles appealed against his sentence of three months imprisonment and a $500 fine, the ensuing legal arguments opened up the whole question of blasphemy's role and status as a viable law. The appeal argued that the State of New York had no statute against blasphemy, and it was only an offence within English Common Law because England retained an established church. Conversely, America's freedom of religious worship should have allowed Ruggles the right of free expression whilst his own religious opinions, such as they were, thus had equal status with those of others.

This case was important, since it was creating jurisprudence where there was no specific statute prohibiting the offence. The distinguished judge James Kent rejected the appeal and chose to rely upon the spirit of the Hale judgement. Dodging the awkward elements of applying English Common Law, he relied instead upon the principle that all blasphemous acts were contrary to public morals and undermined respect for the law. Although he stopped short of adopting English Common Law in its entirety, Kent's, theorizing brought most of the Hale judgement's considerations into American law, especially an assertion that Christianity was the nation's chosen religion. Kent declared attacks upon

---

[15] Schroeder, *Constitutional Free Speech Defined*, 353.

Christianity to be 'extremely impious, but even in respect to the obligations due to society, [they are] a gross violation of decency and good order'.

This judgement was by no means accepted by all lawyers or constitutional commentators, who saw such opinions as dangerously conservative. Writing a century later Theodore Schroeder argued the central question in the Ruggles case, of 'whether or not the common law crime of blasphemy was repugnant to the Constitution', had been forgotten. Schroeder suggested that Justice Kent had shaped theories about religious liberty away from what had been intended by Thomas Jefferson. He also saw Kent as embodying a clerical elite, and that 'through Ruggles Justice Kent retaliated upon those who had done violence to his spiritual aristocracy'. Schroeder further argued that Kent was a conservative outpaced by events and the evolving interpretation of free speech in New York, which he subsequently voted against in 1821.[16] Although for later free-speech advocates it was easy to depict Kent as an out-of-touch conservative, there were other important dimensions to his thinking. Kent was an avowed federalist, and saw the recourse to English Common Law as introducing a standard interpretation which might eventually overwrite the inequalities of individual state laws. Nonetheless, the Ruggles case demonstrated that when blasphemy appeared in American courtrooms it would always reawaken the question of whether the United States professed a religion that should be protected by law.

In England more concrete attacks upon the church–state link continued throughout the nineteenth century. After Carlile the 1830s saw radicalism flourish amid a well-organized, illegal, unstamped press.[17] Anticlerical content was an important mainstay of this form of journalism and the milieu's central figure, Henry Hetherington, had a significant track-record in this area. Hetherington was also notable for exposing some of the quaint anomalies which existed as a result of the law's indifferent operation. A conviction for blasphemy in England removed the protection of the copyright laws, paradoxically ensuring widespread circulation of pirate editions! When Hetherington ensnared a respectable publisher, Edward Moxon, for issuing editions of Shelley's blasphemous *Queen Mab*, he also managed to demonstrate how blasphemy laws could effectively scrutinize all aspects of culture unchecked, while catching the respectable as well as the reprobate.

The illegal unstamped press of the 1830s argued knowledge contained the capacity to change society, and that limitations upon the spread of knowledge were unequivocally dangerous. In particular, access to information about sexuality

---

[16] Ibid. 69–71.

[17] P. Hollis, *The Pauper Press: A Study of Working Class Radicalism of the 1830s* (Oxford, 1970); W. J. Linton, *James Watson: A Memoir of the Days of the Fight for a Free Press in England and of the Agitation for the People's Charter* (Manchester, 1880); Donald Thomas, *A Long Time Burning: The History of Literary Censorship in England* (London, 1969); W. H. Wickwar, *The Struggle for the Freedom of the Press, 1819–32* (London, 1928); Joel Wiener, *The War of the Unstamped* (Ithaca NY, 1969).

and family limitation was deemed immoral and corrupting by governments in England and abroad throughout the nineteenth century. Richard Carlile had been involved in this work, and later Charles Bradlaugh and Australian contemporaries (Thomas Walker and William Whitehouse Collins) were to be the subject of prosecutions for obscenity in the 1870s and again in the 1880s. Although Bradlaugh and these latter individuals were never snared for blasphemy, the connection with freethought and anti-religious opinions was established in the public mind. This connection between blasphemy and family limitation ensnared Abner Kneeland in 1830s Boston, and came back to be an aggravating factor in later cases.[18] By the middle of the nineteenth century many hoped that blasphemy in England had become an anachronistic law, or at least, as a legal concept, one that did more to undermine religion's authority than to promote it. In England during 1857 this was strongly emphasized by the case against Thomas Pooley which excited considerable radical and liberal interest, particularly in London. Pooley was a Cornish well-sinker whose episodes of insanity led him to denounce Christianity in virulent terms. He was imprisoned and confined with only minimal investigation of his mental condition. Pooley's treatment was denounced by J. S. Mill, whose *On Liberty* contained an acerbic reference to the case and indictment of the society that allowed it to proceed. This seemed clear evidence that tolerance and free speech had yet to be formally accepted in Britain.[19]

Colonial imperatives also forced the British government to legislate in pluralistic religious environments. In the aftermath of the Indian Mutiny the renowned jurist James Fitzjames Stephen was responsible for the construction of the Indian Criminal Code of 1860, which contained provisions intended to safeguard the status of individual religions in India. Ostensibly the relevant provisions of the Indian Criminal Code sought to equalize all religions and legitimize their protected status in law. Without direct reference to any particular religious denomination, this part of the Code made it illegal to deface or defame any religious object or text.[20]

Nonetheless, tolerance in England would be extended in the latter stages of the nineteenth century with a liberalizing definition of blasphemy. This particular development was as a result of the notorious Foote case of 1883–84. The case is already well served by a copious series of contemporary works and a number of works by historians, but its impact remains central to our story. George William Foote was a radical journalist with literary aspirations who embarked on a campaign to discredit the blasphemy laws in England. Foote's newspaper, the *Freethinker*, progressively heightened the offensiveness of its written and pictorial content, culminating in a 'Comic Life of Christ' and a disrespectful

---

[18] See Ch. 4.
[19] T. J. Toohey, *Piety and the Professions: Sir John Taylor Coleridge and His Sons* (New York, 1987).
[20] See Ch. 1, n. 47.

MOSES GETTING A BACK VIEW.

Fig. 5. G. W. Foote's ribald depiction of Exodus 33: 21–3 *(Freethinker Christmas Number 1882).*

image of the Almighty's posterior.[21] The resolution of the incident in court created innovative case-law which echoes through English legal history and the numerous colonial legal systems reliant upon the example of English Common Law. Justice John Duke Coleridge dissolved the link between Christianity and the law of the land, arguing that even hard-edged criticism of the religion and its doctrines was acceptable. This was provided the intentions of speaker or publisher were honourable, and the 'manner' of this expression did not contain a conscious desire to offend. In its time, this seemed to be a blueprint for a rational and tolerant way forward. Yet James Fitzjames Stephen argued that it preserved the remnants of an intrinsically bad law which should have been eradicated.[22] This issue of 'manner' was seen by observers in Britain and the colonies as setting the limits of verbal or written debate. It was, however, doubtful that Coleridge, or others happy with this resolution, ever considered that blasphemy's

---

[21] Foote was in the end prosecuted for words written by William Heaford in an article entitled 'What Shall I Do To Be Damned?', *Freethinker*, 21 and 28 May 1882 and 16 July 1882. Whilst the case entered court Foote enraged opinion against himself still further with the printing of ribald cartoons, culminating in the reworked picture of a text from Exod. 33: 23. See Also G. W. Foote, *Prisoner for Blasphemy* (London, 1886), 38, id., *Full Report of the Trial of G. W. Foote and W. J. Ramsey for Blasphemy* (London, 1883).

[22] James Fitzjames Stephen. 'The Law on Blasphemy and Blasphemous Libel', *Fortnightly Review* (Mar. 1884), 289–318.

15. He is run in for Blasphemy.

Fig. 6. Christ is arrested 'for blasphemy'. From the 'Comic Life of Christ' *(Freethinker Christmas Number 1882).*

long-term history would go beyond the written word to be linked with the act of performance.

This apparent growth of religious toleration alongside the, admittedly mixed, success of liberal ideals of individual rights gave birth to a replacement for passive blasphemy. This new form 'active' blasphemy did not necessarily protect the rights of free expression, yet it placed much more responsibility upon those who claimed they were offended by the actions and words of others. As providential belief declined in everyday life, believers had to express their horror as a manifestation of profound personal offence. Legal systems also began to require individuals to demonstrate offence, and would actively test the extent to which material offended. Such systems also began to assert that some criticism was acceptable or justified through the notion of 'manner'. All this required the victims to become 'active' in the pursuit of restitution for their pain.

Many European states, but notably France and Germany, in the years after 1850 witnessed a wildly fluctuating relationship between the church and the state. In Germany this was complicated still further by a sometimes strained relationship between the state and the Catholic religious minority. Blasphemy would frequently figure in the sometimes tortuous battles between religion and the state in these countries. In France the requirements of a secular state power triumphed, whilst in Germany blasphemy was a source of an occasional rapprochement between warring parties. France in the nineteenth century resisted and substantially removed the power of the church or individuals to proceed in the prosecution and conviction of blasphemers. Whilst the Catholic church could not prevent attacks upon its doctrines, and claims to stewardship over aspects of French life, it was at least able to absorb them. On the occasions when French society became more tolerant to the claims of the Catholic church, this was largely at the behest of pious laity or in response to initiatives from elsewhere. In 1801 Pius VII granted a year's indulgence to those reciting prayers in reparation for holy insults. This was followed in 1840 by the initiative of Pope Gregory XVI, from which an oratory in Rome founded an association of prayers against blasphemy. Later associations, like the one authorized by the Bishop of Tours in 1847, enrolled members of the laity and organized prayers to atone for blasphemy and the evils befalling contemporary France.[23] This had followed a twenty-year period in which the French Catholic church had promoted a culture of sacred miracles, whilst its mariolatry had already begun to colonize female piety.

Occasionally a change of government brought a period of prosperity for the church. This occurred under the reign of Napoleon III, who allowed the church significant freedom of expression and oversaw an increase in recruitment to the clergy. However, the tide was equally capable of turning again to make life less congenial for the Catholic church. The 1880s saw the Republic valorize anticlerical individuals and extend toleration to anti-religious views. Civil divorce was reinstituted and military service for the clergy became mandatory. Although the state had exerted exceptional control over the French Catholic church throughout the nineteenth century, separation of church and state was only formalized in 1905.[24]

Although the pious laity prayed to atone for blasphemers, it was a significant discovery on the part of late nineteenth-century governments that prosecuting them was a policy without significant political risk. Preventing blasphemy and punishing it appeased a surprisingly large range of most European populations. It appeared to safeguard morals, it demonstrated the god-fearing credentials of the secular power, and frequently provided a new cohesion to ideals of national identity. This list of advantages looks to the modern eye like the construction of a form of social and cultural conservatism which distrusted innovation and change. Certainly there is a case for seeing these attitudes mobilized against the new tide of cultural modernism, and thus it is scarcely surprising to see blasphemy law used alongside other forms of censorship to attack writers and artists. Writing about drama in the 1840s, Louis Blanc indicated the clear duty societies held to protect populations from unscrupulous artists. To Blanc no

[23] *An Association of Prayers against Blasphemy, Swearing and the Profanation of Sundays and Festivals, under the Patronage of St. Louis, King of France, Approved by the Archbishop of Tours.* Translated from the French by Edward G. Kriwan Browne (London, 1847), 17 and 18.

[24] Michael Burleigh, *Earthly Powers: Religion and Politics from the French Revolution to the Great War* (London, 2005), 210, 340, and 362.

government should 'deliver the souls of the people as fodder to the first corrupter who comes along'.[25]

But as the century wore on Germany took the lead as the European home of censorship. The Imperial Press law of 1874 may have liberalized control of the press, but dramatic productions were still subject to stricter control than existed elsewhere in France or Great Britain.[26] Although such actions seemed philosophically justified, putting them into practice could be highly problematic. In an age where public opinion and the early mass media were becoming intrinsic parts of life, policing this was fraught with difficulty.

Quite often censorship regimes designed to curtail the public performances of plays were unable to constrict their circulation in written form. Nor were they ultimately able to police the numerous private performances of such works staged by enthusiasts. At other times, even the relative sloth of legal proceedings would sometimes defeat their own object. In 1889 authorities in Saxony proceeded against the novelists Willhelm Friedrich Verlag, Hermann Conradi, and Wilhelm Walloth in the co called 'Leipzig Realists Trial'. All were accused of obscenity although Conradi's work, *Adam Mensch* (*Adam Man*), was also accused of blasphemy. By the time all were convicted up to three-quarters of their print run was already in circulation. From the tone of the public response, it became fairly clear that these attempts at censorship did more to promote naturalist writing than hinder it. Several literary associations were formed in response to censorship, and at least two journals also joined this crusade. Moreover, the decision to try the three defendants together made them a group upon whom radical hopes and causes could be focused.[27] In Bavaria, during the 1890s, accusations were levelled against Hanns von Gumppenberg for his drama *Messias* (*Messiah*). In true naturalist style, this depicted a thoroughly well-intentioned human Jesus, whose apparent miracles were fraudulent methods of convincing audiences of his divine power. Von Gumppenberg defended himself from the lecture platform, and escaped prosecution when his precise words could not be established to the satisfaction of the court.

Occasionally the German authorities would prosecute blasphemers as a way of appeasing the Catholic minority, who often argued that protection for their beliefs was generally inadequate. In 1900 Max Von Feilitzsch, the Bavarian Minister of the Interior, stated that he was prepared to see such prosecutions reach court, even if conviction was unlikely. Such occasions would demonstrate that the state took its responsibility for the protection of religious minorities seriously. This policy decision had been prompted by Oskar Panizza's controversial play *Das Liebeskonzil* (*The Council of Love*), which had been written as a means of

[25] Quoted in Goldstein, *Political Censorship of the Arts*, 114.

[26] Gary Stark, 'Trials and Tribulations: Authors' Responses to Censorship in Imperial Germany, 1885–1914', *German Studies Review*, 12: 3 (Oct. 1989), 447–68, at 449.

[27] Peter Jelavich, 'The Censorship of Literary Naturalism, 1885–1895: Bavaria', *Central European History*, 18:3, pp. 326–43, at 327–8.

provoking the Catholic church and offending Catholic sensibilities. The play depicted heaven, hell, and the court of Pope Alexander VI, and it put forward the suggestion that a malevolent God had created syphilis to punish humanity. Amid its portrayal of God as foolish and Jesus as impotent, the Virgin Mary was unnervingly preoccupied with her own sexual allure. Similarly, Panizza's caricature of the corrupt Borgia papacy was intended to make his audience think much more critically about the recent innovations of Papal Infallibility and the Immaculate Conception. Likewise, an impotent Christ was an attack upon the dominance of mariolatry within Catholic teaching. In January 1895 the prosecutor in Munich ordered confiscation of the play's print run. The meagre number of copies that had already been sold were the subject of police searches and pressure was applied to booksellers to identify the purchasers. Panizza was eventually charged with ninety-three instances of blasphemy contravening Article 166 of the Reichsstrafgesetzbuch of 1871. Desperate to produce offended individuals whose responses could be used in court, the Bavarian police cited their Leipzig counterparts as examples of the offended citizenry. This had the desired effect, since Panizza was convicted and served a year in prison. But this was scarcely the last German and Austrian courts were to hear of Panizza or his play.[28]

Athough literary works were carefully scrutinized in the final quarter of the nineteenth century, more obviously philosophical ideas and writings were also by no means free from prosecution. In 1888 Sweden successfully prosecuted the philosophical writer Viktor Lennstrand, who had concluded that: 'What the world has lost by the loss of God, we must restore to it.' Although jurors acquitted him, he was subsequently convicted by official tribunals, imprisoning him for three months for his lecture 'The God Idea'. Lennstrand continued his campaign, editing his newspaper *Fritankaren* (*The Freethinker*) from his prison cell, and later endured another sentence of three months for his subsequent lecture 'Why I attack Christianity' in 1889. However, Lennstrand's case demonstrated that the pace of toleration was scarcely uniform throughout Europe. Unlike the artists who were ensnared by the law in Germany, Lennstrand's work was in no way flippant. Instead it presented a reasoned series of anthropological and ethnographical arguments about the evolution of religion. Clearly such high-handed actions also incensed his British counterparts, who brought the case to the attention of what, in these moments, seemed a manifestly more liberal society.[29]

---

[28] Peter Jelavich, 'The Censorship of Literary Naturalism. Peter D. G. Brown 'The Continuing Trials of Oskar Panizza: A Century of Artistic Censorship in Germany Austria and Beyond', *German Studies Review*, 24:3 (October 2001), 533–56.

[29] Viktor Lennstrand, *The God Idea: A Lecture, for Delivering which the author was sentenced to six months imprisonment for blasphemy in Sweden*. Translated from the Swedish. With an Introduction by J. M. Wheeler (London, 1890).

During this same period the story of blasphemy's development in the Netherlands, a society which had a very different confessional history, is illuminating. Rather than appeasing specific religious groups, the Dutch blasphemy incidents were early explorations of the importance of the public-order dimension. In Holland the French *Code penal* of 1811 had remained in operation well into the second half of the nineteenth century. During the Code's revision in 1881, consideration of blasphemy was strangely omitted, despite the use of the North German League model that clearly recognized it. This was largely because the Dutch Code's emphasis upon public order had tried to define the issue of 'annoyance' (*ergenis geven*) in a religious context. The commission charged with this task, and parliament in particular, did not want a separate offence of blasphemy to be re-created. A minister in the Dutch parliament offered the argument of Tiberius to suggest that 'God was capable of protecting his own laws. No human laws are necessary.'[30] Interestingly, a footnote to policing blasphemy as a moral infringement resurfaced in 1902 in an article of the military law (122b) which forbade the scolding of an officer or NCO in front of other, lower ranks.

As the new century dawned the possibility of using film to portray religious themes began to give censors, governments, and even audiences a series of headaches. Religious cinema quickly moved beyond the portrayal of biblical figures to use religion and its central motifs in new and sometimes challenging ways. This had been heightened by the power of the novel and of the theatre to reach mass audiences. This mass audience began to persuade filmmakers of the potential importance of religion as a theme. Cinema's relationship with religion during the twentieth century was largely to hinge around two related factors. The first was the complicated issue of whether depicting Christianity on film would enhance or detract from the spiritual lives of people in the West. If the depiction was to be laudable, and even beneficial, then how far should the religious establishment accept the influence of this reinterpretation?

The initial signs seemed encouraging, since the very first biblical epics saw themselves implicitly as stories. In these, the Bible was seen as a collection of narratives that were familiar to their audience. Thus many of the earliest biblical films were what we might describe as 'played straight', with a clear emphasis upon the narrative which utilized tableau and visual spectacle in the absence of sound. This group of films contains the work of such cinematic luminaries as Cecil B. DeMille and D.W. Griffith, and it is no coincidence that both of these directors maintained a strong sense of history in most of their other output. Cinema quickly realized the potency of biblical stories as narratives; Ferdinand Zecca was one of the first, producing the *Prodigal Son* in 1907 followed by *Samson and Delilah* in 1908. Religious epics truly reached new heights with DeMille's *The Ten Commandments* (1923). DeMille's subsequent film, *King of*

---

[30] The original Dutch is, 'ik meende dat het sedert lang vastond, dat God zijn geen menselijke wetten noodig'.

Kings (1927), was one of the first to be actively conscious of its impact, and represented the creation of religiously self-important spectacle. Throughout the filming a Jesuit priest was present to advise on all aspects of the film's portrayal of Christianity. The film was notable for the seclusion of the actor playing Christ, with only the director allowed to speak to him whilst he was in costume; similarly, prayers were said before the shooting of each sequence.[31]

However, very quickly film directors found that producing a supposedly factual record of the Gospels and death of Jesus was not without its pitfalls. Some uncomfortable themes contained in the Gospel stories had a potentially damaging impact when committed to the screen. In particular, ascribing responsibility for the death of Christ presented a problem of interpretation for a director seeking to reach a mass audience. *King of Kings* provided the first notable departure in this. This film had the highpriest Caiaphas and the Jewish authorities, rather than Judas, as the central figures responsible for Christ's death. (A similar accusation of anti-Semitism was occasionally made later against Tim Rice and Andrew Lloyd Webber's *Jesus Christ Superstar*, which depicted the Sanhedrin as a body of evil and authoritarian figures, although this probably owed more to popular anti-establishment attitudes of the late 1960s and early 1970s than to any deeper theological point). D. W. Griffith's 1916 epic *Intolerance* caused a scandal around its crucifixion scene, with responsibility for the death of Jesus associated very clearly with anti-Semitism. An original version which showed Jewish religious leaders as culpable had to be discarded, and the relevant scenes reshot with Roman soldiers as replacements.

The arrival of sound in the cinema would even more readily open up the Gospel story, as indeed any other historical narrative, to the possibility of deeper levels of interpretation and characterization. From this point onwards to our present time this has enabled film directors to produce a variety of different images of Christ. He has been portrayed both historically as well as in modern dress. He has also been portrayed as divine as well as unerringly human. All of these interpretations managed to give a new slant to a story audiences thought they were familiar with, and orthodox religion began to feel the impact of the popular religious epic. DeMille's *King of Kings*, coming at the end of the silent era, did good business at the box office and was seen by almost a whole generation of Americans. The first appearance of Jesus in the film is an iconic moment in which a blind girl's sight is restored and the first image she sees is Jesus smiling down at her. This prompted an American minister to declare to the actor that: 'I saw you in The King of Kings when I was a child and now, every time I speak of Jesus, it is your face I see.'[32] Such sentiments suggest that, even for the devoutly religious, the power of the cinema to affect their view of their deity and the

---

[31] I. Butler, *Religion in the Cinema* (New York, 1969), 38, and A. Pavelin, *Fifty Religious Films* (London, 1990), 34.
[32] *Fifty Religions Films*, 40.

incarnation was simultaneously a responsibility and an opportunity. Film-makers were to exploit this power in various ways as the twentieth century progressed.[33]

The first third of the twentieth century saw blasphemy laws and prosecutions become a means of combating the growth of socialist and anarchist threats and their cultural offshoots. This explains action against writers and artists that eventually reached the courtrooms of Europe and the United States. In 1917 a Lithuanian, Michael Mockus, was prosecuted in America for an attack upon Christianity which cheapened the image of the Holy Spirit. Following the Mockus case a Lithuanian communist, Anthony Bimba, was prosecuted in 1926 under the Massachusetts law of 1641. Bimba had been a significant opponent of Christianity amidst the local Lithuanian community in the town of Brockton, Massachusetts, and had attracted the attention of radical workers within the local shoe industry. At a meeting in the local Lithuanian National Hall, Bimba had declared that 'Christ was a Coward and had been afraid to die'. The following day a blasphemy charge was yoked to a charge of sedition which referred to other opinions Bimba had expressed the previous evening. The court eventually acquitted Bimba of the blasphemy charge (convicting him of sedition), yet the association between the two remained in the public mind.[34] Australia also took action against similar material. When *Ross's Monthly* magazine in 1919 carried an article depicting the arrival of Bolshevism in heaven, and its attendant disruption to organized religion, the paper was prosecuted for libelling 'God, the scriptures and the Christian Religion'. The paper's proprietor was eventually fined £50 on appeal. This incident also stimulated the first organized movement in Australia to campaign for the removal of laws against blasphemy.[35]

In the aftermath of the First World War in Germany some anti-militarists fell foul of the law. The artist George Grosz had served in the war and had been profoundly disturbed by what he had witnessed. After a failed suicide attempt, Grosz discovered sketching and drawing as his only means of expressing this anguish. In the 1920s some of his illustrations were prosecuted as blasphemous, in what became probably the most celebrated case in German history. One image depicted a German and an Austro-Hungarian Army officer coerced by an authoritarian shadowy figure with a whip. Alongside these three figures was a pastor balancing a cross and a Bible. A second image, entitled 'The Outpourings of the Holy Ghost' (*Ausschütung des Heiligen Geistes*) was a piece of fairly standard updated anticlericalism. This depicted a preaching minister with guns, grenades, and bayonets spouting from his mouth to shower upon a group of cowering prisoners. Perhaps the most disturbing picture was a depiction of Christ wearing a gas-mask and soldier's boots under the caption 'Keep your mouth shut and

---

[33] This is more fully covered in Ch. 7.

[34] For more on the Bimba case see William Wolkovich, *Bay State 'Blue' Laws and Bimba* (Brockton, 1975).

[35] Coleman, *Obscenity, Blasphemy and Sedition*, 98–9.

De overheid, 1923

Fig. 7. George Grosz cartoon. Church and militarism in partnership (1923).

serve'. Grosz was proud of this anti-militarist inspiration that caused him to imagine Christ coming to preach in the trenches, only to be misunderstood and coerced into the war effort. He publicly stated that he was neither Christian nor pacifist, but was actively motivated by an inner need to create these pictures. Unimpressed by this, the Charlottenberg Municipal Court found Grosz guilty of grossly insulting church institutions. Grosz then appealed to the higher court (the Landesgericht), who upheld the conviction against him. Undeterred, a subsequent still higher appeal to the Reichsgericht in Berlin resolved the issue favourably for the artist. After some deliberation, this higher court decided the works were not critical of fundamental Christian ideas and did not criticize Christ as the church understood him. When acquitted, Grosz saw this as a ringing justification of the artist's right to freedom of expression.[36] Often these forms of artistic expression were hard to equate with outright subversion. Yet this episode demonstrated that blasphemy remained as both a genuine fear and, in some minds, an opportunity to test the limits of censorship.

Alongside the German experience, the Netherlands had to control and police similar violations. In 1931 there were urgent calls for an alteration to the penal code to combat a growing wave of anti-religious propaganda. This had been emanating from communist agitators, and was allied to a systematic campaign of disrupting church services. Seizing upon this, the Justice Minister, Jan Donner,

---

[36] de Roo, *Godslastering*, 70.

Fig. 8. Georg Grosz cartoon. 'The Outpourings of the Holy Ghost' (*Ausschütung des Heiligen Geites*) (1920s).

argued that blasphemy was causing actual hurt to religious feelings and was thus still a dangerous phenomenon in Dutch society. The paper *De Tribune* attracted the attention of the authorities when it published an edition containing an article entitled 'Down with Christmas'. This was complemented by a cartoon revealing

God as the inventor of a poison-gas for use against Soviet Russia. A further cartoon showed a boatload of warmongering industrialists sailing towards Russia with God depicted as blowing the sails. The ensemble was completed with a representation of two labourers chopping up a crucifix, with the dawn of a free, unfettered community pictured in the background.

In response to these challenges Donner succeeded in having a new article (429b) inserted into the Dutch Penal Code which would prevent the display of blasphemous words and pictures on the highway. Such an offence was liable to the penalty of a month in prison or a fine of 100 guilders. Of more importance was the new clause added to Article 147 of the Code. This declared illegal all verbal, written, or illustrated attacks upon religious feelings that were scornful (*smalende*), a concept also relevant to Article 429b. Within this the hurt did not have to be proved, and it was sufficient that the hurt should appear implicit within the content. What gave this a truly political dimension was that such material did not have to be the subject of an actual complaint, allowing the authorities to act summarily against ideological nuisances. Nonetheless, a strange loophole existed in which the scorning nature of the attack had to be intentional. The problems inherent in this became apparent in June 1933, when the authorities wanted to proceed against a Rotterdam coal merchant for a leaflet entitled *Nederland, God en Oranje* (*For the Netherlands, God and the House of Orange*). This jocular leaflet noted that only 10 percent of the Dutch attended church, despite the not inconsiderable financial support given to the churches. Penal laws against scorning God were also portrayed as merely demonstrating his powerlessness. These churches and the authorities were described as hoping they would convince the 'old Dutch God he is worth something despite the fact that his situation was clearly hopeless'. However, the eventual prosecution foundered because the pamphlet's contents pre-dated the revised Article 147, and the coal merchant was not deemed responsible for the leaflet he was distributing. Incredibly, it was also discovered that in practice the law did not cover the actual spreading of blasphemous material, merely its authorship. This was reinforced by an incident two years later in Almelo. This concerned an election address which argued that God's only future was as a political pawn. However, this could not be proceeded against for the same reasons as the Rotterdam pamphlet and led to an amendment closing the loophole. This eventually made distributing or stocking such material offences liable to two months imprisonment or a fine of 120 guilders.

The year 1934 witnessed a further flurry of incidents that seemed to justify the fears of the Dutch authorities. In June 1934 a socialist conscientious objector in Dordrecht had described religion as an error, finishing with a fatal sentence reminiscent of Oskar Panniza: 'A God who created the Tuberculosis bacillus is not a God but a criminal.' This individual claimed his unbelief left him immune from blasphemy, but he was nonetheless convicted, served a month's prison sentence, and was fined 30 guilders. This incident was followed by a two-month sentence for an anarchist journalist who had playfully advertised shop-soiled statues of Jesus and the saints. The advert also attached sexual innuendo to the soiled nature of the Virgin Mary statuettes it had on offer. Such assaults enabled the political Right to take up the matter, and the Dutch National Socialists demanded action. Eventually they goaded the government into prosecution in Rotterdam by displaying *De Tribune*'s poison-gas cartoon on a placard with a caption declaring it to be 'a scandal that is allowed'. The government responded unenthusiastically with token imprisonment, fines, and by ordering destruction of the placard.[37]

The involvement of the Dutch National Socialists in protests was significant, since the pre-war Right in Europe frequently accused some artistic works of blasphemy, identifying this trait with a suspicious foreign cosmopolitanism. The 1936 exhibition of 'degenerate art' which was displayed in the Haus der deutschen Kunst in Berlin provided the occasions for Nazi culture to proclaim avant-garde works as, amongst other things, blasphemous. This and other subsequent instances involved a curious recourse to the medieval conception of shame, where public display, opprobrium, and ridicule were once more called upon to marginalize those felt to be outsiders.

However, in parts of Europe untouched by Nazism the erstwhile remnants of medieval law were starting to fade from view. Even once-theocratic Switzerland by 1942 did not acknowledge blasphemy to be a recognizable criminal offence. Before this, blasphemy had been reduced to a nuisance only punishable in a few cantons. The post-war world began with an optimism that secular rationalism would offer more solutions to the prejudices that had hamstrung and blighted the pre-war world. In this atmosphere organized religion and its attempts to influence governments and the populace seemed a vestige of the old world left behind. Education and welfare services had increasingly moved out of religion's orbit, and many conventional indices of religiosity showed that some element of decline had set in. Many were concerned that this brought with it a loss of respect, but perhaps more pertinent was a desire to explore the potential within new freedoms. The secularized society, analysed and in part proposed by 1960s sociologists, would no longer revere and privilege religion. The duty of government within this equation was to provide a culturally enabling society free from restrictions. Laws that limited freedom seemed less viable when post-war patterns of migration made multiculturalism a new dream for some and for others a necessity. Within this atmosphere of pluralism, crimes of religious offence, and the cultures that surrounded the idea, seemed no longer tenable nor worth defending.

Thus the later twentieth-century history of the offence of blasphemy is in some respects an alternative history of the state. The new agendas fed into this by inward migration of many post-colonial ethnicities also made important contributions to this alternative history. A range of cultural, nationalist, and ideological

---

[37] M. R. Baelde, *Studiën over Godslastering* (The Hague, 1935), 192, 195, 198, and 228.

elements fought back against the homogenization of post-war culture, instead promoting separate identities. A polarization between rights and beliefs gave nation-states a redefined role in addressing the needs of their citizens. This began to represent—and still does represent—a real headache for those who espouse, through the law and wider governance, the modernist ideals of toleration and multiculturalism. Within the last twenty years the attempts by the European Union to produce pan-community standards of laws and human rights in the area of religion have met with considerable opposition and reaction. This was at least partly inspired by a distrust of the 'worth' and 'value' of a pan-European standard of morality. Some more recent reactions have also distrusted the involvement of the nation-state in legislating in the area of religious belief that some argue belongs in the private sphere. Others, conversely, have welcomed the state's involvement and have produced arguments that cite the duty of government to protect the religious beliefs and feelings of others. Interestingly, American society was also confronting both discourses. Those who supported local jurisdictions were opposed by those espousing the power of the federal law and the First Amendment.

Post-war cinema reopened the awkward questions that it had asked about the divine in the first two decades of its existence. Indeed, it was a film that was responsible for ending the possibility of state blasphemy prosecutions in the United States. In 1951 New York State withdrew its licensing mechanism from the Roberto Rossolini film *The Miracle*. Significantly, in this overwhelmingly Catholic state, it had been pressure from the church that ensured the film was labelled as sacrilegious. This had been the cue for the US Supreme Court to dismiss this action, thereby extending the First Amendment rights to film, which now became a category of artistic expression.

Given this, at least partial, vote of confidence, Hollywood still pressed on with filming religious subjects. From a wider historical perspective attempts to reinterpret religion for a new audience placed Hollywood in the tradition of Strauss or Woolston, whose allegories had spoken to a different age. Some post-war portrayals of Christ on film were flawed, not through their interpretative failure, but through the constraints and abilities of the cast and directors involved. Most critics have little praise for Nicholas Ray's *King of Kings* (1961). In an attempt to be inoffensive, all of Christ's miracles were omitted and the whole question of his divinity was deliberately underplayed. In this instance it is even possible to suggest that artistic licence and spiritual neutrality were a form of blasphemy. *King of Kings* skated over the accusation of Christ as a blasphemer, and at no point did the film seek to claim divinity for the central character. Two years later George Stevens's *The Greatest Story Ever Told* also attracted adverse criticism. Stephens had total control over the writing, producing, and directing of *Greatest Story*, and it was to become something of a personal obsession, which critics see as a cause of its inadequacy. The film is flawed by the appearance of improbable guest actors (most obviously John Wayne) who dominate while on screen, not always to the benefit of the film itself. As many have noted, such individuals carried with them the baggage of roles they had previously played, undermining the narrative and cohesion of the film.[38] This was particularly unfortunate, since the central characters, played entirely by unknowns, found themselves overshadowed by 'Hollywood in sandals'.

Human and experimental Christs came in many forms, and were territory colonized in previous centuries by Socinian and Unitarian ideas. With the issue of divinity downplayed, it was possible for modern film-makers and audiences to view the Gospels merely as an inspirational story. Pier Paolo Pasolini, an avowed atheist, produced the naturalistic, low-key *The Gospel According to Saint Matthew* (1964), which saw Jesus as a spokesman for the downtrodden and a quasi-social revolutionary. This portrayal was in distinct contrast to some previously overblown Hollywood productions. Its concentration upon Jesus as an outsider and as an anti-establishment figure, its cinema-verité documentary style, and use of unknown actors made it consciously distinctive. Pasolini treated the Gospel as a species of archetypal myth and epic, whilst his Christ was unpredictable and many-faceted, with moodiness and childlike behaviour juxtaposed with hints of greatness. Jean-Luc Godard went for a modern portrayal of the Gospel interlaced with simplicity in his *Hail Mary* (*Je Vous Salue, Marie*, 1985) which tried to show Mary as an innocent (if almost consistently nude) virgin. This film prompted condemnation from Pope John Paul II and Cardinal Murphy, who saw in it a picture of the Gospel that was too naturalistic and a Christ that was far too human.

Aspects of the counter-culture that western liberalism had produced inevitably wanted to question authority, especially when this seemed to be supported by the power of religion. Thus it is no surprise to discover students and fringe literary figures involved in twentieth-century blasphemy. The responses of legal systems and authorities to this new phenomenon across Europe were scarcely uniform. In June 1959 Reinhard Döhl, a student from the University of Göttingen, produced and printed a profane Mass ridiculing sections of the Agnus Dei, provoking a complaint from two Hanover students. After an initial hearing he was eventually convicted by the Landesgericht, receiving a sentence of ten days in prison and a 100-mark fine. A subsequent appeal to the Bundesgerichtshof resulted in acquittal and a declaration from the court that the rights of artists were more important than any religious offence that they might cause. With this, European legal and policing structures fell back upon the protection and defence of public order. In 1960 there was a demonstration of how this conception would operate in Switzerland. The artist Kurt Fahrner produced a work depicting a naked crucified woman, which was exhibited publicly in Basel. He refused to remove it, but when a crowd gathered at the official opening the police intervened and Fahrner found himself in court. Although convicted and sentenced to ten

---

[38] P. Fraser, *Images of the passion* (Westport, Conn., 1998), 168.

days prison and a 30-franc fine, he appealed to the Swiss Bundesgericht. This dismissed the case, noting, interestingly, that the portrayal of the woman was not obscene, and that artists had considerable freedom in their portrayal of the naked form. Farhner's own motives in producing the work were also exonerated.[39]

Further west, the counter-culture's disdain of religious authority produced the Netherland's most famous case. The satirist Gerard Kornelis Reve, in an experimental work, had imagined God as a donkey, of which he became so enamoured that he speculated about having sex with the animal. Perhaps echoing George William Foote's memory of the ambiguous text in Exodus, Reve described wanting to 'possess God three times in his secret place' (*Zijn geheime Opening bezitten*).[40] When tried, Reve argued that he considered sex to be holy, and that an inability to link God with this act was itself a blasphemy. Reve was acquitted, yet still went to a higher court to completely vindicate himself and his artistic reputation. This higher court argued that the scorning element (*smalende*) could not be proved and that Reve did not exhibit the intention to offend.[41] In the United States a case against *National Lampoon's* cartoon of the Virgin Mary being kicked out of the house by her father for being pregnant was dismissed by a Massachusetts court.[42]

The libertarian advanced guard, however, did not triumph everywhere. South Africa had quite draconian laws regarding censorship, and these in turn were operated in a manner which was, to say the least, inconsistent. Periodically they would be supplemented by emergency legislation that served to confirm the rigour of laws already on the statute book. This made the state an engine of its own protection, operating restrictions that overruled the freedoms of the individual as understood by most other western nations. As late as 1990 soft-core pornography was banned for showing the nipples of white women, whilst the ethnographic context in which black women's nipples appeared meant that these remained uncensored.[43] From the perspective of a country ignorant of many cultures of tolerance, challenges to liberalism abroad seemed capable of altering the climate for change at home, as when calls for a South African Bill of Rights drew upon the turbulent experience of free-speech advocates in America. But most poignantly, the example of the Common Law in Thatcher's Britain was seen as a means of controlling and restricting information and its use.[44]

---

[39] de Roo, *Godslastering*, 72

[40] Foote's most blasphemous depiction of God had been a ribald reinterpretation of Exod. 33: 21–3: 'And the Lord said, . . . I will put thee in a cleft of the rock . . . and thou shalt see my back parts: but my face shall not be seen.'

[41] de Roo, *Godslastering*, 113

[42] See 'Blasphemy', *Newsletter on Intellectual Freedom* (Mar. 1978), 38–41.

[43] Barbara Ludman *et al.* (eds.), *Obscenity, Blasphemy and Hate Speech; How Much Can We Tolerate?* (Johannesburg, 1993), 9.

[44] Ibid. 14.

That such control could be wide-ranging was amply demonstrated for the South African Republic by its Publications Act of 1974. This deemed undesirable 'objects, film(s) or public entertainments if they were indecent, ridiculed the inhabitants of the state, harmed relations or compromised the security of the Republic'. Such measures were drafted in a comprehensive and inclusive way, and in the matter of blasphemy they rather left the particularity of the Common Law behind. Works were undesirable if they were 'blasphemous or offensive or harmful to the religious convictions or feelings of any section of the inhabitants of the Republic'. This was perhaps the ultimate logic of public-order approaches to blasphemy. By labelling it as a species of trouble and yoking it with other species of subversive disorder, government hoped it had undermined the menaces threatening a frightened and enclosed society. Nonetheless, the broad-brush Christianity inherited from Common Law remained in the statement (contained in the preamble) of the 1974 Act. Within this the South African people desired to maintain a 'Christian view of life', despite the manifest religious pluralism that had always characterized the South African nation. Compared with legal developments elsewhere this looked quite old-fashioned, since it identified belief with morals. For example, the 1988 ban on the self-explanatory film *Stripper of the Year* considered it not simply as appealing to lust but also as undermining principles 'commonly espoused by a Christian society'. Some commentators on South African censorship, such as J.C.W. Van Rooyen, argued that the coming of a Bill of Rights would unravel the uncomfortable truth that an inherited Common Law protected only Christianity in an otherwise manifestly pluralist state.[45]

Nonetheless, such catch-all proceedings became identified with detention without trial and the tyranny of the Group Areas Act.[46] Mechanisms of censorship were stewarded by the state that also appointed publications committees to oversee cases, and an appeal body similarly appointed by state fiat. The 1974 Publications Act circumvented the Supreme Court's jurisdiction over appeals that had existed under the previous 1963 legislation. Such repression provoked a response in kind, and the Publications Appeal Board had to take action against a somewhat ironic target. In 1981 it banned Andre Brink's novel *Kennis van die Aand (Looking on Darkness)*, which acquainted Christ's passion with a call to political activism.[47] Here the line between blasphemy and political censorship had become dangerously invisible. Salman Rushdie's *Satanic Verses* was itself later banned in South Africa, once again under such catch-all legislation. Ironically, this protection, at least in practice, for all faiths had come about as a result of the state's desire to take coercive measures in the name of protecting rights. Whilst this upset libertarians, it was a fulsome justification of their arguments about how precarious regimes never flinched from using the apparatus of censorship as a weapon in their armoury of control.

---

[45] J. C. W. Van Rooyen, *Censorship in South Africa* (Cape Town, 1987).   [46] Ibid. 15.
[47] Ibid. 18.

The late 1970s also witnessed controversy in Canada that emerged from a similar species of political subculture. This incident concerned a theatrical production that linked religious portrayals with the agenda of the contemporary feminist movement. In May 1978 the Arts Council of Montreal refused funding for a production of *Les Fées ont soif* (*The Fairies are Thirsty*), which was scheduled to appear at the Théâtré du Nouveau-Monde. In an obviously Catholic society the play took a considerable number of risks. In scrutinizing the cultural models of mother, whore, and the Virgin the play divided the stage into physically separate 'spheres', apportioning one as a neutral space in which all three characters interacted. The play was drenched with the themes of female subjection, with the Virgin spending the whole production holding an outsized and heavy chain symbolizing the Rosary. The Virgin was episodically portrayed as a victim of male patriarchy, but was given the opportunity to pronounce on this alongside the other characters. Her words also made light of the Immaculate Conception, describing the Holy Ghost pejoratively as her 'bird for a husband', suggesting how her 'son' had been 'taken from her' throughout the ages. This line of criticism was a familiar one and had been followed by Oskar Panizza, albeit from a different perspective.[48]

The play was denounced and the media challenged to publish sections of the script, a call answered by the newspaper *La Presse*. This act provoked further indignation from groups who mobilized themselves to shadow the production. When the play opened, the Archdiocese of Montreal organized vigils and it was denounced by the Archbishop of Quebec for its frivolous depiction of the Virgin Mary. After lobbying by Catholic organizations, the printed version of the play was banned. Counter-protests by such literary luminaries as Simone De Beauvoir and Julia Kristeva eventually succeeded in having the ban set aside on a technicality. Although a subsequent round of complaints were tabled whilst the play was staged, the Supreme Court only considered the matter closed in 1980.[49]

This incident overlapped with the revival of blasphemy as a living legal concept within the United Kingdom. This was in response to the notorious *Gay News* case, which not only brought blasphemy back into public consciousness but also entailed a landmark alteration of the law which dissolved the 'manner' distinction which Coleridge had established. This incident involved the prosecution of a poem by James Kirkup which had appeared alongside an illustration in Britain's leading newspaper intended for a homosexual readership, *Gay News*. The poem depicted a Roman soldier having intercourse and oral sex with the crucified body of Christ, although its author argued it discussed the possibility of religious salvation for homosexuals. Kirkup had already written on religious themes, and

[48] Jane Moss, 'Les Folles Du Québec: The Theme of Madness in Québec's Women's Theatre', *French Review*, 57:5 (Ap. 1984), 617–24.

[49] Maria Suzette Fernandes-Dias, '*Les Fées ont Soif*: Feminist, Iconoclastic or Blasphemous', unpublished paper, Negotiating the Sacred II: Blasphemy and Sacrilege in the Arts, 3/11/05. Centre for Cross-Cultural Research, Australian National University.

in this poem sought to explore the role of the outcast in society and their hope for salvation.[50] Most opinions suggest the poem to be of little literary merit, with the defending counsel Geoffrey Robertson recalling it as 'a muddled comment about the mystery of the crucifixion and the empty tomb'.[51]

Despite a robust defence, the editor of the paper, Denis Lemon, was convicted and given a nine-month suspended sentence. The presiding judge, Justice King-Hamilton, had no sympathy at all for Lemon or *Gay News*, and declared the poem to be 'blasphemous upon its face'. The case went to appeal, and this particular judicial process was important for the subsequent history of the law of blasphemous libel. Geoffrey Robertson recalls his surprise at Lord Edmund Davis's support for quashing the conviction, and his even greater surprise at the otherwise liberal Lord Scarman's rejection of the appeal. Robertson noted Scarman's recognition that protection for only one religious group was an anomaly, and his wish to see the law either repealed or extended to other religions. Strangely, this suggested that the law of blasphemous libel was retained in Britain as a potential tool of value for a multicultural future.[52] But the final verdict had the effect of recasting the Common Law of blasphemy. Henceforth Coleridge's distinction between 'manner' and 'matter' was removed from English Common Law, thereafter making almost any controversial religious statement or expression liable to prosecution. This judgement was noted around the world, and provided a path for other former colonial jurisdictions to approach the crime of blasphemy once again. After the *Gay News* case judgement these jurisdictions had the choice of adopting its implications or denying them. In choosing the latter course of action, Australia significantly demonstrated its preparedness to depart from its English Common Law parent.

In England the impact of the *Gay News* case dealt significant blows to both the Gay Rights and the libertarian agendas. With the election of Mrs Thatcher in 1979, the coming of a retrenched society led commentators such as Ronald Dworkin to express their considerable misgivings about challenges to freedom of speech. Dworkin's critiques of the culture of secrecy that surrounded the Thatcher years were acerbic, and in some ways have scarcely abated. In particular, he constructed a theoretical culture of liberty which had a thoroughly conventional political dimension. Dworkin suggested government's ability to balance rights and responsibilities would regularly come under strain, or could be cynically shelved as a matter of policy. Even when faced by European-inspired legal imperatives, the ability of government to stall or deny the power of these

---

[50] St John A. Robilliard, *Religion and the Law: Religious Liberty in Modern English Law* (Manchester, 1984), 34.

[51] A facsimile of the relevant page has been published openly since 2000 in Alan Travis, *Bound and Gagged: A Secret History of Obscenity* (London, 2000), 258. Geoffrey Robertson, *The Justice Game* (London, 1999), 147. For a fuller account of the *Gay News* case see my *Blasphemy in Modern Britain* (Aldershot, 1999).

[52] See *Whitehouse* v. *Lemon* (1979), AC 658. Robertson, *Justice Game*, 153

would persist. Dworkin argued that 'In a culture of liberty, however, the public shares a sense, almost as a matter of secular religion, that certain freedoms are in principle exempt from this ordinary process of balancing and regulation. It insists that government may not dictate its citizen's convictions or tastes, or decide what they say or hear or write. . .'[53] This culture of liberty, which Dworkin argued had considerable support, was so deeply ingrained that it had become 'an attitude'. Seeing liberty as somehow organic and alive was a counter-argument to those who wished to pursue the minimization of harm, felt moved by political correctness, or believed moral rectitude could be measured unequivocally. To Dworkin and many libertarians, 'the value of liberty will always seem speculative and marginal; it will always seem academic, abstract, and dispensible. Liberty is already lost, whatever the outcome, as soon as old freedoms are put at risk in cost–benefit politics.'[54] Dworkin's analysis of how the European Convention on Human Rights would affect Britain's blasphemy law agreed with most other commentators that the existing English law violated Articles 9 and 10 of the Convention. Of greater interest was his suggestion that equalization of the law offering protection for religion in general actually contravened the Convention's stated aims.[55]

From the late 1980s libertarians in America also noticed how the climate for free expression had taken a marked turn for the worse. As Marjorie Heins noted, 'symbols, words, ideas, and images were being blamed for social ills'.[56] Such suggestions give us a glimpse of how earlier fears about expression, sometimes hundreds of years old, could be rekindled. It was not simply an isolated number of challenges to free speech, but an entire change of attitude and approach. Books, films, museum exhibitions, music, and even school literature became embroiled in a struggle for America's moral and immortal soul. Obscenity, unpatriotic sentiment, challenges to so-called family values, and of course blasphemy were seen as creeping and destructive forces poised to inflict untold damage upon a nation already showing worrying symptoms of moral decline. Thus were born what contemporaries in media and academic circles dubbed 'the culture wars'. Such a designation spoke of a deep divide that had opened up between the liberal, secular tendencies within American society and the conservative forces of retrenchment and tradition. This fear of social collapse, and attempts to blame society's ills upon some supposed moral amnesia, had been a cornerstone of the West's major political turn to the Right at the end of the 1970s. Indeed, it had provided something of a crusading impetus to the Thatcher years in Britain. In particular, some spectacular attempts to gag free expression—such as the Clive Ponting and *Spycatcher* affairs—showed how far government was prepared to

---

[53] Ronald Dworkin, *A Bill of Rights for Britain: Why British Liberty Needs Protecting* (London, 1990), 10.

[54] Ibid. 12.   [55] Ibid. 35.

[56] Marjorie Heins, *Sex, Sin, and Blasphemy: A Guide to America's Censorship Wars* (New York, 1993), 1.

go. Ponting, a senior British civil servant, had leaked compromising documents to an opposition MP, Tam Dyell, which challenged the government's account of the sinking of the Argentinian warship the *Belgrano* during the Falklands War. Ponting was prosecuted and, to the delight of free-speech campaigners, was acquitted, despite the hostile direction of the judge. Peter Wright's secret-service memoir, *Spycatcher* was a spectacular embarrassment for the British government, whose attempts to block its publication in Australia and the United Kingdom were eventually overturned. Both incidents indicated the government's willingness to gag uncomfortable facts. Yet they also displayed that individuals would still take risks 'in the public interest', and that they would frequently receive considerable support for such principled stands.

But America's enlightened cultural approach to information was generally supposed to be different. It had a written constitution which protected free expression through its First Amendment. There were stringent freedom-of-information and disclosure laws, whilst federal law could also override the attempts of petty officialdom to limit rights and exert kangaroo justice. Nonetheless, change had been under way for some time. America's obscenity laws had almost lapsed in the mid-1960s, but the election of Richard Nixon had resulted in the less sympathetic appointment of Warren Burger as Chief Justice. Burger was subsequently responsible for the landmark ruling in *Miller* v. *California*, a case of obscenity tried in 1973. To the astonishment of liberals and proponents of the power of federal law, Burger undermined the ideal of national standards of decency and propriety. In what amounted to almost a charter for small-town American decency, Burger argued that individual communities could make censorship decisions without any reference to a perceived national standard. This potentially damaged the First Amendment rights of consumers away from the metropolitan areas of America.

Devolving responsibility for censorship shifted attention to the sources of moral disquiet. The media's alleged culpable position in making America a dangerous place began to be exploited by some in the legal profession. In an especially perilous use of the concept of 'incitement', an individual's parents prosecuted three television networks for the role screen violence had played in their son's brutal murder of an 83-year-old woman.[57] This was important, since King-Hamilton's summing up in the *Gay News* case had cited the potential for Kirkup's poem to incite immoral and illegal action amongst an underage readership. Had this American suit been successful it would have imposed policing mechanisms on broadcast media that would have rendered everything from science fiction to Dostoevsky culpable for social ills. Free-speech watchdogs were concerned that serious consideration of such a suit in court meant that misuse of America's 'harmful to minors' laws remained probable.

Further pressure tried to unpick the integrity of the First Amendment, as society once again debated the unthinkable, as it had over Ruggles and Kneeland

---

[57] See *Zamora* v. *Columbia Broadcasting System* 480 F. Supp.. 199 (S.D. Fla. 1979).

in the previous century.[58] The conservative Right questioned whether American society was certain that the First Amendment was an inalienable and indivisible right. Although there had clearly been logical exceptions to this right of free expression, these had obviously covered patently illegal activity. In practice, moral crusaders found that challenging the First Amendment was not easy. Thus so much action against morally questionable material evaded the use of the law altogether. Picketing, leafleting, boycotting, and various other modern 'shame punishments' were all utilized by pressure-groups that organized themselves to defend morals and religious ways of life. This situation also reflected what American opponents of revealed religion and its claims had really known for years. Their Constitution theoretically protected them from their opponents through the separation of church and state. However, this in itself meant that local informal action within communities became the preferred course of action of these religious opponents.

As the decade wore on a further tactic was found to be more effective still. Some fundamentalist and Bible belt commentators had begun to question the validity and value of the separation of church and state, and sought ways to redefine its meaning. Complaining about the state prohibition of nativity scenes in shopping malls became symptomatic of arguments that the state was not so much neutral as actively secular. This position saw the relationship between religion and the state as a conflict model. The state was thus a secular enemy of Christianity, and the duty to render unto Caesar seemed increasingly to be conditional. Campaigns for freedom of religious expression were one thing, but the state's supposedly antagonistic action also came under scrutiny. Questions began to be asked about precisely how the federal government was bankrolling this assault upon Christianity and its values. The National Endowment for the Arts and the National Endowment for the Humanities thus became leading targets of campaigns demanding clear explanations of their funding policies.

Material that was challenging, potentially offensive, or even mildly ambivalent came to be scrutinized more closely. The accusation that the dollars of godfearing taxpayers were being used to fund blasphemy was an extraordinarily subtle attempt at censorship. Material was not so much proscribed as not seen at all, or potentially not even created in the first place. Moreover, material that was known to be challenging, such as the quasi-pornography of Robert Mapplethorpe or the controversial depictions of Christ by Andres Serrano (*Piss Christ*), would be blacklisted and discover exhibition space was denied to them. Serrano's work in particular was thought to open up new boundaries of offensiveness. His photographs of a crucifix suspended in a vat of the artist's own urine and faeces seemed the most determined attempt yet to degrade Christianity. Opponents argued that free expression carried with it the responsibility to tolerate the objectionable, but this would impress few people on the conservative Right.

[58] For the Kneeland case see Ch. 5.

Fig. 9. Tania Kovats, *Virgin in a Condom.*

What carried more weight was the denial of rights this entailed. Even Supreme Court judges, such as Sandra Day O'Connor, would recognise this, since restricting freedom of speech interrupted personal autonomy in the construction of world views.[59]

Several of these arguments would find themselves mirrored in the response of Australian society when attempts were made to display Serranno's *Piss Christ.* When the work was exhibited in Australia it quickly ran into the same opposition it had encountered in America. When the Archbishop of Melbourne applied for an injunction to prevent an exhibition containing it from going ahead, this was refused, on a technicality, by the Supreme court of Victoria. The Archbishop claimed the work went clearly beyond the discursive, representing instead a calculated attempt to outrage. The court, under Justice Harper, felt that clear proof that the exhibition would incite a breach of the peace was obviously missing, so that he could not uphold a restraint upon free expression. Ironically, the exhibition did incite such action, although conceivably this might have seemed inevitable after all the adverse publicity. When the exhibition opened a man was detected trying to remove the photograph; after a subsequent attack by two youths the exhibition finally admitted defeat, closing its doors in early October 1997. Trouble pursued the exhibit to New Zealand when it was displayed the following year. Here the photograph was shown alongside two other works which were also to attract adverse publicity. Tania Kovats's *Virgin in a Condom* was a critique of the Catholic church's social teachings, whilst Sam Taylor-Wood's painting *Wrecked* depicted a naked woman in ecstasy at the Last

[59] Heins, *Sex, Sin, and Blasphemy,* 6.

Supper. The case containing the Kovats work was damaged and a gallery curator was assaulted. Nonetheless, the Solicitor-General, John McGrath, blocked all attempts to allow either a private or public prosecution.[60]

One important aspect of America's 1980s 'culture wars' that is especially pertinent to the history of blasphemy was its bias. As we have discovered, blasphemy laws rarely captured elite victims, whereas grass-roots profanity would quite regularly be punished. If an item of culture could not evoke significant aesthetic feeling in a judge or jury then it was more likely to suffer punishment. The law even had its own measure of this in discussion of the so-called 'serious value' of anything it was asked to scrutinize. American obscenity law operated with a conception of 'manner' that looks familiar to any student of the pre-*Gay News* case-law of blasphemous libel in Britain. Labelling something as patently obscene involved a test of 'prurient' interest. Thus, wholesome interest in sex was acceptable, although the ability to distinguish between this and the prurient bordered on the eccentric.

Censorship of the American cinema had existed before, but by the early 1990s it had become a distinct memory. Suddenly the early 1930s 'Hays Code' and its mechanisms were hastily revived. Although this was aimed at curbing scenes of nudity or sexual content alongside graphic forms of violence, there were also stringent bans upon the criticism of forms of organized religion. Christian organizations would also join in this idea that art promoted immoral or violent activity. In the early 1990s the Roman Catholic cardinal of Los Angeles, Roger Mahoney, called for a revitalized film code. His objections to some films could be viewed alongside the incitement-to-act cases mentioned earlier. Mahoney was bothered by *Cape Fear* because it glorified revenge, whilst he was later prominent in an attempt to blame the film *Pretty Woman* for causing a teenage girl's involvement with drink and prostitution. Members of the Moral Majority, such as Ted Baehr, in early 1992 pooled their resources to form the National Association of Ratings Boards, who wanted to foist a film censorship code upon the local jurisdictions spread throughout the country. This was explicitly intended as a revival of the Hays Code, and the idea of empowering citizens to police culture was to be potent throughout the western world. In England, from the remnant of Mary Whitehouse's National Viewers and Listeners Association came a much more watchful, and crusading, organization in the shape of Media Watch. There was also, in America, a still more subtle form of censorship at work. This was the censorship of more experimental and fringe films and books that found themselves priced out of their own legal defence. Paradoxically, the more mainstream a film seemed to be, the more legal muscle and arguments it could organize for its own defence. This is yet another 'dark figure' our study should consider. Offended individuals might well have refrained from

---

[60] For a fuller account of the New Zealand episode see Reid Mortensen, 'Art, Expression and the Offended Believer', in Rex Ahdar (ed.), *Law and Religion* (Aldershot, 2000), 181–97.

prosecuting material they found offensive for fear of the legal consequences and costs defeat would bring.

Blasphemy suddenly became a matter of significantly mainstream interest within the public consciousness through the *Satanic Verses* affair. Europe and the English-speaking world had hitherto encountered blasphemy as an attack upon Christian society perpetrated by a succession of individuals that it conveniently labelled as outsiders. The Rushdie incident changed this perception, making blasphemy a part of a globalized world, thereby introducing the West to new religious groups claiming the status of insider. The controversy began with the respected, western-educated author Salman Rushdie releasing his work *The Satanic Verses* to a bemused and startled public. This work involved references to the Prophet Muhammad which Muslims in a number of countries found offensive and blasphemous. Although in describing the blasphemy Islam did not speak wholly with one voice, the incident galvanized opinion around the issue of protecting religious beliefs from harm. Very quickly it became obvious that the matters the Rushdie incident raised in western societies were problematic and liable to be of considerable longevity.

Rushdie's *Satanic Verses* contained sections which many Muslims argued defamed the Prophet, sought to ridicule and mock Islam, and to make it a source of humour to western societies. As part of an affirmation of religious identity Muslims began to ask western legal systems for protection for their beliefs from what they saw as opportunism. In most instances Muslim pleas fell upon deaf ears. In the United Kingdom such claims were short-circuited by the law's historic protection merely for the Anglican church established by law. This put Muslims in a dubious state of equality with branches of Christianity that considered themselves also excluded. Other non-Christian religions, and those countries with strong religious legacies within their own constitutions, reacted in a broadly similar manner. In other European countries, such as France, the secular structure of the state rendered proceedings for blasphemy almost impossible, and technically alien to the state's view of its own role in ensuring civilized behaviour. Countries with strong traditions of freedom of expression (such as the United States) were also unable to countenance limits upon such freedoms.

Certainly, for a time, these polarized opinions pitted East against West in what some came to consider a latter-day episode of Edward Said's 'Orientalism'. Certainly, the two camps' respective images of each other did not help matters. The western liberal and literary world saw Islam as unreasonable and obscurantist in demanding a legal protection which was decidedly anti-modern. Others also argued that Islam did not possess a properly developed concept of the secular. The Islamic world saw hypocrisy in the existing selective protection of a moribund religious tradition, and reminded liberals that all they had done was to elevate freedom of expression to the status of a religious dogma. Moreover, the West had historically been powerful and the printed word carried with it the potential power of cultural imperialism. However, the spell cast by these arguments was abruptly broken by the shattering arrival of direct action and violence upon the scene. Publishers of the *Satanic Verses* were physically attacked in Denmark, Sweden, and Pakistan. Thereafter Rushdie himself became an unwilling player in geopolitics when he was the victim of the Ayatollah Komeini's pronouncement of a *fatwah* sentencing him to death and inviting his assassination. Even Muslims who disagreed with the *fatwah* would be at risk, and the director of the Brussels Islamic Centre, Abdullah al-Adal, was murdered supposedly because his indifference was regarded as itself a species of blasphemy.[61] Demonstrations and visually powerful book-burnings occurred in many western countries, but ultimately to little avail. Although the episode did eventually subside, it left a profound legacy for western governments which has yet to be fully appreciated.

Blasphemy thereafter has had an increasingly perplexing Janus face. It was derided by the liberal and secular portions of society as anachronistic, oppressive, and inhumane. These views gained credence as human-rights agendas and jurisdictions began to cast their shadow over the nation-state and its supposedly parochial view of matters. This was countered with a—some would say belated—recognition that religion was a central right and an indivisible portion of identity deserving protection. Allied to such arguments was a growing suspicion that the human-rights agendas were themselves not actually neutral but actively hostile and secular. Christianity's historic role in supporting sacred and secure government was used to dismiss the claims for sovereignty exercised by pan-national organizations. Perhaps for the first time in the twentieth century, those who actively wanted blasphemy to remain and be a useful concept at last had more rational and irrational arguments at their disposal than ever before.

[61] F. Lagard Smith, *Blasphemy and the Battle for Faith* (London, 1990), 28.

4

Who Were the Blasphemers?

THE BLASPHEMER IN THE COMMUNITY

The blasphemer rarely comes down to posterity through the objective views of contemporary observers. What evidence we tend to inherit comes from sources that are either unequivocally hostile to them, or enthusiastically supportive. Both of these polarized viewpoints are in danger of over-influencing our analysis. The evidence generated by detection, prosecution, and punishment regimes since the medieval period have all depicted the blasphemer as a nuisance, a troublemaker, or an unfortunate. When we add to this the vast literature warning the unwary of the fate of the unrepentant blasphemer, they seem an obvious and ever-present threat to western societies. However, examining the writings praising those prepared to criticize religion, or champion free discussion, makes the blasphemer alternatively emerge as an heroic enlightenment figure. Thus, we need to go beyond this dichotomy to frame a discussion of why people blasphemed or found themselves accused of such a crime against both societies and individuals. More importantly, analysing who blasphemed suggests that the imperative to discipline individuals for their opinions is by no means tied in a simple way to specific historical periods.

Our earliest encounter with blasphemers in the medieval West is sketchy and incomplete. It stems generally from both the very earliest municipal statutes and the work of the mendicant orders we encountered in Chapter 2. Beyond this, fleshing out this picture further involves some guesswork. As we noted, many individuals caught by such by-laws and edicts were socially marginal. Certainly it seems likely that our 'dark figure' of unrecorded incidents of blasphemy must also find room for the use of the accusation against these individuals. In this an accusation of blasphemy may well have functioned in the same manner as slightly later accusations of witchcraft, which targeted those less acculturated to the expectations of an urbanizing and increasingly cohesive society. Petty hostility to these outsiders may well have reached for the nearest means of exclusion to hand. Similarly, those on the margins of society may also have attracted the most attention and scrutiny from their neighbours. This certainly explains the response to the Jews and to Jewish *conversos*. Nonetheless, the very marginality of individuals may also have encouraged blasphemous thoughts and utterances.

Common and catastrophic misfortune could prove a formative experience that made individuals occasionally lash out against a God, and a religion, that had betrayed them and their faith in a benevolent universal order. The temptation to blaspheme must have come frequently to the dispossessed and the poverty-stricken. Just as the powerless genuinely believed that they had made a pact with the devil, so blasphemous words and actions performed a similar function. Cursing and defaming a God who had dispossessed or played an important part in the decline of an individual's own prosperity must have been a common, albeit an unrecorded, phenomenon. As was the case with witchcraft, some local neighbourhood disputes could result in individuals accusing their opponents of the use of blasphemous words.

As was also the case with witchcraft, these incidents often occurred in isolated communities and say much about the dynamics within them. A chronologically late example of this, which nonetheless gives a flavour of much earlier times, comes from the isolated community of Sandwick in the Shetlands Islands off the north-east coast of Scotland. In the 1760s and 1770s a flurry of blasphemy cases occurred which originated from interpersonal disputes that convulsed the neighbourhood. When Adam Sinclair quarrelled with Robert Thomason, their squabble degenerated into an occasion in which both blasphemed 'the Holy Name of God'. This was a scandalous outcome occurring in front of several witnesses, all of whom proved willing to testify against Sinclair and Thomason. Just as in other early modern communities, some individuals were persistent offenders, whilst whole families gained an unenviable reputation for the quickness of their tongues. In 1779 successive members of the Halcrow family were involved in using blasphemous words against their neighbours in the midst of petty squabbles. One incident may even have occurred within the family. Marion Halcrow was cited for blasphemy by Janet Halcrow for having suggested 'the divil' might be within the latter's cow, since it had eaten grass from the former's grazing land. Sometimes blasphemy made an unbidden appearance amongst other acts of violence or affray. In 1784 James Smith broke the Sabbath to attend the house of one Andrew Duncan, threatening to break up the loft doors. Smith distressed Duncan's pregnant wife and, in the course of his tirade, blasphemed. Perhaps less surprisingly, in view of the distress caused, a number of witnesses were again prepared to testify to the truth of these occurrences.[1]

Each of these cases provides useful evidence of how the exclamation of blasphemy could still occur spontaneously, even within a culture which had developed mechanisms designed to expunge it. Nonetheless, the community did readily have one eye on the desire to control these outbursts and the infringement of expectations they represented. In accusing an individual of

[1] Sandwick Parish, Shetland, Church of Scotland, kirk session minutes 1755–1842, Shetland Archive, CH2/325/1 *et seq*. Evidence from 1769, 1771, 1774, 1777, 1779, and 1784. I am greatly indebted to Callum Brown for drawing my attention to this material.

blasphemy the recipient was not rendered powerless, as appears the case in some European evidence.[2] The accusation, on the contrary, gave the 'victim' power, since it ensured that local policing authorities, in this case the local kirk, would intervene. Certainly Scotland's widespread concern to discipline its population has led recent studies of the nature of post-Reformation discipline to note its systematized severity. Confession and shame were not simply central parts of the Church of Scotland's control over morality, but having authentic miscreants publicly confess their sins was a part of its drama of repentence. What Diarmaid MacCulloch termed a 'theatre of forgiveness' common to Calvinist and Reformed Europe, reached its epitome in Scotland, where public confession was most stylized and persisted much later.[3]

Evidence of blasphemy as a component part of neighbourhood disputes also comes from the eastern Mediterranean and demonstrates how it could turn upon particular aspects of religiosity. In late twentieth-century Macedonia anthropologists came across instances where the Orthodox religious icons of a particular village lay at the centre of blasphemous episodes. In the Eastern Orthodox religion a village indulged in blasphemy when it claimed its own local icon was more effective in offering protection from providential disaster than that of a rival village.[4]

However, the medieval period does give us a glimpse of the existence of blasphemy as a species of articulate religious error. Carol Lansing's study of early Cathar heresy uncovered an individual whose blasphemy appeared to consist of uttering aloud his attempt to understand or reconcile his doubts about transubstantiation. When Bartolomeo 'Speçabrage' was sentenced by the Inquisition in Vicenza in 1292 for likening the host to a simple loaf of bread he had elevated, he had, wittingly or unwittingly, parodied the sacrament.[5] We have already seen that other evidence from the Inquisitions of the early modern period tells a story of individuals caught off guard by members of their immediate circle. The overwhelming picture of these incidents is of individuals speaking without rational thought or under extreme stress.[6] Maureen Flynn has investigated the works of contemporary theologians in search of clues to the interpretation of blasphemous outbursts, and what these apparently said about their perpetrators. The theologian Juan Luis Vives suggested that blasphemy more readily sprang from animalistic instinct. Blasphemy could be

---

[2] Françoise Hildesheim noted that blasphemy accusations could function as a smaller part of undermining the character of a neighbour in a wider and deeper local dispute. See Françoise Hildesheim, 'La Répression du blasphème au XVIIIe siècle', in J. Delumeau (ed.), *Injures et blasphèmes; Mentalités*, ii (Paris, 1989), 79.

[3] See Diarmaid MacCulloch, *Reformation: Europe's House Divided* (Harmondsworth, 2003), 596–600.

[4] Michael Herzfeld, 'The Significance of the Insignificant: Blasphemy as Ideology', *Man*, NS 19: 4 (Dec. 1984), 653–64, at 654.

[5] Carol Lansing, *Power and Purity: Cathar Heresy in Medieval Italy* (Oxford, 1998), 100.

[6] See Ch. 2.

contained and controlled within the individual by gaining sovereignty over the appetites. This could be used to justify the attempt to instil religious forms of manners and behaviour within religious populations. Leading Dominicans suggested reflection, or the recitation of aves or paternosters, to relieve stressful thoughts and situations. This interpretation, and the advice dispensed to the unwary, led Flynn to conclude that: 'Blasphemy in the moral literature of the Renaissance came to be regarded for the first time in church history as sensual speech, speech related not to people's rational and volitional powers, but to their imaginative capacities, their passionate nature, and their physiological humors.'[7]

When early modern courts and local jurisdictions discovered blasphemy, the encounter predominantly turned around the desire to re-establish a peace that had been broken. In many respects the attitudes of authority between the sixteenth and the end of the eighteenth centuries can best be summarized by rephrasing Socrates' pronouncement on theft (in Plato's *Gorgias*). Blasphemers were not punished because they offended God and order, but instead, so that God and order be not offended. This attitude seems to be prevalent in the responses that early modern Europe took against what we might term the casual blasphemer. These were individuals who were involved in specific incidents that breached public order through dishonouring God. By far the largest category of such offences involved drink.

Many blasphemers in the pre-eighteenth-century period found themselves in the dock as a result of drink and its consequences. Clearly this indicated that often alcohol and its attendant conviviality gave an opportunity for the release of emotions, idle thoughts, and over-confident scepticism. In 1513 a judgement in Leiden, against a known miscreant Gerijt Jacopsz. (alias 'the hedonist'), declared that he had spoken blasphemous words reviling God and the Virgin whilst drunk. Occasionally such incidents could be treated more seriously. In 1662 a Swedish boatswain, Lars Olufsson, was convicted and executed for cursing the Holy communion whilst in a drunken stupor.[8] Alain Cabantous's study of France showed blasphemy occuring in taverns as a species of bravado by intoxicated men. One such typical intoxicated individual in Trois Rivières (New France) in 1717 uttered loud and uncompromising blasphemies about the name of God in the local town square. Some inflamed by drink acted with others to continue their blasphemies after leaving the tavern. One group performed a mock and ridiculous Mass in Toledo in 1678.[9]

---

[7] Maureen Flynn, 'Taming Anger's Daughters: New Treatment for Emotional Problems in Renaissance Spain', *Renaissance Quarterly* 51: 3 (1998), 864–86, at 872, 874, and 878.

[8] M. R. Baelde, *Studiën over Godslastering* (The Hague, 1935), 109–10. Hans Andersson, 'Brottsliga batsman. En undersökning om båtsmännens brottslighet i Stockholm under senare delen av stormakstiden', in *Forum Navale* (1993).

[9] Alain Cabantous, *Blasphemy: Impious Speech in the West from the Seventeenth to the Nineteenth Century* (New York, 2002), 106.

But drink was not cited as the sole cause of such behaviour, and attention was focused upon the nature of the *cabarets* performed in taverns in eighteenth-century France. This was close to blaming the medium of communication for the message, but certainly authorities felt they had a right to go in search of where profane attacks upon God and the scriptures originated from. A variation of how tavern behaviour could escalate into blasphemy and iconoclasm is demonstrated by an incident that occurred outside Paris in 1701. A group of three young men drinking in a tavern pushed their revels to extremes, with a contest to offer the greatest impieties and profanities with the intention of conjuring an evil spirit. The incentives included exemption from the not inconsiderable bill, yet also clearly these individuals enjoyed the shock and fear they had instilled in onlookers who demonstrably feared divine retribution. One of the group, determined to 'trump' the actions of the others, fried a crucifix in butter. This final event was supposedly ended by a flash of thunder reverberating down the tavern's chimney, which supposedly scattered the three debauchees, never to be seen again. [10]

In colonial America alcoholic excess was also central to many of the earliest cases of blasphemy we know about. American Puritanism could be both more and less tolerant than were European authorities where drink was a mitigating circumstance. Whilst New Haven, Connecticut, in the 1650s was prepared to merely fine and deprive William East of alcohol, in Boston some attitudes were tougher. In 1654 Benjamin Saucer was faced with the possibility of a capital trial for denying God and showing disrespect whilst drunk. The more sensible attitudes of the jury prevailed, and this led to more lenient sentences in this jurisdiction hereafter.[11] However, the association with drunken lower-class misbehaviour resulting in blasphemy was not the whole story. The genesis of what would later become libertinism was evident in some examples from the seventeenth century. Sir Charles Sedley, a noted dramatist and poet, let a drunken revel in Covent Garden go beyond acceptable boundaries. Sedley comes down to us most readily from the memoirs of Samuel Pepys, who noted how his performance on a balcony in front of enraged onlookers degenerated beyond the merely bawdy. Sedley mixed mockery of the scriptures with simulated sexual acts, culminating in a travesty of the Mass which involved stirring wine with his penis and consuming this as a parody of the Eucharist.[12] The connection with libertinism and later Epicureanism meant that for some libertines drink would invariably be involved in their activities. Sedley was fined and imprisoned for both obscenity and blasphemy, and the judge made it clear that he considered this latter behaviour to be an offence against public morals.

[10] Quoted in Thomas Brennan, *Public Drinking and Popular Culture in Eighteenth-Century Paris* (Princeton, 1988), 270–1.

[11] L. W. Levy, *Blasphemy: Verbal Offense Against the Sacred from Moses to Salman Rushdie* (New York, 1993), 253.

[12] Samuel Pepys, *Diary*, 1 July 1663.

However, the relationship between blasphemy and the tavern was also at times more complex. Quite often the tavern was merely the site of meetings between individuals or of interpersonal quarrels amongst strangers. Francisca Loetz noted in Reformation Switzerland how blasphemous words could be used by individuals to establish forms of superiority over those they argued with. The use of such words represented an escalation of any argument, and their effectiveness could enrage opponents still further. In 1545 an argument in a tavern between two individuals, Breitinger and Sprüngli, escalated dramatically. After a tirade of name-calling, which took in remarks about one protagonist's physical appearance, a retort involved accusing the other of having sexual relations with a farm animal. Breitinger, indicating his willingness to use his sidearm, brought these proceedings to a halt, punctuating the exclamation with a blasphemy. Many early modern historians tell us that much quarrelling of this type was quite ritualized, with fairly well understood ground-rules that allowed escape and for weaker protagonists to withdraw with elements of honour intact. Nonetheless, some of these confrontations clearly got out of hand, and frequently occupied municipal authorities throughout Europe. Interestingly, for this plebeian social world, such arguments represented the most likely place that women were to appear in the world of popular blasphemy. Evidence from seventeenth-century Paris tends to suggest that these women were well integrated into the family unit and may simply have been dragged into arguments that got out of hand.[13] These episodes emphasize how the recourse to blasphemy was the culmination of an argument beyond which the slighted protagonist could not go. Honour would thus be demonstrated or satisfied in the sight of the whole community.[14]

Sometimes blasphemous prosecutions arose from nothing more than jokes that misfired, indicating how close the sacred remained to the profane. The persistence of such jokes also suggests strongly that this combination was still effective as a vehicle for risqué mirth. But some jokes could not always communicate safely across cultures and social distinctions, with unfortunate consequences. Our example comes once again from Zurich, a century later than the battle between Breitinger and Sprüngli. A Swabian in 1658 in a tavern told a joke about one of his grasping fellow-countrymen who took the greater share of a meal and money payment away from God, with whom he was supposed to share these items. The punchline involved the Swabian laughing at his own supposed regional characteristics, yet his master chose to distance himself from these proceedings, deciding instead to inform the local magistrates of what had transpired.[15]

Beyond simple tavern and street arguments, blasphemy could also appear as a clear part of threatened or actual interpersonal violence. The records of Old

---

[13] Cabantous, *Blasphemy*, 98.

[14] Francisca Loetz, 'How To Do Things With God: Blasphemy in Early Modern Switzerland', in Mary Lindemann (ed.), *Ways of Knowing: Ten Interdisciplinary Essays* (Leiden, 2004), 142–3.

[15] Ibid. 138–9.

Bailey Proceedings for the seventeenth and eighteenth centuries also suggest that an interjection of blasphemy by an assailant was specifically designed to strike fear into the victim. When Henry Simms confronted Francis Sleep on the highway in 1747, he 'swore in a blasphemous manner' that he would 'shoot him dead'. Similarly, in 1768 the landlord of the *Last and Sugarloaf* in Blackfriars called for the watch when he caught Daniel Asgood abusing another customer. Asgood's threats to scald and 'broil' this individual were accompanied by 'many blasphemous oaths and vile expressions'. Whilst hurrying to the scene, the watch was attacked by Asgood and his accomplices, resulting in the death of one of the watchmen. When George Ward demanded money with menaces from Alice Weldon in 1785, he swore at her blasphemously whilst attempting to throttle her. Women were also prepared to use blasphemy in this context. When Dorothy Holman overheard three women and a man attacking Eleanor Harrison near Cripplegate in February 1745, she heard 'such swearing and sad wicked oaths, vast blasphemous oaths', that she was convinced a riot was in progress.[16] Similar instances of blasphemy as a prelude to the use of physical violence emerge from eighteenth-century France.[17]

A close associate of drink as a source and provocation to blaspheme was gambling. Clearly intoxication was not material in most instances of gambling, but there must surely have been points at which they intersected. Blasphemy would occur either where the individual called upon the divine as an invocation for providential good fortune, or cursed the almighty for failing to grant it. Certainly it is worth noting that the world of the gambler was one significantly divorced from rationality and relying on chance, often bearing little relationship to ideas of either popular or official justice. Arguably gambling was considered by the populace at large to be a point of their lives where they were in touch with the almighty, a conclusion to be significantly repudiated in Counter-Reformation and Jansenist France.

What so frequently worried authorities was that gambling involved a manifest loss of self-control. Thus this profane abuse of providentialism was viewed as sinful and could only mean the individuals involved would eventually blame God for their misfortune.[18] This implies that some early modern individuals viewed their religious belief as a contract with God, in which human worship

---

[16] Proceedings of the Old Bailey Ref: t17470225–18 Henry Symms, theft with violence: highway robbery, 25th February 1747. Ref: t17680114–13 Daniel Asgood, killing: murder, 14th January 1768. Ref: t17850406–61 George Ward, Thomas Connor, theft with violence: highway robbery, 6th April 1785. Ref: t17450424–32 Margaret Mears, otherwise Kirby, Jane Smerk, otherwise Singing Jenny, Catharme (*sic*) Bowyer, theft with violence: highway robbery, 24th April 1745.

[17] Cabantous, *Blasphemy*, 107 and 115. Cabantous cites evidence from mid-seventeenth-century Parisian localities to suggest that almost half of blasphemy instances were accompanied by forms of physical violence.

[18] See Alex Walsham, *Providence in Early Modern England* (Oxford, 1999), 65, 78, 79–80.

had been supposedly exchanged for the promise of good fortune.[19] Ultimately theologians took a dim view of these systematic misuses of providence, because they were symptoms of a failure to accept the natural consequences of a God-given universe.[20] In early sixteenth-century Toledo the Inquisition heard how Juan de la Calle had lost control of his thoughts and strove to 'deny God and the bastard of his lineage'. Similarly, in 1544 a group of bewildered villagers told the Inquisition they had witnessed a gamester pledge his allegiance to the devil, since God had clearly forsaken him.[21] Towards the end of the same century Diego Flores, an inhabitant of Veracruz (New Spain), cursed God for having persistently 'punished' him with poor luck. Gonzalo Hernández de Figueroa, the son of a prominent conquistador, famously maintained a long career filled with similar bravado. He had been tried for verbally abusing the almighty at the tender age of 17, when he had openly threatened to fight with God. Gonzalo had to explain himself before the Holy Office on no less than four subsequent occasions. Each time he had hurled insults at God, and each time these actions had sprung from exasperation and frustration from his failure to prosper at the gaming table.[22] Similar frustration led Antonio Rinaldeschi to hurl horse manure at a tabernacle containing the Madonna in early sixteenth-century Florence. However, a portion of the dung, shaped like a rose, attached itself to the statue and became the object of popular veneration. Rinaldeschi himself was caught and subsequently executed for his crime. This case is especially notable, since it inspired a tableau outlining these events culminating in a depiction of angels and devils competing for the soul of the unfortunate Rinaldeschi.[23]

Gambling as a pastime was also condemned, because it was wasteful of time and energy that could have been supposedly spent more piously. Some historians of gambling equate this with a Protestant, almost Weberian, attitude to profligacy and the growth of bourgeois sensibility. It is even suggested that Catholic societies were somehow lenient about issues associated with gambling.[24] Certainly it is possible to see evidence of such a reforming project in the work of some pamphleteers. This had interestingly moved away from fear of providential cataclysmic judgement. Josiah Woodward's *A Disswasive from Gaming* (1707) suggested that divine judgement would occur around the unwise 'stewardship' of an individual's time.[25] Yet this dichotomy is scarcely exact. Catholic Europe, as we have seen, did proscribe gambling and the blasphemy that surrounded it,

[19] Javier Villa-Flores, 'On Divine Persecution: Blasphemy and Gambling in New Spain', in Susan Schroeder and Stafford Poole (eds.), *Religion and Society in Colonial Mexico* (New Mexico, forthcoming), 120, 140–3, 148.

[20] Flynn, 'Blasphemy and the Play of Anger', 32.   [21] Ibid. 50 and 51.

[22] Villa-Flores, 'On Divine Persecution', 145–7.

[23] William J. Connell and Giles Constable, 'Sacrilege and Redemption in Renaissance Florence: The Case of Antonio Rinaldeschi', *Journal of the Warburg and Courtauld Institutes*, 61 (1998), 53–92.

[24] Gerda Reith, *The Age of Chance: Gambling in Western Culture* (London, 1999), 5.

[25] Josiah Woodward, *A Disswasive from Gaming* (London, 1707), 2.

even equating the phenomenon with idolatrous worship of money.[26] Moreover, the divine nature of punishment against the blaspheming gambler did not disappear amidst an approach to gambling which is sometimes described as a 'secularization'.[27] The stock providential stories concerning the terrible fate awaiting the blaspheming gambler could resurface. In the period of the Jacobin scare in England some of the classic narratives of the reduced and despoiled gambler re-emerge almost totally unscathed. In *The Awful Death of Richard Parsons* (1814), his oath during a gaming dispute—'That he might never enter into the kingdom of heaven, and that his flesh might rot off his bones'—was fulfilled within a few days, leading to his rapid and untimely death. After 'mortification' set in over his whole body, he died 'in a dreadful fit of shaking and trembling'. The pamphlet concluded with a poem indicating the undiluted providential fate that waited blasphemers:

> Stand forth, thou bold blasphemer, and prophane;
> Now feel his wrath, nor call his threatenings vain;
> Sinners awake betimes; ye fools, be wise;
> Awake, before the dreadful morning rise;
> Change your vain thoughts, your crooked works amend
> Fly to the saviour, make the Judge your friend
> Lest, like a lion, his last vengeance tear
> Your trembling souls, and no deliver'er near.[28]

Thus far it is tempting to see blasphemy solely as an issue of control. Again, the nature of the sources can lead us too readily to this conclusion. Court cases and convictions are liable to construct an image of municipal and theological authorities determined to discover and punish such transgressions. Since many court cases and incidents focused upon individuals at the margins of society, this suggests unruly or simple undisciplined populations brought under scrutiny by new social practices.

This emphasis upon subjugating the will of the unruly is seen by Maureen Flynn as a religious counterpart to secular forms of disciplinary establishment amongst the knightly class as outlined by Norbert Elias. In this the act of confession and absolution were part of this religious acculturation.[29] In other words, this looks like a vindication of Elias's 'civilising process', in which changes in the practices and perceptions of the ruling elite detected misbehaviour amongst the lower and marginal members of society. This has persuaded some

---

[26] John Dunkley, *Gambling: A Social and Moral Problem in France, 1685–1792* (Oxford, 1985), 87.

[27] Reith, *The Age of Chance*, 13.

[28] *A Warning to Gamblers and Swearers in the awful death of Richard Parsons whose flesh rotted off his bones, agreeably to his impious wishes, when disputing at a game of whist . . . To which is added an affecting narrative of the death of Joseph Shepherd who was struck with a mortal disease in the same such manner* (London, 1814).

[29] Flynn, 'Taming Anger's Daughters', 868.

historians to investigate and describe blasphemous 'characteristics' evident in parts of the population and specific occupational groups—creating the analytical phenomenon of blasphemous 'archetypes'. Many people accused of blasphemy in French cases are also those who showed evidence of alternative lifestyles which marked them out as profoundly different from the rest of the population they lived amongst. Much of French historiography writes and thinks about a profane populace teetering on the very edge of discipline and control. This approach, however, describes a reformation of manners as a significant cultural project undertaken by French society during the seventeenth and eighteenth centuries. Moreover, certain professions, namely soldiers and sailors, are seen as especially prone to blasphemous forms of behaviour. Public-order and decorum issues argued for the segregation of these people from the vast majority of the population that they might upset or infect with the contagion of blasphemy.

Oliver Christin and other historians have found blaspheming matelots scattered across Europe. Alain Cabantous found edicts against blasphemy to be a central component of merchant and military naval codes in seventeenth- and eighteenth-century Europe. A boatman in early sixteenth-century Meaux (a district east of Paris) was prosecuted and burnt in 1528 for denying the Virgin had any more power than her own statue.[30] Further east, Hans Andersson's study of seventeenth-century Sweden uncovered remarkably similar evidence. We have already encountered the drunken boatswain Lars Olufsson, but he was scarcely an exception. In 1699 two members of the Swedish royal navy were condemned to death for having changed the words 'I have Jesus in my heart' to 'I have the devil in my heart'.[31] Andersson associated these acts unequivocally with occupational factors, to suggest that these marginal people and their transient lifestyle rendered them beyond effective control. Although these elements were clearly important, it is worth remembering that this approach assumes profanity and blasphemy to be simply endemic amongst particular groups. Similarly, Alain Cabantous noted the high number of artisans and tradesmen accused of blasphemy, but was unable to offer any conclusive explanation for this occupational trend. Cabantous was more certain of his conclusions about gender and age, noting the masculinity of the practice and its prevalence amongst the 20-to-40 age-group.[32] Yet there is a more complex equation to be constructed around this evidence than a simple association of behaviour with lifestyle, gender, age, or occupation. Factors such as the freedom to speculate about the nature of the universe, the distance from moral and social constraints, simple public visibility, or the proximity to danger may also have been significant. However, we need to know much more about precisely how such behaviour was transformed into an authentic case of

---

[30] Cabantous, *Blasphemy*, 2. Olivier Christin, 'L'Iconoclaste et le blasphémateur au début du xvie siècle', in J. Delumeau (ed.), *Injures et blasphèmes; Mentalités*, ii (Paris, 1989), 39–40. Christin links this particular incident with more classical Protestant iconoclasm.

[31] In Swedish 'har jag Jesum i mitt hjärta' and 'Jesum mot fanen'.

[32] Cabantous, *Blasphemy*, 99 and 101.

blasphemy requiring judicial action. This suggests that there may be more to be added to this equation through examining the precise incidents of blasphemy and their context.

I opened the first chapter of this book with the example of the Dutch boatman Robert Adriansz. Van Hoorn from 1728. I noted how his reckless actions in goading the almighty during a storm, and failing to take evasive action, resulted in him being detained on a charge of blasphemy. As we discovered, Van Hoorn's offence was treated seriously and he received the ultimate punishment. At the outset we concentrated upon his precise actions and their implicit effect. This particular incident is also important in that it shifts our attention a little away from the blasphemer as simple perpetrator. It also gives us potential insight into the motives of those who complained about Van Hoorn's actions. These are the people 'hidden' in conventional histories of blasphemy, yet here their contribution is central to our understanding of the relationship between blasphemy and the operation of the sacred in everyday life. Van Hoorn's blasphemy might have been forgiven by his audience had he not been straining their relationship with God quite beyond acceptable limits. Sea-travel was hazardous, and some of Van Hoorn's unfortunate audience certainly maintained the belief in providence we met elsewhere in the gaming hall. This providentialism had considerably widespread currency, and fiercely exercised the pre-enlightenment mind.[33] If we imagine a dangerous sea-passage, that conceivably tested the nerves of all passengers, these unfortunate people were aggravated still further by an individual whose actions were objectively dangerous to life and limb. Of still greater concern were his invitations to the almighty to intervene in worldly affairs in the worst possible way. Although Van Hoorn was tempting fate, perhaps even craving destruction, his passengers may have taken subsequent legal action against him in thanksgiving for their own deliverance. That boatmen were predisposed to blasphemy cannot function solely as a free-standing explanation; but their occupational position was a pivot around which many other issues turned. The nervous and anxious, with their notion of God and the sacred in the forefront of their minds, were confronted by reckless behaviour.

Here was a real instance in which the nature of the universe and God intervening in it became an issue of pressing speculation in everyday life. This suggests a series of 'moments' for early modern populations in which the mind was focused upon this great matter. Thus it becomes easy to envisage this 'underworld' of providentialism infecting the thoughts and behaviour not only of our sailors, gamblers, and soldiers, but also the audiences for their words and actions—ultimately the people who complained and bore witness against them. We should also be wary of how much a reputation for blasphemy was a consequence of its visibility. In the case of soldiers, Élizabeth Belmas noted that blasphemy was punished especially severely in the French military, and certainly

---

[33] See Ch. 6.

it appears in the disciplinary codes of armed forces elsewhere in Europe until the dawn of the twentieth century.[34]

THE BLASPHEMER AS RELIGIOUS RADICAL

Thus far we have encountered the portrayal of blasphemy as a plebeian, culturally abhorrent misdemeanour. Individuals attacked the name of God, invoked his power, or set themselves above him in ways which shocked and sometimes terrified pre-modern populations. So how precisely does the historical picture change from the world of the medieval and early modern street to the modern world of a literate public offended by the cultural products of others? We should remember also that experience of blasphemy, from the point of view of the victim, altered considerably after this change to modernity. The suddenly explosive and rash incident became a world of internalized blasphemy. This had the capacity to be premeditated and to be repeated, with the subsequent and possibly repeated viewing of offensive material. Understanding the transition between the two requires us to forget the notion of a rigid divide between the popular and the learned.

Tavern-room apostasy became enlightenment deism not through the former's disappearance, but because the latter came to reflect the erosion of authority that the former had haphazardly scorned for centuries. We are also aware of enough evidence to suggest that these doubts, which scrambled to the surface in the tavern, were nurtured by popular culture and access to the ideas contained in texts that authorities would rather have seen banned. Two of our most celebrated expeditions into the unknown of pre-French Revolutionary cultural history, Carlo Ginzburg's *The Cheese and the Worms* and Robert Darnton's *The Literary Underground of Pre-Revolutionary France*, have illuminated precisely this territory. Ginzburg's work showed an individual's defiance against the power of the Papal Inquisition to assert his own world-view, constructed from personal experience and ideas traced from his own wide-ranging and copious reading. Although these insights were gleaned from the testimony of an extraordinary individual, they invite us all to reconsider our image of religious orthodoxy. Unbending obedience could not be guaranteed, because the population of Europe at large had (literally) other ideas. Religious authorities and the state did not even have to go as far as to be fearful of active religious dissidence. Sometimes even the superstitions of the populace at large offered a picture of allegiance to the established order as fleeting and conditional. This perhaps partly explains why bishops in England were quite so concerned about the birth of monstrous objects to humble serving-women, merely in search of an excuse to hide an illegitimate birth or an infanticide.[35]

---

[34] Élizabeth Belmas, 'La Monteé des blasphèmes', in J. Delumeau (ed.), *Injures et blasphèmes; Mentalités*, ii (Paris, 1989).

[35] See David Cressy, *Agnes Bowker's Cat* (Oxford, 2000), 9–50.

The influence of many of the late medieval French heresies, alongside the scholasticism and anticlericalism inherent in the Lollard teachings of Wyclif, meant that informed protest against authority had notable ancestors. Their rejection of clerical power and religious belief dispensed from above had been inherited by antinomian and independent sects in the English Revolution, and this also had an important impact in colonial America. At this point the questions and scepticism which emerged in the early modern tavern began to get some rather more disturbing and convincing answers. Similarly, the religiously plural establishments of the New World were also founded with an intense hunger for religious self-determination which, as we have seen, constituted powerful arguments for judging authority against the yardstick of the scriptures. This was some degree beyond the misuse of religion as lower-class misdemeanour and habit. By the seventeenth century significant sections of blasphemy had become an attack upon authority. They emanated not from drink or bravado, but from sincere religious conviction. As such, they were a greater challenge to even the highest religious and secular authority. We get something of the flavour of this in the exchanges between King James I and the Anabaptist Bartholomew Legate, who proved a more durable opponent than some of the witches the King confronted in Berwick. Legate had a number of beliefs that all essentially sprang from a denial of Christ's divinity, and even emphatically argued that to believe God became flesh was itself a 'monstrous blasphemy'.[36]

The Ranters demonstrated the epitome of antinomianism, with their elect status confirmed by the ability to sin without it being recognized as such. The Ranters denied the validity of existing churches and religious dogma, and believed the world to be corrupted and beyond the reach of God. This made them some of the first to assert a materialist view of the world. They regularly parodied the Eucharist and shifted theological attention away from the incarnation to the idea of God. This belief regularly strayed into the assertion that Ranters had God within themselves. Moreover, they saw themselves as bound by no human laws and considered that perfectability was attainable on earth. Many of these suggestions come through in a case tried in 1678 concerning a serving-maid whose name is not recorded. This woman was a member of the Ranter group called the Society of Love, and she variously claimed to be able to pronounce who was damned and who saved, as well as acquiring sacred attributes and declaring herself the Virgin Mary. Her various religious identities would come to alter over time, as her prosecutors discovered. At her initial trial she was found guilty of 'religious offences against the king' and imprisoned for having 'taken upon her to be God'. She was eventually released from prison, having obtained sureties, yet three months later had broken the terms of these and was once again in the dock. The court judged that she had considered her release as a further licence to blaspheme and she had thus resumed the objectionable

---

[36] Hypatia Bradlaugh-Bonner, *Penalties Upon Opinion* (London, 1934), 15.

practice. This time the 'maid' had ceased to be God himself but claimed to have become 'the Third person in the Trinity, and that her Father was that Christ, who was with God at the Creation'. For this the court declared she was to be 'Whipt into better Manners of Religion'. Theodore Schroeder later declared this woman to be clearly demented, but her numerous declarations sit comfortably with Ranter antinomianism, Muggletonianism, and the Quaker perception of the spirit within.[37]

Muggletonians themselves could be a considerable nuisance to the authorities. Lodowick Muggleton's and John Reeve's religious mission was clearly disruptive of the peace within society, since both regularly cursed individuals in public situations. They also declared themselves, in classic antinomian style, to be exempt from the spurious laws of men. Reeve went so far, in his *Divine Looking Glass*, as to declare that the scriptures were the invention of the rich and powerful to coerce and oppress the poor. When Reeeve and Muggleton stood in the dock in 1653 they denied the judge had any clear commission to try them, instead arguing that they alone had been appointed to try crimes of blasphemy. When Muggleton was tried alone in 1677 he was still unrepentent, and claimed: 'the whole power of Witnessing, Blessing, and Cursing, devolved into his hands, which he as impiously practised upon the least affront or opposition; pronouncing persons damn'd by their particular Names, blasphemously adding, That God, Angels, or Men could not afterwards save them.' This was simultaneously blasphemy in itself and an assault upon the state's authority to protect the religious peace.[38] Ranter and Muggletonian ideas could still be influential in blasphemy trials until the end of the century. William King, a cooper in Salem, Massachusetts, regularly fell into demented rages in which he claimed to see his God 'in a third heaven'. Interestingly, King's prosecution and trials were seen as a political embarrassment, since then suggested obscurantist legal practices just as the colony's charter was on the verge of being renewed.[39]

It was perhaps the Quakers who posed the greatest danger for those in authority. Their set of beliefs, and the particular actions of individuals who believed them, had considerable impact on both sides of the Atlantic. Originating in England, the ideas of George Fox, James Nayler, and the circle which clustered around Samuel Gorton in New England showed that piety and the semi-defiant gesture might provoke the wider spread of disobedience. Quaker beliefs seemed deliberately intended to undermine and smite civil authority through conducting

---

[37] The Proceedings of the Old Bailey, Ref: t16780828–14. Maid, offences against the king: religious offences, 28th August, 1678.

[38] Theodore Schroeder, *Constitutional Free Speech Defined and Defended in an Unfinished argument in a case of Blasphemy* (New York, Free Speech League 1919; De Capo Press edn. 1970), 290 and 295 For Muggleton's subsequent trial see Lodowick Muggleton, offences against the king: religious offences, 17th January, 1677. The Proceedings of the Old Bailey Ref: t16770117–1.

[39] Carla Gardina Pestana, 'The Social World of Salem: William King's 1681 Blasphemy Trial', *American Quarterly*, 41: 2 (June 1989), 308–27.

their so-called 'Lamb's War'. Their refusal to practise hat honour (i.e. to take off their hats before social superiors) or to swear oaths marked these individuals out from their society and enraged those who were still fundamentally a part of it. The Quakers regarded all religious authority other than their own inspired inner light as a form of Antichrist, and spoke against it with military metaphors that challenged public order.[40] Moreover, their relentless quest for forms of martyrdom would make them look like an especially austere version of Ranter antinomianism, a group with whom they were initially compared.

Whereas for the Ranters the ability to sin innocently was a sign of election, for Quakers the pursuit of martyrdom was essential to the same kind of conviction. Moreover, their behaviour teetered between the apparently insane and the dangerously messianic, with some actions provocatively blasphemous in their implication. Going naked for a sign (as many did in market-places throughout England and America) was a barbed and dangerous eccentricity, but it was generally accompanied by declarations that the individual was one with God. When Nayler entered Bristol in an imitation of Christ, this went some distance beyond such acts. Denouncing and causing a nuisance to congregations and church premises tipped the issue into a day-to-day public-order problem. Not only did Christ appear mocked by these actions, but they also cast authority as oppressors of the new messianism. Quakers were also indicted for denying obedience to the magistracy.[41]

Cromwell moved against the Quakers because they constituted a species of intolerance. In their disruption of church services and their attacks upon ostentatious church premises they actively violated the Commonwealth's otherwise relaxed attitude to religious tolerance. Quaker anti-trinitarianism struck dangerously at much Puritan theology, and it was Cromwell's religious advisor, John Owen, who stated how far such views posed a threat. He declared: 'The liberty of men's rational faculties having got the great vogue in the world,' men were deciding 'that religion consists solely in moral honesty, and a fancied internal piety of mind towards the deity.'[42] Ranters, as we have discovered, undermined morality, and the blend of social and religious dissidence represented by the Quakers was deemed an equal danger. It was proceedings against the Quaker leader James Naylor that made Parliament confront the unresolved issue of who should regulate religious morality and how it should be controlled.

The blasphemy cases against Best and Biddle had provoked controversy about the nature of religious tolerance, but also about the power of Parliament to proscribe and enforce any form of religious orthodoxy. John Biddle espoused anti-trinitarian doctrines and had expounded these in a book that had been

---

[40] Leonard Levy, 'Quaker Blasphemy and Toleration', in *Constitutional Opinions: Aspects of the Bill of Rights* (Oxford, 1986), 40–71.

[41] William Warren Sweet, *Religion in Colonial America* (New York, 1943), 148.

[42] Blair Worden, 'Toleration and the English Protectorate', in W. J. Shiels (ed.), *Persecution and Toleration: Studies in Church History*, Vol. 21 (Oxford, 1984), 199–233.

publicly burned in 1647. He was imprisoned for a final time in the reign of Charles II and died in prison. The Biddle case had been an especially important touchstone of religious liberty, since such action reminded many of Laud's hated Star Chamber. This embarrassingly left Parliament with no option but to allow both Best and Biddle to rot in prison. The Naylor case, however, was brought immediately to the attention of the House of Commons, where it is sometimes possible to get a real flavour of the millennialism that persuaded many members that they were living in the last days. Reactions to Naylor's behaviour ranged from the relatively tolerant to a desire to have him executed through the biblically prescribed method of stoning. In the event, Naylor was spared the death penalty through a narrow parliamentary majority. Nonetheless, he was sentenced to be whipped through Westminster, pilloried, branded, bored through the tongue, and to be detained indefinitely.[43]

This pattern was substantially repeated in America. The obstinate actions of Samuel Gorton's followers in New England signalled their intention to convert and 'win over' the population of particular states that sought to exclude them. They were prepared to actively court martyrdom, and were granted it by an exasperated succession of state authorities. William Robinson, Marmaduke Stevenson, William Leddra, and Mary Dyer all eschewed self-preservation and stridently returned from exile to undergo martyrdom in the form of execution. Quakers on both sides of the Atlantic made a range of powerful and articulate enemies who denounced their actions to a wide readership. Much of this criticism appeased many who felt that more moderate forms of religion and the Established Church were mocked and ridiculed by Quaker actions. In numerous pamphlets Quakers were denounced as all-purpose deviants, who indulged in everything from the politically threatening doctrine of extreme justification through to explicit homosexual acts.[44]

In this respect Quakers as a group constitute a useful place to organize our a study of the types of crime and misdemeanour early modern blasphemers were thought to perpetrate upon their society. Dissent from established religion was certainly not a crime in itself, as the Act of Toleration came to grudgingly recognize. Nonetheless, it was still important to consider the reactions of society at large to the interpersonal threat Quakers seemed to pose. Their anti-trinitarianism was to be an enduring theme in prosecutions and indentifications with blasphemy throughout the West. Whilst this doctrine was by no means permissible, it could at least be hidden if such individuals maintained seclusion and an inward-looking, sectarian character. However, this was shattered utterly by the heady cocktail of set-piece activism which the Quakers promoted vigorously,

[43] The Netherlands also proceeded against Quakers. John Marshall notes an edict in Friesland dating from 1662 aimed at Quaker doctrines alongside outbreaks of interpersonal violence against them, notably in Rotterdam in 1675. See John Marshall, *John Locke, Toleration and Early Enlightenment Culture* (Cambridge, 2006), 169.

[44] For a recent discussion of accusations against Quakers see ibid. 304–6 and 454–7.

since their salvation arguably depended upon it. Moreover, their determination
to pull down Antichrist wherever they saw it meant that they constituted a basic
public-order problem for any authority unlucky enough to uncover them in its
midst.

Fox and Nayler's own pronouncements suggest that they were well acquainted
with the language that would destabilize and undermine confidence in the
Established Church, as well as the forms of government that would undertake its
bidding. Indeed, the Quakers themselves spawned a veritable industry of hostile
and venomous pamphlets which educated the population at large about their
dubious practices. Thomas Jenner's fiercely anti-Quaker tract, in 1670, took
exception to James Naylor's equation of himself with Christ in Bristol, and still
worse the worship of his deluded followers.[45] Jenner's tract is peppered with
references which reduce their beliefs to blasphemies of one kind or another.
Their refusal to recognise the Trinity as three distinct persons caused affront,
whilst 'confutation'—the identification of God with the spirit within each
Quaker—was rendered still more blasphemous by the alleged assertion that
Christ himself was imperfect. As far as Jenner was concerned, this allegedly
placed Christ in a fallen state below the average perfected Quaker. Later
commentators would pick upon this last article of faith especially to argue it
was both blasphemous and a species of vile intolerance. Writing in 1716, Henry
Pickworth reiterated that 'it is no less than Blasphemy in them to pretend that
the name Jesus and Christ belongs to the whole body, and every member of
the body, as well as to Christ the head'. Pickworth suggests that it was also
blasphemy to put themselves above God as the judges of others, wielding divine
laws, 'under the penalty of our Exclusion from Church communion, whether or
no we consent to them'.[46]

Timothy Taylor, writing a preface to Jenner's pamphlet, gives an especially
interesting flavour of what it was like for the orthodox to encounter Quakers
in real life. It also conveys a clear picture of how these encounters destabilized
the existing order to upset real people in real situations. Taylor records meeting
an individual Quaker who actively 'scoffed' (a word later to be intrinsic to
blasphemy) at the orthodox conception of Christ. Jenner conveys this as an
uprovoked approach and mentions the Quaker declaring, with real desire to
cause offence, 'I believe thy Christ is above the clouds'.[47] He also records other
instances where blasphemies such as Christ's creation alongside Adam, and
Christ's death with Adam's sin, were both 'uttered in the hearing of myself'.
These blasphemies were capped with the suggestion that Christ's own suffering
was merely intended as an example. From this point Jenner's work slides into

---

[45] Thomas Jenner, *Quakerism Anatomised and Confuted* (London, 1670), 27.
[46] Henry Pickworth, *A Charge of Error, Heresy etc. . . . and offered to be proved against the most noted leaders &c of the People called Quakers* (London, 1716), 170
[47] Jenner, *Quakerism Anatomised and Confuted*, preface.

using blasphemy as a blanket term for all other Quaker beliefs he encountered. These ranged from attacks upon the unregenerate, denying the separate person of the Holy Ghost, and individuals taking the role of Christ upon themselves. These were all doctrinal attacks, but this work gives us an insight into how Quakers made sure they caused upset and forced their works and opinions upon others.

The Quakers were such a threat to the New England Puritans because they attacked both the churches and the civil government. Eventually the will to act against them collapsed under the weight of public revulsion at the enactment of the capital sentences on Gorton's followers. When this was allied to the fear of arousing the opposition of the English government, the way was ostensibly cleared for this group to become rehabilitated, with their persecution ceasing after 1677. Yet the influence the Quakers wielded was sporadic and fleeting, since Foster describes the mass of the population as 'so much damp powder when exposed to the Quaker spark'.[48]

The Quakers' abortive career as scriptural revolutionaries also coincided with the rise of deist and materialist beliefs that would spawn eighteenth-century concerns about blasphemy. The end of the seventeenth century saw a particular interest in the ideas of the Epicureans. The Epicurean position argued for a view of the natural world which would undermine the concept of supernatural intervention. The Greek Philosopher Epicurus argued that all creation was the product of mechanical causes and was ostensibly matter alone. Beyond this, accepting the supernatural explanation exclusively was a mistake. Even if natural explanations could not be found for events or phenomena, Epicureans argued that they could be imagined legitimately without recourse to ideas of divine providence. Immediately it is possible to see how Epicureans were a significant challenge to a world that believed in providence and the operation of laws against blasphemy. Epicureans blasphemed by denying divine intervention, whilst their belief in natural explanations demonstrated how the universe operated without such intervention or punishments. Epicureans also argued that there was no reality beyond the existence of the body. When they considered religion and the nature of God, Epicureans would demonstrate their credentials as the forerunners of the modern atheist position. They denounced providence and focused upon the problem of evil, arguing that the nature of malevolence within creation denied an intelligence at its core. There were no gods and no devils, and thus belief in providence and prayer were delusions. Epicureans therefore argued that the whole notion of religion was based essentially upon a species of fear. Human individuals thus had a duty to rise above this and celebrate every aspect of their material being. Yet importantly, Epicureans stopped short of a fully determinist position and noted that atoms could act or 'swerve' without obvious explanation.

---

[48] Foster, *The Long Argument*, 190, 193, and 199.

Deism was a theological position that deliberately detached itself from the religious authority represented by churches and religious establishments. It was especially fashionable in aristocratic circles, arguably for this reason. Initially such beliefs were conflated with forms of atheism and some sixteenth- and seventeenth-century French commentators almost invariably yoked them together.[49] Certainly there was considerable scope for linking deism with views that could loosely be termed libertine, since the latter seemed an almost inevitable consequence of deism and Epicureanism. If God had retreated from simple intervention in the lives of individuals, then the moral codes Christianity enforced were nothing more than the crude exercise of power without justification. Such approaches fuelled the attitude that came to be described as libertine. This attitude not only spoke out against authority but actively argued for the individual's right to transgress moral codes. Such views were personified in Italy by the renegade former priest Giulio Cesare Lucilio Vanini, and in France by the literary libertine Théophile de Viau. Some see Vanini as a pantheist who was nonetheless the unfortunate victim of a systematic crusade against blasphemy, deism, and Protestantism. This persecution followed something of a local moral panic, which became embroiled in a wider crisis of religious authority extending into the early 1620s.[50] Despite warnings as to his behaviour, he refused to desist from public denunciations of the scriptures and his *De Admirandis Naturae Reginae Deaeque Mortalium Arcanis* was ceremonially burned. Vanini was arrested and executed in 1619 in Toulouse, and would later come to be seen as a freethought martyr in the manner of Giordano Bruno. The pursuit of deists continued for a time, resulting in the imprisonment of the homosexual libertine Théophile de Viau. His 1622 collection of poems, *Le Parnasse satyrique*, led to his pursuit and a capital sentence passed and enacted in effigy in his absence. His imprisonment was followed by banishment, where he was protected by influential patrons until his death in 1626.

This express wish to start with new conceptions of how society and the universe operated was an important driving force behind the acceptance of deism in philosophical circles. In England deism combined two important elements that ensured its importance and popularity with this audience, but would also ensure the inevitability of its clashes with authority. First, it was diverse and at no time resembled a coherent and unified religious doctrine or position. Some deists still believed in eventual punishment at the hands of God, whilst others thought this untenable. Its advocates espoused views which included materialism, a pantheistic creation of nature as religion, forms of simple anti-trinitarianism, and the natural religion which would later give birth to the notion of the universe overseen by Paley's 'watchmaker'. This diversity made deists strong advocates of religious toleration at precisely the time when the Restoration was becoming

---

[49] C. J. Betts, *Early Deism in France* (Kluwer, 1984), 6. See also Alan Charles Kors, *Atheism in France 1650–1729* Vol. 1: *The Orthodox Sources of Disbelief* (Princeton, 1990).
[50] Betts, *Early Deism*, 22.

once again concerned about deviant religious groups. The Anglicanism that came with the Restoration was 'broad if oppressive', and sought moral conformity as an ideal in answer to the philosophical conclusions of some deists and the antinomian misbehaviour of the past.[51] However, the scientific philosophy that also underpinned deism, arguably making its survival possible, was the scientific revolution ushered in by Isaac Newton. This introduced a striving to make the universe ultimately explainable purely on its own terms, and potentially reduced all of creation into inert matter.

Representative of this tendency to reduce all to a material reading of the universe was Charles Blount who, in the 1670s, concluded that reason was the ultimate pilot of all mankind. In a number of texts he laid waste the existing orders of religion, in dismissive fashion. Blount's work saw duplicity in religion's claims to reveal truth that was also supposedly mysterious. His work thus formed, as one commentator has put it, a 'pandemonium in which the unifying theme is the rejection of all revealed religion and Christianity in particular'.[52] The work of deists like Blount denied revelation and the supernatural, and thus constructed and fostered doubt about the doctrine of a future life. This compromised religion's relationship with the state, and its position as a part of society suddenly seemed purely a matter of form and function. As Roger Emerson puts it: 'Religion might be a social cement but it was also the promise of pardon and redemption, a promise unavoidably tied to the mysteries of the incarnation and the Trinity.'[53]

Deists found themselves arguing for a philosophical tolerance, although they equally actively shunned prosecution. They may have argued that they held the moral high ground, but nonetheless they were also prepared to acknowledge the basis of some of established religion's claims. Writers like Blount accepted elements of the Anglican church and its functions as an intrinsic part of citizenship, whilst others saw the unique nature of Anglicanism as implying and imparting a sense of benevolent national identity. Writing in the first years of the eighteenth century, Authony Ashley Cooper, the third Earl of Shaftesbury, made further contributions to deist thought. Explicitly he argued against the individualized conduct choices that had been argued for earlier by Thomas Hobbes and Bernard de Mandeville. Shaftesbury viewed virtue as natural to humans, and held that vice arose from deficiencies in the public expression of relationships. Virtue did not reside with God but was manifest in human interactions. In this Shaftesbury was a prophet of moral behaviour seeking a balance of the appetites and drives within mankind. Such a balance instilled morality and politeness, and would also sidestep the debate about free will and determinism. This was a further removal of responsibility from God that characterized the deist position. Allied to this, Shaftesbury believed in unfettered

---

[51] Roger L Emerson, 'Latitudinarianism and the English Deists', in J. A. Leo Lemay (ed.), *Deism, Masonry, and the Enlightenment* (Newark, 1987), 19–48, at 20–1.
[52] Ibid. 25.   [53] Ibid. 31.

freedom of thought, arguing that excesses would be self-correcting when the balance of virtue was restored within mankind. He was even prepared to accept the utility of humorous attacks upon religion, since they were the ultimate test of its value and durability. Such propositions were steeped in a quest for politeness and the display of virtue in debate which placed religious matters in the hands of laymen.

From a position of sociability and politeness, the whole tenor of deism's implications, and the ideological standpoint that others made of it lower down the social scale, were to be radically transformed by the end of the eighteenth century. It would become at once more popular, more materialist, and more dangerous as it came to focus upon the tyrannical nature of religion operating in tandem with the state. No longer would the language be quite so polite or the arguments be so referenced and rhetoricized. Deism was to become coarser, but it was also to become emphatically more political. Much of this explains the actions of individuals like Peter Annet, who was the first to make an attempt to publish deist and freethinking views in a popular and journalistic manner. Increasingly, skilled artisans were coming into contact with, and debating, the stock of philosophical arguments that had been the intellectual diet of their betters merely a generation earlier.

This might have been a slow process, with little by way of discernible results, had it not been for the massive acceleration provided by the French Revolution. We know a considerable amount about how this event revolutionized political thinking in England. However, it also sharpened the ideological consequences of deism, to make the church–state link a unique subject of criticism. Seventeenth- and eighteenth-century deists fondly imagined the withering away of spurious religious authority, and a similarly gradual evolution of religious tolerance. They scarcely thought that such a drastic change could come upon a familiar society almost overnight.

The French Revolution reached England in a variety of disparate and unexpected ways. In particular, the challenge to the establishment intrinsic within the revolution meant that all sorts of linguistic tools and cultural genres were potentially available for the disaffected to exploit. Pitt's prescriptions against meeting and forms of publishing show evidence that authority in Britain saw revolutionary potential almost wherever it cared to look. Assaults upon English society could thus be expected to come from any quarter at any time, and were liable to use anything from humour to pornography to overturn morals and the social system. This would produce a new society that was eclectic and heterodox: two terms that were to become riddled with foreboding in the first half of the nineteenth century. Both presumed odd and bookish individuals delighting in the pursuit of esoteric knowledge and enlightenment that they would communicate to others. In the manner of Voltaire, there was a presumption that such ideas would not harm elite audiences but could only reach the populace with potentially dangerous consequences. The French Revolution convinced the authorities in Britain that the possibility of individuals being at once political, social, and cultural radicals was coming to pass. The numerous attempts to make blasphemers into enemies of society and the state was a characteristic feature of the use of the Common Law of blasphemous libel in England. This became especially prominent in the early nineteenth century as an explicit attempt to combat the social and political effects of Jacobinism.

Those who held deist views could be swept up within the umbrella of the blasphemy laws, and legal attacks upon anti-trinitarian views were also a central part of the establishment view of Unitarianism.[54] It is possible, to see this paradigm of judgement in action in the treatment of two individuals. First the trial of William Hone in 1817 ended as a farce in which the government appeared to have committed a number of serious miscalculations over the inventive uses to which conceptions of legal propriety, justice, and 'Englishness' might be put. Hone himself held views which, although by no means deist, were some distance from orthodox established Christianity. He was certainly anticlerical, and penned a 'Parody on the Athanasian Creed' which attacked corruption and the systematic abuse of governmental power. Nonetheless, this work also parodied the Trinity in its description of 'Old Bags' being 'One Doctor not three'. Hone also described Derry Down Triangle, a knave and fool, as having 'descended to kiss the Nethermost End of Tally-high-ho; and rose again as a giant refreshed'.[55] For an unprepared audience this must have been shocking, and Hone in all faced trial in response to three ex-officio informations. Yet defence of the work was both possible and unexpectedly successful. Hone drew sympathy when he highlighted the judge's frequent interruptions of his case. He also claimed that he was using a familiar literary form to attack wholly secular abuses and intended no blasphemy. Hone cited other secular and parody creeds, including those intended for excisemen, freeholders, and married women.[56]

The real embodiment of this Jacobin-inspired threat in England was Richard Carlile. Carlile was swept up in the tide of indictments which the government and the Society For the Suppression of Vice enacted during 1819. This year was the highpoint in the nineteenth century of government action against the blasphemous and seditious, with sixty-three prosecutions for seditious and blasphemous libels defaming the king and other officials. This is double the

---

[54] David Nash, *Blasphemy in Modern Britain: 1789–Present* (Aldershot, 1999), 79, 85, and 86.

[55] William Hone, *The Sinecurists Creed, or the Belief as the same can or may be sung or said throughout the Kingdom* (various editions), 5–7. Carlile also imitated this work in a 'Bullet Te Deum' of 1817 which sought to link religious with state power in his final assertion that: 'O Bullet, in thee have we trusted; let the Reformists for ever be confounded.'

[56] See William Hone, *The Third Trial of William Hone on an ex-officio information at Guildhall London December 20, 1817 before Lord Ellenborough and a special Jury, for publishing a parody of the Athanasian Creed* (3rd edn., London, 1818), 26–8. See also F. M. Hackwood, *William Hone: His Life and Times* (London, 1912); Robert Hole, *Pulpits, Politics and Public Order in England 1760–1832* (Cambridge, 1989); Olivia Smith, *The Politics of Language, 1791–1819* (Oxford, 1984).

number of prosecutions for either 1817, 1820, or 1821—all years of similar government concern. In many respects Carlile probably serves as a representative of the enlightenment agitators and their especially close link to cheap and seditious publishing. Carlile effectively acted as the crossroads for many ideological challenges to moral and religious authority. He was a west-country artisan and political radical who had witnessed the carnage at Peterloo and, like others of his generation, had been deeply influenced by that event. But Carlile had also imbibed a great deal from French anticlericalism, demonstrating immense pride in repeating Diderot's desire to see the last king strangled with the entrails of the last priest. But his work also took him into other culturally challenging areas, from providing alternative medicine through to the printing and distribution of England's first widely available family-limitation manual, *Every Woman's Book*. Carlile also advocated free sexual union and an end to the tyrannical nature of marriage, a situation he practised in his own domestic arrangements. All were forms of liberation from spurious authority and tyrannical control exercised by superstitious practices. Carlile went further in linking the opponents of birth-control knowledge with priestcraft.[57] Carlile was dogged and determined, and occasionally allowed himself to emphasize these parts of himself, rather than using more accommodating strategies and tactics that might have served him and his causes somewhat better. His decision to read the whole of Paine's *Age of Reason* during his court appearance as a means of getting it published in the press reports of the case was both ingenious and tedious. Nonetheless, it was precisely this doggedness that inspired a whole generation of shopmen to publish and sell his works, as well as to endure imprisonment alongside him in the same causes he espoused.

What was significant about Richard Carlile and his shopmen was their persistence in seeking to put forward deist, socially radical ideas whilst at the same time upsetting almost all figures in authority. He recruited a tightly knit and dedicated group of 'guerrillas', such as James Watson, Susannah Wright, and William Tunbridge, who were prepared to suffer imprisonment and sporadic confiscation of their literature in the cause of press freedom and liberty of opinion. Carlile's compatriots, to a man and woman, took the epigram 'Publish and Be Damned' to quite extraordinary lengths. Prepared for seizure of their stock, arrest, conviction, and imprisonment, the action against Carlile's form of deism resembled a war on several fronts. Neither these individuals nor the authorities themselves would give any quarter.

Many of the defences offered by these individuals and, to a large extent, the example of their defiance, offered a critique of English justice that was potentially worrying for those in authority. Defendants in the dock frequently argued, as

---

[57] For more detail here see Angus McLaren, 'Contraception and the Working Classes: The Social Ideology of the English Birth Control Movement in its Early Years', *Comparative Studies in Society and History*, 18:2 (Apr. 1976), 236–51, at 243–4

William Campion did, that the Anglican religion was a monopoly enforced purely because it was powerful. James Watson, meanwhile, challenged the court to produce evidence of harm or injury perpetrated by his views.[58] Susannah Wright saw the work of the Vice Society, particularly its use of a law outside statute, as partial and a law of 'whim, caprice, and tyranny'.[59] Others copied Carlile's strategy of reading freethought works or haranguing the courtroom with their defiance. In 1822 William Vamplue read the whole of the pamphlet that he had been arrested for selling, and stated his approval of the sentiments there expressed. William Campion's defence was 'an exceeding long one, consisting of a most profane and appalling attack upon the grand doctrines and precepts of Christianity'. When convicted for selling Carlile's *Republican* on the same day in 1824, James Clark's defence lasted for five hours, in which he 'ridiculed most of the prophecies and miracles contained in the Holy Scriptures, and made the most indecent and shocking reflections upon the characters of the prophets and apostles'.[60]

In the end it is quite difficult for history to decide whether there were winners and losers from this action. Nonetheless, the image of Carlile almost constantly in prison, occasionally sharing a cell with both his wife and his sister, looks like defeat. Authority, on the other hand, did not necessarily look particularly victorious when individuals like Shelley could attack its heavy-handed action. Those who spoke out against tyranny had expressed important arguments about whether the liberties of England seemed to be in the safest of hands. In the end, the people were not wholly pulled away from their religious 'delusions' by the work of Carlile and his shopmen. But this work did establish a network of radical publishing which was to be important for later culturally and politically radical movements, like Chartism and Owenism. It was the latter of these, Owenism, which was to be crucially important in the future, and would further the spread of freethinking and atheist ideas.

Carlile's freethought career operated with a conflict model foremost in his mind, and that was certainly the way his shopmen also viewed the situation. Christianity and its pretensions to power were to be challenged at every turn. The rationalist ideas of Robert Owen, the man who wanted to create a science of society, emphatically rejected the conflict model of politics and the relationship between individuals and authority. When Owen spread his radical rationalist message it was with a network of social missionaries, rather than through a campaign of systematic and confrontational anticlerical publishing. Nonetheless,

---

[58] R. Carlile, *The Trials with the Defences at Large of Mrs. Jane Carlile, Mary Ann Carlile, William Holmes (etc.)* (London, 1825), Tunbridge Report, pp. 15–28.

[59] Ibid., Wright Report, pp. 15, 17, and 56.

[60] Proceedings of the Old Bailey Ref: t18220220–125 William Vamplue, Breaking the Peace: libel 20 February 1822. Ref: t18240603–247, William Campion, offences against the king: religious offences, 3 June 1824. Ref: t 18240603–252 James Clark, offences against the king: religious offences, 3 June 1824.

enthusiasm and the anticlericalism of over-excited youth could also play its part. It was a combination of these that led the young and impressionable George Jacob Holyoake to declare in a lecture that the almighty had been doing his job so badly he 'ought to be placed on half pay'. For this Holyoake served a six-month prison sentence for blasphemy, during which his wife found herself and her family in considerable distress.

This particular experience was to be a formative one in shaping mid- and late nineteenth-century freethought and freethinkers. As a result of it Holyoake's mind turned to constructing and elaborating a series of defensive measures. He founded an Anti-Persecution Union which was aimed at assisting freethinkers and deists (and even the religious) who found themselves the victims of the tyran-nical church–state establishment in both Britain and further afield. Holyoake also created the secular movement in Britain, which was to be the umbrella organization of all those who challenged Christianity to tolerate freethinkers. No more could freethinking and secularist views be associated with the trou-blemaking of a Richard Carlile or the apparent naivety of the early Owenite programme. This classic mid-Victorian position was in place long enough to impress J. S. Mill, who declared blasphemy prosecutions to be an anachronism. But Mill also upheld the libertarian ideals for which secularists had been arguing. Mill viewed this as the complete and final stage of a society dragging itself from ignorance and barbarism to knowledge and enlightenment.

However, the atmosphere changed in Britain when a new generation that had not experienced the repression of the 1840s and 1850s began to assert itself in the secular movement. Amongst these was Charles Bradlaugh, a man who could not comprehend the social harmony-style model Robert Owen had offered through his versions of rationalism. Bradlaugh took a more individualistic slant, and was joined by many others who saw Christianity as a form of collective dependency. Bradlaugh, and others who might be described as liberal individualists, believed in producing a society which would be enabling for the individuals within it. Forms of privilege and paternalism of all kinds (whether from the political Left or the Right) were enemies to individual forms of liberty. Bradlaugh's campaign for the publication of the Knowlton pamphlet (a tract which carried birth-control information) in 1878 was very clearly an attempt to advance the rights of individuals to control their own fertility. Such issues also provoked a storm in Australia, where Knowlton's works were held to advocate the overthrow of decent society. New South Wales's leading advocate of Malthusian knowledge, Thomas Walker, was prosecuted for his lecture which would invariably lead youth astray and outrage public decency.[61]

When Bradlaugh turned his attention to the laws against blasphemy, he saw these as a further check upon the liberty of the individual. Not only were they denied the right to express their perfectly proper views about religion, its place,

---

[61] Peter Coleman, *Obscenity, Blasphemy, Sedition* (Brisbane, 1966), 69–71.

and its power structures, but this same religion was protected on a privilege basis by the law of the land. Bradlaugh actively wanted to encourage people to break such laws and bring them down. Thus, one of his pamphlets argued the necessity of heresy and, by implication, blasphemy. In this work Bradlaugh suggested that the world was starting to march to a materialist tune, since anthropologists, geologists, ethnographers, astronomers, and even clergyman were all actively heretical. Bradlaugh also identified Christianity with anachronism and decay, suggesting that it fostered and encouraged a retarded approach to the modern world. Thus, all methods of attacking this religion and its hold over the people were justified.[62]

Bradlaugh devoutly wished for a blasphemy trial that would highlight this obvious anachronism, yet he always managed to avoid blasphemy prosecutions aimed at him personally. Others were, however, prepared to take up the gauntlet he had thrown down. The most important amongst these was George William Foote, an otherwise cultured and urbane individual who chose to neglect penning his Shakespearean criticism in favour of acquainting himself with, and reworking, a rich vein of French anticlericalism. It is certain that Foote actively courted prosecution. His newspaper, the *Freethinker*, contained serious journalism but nonetheless specialized in irreverent and scurrilous portrayals of biblical subjects. Sometimes these attacked biblical stories and their failure to illuminate moral truths, whilst at other times he lampooned some biblical passages and the images they conjured up. Foote would sometimes display a contempt for the primitive nature of Christianity's origins, distinguishing between the modern conception of an almighty God and the vengeful barbarism of the Hebrew deity.[63] Sections of continental-style anticlericalism were plundered for their shock value, and it was precisely this element which led to the Home Office taking such a significant interest in George William Foote and his works. Foote was very clear that he drew his ideological mandate from past struggles, declaring:

I tell you that you could not suppress the *Freethinker* if you tried. The martyr spirit of Freethought is not dead, and the men who suffered imprisonment for liberty of speech a generation ago have not left degenerate successors. Should the necessity arise, there are Freethinkers who will not shrink from the same sacrifice for the same cause.[64]

The mood Foote and his fellow defendants, Ramsey and Kemp, tried to create was sporadically infectious, successfully focusing upon the anachronism the law and its punishment represented. Foote also put into action the logic of Bradlaugh's arguments about bringing down the blasphemy law. Through a landmark prosecution, conviction, and imprisonment England would be shown

---

[62] C. Bradlaugh, *Heresy, its utility and Morality: A Plea and a Justification* (London, 1870).
[63] George William Foote, *Defence of Free Speech: Being a three hours Address to the Jury in the court of Queen's Bench Before Lord Coleridge on April 24th*, 1883 (London, 1932 ed.), 37.
[64] Foote, *Prisoner for Blasphemy*, 23.

" *And it came to pass after these things, that God did tempt Abraham* . . . *And he said, Take now thy son, thine only son Isaac, whom thou lovest, and get thee into the land of Moriah; and offer him there for a burnt offering.* . . . ."—Genesis xxii., 1, 2.

Fig. 10a. G. W. Foote borrows from French anticlericalism. The *Freethinker* (above) and Leo Taxil's 'version' of the sacrifice of Isaac (facing page).

Fig. 10b. Leo Taxil's 'version'

that laws against blasphemy were unreasonable and anti-modern. He declared: 'as the *Freethinker* was intended to be a fighting organ, the savage hostility of the enemy is its best praise. We mean to incur their hatred more and more.'[65] Foote effectively stage-managed all aspects of the case which was eventually brought against him. Accounts of his trial and incarceration appeared in his own and other freethought newspapers, whilst different aspects of the case also appeared in pamphlet form. All these were intended to demonstrate the futility and partisan nature of the law. If England did not live in an age of reason, then certainly most commentators contended it should live in an age of tolerance.

But it was not simply England that was trying to live in an age of reason, as the 1870s and 1880s witnessed a minor revival of similar blasphemous activity in Australia and America. The incidents in Australia were a direct offshoot of the work of secular organizations in England. One of the vice-presidents of Charles Bradlaugh's National Secular Society, the former Methodist minister Joseph Symes, continued his work for freethought upon his emigration to Australia in 1884. Symes found a warm welcome in the Australian freethought movement, and continued his work in Melbourne through his weekly newspaper the *Liberator*. Symes adopted the confrontational and invasive style of George William Foote, and the paper regularly promised (or alternatively threatened) significant and offensive levels of blasphemous content. Symes borrowed some of Foote's language and some of his motifs, referring waspishly to clergymen as 'skypilots'. Interestingly, Symes also tailored his message to an Australian audience of radicals, with semi-republican attacks upon the British monarchy and upon imperial ideals.

The Australian authorities quickly noticed the connection with British freethought agitation when it confiscated and destroyed Symes's own stock of the *Freethinker*. This, however, did not bring matters to an end, since Symes took his blasphemy onto the lecture platform. At a number of meetings he lectured in detail against the Christian religion and, with an eye clearly on prosecution, parodied and lampooned religious services. At his trial before the Criminal Court in October 1884, Symes tried to argue that his own Secular Association was a religious denomination and thus entitled to equal protection under the law. Whilst Symes had adopted the language of religious toleration, he also drew upon the libertarian agenda that the freethinkers in England had pioneered. When the authorities tried to proceed against him using an act requiring publishers to submit sureties for their own good behaviour, Symes defied them. In doing so he echoed the struggles of an earlier generation of anti-censorship and knowledge-taxation campaigners in Britain. Although convicted, Symes eventually received only a derisory fine which scarcely vindicated the actions of the authorities in this instance. Just as in England, Australian

---

[65] Foote, *Prisoner for Blasphemy*, 21.

Fig. 11. Portrait of George William Foote.

police authorities thereafter held back from prosecuting Symes who, like Foote, continued to defy authority by maintaining his own publishing programme. A number of the leading Christian organizations throughout Australia complained about this apparently partial treatment, but to no avail. Throughout this period Symes goaded his opponents, even introducing one of them into his mock sermons and lessons. As with Foote, these actions introduced levity into a realm of knowledge and experience that had otherwise been accepted as serious and beyond question.[66]

America arguably had earlier spawned its own answer to the likes of Carlile and G. W. Foote, in the guise of the freethinking lecturer Abner Kneeland, who had once been (like Symes) a clergyman. Kneeland displayed attachment to the ideas of both Thomas Paine and Robert Owen, and through his journalism supported the argument for the liberation of women promoted by the campaigner Frances

---

[66] See Coleman, *Obscenity, Blasphemy, Sedition*, 92.

Wright.[67] He was also a friend of Charles Knowlton, whose family-limitation pamphlets were already causing a stir in New England, and was a noted political radical. Kneeland's tirades against the privileged, the clergy, and judges made him appear a descendent of Jacobinism. Espousing some of the same criticisms offered by all these influences, Kneeland lectured at a phenomenal rate. His state-to-state lecture tour was expressly designed to show the various discrepancies between local and federal law. The combination of his lectures and the growing popularity of his journalism awoke the fear that materialism, family limitation, and infidelity (atheism) would be proselytized through the power of the mass media.[68] It is possible to conclude that cases brought against Kneeland were formative experiences in the construction of wider state neutrality.

Like Foote and Carlile, Kneeland found that it was his publications that were most feared, and ultimately most vulnerable to prosecution. Thus, his *Investigator* was prosecuted in Boston, Massachusetts, in 1833 on three counts under the state's Blasphemy Act. Kneeland's blasphemy had involved an article criticizing the Virgin Mary and denying what he termed 'the God of the Universalists', seeing their beliefs as 'nothing more than a chimera of their own imagination'. After also denying the power of miracles, Kneeland avowed himself to be a materialist, with death constituting 'an eternal extinction of life'. Kneeland's defence counsel was the Democrat former state attorney-general Andrew Dunlap, who tried to make the issue appear one of persecution, and ultimately of free speech. Dunlap claimed that the article concerning the Virgin Mary was not denying or cursing the sacred doctrines of Christianity, but that criticism should merely be inferred from the tone of the article. This was a closet argument for the defence of free speech. Dunlap declared the piece to be no more than a statement of the doctrine, and that Kneeland 'had a right, I mean a strict legal right, to assail that doctrine, by the power of argument, and the force of satire'. He suggested that if Kneeland was guilty he was worthy of pity rather than punishment. Finally, pleading for compassion, Dunlap asked whether Jesus would send a 'monomaniac, grey-headed atheist, of some three score years' to jail for blasphemy. This suggests that many saw Kneeland as being prosecuted for his opinions, not for the precise nature and damage done by his pronouncements.[69] Judge Wilde further argued, in

---

[67] See *Boston Investigator*, 2 Apr. 1831 and others.
[68] Lori D. Ginzberg, '"The Hearts of your readers will shudder": Fanny Wright, Infidelity and American Freethought. *American Quarterly*, 46:2 (June 1994), 195–226. See also Helen Horowitz, *Rereading Sex: Battles over Sexual Knowledge and Suppression in Nineteenth Century America* (New York, 2003), ch. 4.
[69] Andrew Dunlap, *A Speech delivered before the Municipal Court of the City of Boston in defence of Abner Kneeland on an Indictment for Blasphemy January Term 1834* (Boston, 1834), 7, 8, and 25. Abner Kneeland, *A Review of the Trial, Conviction, And Final imprisonment in the Common Jail of the County of Suffolk of Abner Kneeland for the alleged crime of blasphemy* (Boston, 1838), 83. See also Robert E. Burkholder, 'Emerson, Kneeland, and the Divinity School Address', *American Literature*, 58:1 (Mar. 1986), 1–14.

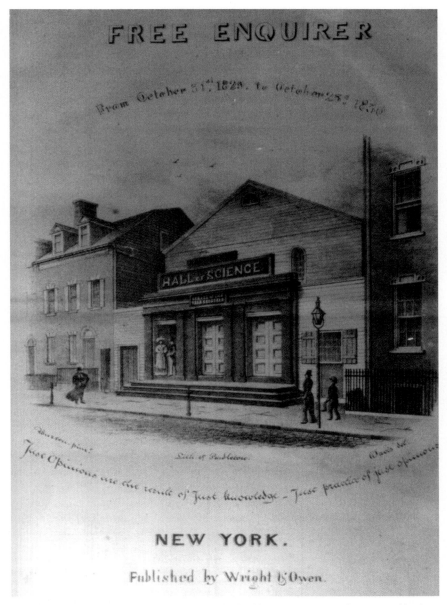

Fig. 12. Abner Kneeland's headquarters. The building was rumoured to conceal beds in which immoral family-limitation practices were indulged!

the third case against Kneeland, that his approach and his manner were of
supreme importance and influenced the protection the constitution would
offer him:

> When he engages in the discussion of any subject in the honest pursuit of truth, and
> endeavours to propagate any notions and opinions which he sincerely entertains, he is
> covered by the aegis of the constitution; but when he wantonly or maliciously assails the
> rights and privileges of others, or disturbs the public peace, he is the proper subject of
> punishment.[70]

Thus, blasphemers like Kneeland were considered to be in the business of
undermining polite society and its structures, a conclusion made more credible
in Kneeland's case because of his association with Fanny Wright and family
limitation. As Foote was to do later, Abner Kneeland used the fact of his
imprisonment as a means to generate further publicity and to discredit the
concept of legal trials for blasphemy.[71] His journey to the county jail turned
into a popular procession, and his supporters ensured that his confinement
was comfortable, with extra furnishings and additional food supplied to him
on a daily basis. His conviction had provoked harsh comment from journalists
throughout Massachusetts, and some, in an exaggerated manner, likened the
treatment of Kneeland to the harsh execution of the 1659 Quakers.[72]

Enthusiasts for forms of social and socialist revolution replaced those who
came out of a tradition of anticlericalism, as the nineteenth century turned into
the twentieth. In Europe many socialists and anarchists had been involved in
movements expressing protest against organized religion. In Germany, Johann
Most was instrumental in organizing a boycott of the Christian churches during
the 1870s. However, a later generation chose a different target when it rounded
upon religion's doctrines. The various cases against J. W. Gott, T. W. Stewart,
and Ernest Pack in England, as well as Mockus in America and the magazine
L'Asino in Australia, were all representative of a fear of foreign influences on
western culture. The legitimate anticlericalism of one country was in danger
of becoming the cultural invasion of nations that had foolishly accepted the
dangerous apostate as a legitimate and peaceable immigrant. Where this was
not the case, the simple fear of foreign literature often remained. This could be
seen as simultaneously imperilling both religion and the morals of the mother

---

[70] *Commonwealth* v. *Kneeland*, 37 Mass. 206–246 (1838) 242.

[71] See *A Review of the Trial, Conviction, and Final Imprisonment of Abner Kneeland, for the Alleged
Crime of Blasphemy, By himself* (Boston, 1838). Kneeland addressed his letters from Boston Gaol as
coming from 'Hades—alias Hell'.

[72] Roderick S. French, 'Liberation from Man and God in Boston: Abner Kneeland's Free-
thought Campaign, 1830–1839', *American Quarterly*, 32:2 (Summer 1980), 202–21. Henry Steele
Commager, 'The Blasphemy of Abner Kneeland', *New England Quarterly*, 8:1 (Mar. 1935), 29–41,
at 39. The central documents of the trial have been usefully collected together in Leonard Levy,
*Blasphemy in Massachusetts: Freedom of Conscience and the Abner Kneeland Case, a Documentary
Record* (New York, 1973).

country. The early 1890s witnessed a panic in Australia centring on the arrival of unsuitable French literature. Although in America it appears that it was customary for liberals to appeal against the tyranny of religious censorship, the situation in Australia was rather different. On occasions attempts to placate religious minorities within Australia would be attacked and denounced by other, similar groups, who saw themselves as defending emerging Australian nationhood from 'foreign' influences. Sometimes such views could strike peculiar alliances with others. This was evident in the attempts to prevent the Australian government's censorship of the Italian anticlerical newspaper *L'Asino* in 1911. Both the newspaper *International Socialist* and Protestant Orange organizations in Melbourne saw the hand of Catholic influence in the ban, demanding it be rescinded. Ultimately, all clerical authorities found themselves unable to deny that the paper was blasphemous. Occasionally arguments against foreign influences caught the socially conservative in the web of blasphemous speech. A potent example of this is a case in 1932 which mixed anti-Semitism with anti-capitalism. A representative of the New South Wales Rationalist Association, Ann Lemon, was arrested and fined for declaiming in a public park that '. . . This God of you Christians is a Jewish God, not an Aussie God, not a fair dinkum Aussie God, just a Jewish god with his money bags around his neck'.[73]

In England, John Gott, Thomas Stewart, and Ernest Pack were all caught up in the challenges to social and political attitudes that characterized the *fin de siècle*. For these socialist libertarians interest in the issues around family limitation, and access to information about it, were constrained by the power of vested religious interests. Family limitation also appeared to address a variety of social and political problems. Not only would the redistribution of resources within society be better achieved through this measure, but it would also significantly emancipate women. This stance brought Gott, Stewart, and Pack onto the fringes of the socialist movement with the establishment of the Freethought Socialist League, which had its headquarters in Bradford.[74] This organization planned an ideological assault on both Christianity and capitalism that the three considered to be mutually supportive, in a manner reminiscent of the early modern church-and-state relationship. The freethought tinge to their socialism was also an obvious criticism of religion's ideological place within the socialist movement. Quite regularly members of the league would express sentiments which claimed that Christianity had emasculated the labour movement. Pack suggested that the league's pamphlets had only been sold at atheist and socialist meetings with one purpose: 'I have always made it perfectly clear when offering it for sale that it was an Anti-Christian pamphlet. My usual cry being that it was the new plan for getting rid of the Black Army, the Sky Pilots, the Devil Dodgers, the

[73] Coleman, *Obscenity, Blasphemy, Sedition*, 4, 94–6, and 100.
[74] See Ernest Pack, *The Parson's Doom* (Bradford, Freethought Socialist League, n.d), 13.

Fig. 13. J. W. Gott.

Fakers and the Humbugs—the parsons.'[75] Such an attitude led Gott, Stewart, and Pack to court high-profile American anarchists such as Melfew Seklew and Moses Harman as allies.[76] When Gott began selling his caustic and satirical 'Rib Ticklers' pamphlet at meetings discussing family limitation, presided over by Stewart, the die was cast. Local authorities in Leeds and Wolverhampton had no option but to prosecute.[77]

The *fin de siècle* which had inspired political activity also influenced the gradual appearance of the modernist style of literature which brought new agendas and new forms of subject-matter to the fore. From the 1880s onwards a number of authors speculated on and explored the nature of the universe and the idea of

[75] *The Trial and Imprisonment of J. W. Gott for Blasphemy* (Bradford, Freethought Socialist League, 1912), 41.

[76] Moses Harman had been imprisoned for his anti-religious views in America. Seklew described himself as 'an iconoclast, atheistic, anarchistic, hedonistic individualist'. Ibid. 153.

[77] See HO 45 10665/216120: Stewart and Gott. For Leeds see 216120/6 Report from the Leeds Chief Constable on the conviction of these Men dated 10/12/11 and 216120/18. Shorthand notes of the trial, Town Hall, Leeds, Tuesday 5th December 1911. For Wolverhampton see 216120/51, Newspaper report of Stewart's conviction at the Stafford Assizes from *The Times* 19 Nov. 1913.

God. Authors like Hardy, Lawrence, Zola, and Whitman produced a tarnished and ambivalent view of the world. They speculated about the nature of God, but did not go as far as to ridicule or lampoon his existence. August Strindberg and Henrik Ibsen would go further, to outline a hostile universe which regularly trapped and punished mankind. Strindberg's brush with the Swedish law of blasphemy was wholly unexpected. He had espoused socialism and in his early thought shown support for feminist ideals. His collection of stories, *Getting Married*, was a work which undermined the sanctity of bourgeois relationships, with a pessimism which would become identified with other modernist works. At least one biographer has seen a deliberately iconoclastic hand at work during these years, describing Strindberg as 'having taken on the function of a destroyer'.[78] Strindberg's book had railed against marriage and had been scathing about the demands women would potentially place upon this institution. When it was published in 1884, Strindberg had braced himself for the outrage of feminists and others who considered the work's discussion of sexuality and venereal disease unacceptable. He was thus surprised when his publisher was approached by the Swedish minister of justice, intent on confiscating the work for its blasphemous content. The first story in the volume, 'The Reward of Virtue', described the Eucharist and its theology as 'an impudent deception', in which the faithful are persuaded that it constitutes the body and blood of 'Jesus the rabble rouser'. Strindberg also speculated idly upon the supposed commercial value of the Sacrament.

These sentiments supposedly scandalized the queen of Sweden and a number of feminist organizations into pressing for action against Strindberg. The Justice Ministry intended to prosecute for an offence of 'blasphemy against God or mockery of God's word'. Strindberg then vacillated over his next actions, but eventually undertook to appear in court himself to answer such charges. His arrival at Stockholm station was greeted by large crowds, and a significant body of opinion was in favour of Strindberg's right to free speech. More conservative views suggested that he had been paid to reappear in Stockholm as a means of promoting the book. The jury eventually acquitted Strindberg, and he received many celebratory messages, the most poignant of which came from the Swedish community in America's most religiously tolerant state, Rhode Island. But Strindberg's victory was eventually to be marred by attempts to limit the book's subsequent distribution. Printers for this controversial work were hard to find, and Strindberg was placed under considerable pressure to delete sections of the story in question, or omit it altogether. Eventually an unabridged version appeared, although the work remained a commercial disappointment.[79]

---

[78] Elizabeth Sprigge, *The Strange Life of August Strindberg* (London, 1949), 97.
[79] Michael Meyer, *Strindberg* (Oxford, 1987), 130–42 and G. A. Campbell, *Strindberg* (London, 1933).

Other writers who went beyond decorum would inevitably find themselves echoing anticlerical styles. Oskar Panizza's depiction of clerical hypocrisy, and God's gift of syphilis to unregenerate man, in *Das Liebeskonzil* recalled the more vulgar forms of French anticlericalism. The success of some of these writers clearly indicated that the nature of God was not simply available for discussion, but was now a legitimate form of artistic inspiration. Panizza himself reacted violently against official censure of his works, to produce strident arguments in favour of the sanctity of the artistic vision. Panizza equated his ostracism from mainstream German culture with a species of insanity, which also ironically provided a type of freedom for the artist. Arguing that poets had a 'divine right' to express their insights into the human condition, Panizza found a new reason for considering the blasphemer to be insane.[80]

However, popular support for the artist's stance had come to be an important phenomenon, and this could occasionally eclipse the work itself, as Strindberg discovered with *Getting Married*. Nonetheless, what Strindberg had also discovered, as others would later, was that being a writer of blasphemy conveyed a degree of celebrity status that would guarantee a certain level of interest in the artist's subsequent progress.

Whilst the work of Christianity's refuseniks like Foote, Symes, Kneeland, and the socialist radicals had a clear intention of offending sensibilities, charting the attitudes of novelists and other artists was manifestly less straightforward. Depictions of God, of Christ, and of the sacred were still to be looked upon as they always had been. But issues of reverence and awe had altered somewhat. The chance to individualize a relationship with God (one's own God) had become increasingly acceptable since the Reformation. With an emphasis upon a Christianity of the word and the text, the idea of God was more readily individualized. A medieval and a coercive early modern age had argued that control ensured conformity, but an individualized Christianity argued for degrees of freedom within limits. This would sometimes resurface in a collision between artistic expression and the providential. Australia witnessed an example of this in 1945, when Lawson Glossop's novel *We Were the Rats*, based upon the exploits of Australian soldiers in Tobruk, provoked a prosecution for obscenity and blasphemy. Glossop's intention was to re-create the lifestyle and attitudes of soldiers under fire in a battle that had become an icon of Australian bravery and masculinity, but had not counted on the public's desire to see such experiences remain untarnished.[81] This 'denial' of the soldier's potential for providential thought also provoked a case in New Zealand, when Siegfried Sassoon's poem 'Stand To: Good Friday Morning' was prosecuted when it was reprinted in the 1920s by the *Maoriland Worker*. This particular poem spoke of the soldier's

[80] Gary Stark, 'Trials and Tribulations: Authors' Responses to Censorship in Imperial Germany, 1885–1914', *German Studies Review*, 12:3 (Oct. 1989), 447–68, at 451.
[81] Coleman, *Obscenity, Blasphemy, Sedition*, 47–52.

desire for safety and deliverance in his promise to believe in the Eucharist if his life should be spared:

> O Jesus, send me a wound to-day,
> And I'll believe in Your bread and wine,
> And get my bloody old sins washed white!

However, a greater individualization of the idea of God meant that such orthodoxy began to seem something of an anachronism. Steps were taken to soften such orthodoxy from 1960 onwards, with the reforms initiated in Catholicism by Vatican II and in Anglicanism with the appearance in 1963 of the groundbreaking theological work by J. A. T. Robinson, bishop of Woolwich, *Honest to God.* The freedom to formulate ideas about the universe meant that the limits of legitimate discussion of the religious were not always clear. This led artists to argue regularly that such limits needed investigation and further exploration. Even the desire to explore meant that artists would thus regularly find themselves misunderstood.

What this amounted to was a significant difference around how the sacred was to be (and in some arguments, should be) viewed. The sacred had now become the object of a 'gaze'. This involved individuals bringing their own cultural expectations and prejudices to the exploration of a religious subject. In the past devoutly religious viewers had brought a pious gaze to such subjects. Some of the individuals we investigated in the medieval period could manage only a confused gaze, or a penitent one, in front of their inquisitors if they had blasphemed whilst not in their right mind. In the world of the late twentieth century it was now possible that individuals not brought up with a Christian legacy would want to discover its significance. Such individuals came to the religious with a 'questioning' gaze which seemed far more dangerous than a secular, 'indifferent' one.

Empowered by centuries of Christian iconography, individuals could pick their way through a myriad of images in search of those which were most in tune with the ideals of the beholder. The 'gaze' was different for artists, however, since it provided inspiration and problems to be 'worked through' by artistic endeavour. The nature of God became a question tackled in a creative way that had previously been consigned to arcane works and volumes with a deliberately restricted audience. Artists believed they had an intrinsic duty, as those who expand the horizons of perception and explore society's taboos. Moreover, with the limitation being only the creative instinct of the artist, what should be, or should not be, said about God?

Such an open-ended questioning of the religious and its meaning created something of a religious backlash with the arrival of newer forms of militant fundamentalism. As the religiously uncommitted wanted to explore, the religiously committed wanted belief to be restated and reaffirmed. This fundamentalism argued for a complete focus upon the sacred and wished for its reappearance in public life. Fundamentalist versions of Christianity denied multiple readings or nuances, instead introducing new, assertive versions of orthodoxy. These were frequently at odds with some permissive and so called 'godless' laws and statutes.

Some artists or filmmakers had their motives profoundly examined through this process, and some were more readily dismissed than others. Jens Jurgen Thorsen's credentials as a Situationist artist were scarcely able to save him from the opprobrium of governments and from successful attempts to prevent the filming of his script, 'The Sex Life of Christ'. Like Thorsen, Nigel Wingrove's *Visions of Ecstasy* was readily dismissed as opportunistic religious pornography rather than anything more meaningful.[82] Andres Serrano, an artist who redefines the word visceral, produced a sculpture that strongly emphasized these essential elements of ambiguity. Serrano's *Piss Christ* was an emblem of the unacceptable. It was certainly possible to argue, as some critics did, that his very direct association of the Christ figure with human ordure was blasphemous; counter-arguments nonetheless existed. Many suggest that Serrano wanted to emphasize, or represent, the dangerous ubiquity and multiplying misuse of Christian symbols. This suggested that the 'gaze' and consumption of the sacred were means of cheapening its impact. If so, this was a valid artistic statement to make, even if its execution appeared cynical and exploitative. Subsequent photographic artists like Bettina Reims also expanded upon and redefined the idea of Christs' passion. Her *INRI* was the exploration of the passion as an almost sexual event. Both the Virgin Mary and Mary Magdalene were pictured nude in this work, alongside strong images of blood and sacrifice. It was not seized or prosecuted, but must rank alongside the works of individuals like Serrano as an exploration of the sacred for a modern world. Sexuality and religious ecstasy have never been far apart, and in Reims's work the connexion was considered more than merely titillating, since extracts from religious devotional texts were juxtaposed with the pictures. Similarly, the directors of the Canadian play *Les Fees ont soif*, who patently offended Catholic sensibilities, had as much to say about an exploitative patriarchal society as they did about the sacred. Diamanda Galás's performance of her own *Plague Mass*, which contained nudity and violent screaming, was also seriously intended to be an indictment of the Catholic church's teaching on the AIDs epidemic.[83]

In more recent years Martin Scorsese's *The Last Temptation of Christ* and Mel Gibson's *Passion of the Christ* were less easily dismissed, even by devout believers. Both film-makers claimed legitimate motives and inspiration in their desire to film the sacred. Whilst acceptable to some, Scorsese's film was dismissed as a blasphemous humanizing of Christ. Gibson's film, with its uncompromising concentration upon the suffering of Christ, was familiar territory to

---

[82] Wingrove's *Visions of Ecstasy* is discussed in Ch. 7.   [83] *Bizzarre* (July 1998), 59.

Catholics, yet its failure to describe Christ's mission upset fundamentalist Protestant groups.[84] Perhaps the individual most caught between the 'pious' gaze and the 'questioning' gaze was James Kirkup, the poet involved in the *Gay News* case of 1978. Kirkup had been awestruck and terrified by the suffering inflicted upon Christ at the crucifixion. Bringing artistic licence to bear, he constructed a poem which spoke to a homosexual audience, offering it the chance of salvation. It described both Christ as an active homosexual and the salvation available to the Roman centurion through his sexual intercourse with Christ's broken body. Such a poem supposedly took Christ's message to a new audience, and was never intended to offend the traditionalists. This emphasized just how individualized responses to religion had become. If the gay community wanted their own Christ, then the principles of religious tolerance suggested that there was no reason why this should not be permitted.

For writers like Salman Rushdie the problem was complicated still further by uncomfortable and unavoidable events of human history. Rushdie himself carried the legacy of the British Empire, of eventual decolonization, and the subsequent history of the post-colonial Indian subcontinent. Having an Islamic heritage combined with a western liberal upbringing, he would also have understood the Orientalist debate from both sides. With such a hybrid range of influences, it is no wonder that some have almost removed motive from Rushdie's actions, identifying his position as riddled with doubt. These commentators suggest that Rushdie is a postmodern individual, unable to do more than distrust monolithic systems and to reflect the contradictions of all the influences that impressed themselves upon him unbidden.[85]

In the medieval and early modern periods blasphemers were considered victims of circumstance, delusion, or drink. These societies paid little attention to the alleged motivation of the blasphemer, because such societies could scarcely conceive of precisely what this might entail. For many species of authority blasphemy was an unpleasant and occasionally dangerous habit that could provoke breaches of the peace. The modern world regards blasphemers as (occasionally wayward) committed seekers after a spiritual or artistic truth. Their right to pursue this truth has generally been enshrined in human-rights legislation and laws to protect freedom of speech. However, their pursuit of this truth has not been universally accepted, nor has their ability to assault the beliefs of others been acknowledged everywhere as an absolute right. Thus, there stands a shaky truce between contemporary blasphemers and their victims. The individual now possesses an enhanced capacity to be more and more offended by what he or she encounters. We might ask where the law and culture place

---

[84] The Scorsese film is discussed more fully in Ch. 7.

[85] M. M. Slaughter, 'The Salman Rushdie Affair: Apostasy, Honor, and Freedom of Speech', *Virginia Law Review*, 79:1 (Feb. 1993), 153–204, at 202.

God when we have emphatically arrived at our regime of rights and free-doms? Societies in the West have been alarmingly confused about answering this question. Whilst ignoring it may seem a short-term panacea, the question will not go away, and relying upon social developments and 'understand-ing' to replace positivist ideals or active hope looks less tenable as each year passes.

5

Controlling the Profane

This chapter attempts to investigate how societies have striven to cope with and control the blasphemer. It investigates the laws and edicts as well as the punishments which western societies have considered appropriate to and suitable for this crime. The Bible gave western societies an important example which legislators and theologians relied upon in the creation of a modern offence of blasphemy. The people of Israel had been chosen by their God, who aimed and directed the lives of his people, and their obedience and worship was expected accordingly. To this community, denying God, or more importantly even profaning him and his name, appeared to be a form of behaviour that lacked meaningful logic. Such an individual, in dishonouring God dishonoured the community.

The worship of false idols was not originally considered to be the offence of blasphemy, since it appeared to be grounded in the nation's identity and relationship with its deity. This instilled a deeper reverence for the nature and the name of God, so that to even speak his name was an especial type of offence. Interestingly, its threat to the stability of the whole community made this a public offence, tried and punished amid ceremony and ritual tearing of garments to mark the retelling of the blasphemy in court. The offence of blasphemy was explicitly that the name of God had been taken in vain. Individuals convicted of this offence were to be summarily executed through the biblically prescribed punishment of stoning.

Such a view made the community take part in restoring honour to their deity, and was a defence of the sacred rather than a defence of specific beliefs. Leonard Levy has highlighted the distinction between this view and the later view in the West, that blasphemy was a disturbance of the civil peace and security. He goes as far as to say that the Judaic approach constitutes a road not taken in the West. Certainly the suggestion is intriguing when considered alongside the West's later developed conception of a social and cultural offence. The Judaic conception of blasphemy identified blasphemers as being beyond the community of which they had previously been offered privileged membership. This dishonour would lead to God breaking his bond with his people unless dissident voices were silenced. If Levy is right, then the West supposedly lay much less emphasis upon the power of God to intervene, instead seeing remedies and punishments as being almost wholly within the realm of men.

However, much of our evidence suggests that the divide Levy argues for is, to a great extent, illusory. The resilience of popular belief in God's capacity to intervene is a particular feature of blasphemy in the West. We noted in Chapter 1 a number of instances in early modern Europe where the audience for blasphemy and the community at large still believed the almighty was capable of intervening in human affairs to punish those present. Certainly, in the seventeenth century some cases involving soldiers, sailors, and gamblers suggest that the providential intervention of God was considered an omnipresent possibility. This impression is further confirmed by the vast didactic literature which promised the vengeance of the almighty upon those who blasphemed his name. Even as late as the mid-nineteenth century, the English translator of the French 'Association of Prayers against Blasphemy's' order of service saw England's descent into the 'hungry forties' as 'a chastisement for her daily blasphemies'.[1]

In the medieval period the treatment of heretics could be considered as a system in which the aim was to restore the spiritually deranged to health and return them to the ideological community of Christendom. Such an approach required ruthlessness and ideological conviction. In undertaking this responsibility, churchmen were seeking to root out and suppress error, hoping to 'save' its victims in the process. In this equation, blasphemers—those committing the error of expressing wilful attacks upon the central beliefs of Christendom—only occasionally appeared as a separate category. As was to become the case with witchcraft, heresy, and subsequently with blasphemy, accusing individuals could be a matter of political ambition as much as religious orthodoxy. Such attacks often mask other pressures prevalent in a community, and explain why some historians are so ready to see heresy, witchcraft, and blasphemy alternately as precursors or manifestations of rapid social and economic change.[2] It was also possible for a developed sympathy for heretical ideas to be a motivating factor in the political struggle of urban communities against state and papal power. A changing social order created by growing individualism and the failure of established religion to offer answers, and comfort, for certain aspirations created a form of discontent with God. This dissatisfaction was a way in which heresy started to resemble forms of blasphemy. Ultimately, those who claimed the authority to take action against heretics saw their disobedience as a crucial demonstration of their threatening nature.[3]

Although the church did not proceed uniformly against heresy until the high Middle Ages, the justification for doing so was somewhat older. Augustine had constructed a series of elaborate arguments which pressed Christendom to

---

[1] *An Association of Prayers against Blasphemy, Swearing and the Profanation of Sundays and Festivals, under the Patronage of St. Louis, King of France, Approved by the Archbishop of Tours.* Translated from the French by Edward G. Kriwan Browne (London, 1847), 14–15.

[2] J. Nelson, 'Society, Theodicy and the Origins of Heresy: Towards a Reassessment of the Medieval Evidence', in D. Baker (ed.), *Schism, Heresy and Religious Protest* (Cambridge, 1972).

[3] R. I. Moore, *The Formation of a Persecuting Society* (Oxford, 1987), 133.

act against those who threatened the purity of faith. Those who rejected the truth of the Gospels were manifestly less deserving of mercy and consideration than the Jew or infidel who had been given no such luxury. Moreover, the heretic's stubborn apostasy made a mockery of the church's wish for uniformity and the state's support for such aims. It was even argued that toleration transferred the guilt to the authorities who permitted such laxity and intensified the awful fate of the guilty.[4] Thus, in all of this was the logic of what Robert Moore has described as a 'persecuting society'. Combating heretics could clearly be seen as a holy duty. A flavour of this is given by St Bernard of Clairvaux, in his preparations for work against heretics in the Languedoc towards the middle of the twelfth century. His expressed motivation emphasized that he was appalled at the profoundly pernicious effects of heresy: 'Men are dying in their sins, and souls are everywhere being hurled before the awesome tribunal unreconciled by repentance, unfortified by communion.' Bernard went still further, to assert his own sorrow at allowing error to spread and contaminate. He must have spoken for all the pious who would become involved in detecting and suppressing heresy, when he declared: 'At the voice of one heretic you close your ears to all the prophets and apostles who with one spirit of truth have brought together the Church out of all nations to one faith in Christ.'[5]

The systematization of heresy-hunting involved greater levels of professionalism amongst practitioners. The keeping of meticulous records marked out regions, communities, families, and even their descendants as potentially culpable in future heretical episodes. Such records also effectively kept track of individuals, enabling harsher treatment of them for subsequent relapses. Moreover, the Inquisition's mode of investigation and questioning involved building up a picture of heretics and their circle. Through questions intended to learn about beliefs in a community, the system offered escape, leniency, and forms of mitigation to the defendant who would denounce or implicate others. Lambert suggests that this quality of information gave inquisitors 'power comparable to that of a modern police officer'.[6] In this way heresy was constructed in the official religious mind as an activity indulged in by communities of believers. Even subsequent historians have followed this tendency, with most accounts of medieval heresy containing maps indicating areas and regions where it was most prevalent. From such studies, the movement and progress of the Papal Inquisition, and even the length of its sessions in specific localities, give

---

[4] For an account of Augustine's influence in the formulation of heresy see John Marshall, *John Locke, Toleration and Early Enlightenment Culture* (Cambridge, 2006), 204–15, and L. W. Levy, *Blasphemy: Verbal Offense Against the Sacred from Moses to Salman Rushdie* (New York, 1993), 47–50.

[5] R. I. Moore, *The Birth of Popular Heresy* (London, 1975), 39–40.

[6] M. Lambert, *Medieval Heresy: Popular Movements from the Gregorian Reform to the Reformation* (Oxford, 1992), 102–3.

us a flavour of this dynamic of heresy as an infestation. Most accounts of
the Waldensians, Cathars, and Lollards indicate their existence as underground
networks of connections and places of shelter spanning considerable geograph-
ical distances and with extraordinary longevity. It is, however, important to
heed the warnings of some who see heresy as sometimes only the confluence
of unrelated and inarticulate discontent. This only gathers coherence in the
hands of inquisitors, who possess the ability to turn them into a heretical
system.[7]

Heresies were not simply quiet beliefs mercilessly harried and broken by
religious authorities fearful of power and jealous of devotion. They were also
opposed by ordinary laymen and women, who themselves wanted protection
from the dangers such beliefs posed. Indeed, enough accounts of heretical
episodes suggest that the intervention of secular and religious authorities saved
heretical individuals and groups from mob violence and justice on numerous
occasions. Robert Moore found evidence of popular violence against heretics and
religious outsiders scattered throughout the eleventh century, although clerical
intervention was not always successful.[8] However, there were also instances where
the populace reacted badly to the imposition of capital sentences upon members
of the local community. Serious rioting occurred in Parma in 1279 and Bologna
in 1299 as a result of the actions of the Papal Inquisition.[9]

The action of authority around heresy involved the religious taking the
secular into partnership. Although all the defendants in heresy cases were tried
by ecclesiastical courts, when the capital sentence was confirmed they were
invariably handed over to the secular authorities for their sentence to be carried
out. This was the start of an uneasy, yet strangely enduring, relationship that
allowed religious agencies to judge and comment upon the secular state's moral
approach to the policing of its population. In turn, the state itself would come
to believe that religious orthodoxy was some guarantee of social peace as well as
a species of security.

The early signs of this relationship becoming a partnership, significantly with
the state as the senior partner, were evident towards the end of the medieval
period. The most obvious manifestation of this is in the number of secular
authorities who enacted their own independent statutes intended to deal with
the heretic. Jews were initially targeted through their denial of Christ as the
Messiah, but also because of their supposed falsification of the holy scripture.
This grew in the first half of the thirteenth century, as Christian attitudes to
European Jewry hardened. In this atmosphere the first significant laws against
blasphemy were passed, commencing with the Town Ordinances and Privileges of

---

[7] Moore, *Formation of a Persecuting Society*, 151.

[8] R. I. Moore, 'Popular Violence and Popular Heresy in Western Europe, c1000–1179', in W. J.
Shiels (ed.), *Persecution and Toleration. Studies in Church History*, Vol. 21 (Oxford, 1984), 43–50.

[9] Carol Lansing, *Power and Purity: Cathar Heresy in Medieval Italy* (Oxford, 1998), 151.

Vienna in 1221. These were followed by laws promulgated by the Emperor Frederick II in 1231.[10]

Other European countries, to a limited extent, followed suit, with blasphemy becoming an offence that required the intervention of secular authorities. In France the involvement of the French monarchy in policing blasphemy could technically date itself to Louis IX's statute of 1263. Later medieval monarchs reconfirmed statutes and ordinances against the crime in the fourteenth and fifteenth centuries. These uniformly specified mutilation as a punishment, increasing the severity of such punishment with subsequent offences. In the late fourteenth century a first offence would result in a month's confinement and an appearance in the pillory. A second offence would result in a subsequent appearance and slitting of the upper lip, to be matched with disfigurement of the lower lip for a third offence. A fourth would result in the complete removal of the lower lip, whilst a fifth would result in the removal of the tongue.[11] Parts of Germany, as well as Spain and the Low Countries, began punishing blasphemers in a similar fashion, but the coherent and sustained campaigns against them would have to wait until the fifteenth century. When these coherent campaigns came they were intended to reinforce religious orthodoxy. This was a product of the Reformation's confessional divide acquiring a systematic interest in religious discipline. In the Reformed churches, replacing a religious vocabulary of symbols with one of texts was not an easy or uniform process. Similarly, a greater level of attention upon the spiritual condition of the individual, on both sides of the confessional divide, fed conceptions of blasphemy.

Detection and policing of blasphemy became just as central to the Counter-Reformation as the need to locate unorthodoxy. In bringing blasphemy laws back into use the catholic church had allowed an important shift to take place, since individuals were increasingly becoming the unit of guilt and responsibility, rather than whole communities. After the Council of Trent, part of the Counter-Reformation push involved a need to establish the bounds between earth and heaven. Where they had blended more obviously before the Reformation, this linkage became a species of laxity and slovenly spiritual practice. Poor, lazy, and incomplete religious observance cheapened the sacred, and an increasingly structured divide was also behind attempts to reform and re-sacrilize the Catholic liturgy during this period. The greater stress upon doctrinal orthodoxy that resulted from Jansenism in France provoked a whole new climate of religious discipline. Many studies of the phenomenon of blasphemy in France begin from this point, and tend to emphasize that blasphemy was a challenge to conceptions of God and the public peace. But it was more obviously a category of behaviour than the fully worked-out ideological objection to the Christian world which

---

[10] Gerd Schwerhoff, *Zungen wie Schwerter: Blasphemie in alteuropäischen Gesellschaften 1200–1650* (Konstanz, 2005), 300.

[11] Dean, Trevor, *Crime in Medieval Society* (London, 2001), 56.

it would later become. Thus, a portion of the history in France is one of local agencies of control seeking to regulate and proscribe against an offence which occurred in everyday life, most frequently as a part of unacceptable behaviour by marginal or unruly groups in society. Whilst agencies of government, from the Crown down through local municipalities, were to exercise their own judgement, the most fundamental agency of control, the church itself, considered prevention to be much better than cure. The identification of blasphemy as a potential sin and its seriousness as a crime gave it an enhanced prominence. It entered discussions about discipline and holiness, to become identified not just with poor behaviour but also neglect of observance. In this respect it resembled a catch-all term intended to stimulate and sustain discipline. In the 1530s Johannes Brenz advocated the sustained use of excommunication and deprivation of the Eucharist to discipline the unruly elements of society within Württemberg.[12] Similarly, the populace of Valangin in Switzerland from the 1570s onwards found that their local consistory court punished non-attendance at church and poor behaviour towards their pastors.[13]

This meant that important disciplinary mechanisms were constructed to prevent blasphemy becoming endemic in the populace at large. The detection and search for blasphemy became a part of the theological training of the French priesthood, and this search for conformity and species of discipline is also evident in a number of seventeenth-century treatises and manuals. Nonetheless, discipline was a holistic concept, of which blasphemy represented merely a facet. Alain Cabantous concluded that disciplinary manuals, at least in sixteenth-century France, under-treated the issue in their advice.[14] The priest was seen as a component part of a great chain of patriarchal discipline, in which fathers, masters, and overseers would exert the legitimate pressure of wisdom and superior status over children, servants, and latowers—all presided over by the steadiness of the parish priest. The machinery of self-discipline in this area was heavily reliant upon compelling those at risk to pray and seek discipline within themselves, even to the point of chastisement.[15]

Whilst the Council of Trent and the Counter-Reformation made the control of religious opinions a matter for the Catholic church to address, the sixteenth century witnessed a quickening of secular government's involvement in the issue of policing and punishing blasphemy. In France the number of ordinances, declarations, and edicts increased dramatically, with no fewer than

[12] James M. Estes, 'Johannes Brenz and the Problem of Ecclesiastical Discipline', *Church History*, 41: 4 (Dec. 1972), 464–79.
[13] Jeffrey R. Watt, 'The Reception of the Reformation in Valangin, Switzerland, 1547–1588', *Sixteenth Century Journal*, 20: 1 (Spring 1989), 98–104, at 94–5.
[14] Alain Cabantous, *Blasphemy, Impious Speech in the West from the Seventeenth to the Nineteenth Century* (New York, 2002), 9 and 10.
[15] See John Bossy, *Christianity in the West, 1400–1700* (Oxford, 1985), 155–6. Bossy sees Jean Bodin as instrumental in forwarding the ideal of family discipline within a wider chain of authority.

fifteen spanning the whole of the sixteenth century. Spain witnessed a flurry of similar legislation in the first couple of decades of the sixteenth century, and analogous provisions were also made in the territories of the Holy Roman Empire in the middle third of the sixteenth century. Venice went so far as to establish its own bespoke apparatus for combatting blasphemy, the *Esecuttori controla bestemmia*, which was ostensibly a judicial council of elders whose pronouncements were beyond appeal. This device to fight the menace of blasphemy, and the subsequent extension of its jurisdiction, suggests a particularly early realization that blasphemy, as both act and offence, had specific public-order dimensions. Certainly, this century's tide of religious wars and dynastic changes meant that blasphemy was a challenge to the monarch's role as guarantor of confessional stability. Moreover, the enduring belief in providence allowed rulers to seek explanations or scapegoats for the misfortunes of society.[16]

Certainly, shame and contrition loomed large in the punishments exacted throughout the early modern world. Some punishment regimes in use against blasphemers show a combination of what we might term ridicule punishments and shame punishments. This blend of shame and ridicule focused both the opprobrium and laughter of the community upon the convicted individual. This made communal opinion stronger than miscreants and their words. Levity, in this sense, strengthened the community against a potential danger, and more readily allowed community-wide participation in the punishment of the blasphemer. This partnership between the community and authority has been described by one historian as a sharing of strategy and tactics, if not wholly of values. Yet we should be cautious about ascribing one-dimensional effectiveness to this regime, since evidence suggests that shame punishments could elicit everything from indifference to psychological pain.[17] The gaze upon such a miscreant could be mocking or reproving, with those convicted clearly expecting and experiencing both reactions. The Leiden hedonist Gerijt Jacopsz. was sentenced to be whipped in the town prison and made to parade, and attend church on Sunday, with a barrel around himself as a shame punishment. This particular punishment was renowned throughout German lands, and Gerd Schwerhoff has uncovered a woodcut of 1618 threatening the townsfolk of Cologne with the 'barrel jacket' punishment.[18] The roof-tiler from Warmond convicted in 1526 underwent an array of degrading shame punishments. He was sentenced to wear a chalice painted on his front and back for a year, and to stand on the scaffold wearing a woman's skirt, whilst carrying a one-pound candle. This he had also to bring with him every Sunday to the Pieterskerk in Leiden. In Catholic Spain it was

---

[16] This is covered more fully in Ch. 6.

[17] David Postles, 'Penance and the Market Place: A Reformation Dialogue with the Medieval Church (c.1250–1600)', *Journal of Ecclesiastical History*, 54: 3 (2003), 441–68, at 467, 464–5.

[18] M. R. Baelde, *Studiën over Godslastering* (The Hague, 1935), 109–10. Schwerhoff, in *Zungen wie Schwerter*, 144.

common for a petty blasphemer to be muzzled and made to ride backwards upon a donkey.

These incidents of public shame were, in Calvinist countries, a part of the consistory court's power to control access to the rite of communion, which had been increasingly limited by Reformed liturgies.[19] Blasphemers convicted in Valangin found the local consistory court capable of imposing fines, imprisonment, or the humiliating punishment of being required to kiss the earth.[20] Post-Reformation Saxony used the stocks and neck-irons to discipline convicted blasphemers, as well as, on occasion, tying them to a wooden crucifix during church services.[21] The neighbourhood squabbles in eighteenth-century Shetland, described in Chapter 4, had been latent appeals for the kirk to intervene. These issues were resolved through public penance before the community and the payment of a fine to assist the poor.[22] The publisher or bookseller of blasphemous works could expect to have their stock destroyed. In France this became a shame punishment in itself, since the burning of such books became a public ritual to rival the English practice of having a single copy burned by the common hangman. However, such events represented only small victories for the authorities, since it became impossible to control material already in circulation, particularly since attention could actively stimulate demand for blasphemous works.[23]

Nonetheless, stricter punishments also existed within these same jurisdictional cultures. When religious changes came to the northern Netherlands, the legislation of Charles V was maintained under the Calvinist republic and came to be enhanced. In 1518 there had been an edict preventing swearing and blasphemy, but a subsequent police edict of 1531 went further and was altered to reflect the new religious ideas. This originally declared: 'As a cure against blasphemers we forbid blasphemy against the holy names of God the Virgin and the Saints. It is also forbidden to deny, scorn, or belittle them.' The penalty for this offence was imprisonment for a month with bread and water. If real vehement intent could be proved, then boring through the tongue would ensue. The Province of Utrecht continued with a degree of leniency, imposing whipping in the stocks for a second offence before boring through the tongue for a third. The imposition of religious discipline in the army and the fleet were also a feature of Dutch provision. In 1590 a military ordinance showed a sliding scale of

[19] Charles Parker, 'The Moral Agency and Moral Autonomy of Church Folk in the Dutch Reformed Church of Delft 1580–1620', *Journal of Ecclesiastical History*, 48: 1 (1997), 44–70, at 55.

[20] Watt, 'The Reception of the Reformation in Valangin, Switzerland', 102.

[21] Susan C. Karant-Nunn, 'Neoclericalism and Anticlericalism in Saxony 1555–1675', *Journal of Interdisciplinary History*, 24: 4 (Spring 1994), 615–37, at 624.

[22] See also Cabantous, *Blasphemy*, 23, which emphasizes how a return to orthodoxy was sometimes more important than punishment.

[23] Alfred Soman, 'Press, Pulpit and Censorship in France before Richelieu', *Proceedings of the American Philosophical Society*, 120: 6 (Dec. 1976), 439–63, at 452–3.

punishment for the offence of blasphemy. A first offence demanded three days on bread and water; a second offence was treated much more seriously, with boring through the tongue and banishment from the United Provinces. This last sentence was rare, since instances were especially noted only in 1635 and again in 1728.[24]

Spain, meanwhile, imposed progressive penalties of whipping, branding, and finally removal of the tongue for a third offence. Civil law in Spain during the same period imposed tongue-piercing, imprisonment, and service in the galleys accompanied by an *auto da fe*.[25] Jurisdictions in Germany and France followed this pattern, but were renowned for an altogether harsher approach to the offence and its perpetrators. Blasphemy was considered a serious felony in early modern Germany, and thus the initial stages of punishment strongly emphasized shame rather than ridicule. Blasphemers punished in the pillory were required to hold a rod and candle as emotive symbols of penance. An alternative sentence was to stand outside a church door, or on a stool of repentance, to hear a sermon on the subject. Ecclesiastical systems of punishment involved public penance that was supposed to provide reconciliation with God. These systems of disgrace became gradually more incorporated into the system, and were a feature of Protestant countries, especially in southern Germany and Switzerland. Penalties could also be imposed by secular courts, and were linked to the punishment of mortal sins, including blasphemy. As the historian of German early modern punishment, Richard van Dülmen, puts it: 'it was crucial that all punishments and combinations of punishments were carried out in public. . . holding up to the delinquent a mirror of dishonesty reflecting the norms of the society from which he or she was on the verge of being expelled.'[26] Although van Dülmen found blasphemy to be only a sporadic offence, he was able to trace the pattern of punishment in several localities. Between 1562 and 1692 Frankfurt sent all of its six convicted blasphemers into exile, compounding the punishment with flogging for two of them and an ordeal with an iron collar for another. Nuremberg however, used birching, branding, boring through the tongue, and the pillory to punish its small number of offenders between 1578 and 1615.[27]

During a similar period in France punishment generally tended to be of a more draconian nature. Blasphemy had been a preoccupation among French monarchs since St Louis, who first introduced legal penalties of such severity (mutilation and death) that Pope Clement IV urged him to moderate them. Successive monarchs up to the beginning of the eighteenth century periodically renewed these measures. During the sixteenth century new edicts were introduced at

[24] Baelde, *Godslastering*, 110–12.

[25] Flynn, 'Blasphemy and the Play of Anger', 30. Elizabeth Belmas, 'La Monteé des blasphèmes', in J. Delumeau (ed.), *Injures et blasphèmes; Mentalités*, ii (Paris, 1989), 15.

[26] Richard van Dülmen, *Theatre of Horror: Crime and Punishment in early modern Germany*, tr. Elisabeth Neu (Cambridge, 1990), 56.

[27] Ibid. 142, 143, and 156.

an accelerating rate, emphasizing the monarch's roles as protector of his realm from divine punishment and dispenser of punishment upon the blasphemer. Occasionally the equation would be altered when the prosecution of blasphemers was offered in thanksgiving for royal victories, such as those by Louis XII in Italy during 1510.

In early modern France blasphemy laws tended to move between two fundamental extremes. The more moderate approach was characterized by the ordinance of 1510, subsequently renewed four times (in 1514, 1546, 1651, and in 1666). Conviction for a first offence incurred a fine which was doubled, tripled, and quadrupled for successive offences. Defaulters were imprisoned on bread and water and detained at the court's pleasure. A fifth offence was punishable by the *carcan*, a form of public torment and humiliation resembling the pillory. Subsequent offences incurred heavier penalties, involving mutilation and branding of the lips and, ultimately, removal of the tongue. The more extreme end of the spectrum is represented by laws introduced by Charles IX in 1572, and reconfirmed by numerous monarchs over the next century. Corporal punishment of various kinds was introduced after the third blasphemous offence (1572, 1594). The law was relaxed slightly in further edicts, but from 1681 piercing of the tongue was practised on the first offence and further infractions were dealt with more severely. Punishment in all cases was preceded by a compulsory public recantation of the offender, who was to be clothed only in a shift.[28]

Much of the evidence which comes from France suggests that municipal and seigneurial justice unconciously embraced the fundamentals of a public-order dimension. Clerics sought to link blasphemy to observance and crimes of thought or spiritual inadequacy. Secular authorities, as they have always been apt to do, saw such behaviour as crimes associated with the public arena and breaches of public codes of behaviour. Alain Cabantous has concluded that this approach provides evidence of proto-bourgeois and seigneurial attempts to attack the blasphemous culture that thrived in lower-class sociability.

In England the interest in blasphemy exhibited by the state was of much greater longevity, and ultimately of much greater seriousness. The statute *De Heretico Comburendo* (1400) really gave a warrant for secular authority to interest itself in matters of religious orthodoxy. It was also able to assume final authority in such matters through this act (and a subsequent one in 1414), solidifying the status of heresy as a crime punishable by burning at the stake. These changes brought England into line with the rest of the Christian West, and were instrumental in identifying treason with sedition. Lollards, Hussites, Anabaptists, and others all seemed to pose this threat throughout the different countries of Europe. Moreover, the religious and dynastic history of England during the sixteenth and seventeenth centuries would invariably see matters of ideological, religious, and political discipline become intertwined.

[28] Belmas, 'La Monteé des blasphèmes', 13–16.

The legal history of the sixteenth century shows this process in evolution. Legal enactments of the reign of Henry VIII made real the connection between the ideology of religion and its potential link with treasonable opinion and activity. An act of 1533 rejuvenated the act of 1414 (subsequent to *De Heretico Comburendo*), enhancing its penalties whilst defining more carefully its use. In 1547 a statute protected the sacrament from 'any contemptuouse wordes or by anny wordes of depravinge dispisinge or reviling'. The statute outlined an offence to be tried at quarter sessions, with penalties of imprisonment for offenders. A year later the Book of Common Prayer was given legislative protection from 'derogation, depraving or despising'. It was, however, the Elizabethan period which provided a significant break with the past through its repeal of the older statutes against heresy. This same act also extended lay involvement in such matters, by allowing lay commissioners the opportunity to enquire into certain offences, previously within the ecclesiastical realm of jurisdiction. Drawing a clear line between blasphemy and heresy had been central to the work of Thomas Cranmer.[29] Nonetheless, this was not a wholly clean break with the medieval past, since elements of heresy blended with blasphemy in cases beyond this date. Heresy only took its last victims in England in the first years of the following century, when Matthew Legate and Edward Wightman were burned in the reign of James I.

This period saw the machinery of ecclesiastical uniformity and discipline become intensely unpopular, through its use as a weapon of coercion by political interests allied to the state. The Common Law of blasphemy appeared in 1617, with a decision that temporal courts could act because blasphemy constituted a disturbance of the peace. The reign of James I also brought systematic prosecution under Archbishop William Laud for a range of religious offences. Laud's power was essentially vested in the Court of Star Chamber and the Court of High Commission for Ecclesiastical Causes. This was viewed by opponents as a hostile development with political consequences, since the Court of Star Chamber had discretionary power over any matter in which it expressed an interest. Moreover, it would regularly extend this jurisdiction in matters of seditious libel when it perceived threats to good order and stability.[30] This might be construed as the closest England came to adopting the tools of the Inquisition. It is at least interesting to speculate what the cultural history of policing religious opinion and behaviour might have looked like had Laud succeeded in retaining control of religious and secular authority for any length of time. Nonetheless, this period did demonstrate that legal minds had made the link between sedition and attacks upon the church of which the monarch was head. Both represented potentially

---

[29] Levy, *Blasphemy*, 96–100.

[30] Stephen Foster, *Notes from the Caroline Underground: Alexander Leighton, the Puritan Triumvirate and the Laudian Reaction to Nonconformity*. Studies in British History and Culture, Vol. 6 (Hamden, Conn., 1978), 35–6 and 54–6.

revolutionary and disturbing elements that threatened the security of the realm. Again, it is possible to see here the start of recognizably modern conceptions of breach of the peace, albeit constructed in this example around protection of the regime in power.

But William Laud's ecclesiastical jurisdiction followed him into oblivion. Its eventual abeyance after 1641 left the offence of blasphemy in a thoroughly ambiguous position. This was to prove dangerous for English society as the Civil War developed revolutionary potential. Ecclesiastical and other forms of supposedly arbitrary power were dissolved, yet society and property still needed protection, and decisions about the limits of toleration were still required. The proceedings in 1645 against the Socinian Paul Best were inconclusive and he was, somewhat embarrassingly, released, since the lawyers of the day concluded that the machinery to try and punish him had been destroyed.[31] The more famous case, against the Unitarian John Biddle, a matter of two years later, made Parliament undertake to resolve the confusion, and the outcome was the return of control and restriction. The Blasphemy Act of 1648 introduced capital punishment for denying the Trinity, the Resurrection, and the Day of Judgement. Interestingly, this particular legislation became an opportunity to outline religious doctrine that was acceptable to the state, whilst ostracizing doctrines associated with Catholicism and Arminianism. The religious turmoil sweeping the country meant that a further alteration was required within two years, and the 1650 Blasphemy Act was framed to deal with the Ranter menace.

This ordinance of 1650 gave justices and heads of corporations the power to imprison for periods of six months when they identified blasphemies and religious errors. A subsequent offence would involve trial by a higher court, namely the Justices of Assize and Gaol Delivery. This higher court could impose sentences of banishment and label those so convicted as felons.[32] Such steps appear to run counter to the religious toleration that otherwise was a feature of the Commonwealth years. Nonetheless, individuals and groups such as the Muggletonians and Quakers posed a significant threat to public order. Through their active denial of toleration, they demonstrated the danger of religious groups who tried to claim supreme authority.

The Biddle case had brought into focus the entire issue of jurisdiction over religious opinion in England, and it was no surprise that it generated important ripples. Of even more importance was the subsequent Naylor case, which had an impact upon heresy and blasphemy in England thereafter. For the first time judges and lawyers investigated the precedents for the law and drew distinctions between blasphemy and heresy that were far-reaching, heralding the final removal of the latter from the law. Lord Commissioner Bulstrode Whitelocke, in the

---

[31] See Alex F. Mitchell and John Struthers (eds.), *Minutes of the Westminster Assembly of Divines* (Edinburgh, 1874), 214.

[32] G. D. Nokes, *A History of the Crime of Blasphemy* (London, 1928), 37–40.

context of the Naylor case, quarried the Hebrew texts of Leviticus searching for an answer that would lead Parliament away from its problem. His answer was that capital punishment was not justified by Mosaic law for the offence of blasphemy, since Naylor's behaviour could scarcely be described as directly misusing the name of God.[33] Largely from here, English law began to evolve away from its medieval past, since Whitelocke identified a clear difference between blasphemy and heresy. Blasphemy involved the act of 'cursing the name of God or of our neighbour', whilst heresy was more obviously the expression of erroneous opinion.[34] In particular, we might note Whitelocke's inclusion of man as a potential victim of the process of blasphemy. Here, more than anywhere, was evidence of a growing conception that religion needed to be protected because it was embedded in society, and not simply because it was the source of authority. Yet, as we discovered at the very start of Chapter 1, Whitelocke still took blasphemy very seriously, and even in the last years of his life he anxiously urged magistrates to combat its presence.[35]

The situation for blasphemy in seventeenth-century France was also a function of struggles for power and control over jurisdiction. A statute against blasphemers had closely followed Henry IV's assumption of power at the end of the sixteenth century. Similar situations occurred again in 1617 and 1631, when internal threats to the monarch saw similar statutes enacted in the wake of the defeat of political opponents. The year 1651 witnessed a blasphemy statute that coincided with Louis XIV reaching his majority and vanquishing enemies that threatened royal authority. The more draconian statute of 1681, confirming mutilation and capital punishment, was eagerly implemented by the diligent lawyers and magistrates prepared to do the royal will. Whilst this may appear a cheap exercise in establishing authority over a group who were already considered pariahs, there is a significant ideological dimension in the French example that should not be missed. The French monarchy's belief in divine right gave the incumbent monarch a clear and concrete mission to be God's representative on earth, and to be the instrument of divine rule and punishment.[36] Effectively, this form of modernization did not so much replace ecclesiastical authority with secular authority as it sought to fuse the two into one. Norbert Elias's interest in the 'civilising process' suggested that the French court became the model for the monarch's ability to marshal and maintain 'monopoly' power.[37] He also noted that the personal power of the monarch was often a substitute for the power of an administrative bureaucracy.

[33] Levy, *Blasphemy*, 199.

[34] Hypatia Bradlaugh-Bonner, *Penalties Upon Opinion* (London, 1934), 19.

[35] Bulstrode Whitelocke, *The Charge to the Grand-Jury, And other juries of the County of Middlesex at the General Quarter Session of the Peace, held, April 21st at Westminster Hall* (London, 1718), 12, 3–7. And *The Second Charge to the Grand-Jury, And other juries of the County of Middlesex at the General Quarter Session of the Peace, held, April 21st at Westminster Hall* (London, 1718).

[36] Cabantous, *Blasphemy*, 67, 78–9.

[37] Norbert Elias, *The Civilising Process* (rev. edn.), tr. Edmund Jephcot, ed. Eric Dunning, Johan Gouldsblom, and Stephen Mennell (Oxford, 2005), 268.

As one commentator has put it, 'the deification of the king served to link past and present, people and deity'.[38] Such responsibilities, which still embodied a sacred component, meant that tolerating challenges to God and this 'link' was advertising the weakness of the monarch's power.[39] Maintaining such power required absolute faith and adherence to the notion of majesty and respect for hierarchies. The monarch was involved in the manipulation of people, and this was central to charismatic rule and the increasing focus upon long-term behavioural goals.[40] The monarch's power also, however, was predicated upon his or her ability to be a mediator of conflict. Blasphemers simultaneously challenged such authority and gave rulers an easy target to demonstrate their power to end conflict and threats to the community's identity. Thus, it is no surprise to see the personal proclamation of *ancien régime* rulers levelled against such a menace, although the long-term success of such assaults upon blasphemy must be seriously in doubt.[41]

Perhaps the most articulate statement of the intention behind statutes against blasphemy was made in England through the Hale judgement of 1675. As Sir Matthew Hale suggested, 'Christianity is a parcel of the laws of England; and therefore to reproach the Christian religion is to speak in subversion of the law'.[42] Many argued about whether Hale had been justified in pulling together the strands of Common Law precedent to make this statement about the offence of blasphemous libel. This was because his definition offered to make both the monarchy in Parliament and sacred institutions deserving of protection.[43] The jurisprudence developed by Sir Matthew Hale and Sir Edward Coke has been described as 'the balancing of morality and politics in the light of history; it is the balancing of justice and order in the light of experience'. It has also been noted how this displays remnants of Trinitarian thinking.[44] It came to rest, too, upon the ideal of precedent which reflected the customs and history of the English people, and such a doctrine also had an impact upon American jurisprudence. Many noted how both Hale and Coke dwelt upon the pre-Norman Conquest antiquity of the law, which was in itself an appeal to custom as an important element in the law's legitimacy.[45] This also injected a degree of chauvinism which would later appear in Blackstone.[46]

---

[38] Jeroen Duindam, *Myths of Power* (Amsterdam, 1995), 108.   [39] Ibid. 132.

[40] For an extended discussion of this see ibid. 137–58.

[41] Norbert Elias, *The Court Society* (Oxford, 1983), 128, 124, and 148. See also Jonathan Fletcher, *Violence and Civilisation: An Introduction to the Work of Norbert Elias* (Cambridge, 1997), 34–6; and Duindam, *Myths of Power*, 32–4.

[42] Nokes, *History of the Crime of Blasphemy*, 48.   [43] See Marshall, *John Locke*, 132.

[44] Harold J. Berman, 'The Origins of Historical Jurisprudence: Coke, Selden, Hale', *Yale Law Journal*, 103: 7 (May 1994), 1651–738, at 1731.

[45] Anon., 'The extent to which the Common Law is applied in determining what constitutes a crime, and the nature and degree of punishment consequent thereupon. Part 1. Of the Origin Early History, and General Principles of the Common Law', *American Law Register* (1852–91), 15: 2, NS 6 (Dec. 1866), 65–79, at 66.

[46] John W. Cairns 'Blackstone, an English Institutist: Legal Literature and the Rise of the Nation State', *Oxford Journal of Legal Studies*, 4: 3 (Winter, 1984), 318–60, at 354–7.

Opponents of the blasphemy laws would later suggest that the authoritative precedents cited to defend a law of blasphemy were substantially a fabrication. This argument claimed that a series of mistranslations and copy-editing errors had left England with an establishment that defended its own interests through the use of legal sleight-of-hand. Certainly, the focus of subsequent critics meant that there was no denying that what Hale had achieved was nothing less than the creation of a coherent legal philosophy of blasphemy within the English Common Law. He had made this judgement from earlier precedents, and subsequent judgements would draw on Hale as a part of the Common Law's process of organic evolution. Although Hale's judgement was open to interpretation, it is striking how far (and for how long) judges and lawyers would accept and promote the 'part and parcel' argument.[47]

The importance of the Hale judgement was perhaps brought into sharp focus by the English monarchy's attempt to re-establish statute power at the end of the seventeenth century. The 1698 act of 9 & 10 William III c. 32 looks remarkably like many of the pronouncements made on the European continent, and in particular resembles some of the French statutes. This made it a criminal offence to hold anti-trinitarian views, to espouse polytheism, to deny the truth of the Christian religion, or to mock or question the truth of the scriptures. Its preamble saw blasphemous opinions as 'tending to the dishonour of Almighty God' and potentially 'destructive to the peace and welfare of this kingdom'.[48] Punishments similarly resembled the graduated severity of French examples, with an emphasis upon the denial of civil rights in the first instance. Conviction for blasphemy would entail imprisonment as well as preventing the criminal from employment and office-holding for a first offence. Alongside this punishment, the protection of the law as a guarantor of property, good name, and inheritance would also be denied. The blasphemer who persisted could expect a sentence of execution upon a third offence.[49]

The remarkable similarity of approach adopted by the monarchies of the seventeenth century in their desire to assume responsibility for the religious component of moral government is striking. In England this statute was never used successfully, and this suggests the importance of the Hale judgement and the power in this area that it had given to Common Law. Although statutes in England and France would look similar, it was this capacity for organic growth that would make the English history of the offence part company with the experience in France.

---

[47] For a more detailed discusion of Hale and problems seen by critics see my *Blasphemy in Modern Britain: 1789 to the Present.* (Aldershot 1999).

[48] John Marshall suggests that contemporaries (namely Burnet and Locke) debated whether the Act should be used to protect sexual morality which stemmed from religious unorthodoxy. Marshall also notes that the Act was also seen by many as a deterrent. See Marshall, *John Locke,* 716.

[49] 9 & 10 William III, c. 32.

In England the Hale interpretation of the law was reconfirmed a matter of fifty years later in the case against Thomas Woolston's allegorical interpretation of the scriptures. The judge, Lord Chief Justice Raymond, considered this to be a direct attack upon the heart of Christianity, but in passing sentence suggested that only such direct attacks were the business of the law. The introduction here of a distinction between attack and opinion was effectively bringing the issue of intention into blasphemy. This was occurring throughout Europe in the fifty years that straddle the end of the seventeenth and start of the eighteenth centuries.

The colonial prehistory of blasphemy in America provided local communities with the ability to determine and prescribe the religious character of that community. Many of the colonies themselves had been established as attempts to create the godly commonwealth in the New World. Having brought with them a belief that the established church had diverged from biblically prescribed society, many New England states took their own flexible and in some places pragmatic approaches to law. In the initial phases of settlement many of the colonies were content to continue in a manner that was partly organic, like the English Common Law. Many actively revered the Common Law and its claims to ancient provenance. Magistrates administered justice in consultation with church elders, who established a regime of penalties tailored to fit individual crimes. These were sometimes flexible enough to allow for degrees of clemency, mercy, and mitigating circumstances. Virginia's first Code of Laws, established in 1610, made action against blasphemy an especial priority. Blasphemy was listed as the second law within this code, which also aimed to catch those who neglected religious observance. This codification of the crime of blasphemy displayed some of the traits that we have already observed in European statutes and edicts. Although intended to protect society from those denying the articles of the Christian faith or displaying contempt for the Bible, there was, once again, a specific focus on those who denied the Trinity. Although these were the most serious of crimes, there was recognition of lesser misdemeanours and the desire to police and punish such offences as profanity, swearing of false oaths, and the misuse of God's name. For the full offence of blasphemy, there was again the three-step scale of punishment, starting with whipping, gravitating through severe mutilation of the tongue, and culminating in the death penalty for a third offence. Although this criminal code was repealed within ten years, its provisions were influential for a time upon the thinking of other jurisdictions.[50]

The colony of Massachusetts, in its so-called 'Body of Liberties' of 1641, recognized the crime of blasphemy, linking it to denial of the Bible a year later. This became a distinct law in 1646, which protected 'the true god' of Christianity and decreed the death penalty cited in Leviticus 24: 15, 16. This 1646 law also

---

[50] Sir Thomas Dale's Code is reproduced in Sanford Cobb, *The Rise of Religious Liberty in America* (New York 1902; 1968 edn.), 78.

covered the behaviour of the native population and other non-Christians.[51] Importantly, this required the perpetrator to display elements of wilfulness and excessive pride as a symptom of the blasphemer's intention. The effect here was to trivialize the milder profanities produced by drink and the heat of the moment, turning them into misdemeanours. Massachusetts adopted the standard punishments of whipping and mutilation of the tongue, adding to this a novel echo of medieval practice. One woman convicted in 1656 was condemned to wear perpetually a large red letter 'B', in a manner reminiscent of the Cathar yellow cross.[52] Connecticut constructed its own statute against this crime, borrowing the wording and intentions of the Massachusetts provisions, and Maryland eventually followed suit. Maryland however, went further in 1649 by separating lower-level profanity (cursing and deriding) from doctrinal denial or anti-trinitarianism. The former henceforth merited fines and corporal punishments, whilst the latter was a capital crime.[53] Other jurisdictions would prescribe the pillory, mutilation, and eventual removal of the tongue. The Lake Michigan area also required those who heard and experienced blasphemy to report its occurrence, on pain of a fine for failing to do so.[54]

Despite the obvious fact that this was a biblically inspired and fuelled system of retribution to please the God of the Bible, justices in America were not always comfortable with the administration of such laws. In some states, such as Maryland, which had been harsh on blasphemers, tolerance to all forms of trinitarian Christianity actively flourished. Most magistrates were similarly loath to carry out the ultimate sentence or even banishment in cases of blasphemy. Ten years before the Salem witch-hunts commenced, this same community treated the serial offender William King comparatively leniently, commuting a possible sentence of execution to whipping and imprisonment.[55] Occasionally individuals or groups who actively courted martyrdom would tie the hands of magistrates and judges. This seems to have been the case in Massachusetts, where the actions of Samuel Gorton's Quakers resulted in laws intended to exclude them, with corporal punishments and imprisonment for unlawful entry into the state. But sentences of corporal punishment and banishment were tried with limited success, and Massachusetts in 1659 felt obliged to execute

[51] The merits of these provisions are discussed in Theodore Schroeder, *Constitutional Free Speech Defined and Defended in an Unfinished argument in a case of Blasphemy* (New York, Free Speech League 1919; De Capo Press edn. 1970), 78–80. See also Andrew Dunlap, *A Speech delivered before the Municipal Court of the City of Boston in defence of Abner Kneeland on an Indictment for Blasphemy January Term 1834* (Boston, 1834) 59.

[52] Louise Taylor Merrill, 'The Puritan Policeman', *American Sociological Review*, 10: 6 (Dec. 1945), 766–76, at 770.

[53] Leo Pfeffer, *Church, State and Freedom* (Boston, 1967 edn.), 82–4, and Levy, *Blasphemy*, 238–59.

[54] George Packard, 'The Administration of Justice in the Lake Michigan Wilderness', *Michigan Law Review*, 17: 5 (Mar. 1919), 382–405.

[55] Carla Gardina Pestana, 'The Social World of Salem: William King's 1681 Blasphemy Trial', *American Quarterly*, 41: 2 (June 1989), 308–27.

the four Quakers who disobeyed sentences of banishment on pain of death. This is a reminder of how the actions of determined martyrs could confer the responsibility for repression and judicial murder upon what they viewed as an ungodly commonwealth. Indeed, at least one historian has suggested that the executions provoked an outcry which began the process of extending toleration to the sect in Massachusetts.[56]

Yet many judicial actions against blasphemers were more routine than this and persisted here for far longer than in other localities. Early eighteenth-century Connecticut had penalties for inappropriate behaviour in church, and these were frequently prosecuted within local communities. Sabbath-breaking was also prohibited, and the actions of some individuals who did this could shade into blasphemy. One individual in the district of Farmington in 1763 sat outside the church dressed inappropriately, uttering profanities that scared churchgoers and their horses. This individual may have been attached to a Ranter-like sect which took pride in profaning the Sabbath.[57] Evidence from many Connecticut counties suggests that the close control of public morals was still considered important at the turn of the eighteenth century. The prosecution of Sabbath-breaking remained a useful method of exerting control upon itinerant workers and socially dangerous groups.

Some colonies actively stepped away from forms of religious persecution, seeing this as anathema to the whole concept of religious toleration. The religious radical Roger Williams had been banished from Massachusetts for expressing such ideas in 1636. Williams himself eventually founded the Rhode Island colony, which placed religious tolerance at the heart of its legislative provisions. He went further, to argue in print that the civil power had no right and should have no power to influence individual conscience. Nonetheless, Rhode Island did consider blasphemy a criminal offence and protected only those whose beliefs were theistic.[58] Williams also condemned the intolerance of Massachusetts and Connecticut, collecting these arguments in *The Bloody Tenet of Persecution*. Williams's views were eventually incorporated into the later arguments of church-and-state separation advocates.[59]

Attempts to use blasphemy prosecution as the enforcement of a godly commonwealth in Scotland had broadly similar results. In the 1690s the actions and influence of Calvinist ministers secured the execution of Thomas Aitkenhead in1698. This was a particularly disturbing case, since it offered secular

---

[56] Cobb, *Rise of Religious Liberty*, 217–18.

[57] Richard Gaskin, 'Changes in the Criminal law in 18th Century Connecticut', *American Journal of Legal History*, 25: 4 (Oct. 1998), 309–42, at 319 and 332.

[58] See Frank Swancara, *Obstruction of Justice By Religion* (Denver, Colo., 1936), 214. See also Cobb, *Rise of Religious Liberty*, 422–40. See also Charter of Rhode Island and Providence Plantations, 1663 in C. H. Moehlman, *The American Constitution and Religion* (Berne, Ind., 1938), 27.

[59] Schroeder, *Constitutional Free Speech Defined*, 367.

Fig. 14. Roger Williams, the pioneer of terationist arguments. As celebrated by the American *Truthseeker*, c.1910.

government a glimpse of how clerical involvement in the issues of restoring ideological and moral order might yet bring punishment into disrepute. Aitkenhead was a naive student whose recantation fell upon deaf ears and whose death influenced a generation of jurists against wholesale religious involvement in this area of justice. If this was the theocratic state, jurists were sure they did not want it, at least not on Calvinism's terms.[60]

Although many American states retained the death penalty for blasphemy, from the end of the seventeenth century there was a growing unwillingness to use it. Many instances exist of individual states passing such sentences and commuting them to banishment, or forms of corporal punishment and lengthy imprisonment. A number of constructed and reconstructed state criminal justice codes from the end of the seventeenth century also recognized capital punishment's limitations. New Hampshire's redrawn code of 1702 removed the capital sentence, and a still later one focused upon corporal punishments and mutilation. Most others either downgraded the offence or redrew their existing criminal codes to adopt this new policy, the last being the state of Vermont at the end of the eighteenth century. Other states translated the death penalty into

---

[60] John Locke was severely critical of the Aitkenhead prosecution and made his views on the matter plain enough. See *State Trials*, xiii. 925–9.

a punishment of shame by merely symbolically carrying it out. Those convicted were taken to the place of execution and waited whilst the noose was placed around their neck. They would then stand in the sight of the whole community in that position for several hours. Such instances occurred occasionally in the seventeenth century and became more commonplace after this. These sentences indicated how the tenor of public and judicial opinion was moving away from the use of the ultimate penalty. The Massachusetts Blasphemy Act of 1782, for example, formally recognized how far the severity of sentences had been reduced. The act included provision for penalties of symbolic hanging, twelve months' imprisonment, the pillory, whipping, or binding over for good behaviour.[61] When New Jersey reconfirmed its blasphemy laws in 1800, those convicted would be subject to a fine of $200 and one year's imprisonment with hard labour.[62]

At first glance the growing leniency extended to blasphemers looks superficially like a process of liberalization. However, we should remember that the end of this period witnessed the construction of the American Constitution which unravelled the idea of a nationally established church, allowing instead freedom of conscience for the religious. Jefferson confirmed this in Bill No. 82 of 1779, which eventually became the model for the First Amendment. The philosophy behind this was designed to reflect freedom of choice and to make religious participation a matter of conscience rather than compulsion.[63] Thus, by the end of the eighteenth century there was substantial agreement that government did not have the legitimate power to impose any form of religious belief or attendance requirement upon its citizens. Although states were permitted their own laws, including support for religious establishment, this was of a plural nature. Thus, unlike their counterparts in Europe, American citizens were permitted to seek out the religion of their choice and engage with it rather than finding themselves co-opted members of a national church. This freedom, and the de facto pluralism of the American religious landscape, also began the enduring struggle between local, state-inspired rights and the federal, centralized law. This was to become an argument about local societies struggling against centralizing, cosmopolitan tendencies. These sometimes appeared to make local law seem virtuous and state law remote and condescending.

This also meant that the role of the English Common Law in America was ambivalent. As we have discovered, this law was considered organic, responsive, and sensitive to the finer points of individual cases. It also demonstrated that local justice could restore the community to order after a damaging experience. However, federalists who liked overarching precedent were also enamoured of

---

[61] Dunlap, *A Speech delivered before the Municipal Court of the City of Boston in defence of Abner Kneeland*, frontispiece.

[62] Laws of New Jersey 1800.

[63] John Ferling, *Setting the World Ablaze: Washington, Adams, Jefferson and the American Revolution* (Oxford, 2000), 158–9.

the English Common Law's ability to create and draw upon reliable case-law. In this respect, the Common Law felt distinctly like community law to both local individuals and state law officials. Leonard Levy notes the comparative absence of blasphemy prosecutions in America as indicative of a tolerance amongst those who constructed the federal law. We might also consider further his suggestion that those who lived within these societies encountered a variety of religious ideas and beliefs more easily and readily than their European counterparts.[64] The sparseness of population and its low density meant that the opportunites for the array of gambling and tavern disagreements or urban argument and encounter that characterized some blasphemy 'outbreaks' in Europe were much less likely to have occurred. Certainly, America's status as a haven of political and religious tolerance became something of a utopian fable amongst English radicals, and it periodically played an important role as a haven and refuge for religious heterodoxy. America may also have witnessed its own mitigation of the effects of procedural justice and the punishments laid down by Common Law. Just as judicial pardon was used in England to save individuals selectively from execution, it seems that benefit of clergy may have alleviated the severity of the law in some American colonies. A law of 1723 in Maryland removed benefit of clergy from the offence of blasphemy, prescribing the death penalty for a third offence.[65]

However, the American Constitution remained a reaction against the power of arbitrary government exercising arbitrary laws. Thomas Jefferson in particular considered the blasphemy law to be an especially pernicious example of such legislation.[66] In 1824 Jefferson wrote an angry letter to the radical Major Cartwright which was subsequently to become famous to students of American constitutional law. Jefferson argued that the Common Law had existed in the pagan Anglo-Saxon world, and that its later equation with the Christian state stemmed from the famous seventeenth-century mistranslations of Sir Henry Finch. This had mistakenly assumed Common Law to be a specific product of Christianity in England, when later analysts were satisfied it pre-dated this religious establishment. Such mistakes, Jefferson had argued, compounded in subsequent works and case-law, were capable of profound misuse in the hands of lawyers who were building legal castles in the air. Through them, the spurious doctrine expounded by Sir Matthew Hale became central to English Common Law. Towards the end of this letter Jefferson stepped out of his scholarly attitude to offer an enlightenment swipe against such pretensions: 'What a conspiracy this, between Church

---

[64] John Ferling, *Setting the World Ablaze*: 268.

[65] Jeffrey K. Sawyer, '"Benefit of clergy" in Maryland and Virginia', *American Journal of Legal History*, 34: 1 (Jan. 1990), 49–68, at 64. See also George W. Dalzell, *Benefit of Clergy in America* (Winston-Salem, 1955).

[66] For more on Jefferson's separation of religious and social obligation see J. William Frost, *A Perfect Freedom: Religious Liberty in Pennsylvania* (Cambridge, 1990), 92–5.

and State! Sing Tantarara, rogues all, rogues all. Sing Tantarara, rogues all.'[67]

By the eighteenth century judicial consideration of blasphemy in England was wrapped up with publication and dissemination. Whereas previous centuries had seen the sermon as the primary method of disturbing the public peace, seditious and dangerous writings were increasingly seen as a more pressing danger. The eighteenth century saw the suppression of translations of Servetus and other works critical of established religion. This was, however, piecemeal and only became actively systematized as late as the Napoleonic era. However, the eighteenth century saw England enact punishments upon infamous deists like Jacob Ilive and Peter Annet. Ilive was imprisoned, with hard labour and confinement in the pillory, whilst Annet had his sentence commuted under an array of mitigating circumstances which included his advanced age, pleas for mercy, and consideration of his extreme poverty.[68]

With the later association of deist and freethinking opinions with Jacobinism, government was much more ready to associate blasphemy with sedition.[69] Thus began a series of prosecutions of booksellers, publishers, printers, and eventually lowly shop-assistants, who could all be implicated in the writing and dissemination of such unpopular views. The prosecutions of individuals, such as that of Thomas Williams in 1797, were careful to equate press freedom with English liberty and to suggest that one crime Thomas Paine's deistical views perpetrated was to abuse such freedom. Throughout, prosecuting counsels would argue that tempered and mannered criticism was thoroughly acceptable, whilst invective and outright denial were clearly not. In asserting this, the argument of Hale, that religion was 'part and parcel', would readily come to the aid of most prosecution arguments in cases of blasphemous libel.[70] Seditious publications that attacked religion thereby attacked the law. Defence arguments were eager to show honourable motives, and Paine's *Age of Reason* was cast by defendants as a deist work, intended to combat the French slide into outright atheism.

The use of blasphemous libel initially appeared a useful weapon in the armoury of governmental control and repression. The English constitutional link between church, state, and prosperity, a situation abandoned by the unfortunate French, meant that it was casting defendants upon the mercy of (hopefully) loyalist juries in England. Philip Harling suggests that most libel prosecutions occurred during crisis-points for the government. Eventually the authorities gave up prosecuting individuals for blasphemy and seditious libel, because it was sometimes difficult to

---

[67] Dunlap, *A Speech delivered before the Municipal Court of the City of Boston in defence of Abner Kneeland*, 82.

[68] Bradlaugh-Bonner, *Penalties Upon Opinion*, 36–7.

[69] See esp. Robert Hole, *Pulpits, Politics and Public Order in England 1760–1832* (Cambridge, 1989), 200–1.

[70] *Howell's State Trials* (1797), 'Proceedings against Thomas Williams for Publishing Paine's "Age of Reason"', 653–720. 26, p. 661.

secure a conviction. Fox's Libel Act of 1792 gave much power to juries to establish the tendency of an opinion to provoke a breach of the peace. Yet the unreliability and arbitrary nature of the law of libel made its use against seditious nuisances a considerable risk. Harling suggests that it was more successful as 'a formidable instrument of harassment'. The method of targeting individuals with ex-officio informations could make life very difficult for anyone caught by them. These could be used to arrest suspected libellers, who then found mounting a defence fraught with difficulty. The cost of sureties could be crippling, and sometimes the legal costs of answering such an information were also prohibitive. The mechanism also deprived the defendants of even remotely adequate knowledge of the information laid against them. When these eventually arrived in court they were well-prepared and comprehensive. The information laid against Carlile in 1819 for publishing Paine's *Age of Reason* contained eleven separate counts, indicting him for describing the Bible as obscene and vice-ridden, and for questioning the Virgin Birth and the authenticity of the scriptures.[71] Courtroom procedures could also be heavily stacked against the defendant. Harling notes that the court was not obliged to inform the defendant of the order in which informations would be heard. Similarly, the dates and venues of trials could be hastily rearranged without notice. Libel cases were also tried before hand-picked special juries. These could be strongly influenced by government pressure, and their composition shaped to secure a desired result. It seems clear that the perils of being imprisoned at the behest of an ex-officio information terrorized those who had sold blasphemous newspapers rather than the authors of them. It also seems likely that this became fused into government policy. It might well be difficult to muzzle individual writers, but the ability of the government to constrain the supply of such writings seemed an important consolation.[72]

But not everything always went quite so smoothly for government and its unofficial supporters. Even before prosecutions foundered, successful ones produced unwelcome publicity and the courtroom too often provided a further platform for the views which had been the source of prosecution. However, the single biggest mistake occurred when government and the Vice Society between them were significantly over-zealous in their pursuit of the radical William Hone. This satirist's *Sinecurist's Creed* attracted attention because of its obvious rewording of an article of faith. Hone's case indicated how arbitrary the decision to prosecute could be in practice, and his defence of citing similar unmolested material in circulation made precisely this point. Such prosecutions functioned as a form of low-level terror aimed at trapping destitute shopmen, who often cowered in the dock. In this respect these laws appeared to function in a manner

---

[71] *A Copy of the Information exhibited ex officio, January 23, 1819, by His Majesty's Attorney General, Against Richard Carlile, for Publishing Paine's 'Age of Reason'* (London, 1819), 3–14.

[72] Philip Harling, 'The Law of Libel and the Limits of Repression, 1790–1832', *Historical Journal*, 44: 1 (2001), 107–34.

that the first generation of Marxist historians ascribed to the eighteenth-century 'bloody code'. Procedural intimidation, alongside the monetary cost of being caught up in a prosecution, deterred all but the most determined. Such tactics and procedures may have worked against the desperate, but articulate radicals like Hone were more than the authorities bargained for, and could also prove a nuisance.

The dominant theme of depriving blasphemers of civil rights was pervasive in the early nineteenth century—but it could take peculiar, or indeed laughably counter-productive, forms. One particular tactic was to refuse the protection of copyright to material found to be guilty of blasphemous libel. This was aimed at the commonplace Vice Society concern that radicals cynically made money out of dangerous material. This also elaborated loyalist views that there could be precious little other reason for individuals to embark on such activities. Such a view also inordinately influenced the prosecution of the lowly, as the association between poverty and infidelity became self-fulfilling prophesy in the courtroom. Deprivation of copyright was intended to ensure that incomes could not be made out of dangerous material by the especially unscrupulous. This unfortunately forgot that unscrupulousness was not the monopoly of the blasphemer, as booksellers and printers saw blasphemous works as fair game and a guarantee of sales. Not paying the author for the privilege of publication made the economics still more attractive, and ensured that, paradoxically, numerous pirated editions of dangerously blasphemous works would circulate still further.

However, leading jurists and philosophers had already interested themselves in how far prosecuting and punishing blasphemy benefited society and fostered respect for the law's workings. No less an individual than John Locke had openly questioned the conduct of the Aitkenhead case in Scotland at the end of the seventeenth century, and, in the spirit of the enlightenment, he noted that it was a clear instance of what could happen if notions of a godly commonwealth were allowed to run amok over the proper rational application of the law. In this instance religion was not seen solely as a dangerous form of interference but also as a system of interpretation that had no mandate within a modern community. Similar tests of social utility had been conducted upon the criminal law by the impact of philosophical radicalism at the Home Office, and the issue of respect for the law began to creep into discussions about blasphemy.

This heightened level of scepticism certainly influenced those who oversaw the new constitutions that were constructed during the age of nineteenth-century revolutions. Perhaps the earliest of these was the Belgian Constitution, which removed a blanket offence of blasphemy in 1815 to replace it with more specific, public-order style offences. One grievance which especially highlighted the problems of utility and respect for the law was the tendency of the legal system to target and make an example of the weak. Thomas Erskine had reacted violently against the Vice Society's hounding of the poor, and he refused his fee, on one occasion, for having conducted a prosecution on their behalf. Of greater significance was the unfortunate tendency of the law to demonstrate its full force against the insane and feeble-minded. The end of the seventeenth century had witnessed the case against Susannah Fowles, an individual who attacked the Lord's Prayer in the course of a series of episodes that could only have been the product of mental illness. Similarly, one of Richard Carlile's associates, Robert Taylor, was prosecuted and imprisoned where modern opinion would probably seek psychiatric reports on his mental condition. Perhaps more influential than these cases of insanity was the Victorian case which most readily put the laws themselves in to the dock.

The Foote case of 1883–4 in many respects displayed simultaneously the wisest and most ill-advised application of justice in this area. The fact that the case came to court at all was largely due to the obstinacy of the home secretary Sir William Harcourt. It was he who insisted that an example was to be made of Foote and his outrageous attitudes. Prosecution was imperative, at every stage the Home Office under Harcourt opposed bail, and even after conviction insisted upon overseeing the prisoner's visting arrangements whilst he was incarcerated. Most tellingly of all, Harcourt's actions did not remove, or significantly counter, the impact of Foote's blasphemy, since his case became a cause célèbre. This involved a campaign of petitions from the world of letters as well as dramatically enhanced notoriety and circulation for Foote's newspaper the *Freethinker*. Whilst rationalists could be expected to complain, the attitude of liberal Christians suggested how far the tide was running against a blasphemy law that would imprison and punish. Canon Shuttleworth, on behalf of the socially progressive Anglican Guild of St Matthew, argued:

If blasphemy be an offence against God, then, surely, it is not for man to measure guilt, or to apportion its punishment. . . . The only essential difference between Mr. Matthew Arnold's sarcasms and the caricatures of Mr. Foote is one of refinement. The one is polished, keen, suggestive, the other rough, outspoken, and course [*sic*]. One wields the rapier, the other brandishes the bludgeon.[73]

Unequivocally, the Common Law of blasphemous libel was discredited by this whole affair. Advice to over-enthusiastic home secretaries or civil servants after this was to exercise caution and restraint. Although monitoring of Foote and his works continued, the policy was to allow scoffing and ridicule to have its short moment in the public eye, which would pass just as rapidly.

When Justice Coleridge presided over the last of the three trials Foote faced in 1883, he set aside the verdict against him. His pronouncement, in so doing, became for almost a century the last word of guidance about blasphemous libel. Modernization weighed upon his decision to set aside the ideas of Sir Matthew Hale and to declare, in tones that must have shocked traditionalists in the

---

[73] HO 144 114/A25454, letters protesting against the treatment of Foote and the verdict against him and Ramsay. Item 503, London, Mar. 1883.

JESUS CANOEING.

" *And in the fourth watch of the night Jesus weut unto them walking on the sea.*"—MATTHEW xiv., 25.

Fig. 15. G. W. Foote's rendering of Matthew 14: 25.

established church, that Christianity could no longer be considered 'part and parcel' of the law of the land. This gave up the church-state link in this area of jurisdiction, and set the two upon divergent courses. Henceforth the test of whether a publication, or speech; was blasphemous did not rely upon the words constituting an attack upon beliefs or doctrine. Such attacks were now considered a part of free speech, the offence lay in the intention behind such actions. If maliciousness, a patent desire to upset or wound, or the display of arrogant scoffing were present then these would constitute the offence. Many were to sum this up in assertions that the offence of blasphemy had been transformed from an emphasis upon 'matter' to an emphasis upon 'manner'. This was perhaps more far-sighted than it appeared to contemporaries, and it was to endure as an influential path in English law.[74] What seemed to opponents to be a simple updating of anachronistic practices was asking new things of the Christian religion and its practitioners. Henceforth other forms of protection would have to fortify the believer against those who might offend. Ending this church–state link encouraged some to find more concrete and credible defences for their beliefs. Others on both sides of the offence must clearly have learned to tell the difference between debate and scurrility.

The logic of the Coleridge judgement was that religion was an area that was ripe for free and, if necessary, heated discussion. American law reached surprising conclusions when it grappled with the legal legacy that it had been left by its erstwhile colonial status, alongside its patchwork quilt of state jurisdictions. Since America was intent upon resolving the church–state issue, it is scarcely a surprise that it concluded, almost seventy years earlier than Justice Coleridge, that intention was important. The case against Ruggles involved a defence that the state lacked a statute enforcing blasphemy. There were also important arguments about how far English Common Law had infiltrated the state constitution of New York. Ruggles's defence clearly focused upon the American Constitution's denial of a church established by law. In the absence of this it could have been argued that the Constitution therefore guaranteed religious liberty. However, Chief Justice Kent acknowledged and promoted the spirit of the Hale judgement and its construction of religion as 'part and parcel'. Nonetheless, there remained the vexed question of whether the Constitution's rights of free speech could be used to protect a blasphemer. Once again the ghost of Sir Matthew Hale hung over the decision in this instance, since Christianity was seen as enabling good order to prevail. Whilst a case could be made for the blasphemer possessing such rights, the judgement in this instance argued that these impinged upon the rights of those wishing to follow their own religious observance. This argument about conflict of rights in relation to free speech asked how differing opinions would live and coexist in the community. Individuals had the right to worship, yet other individuals had the right to criticize and attack the beliefs of Christians which they might find abhorrent. Justice Kent eventually argued that these issues could be reconciled by focusing upon the intention and manner of those who

---

[74] Interestingly, the law in Ireland had been forced to exonerate a Catholic friar for burning a pile of books which, he was unaware, contained copies of the Protestant Bible. His acquittal clearly turned on the issues associated with intention. See Paul O'Higgins, 'Blasphemy in Irish Law', *Modern Law Review*, 23: 2 (Mar. 1960), 151–66 at 162.

would speak. Opinions were one thing, but attacks were quite another, and this invented the concept of 'manner' which was eventually to be so influential in England.

This clearly demonstrated a pattern of how the Common Law of blasphemy was capable of unravelling, a process which would potentially take it away from governments, discipline, and the control of morality into the realm of protecting the rights of speech and belief in communities at large. A case in Pennsylvania in 1824, in which the judge adopted a similar stance to that of New York, took this further. This co-opted English Common Law also, making the distinction between honest doubt or belief and scoffing contemptuous opinions. The constitutional guarantee of free speech in this instance was seen as something that came to the rescue of marginal but otherwise responsible religious groups like the Unitarians. A later decision in the state of Delaware further confirmed that Christianity was to be given preference in practice over both other religions and the rights of individuals to free speech as defined and confirmed by the Constitution. Each of these cases showed a different jurisdiction coming to terms with problems bequeathed to it by the legacy of English Common Law and its own, very different aspirations.[75]

The issue of whether English Common Law had been transmitted into these new jurisdictions would arise again, not simply in the American context but also when other dominions, such as Australia, asked whether such crimes existed within their boundaries. Several issues were refined in the light of the case against Abner Kneeland and the judgement of Justice Shaw in this case. This reconfirmed the surreptitious creep of English Common Law into the laws of individual American states, bringing a number of qualifications to bear on the open-ended nature of individual rights. For example, the case illuminated the fact that judges could suggest that liberty of the press was only the licence to publish without prior consent from a legal officer. Individuals who then exercised their rights through publication nonetheless remained responsible for the material they published. This had wider dimensions, since it was argued here that permitting blasphemous opinions to appear in print might act as encouragement for incitement to a range of other heinous criminal acts. The issue of individual religious liberty was also answered through reference to the manner of individual utterances. Again the issue of style and context raised its head, so intention became an important test of this issue, reinforcing a strong public-order dimension.[76]

However, the tide of opinion did not always run in a direction that would support the adoption of English Common Law or its assumptions. A case in

---

[75] For further discussion see Stewart Banner, 'When Christianity was Part of the Common Law', *Law and History Review*, 16: 1 (Spring 1998), 27–62.

[76] 'Blasphemy. What Constitutes Offense under Maine Statute', *Virginia Law Register*, 7: 11 (Mar. 1922), 855–8, at 857.

Kentucky in 1894 against Charles Moore demonstrated that the failure to have an earlier precedent meant that states confronting this problem in the later part of the nineteenth century would do things differently. Moore was prosecuted for having published in a newspaper, *Blue Grass Blade*, a ribald portrayal of the incarnation 'as the result of a sort of Breckinridge–Pollard hyphenation between God and a Jew woman'. This reference alluded to a recent breach-of-promise case in which a Colonel Breckinridge had conceived a child with a significantly younger woman. The Moore case was interesting since it overturned Justice Kent's ruling in the Ruggles case. Judge Parker, presiding, argued that a law of blasphemy was clearly associated with a church–state link that was nowhere a reality within the American Constitution. Thus, English Common Law did not creep seamlessly into the state law of Kentucky. Indeed the judge, Justice Parker, inevitably concluded that a law of blasphemy was effectively unconstitutional, pronouncing, 'this crime must be considered a stranger to the laws of Kentucky.'[77]

That the tide had turned decisively was emphasized by the first US blasphemy case of the twentieth century, in which a Lithuanian immigrant, Michael Mockus, was prosecuted in Connecticut in 1916. He was also prosecuted in Illinois, where the judge denied that a statute of blasphemy existed and excluded English Common Law from the legal agenda. Mockus also found himself in trouble in the state of Maine when he continued to lecture. In this state he was finally brought to account and convicted on eight counts of blasphemy. The reaction to him as a communist social revolutionary resembled the treatment of Aldred, Pack, Gott, and Stewart in England.[78]

Theodore Schroeder, the constitutional expert and co-founder of the Free Speech League of America, saw the Connecticut prosecution of Mockus as an opportunity to test the limitations and credibility of American jurisprudence upon blasphemy. Schroeder, in stating the defence in this case, noted that the protection of constitutional rights seemed to be extended to the respectable more readily than to others. This echoed the 'buckram bound' argument that opponents of blasphemy laws used in England to assert that it was a crime which punished coarseness rather than wounding.[79] He also reminded American Society that maintaining free speech was occasionally a calculated but necessary risk. As Schroeder put it: 'the constitutional guarantees for equality, for religious liberty, and for freedom of speech were not limited in their operation to those who possess any particular degree of culture, or a polite and approved literary style, or for the protection of persons expressing only 'safe and sane' popular opinions.' But Schroeder went further, suggesting that constitutional rights were intended precisely as enabling mechanisms, rather than limitations that required

---

[77] Schroeder, *Constitutional Free Speech Defined*, 60.
[78] For Mockus's conviction in Maine see *State* v. *Mockus*, 120 Maine 84, 113 Atl. 39 (1921).
[79] See 'Blasphemy Analyzed', *The Truthseeker*, 45:12 (New York), 23 Mar. 1918.

policing. In this he was especially critical of Blackstone. Reworking the suggestion that blasphemy laws constituted an anachronism, Schroeder declared:

I believe the future historian will say that this case is the most important prosecution that has come before a Court of this State for a century. I know that if this case is not terminated in accord with the sentiments of the more enlightened portion of the community, your decision will necessarily place a club in the hands of the intolerant and bigoted, whereby the intelligent ones can be cowed and silenced in matters of religious controversy.[80]

The potential ambiguity of law within different American states, further complicated by constitutional amendments guaranteeing freedom and rights, made navigating a way through the legal status of blasphemy a complicated project for any lawyer. In the Mockus case, Theodore Schroeder's defence (mindful of unhelpful precedents set by the Ruggles case) had to encourage the court to be prepared to make precedent anew. Other rhetorical devices could also be called into play. Schroeder compared different interpretations of the Constitution and differences over religious doctrine, allying these to 'temperament' and 'disposition'. In this he hoped such arguments would destabilize the existing 'certainty' about the law in favour of setting new precedents from what he termed 'scientific' method. The use of a 'scientific method' allowed Schroeder to argue that the Constitution was in a constant state of evolution, so that: 'We must see each of the guarantees as a fragmentary means of accomplishing a unified purpose, which in this case is the protection of an ever-perfecting concept of enlarging intellectual freedom.'[81] However, the Supreme Court turned against this view, with the conservative suggestion that religion determined the nature of civil government, so that reverence for this religion was a safeguard of its stability.[82]

Schroeder eventually distilled his experiences into a Free Speech League pamphlet instructing juries upon their duties in blasphemy cases. In stressing the implications of equality of liberty, Schroeder noted that Christians who objected to blasphemous words were claiming special privileges akin to those of established churches:

Before our Revolution it was always the privilege of the orthodox Christians to hold up to ridicule and contempt the false conception of God or of religion as entertained by the heathen. Our constitutional guarantees of free speech did not take that right away from the Christian. It rather confirmed it as a legitimate weapon against whatever a Christian may consider pernicious error.[83]

Beyond this, the United States' experience of blasphemy in the twentieth century remained a guerrilla war between federal and state individual conceptions of

---

[80] See 'Blasphemy Analyzed', *The Truthseeker*, 19.   [81] Ibid. 24–37 and 43.
[82] *State* v. *Mockus*, 120 Maine. 84, 113 Atl. 39 (1921), p. 93.
[83] Theodore Schroeder, *Law of Blasphemy: The Modern View Exhibited in Model Instructions to a Jury.* (New York, Free Speech League, 1919), 11.

law. Although local systems of justice displayed greater levels of enthusiasm for pursuing blasphemers, such pursuit could prove embarrassing. When the freethinker Charles Smith protested against the putative Arkansas state statute prohibiting the teaching of evolution in public schools, legal action was taken against him. Signs displayed in the windows of his headquarters declaring the Bible to be a fabrication were considered an act liable to breach the peace. When a small fine was imposed, Smith refused to go quietly and was subsequently jailed, where he opted for a very public hunger strike. After the police became embarrassed about this, Smith was quietly released and was able to continue his activities. This showed that, however much local jurisdictions might want to defend their own community morality, enforcing this could bring the law into disrepute. Occasionally there were instances where a community defended itself with some success. In 1942 a Jehovah's Witness in New Hampshire was tried under a section of the state's public laws which forbade the use of 'offensive or annoying words' or the use of 'derisive names' against individuals who were lawfully in a public place. The defendant had denounced all religions as a 'racket' and insulted a local marshal as a 'God damned racketeer' and 'a damned fascist'. The appeal court waved away the appellant's claims to Fourteenth Amendment protection by acutely observing that 'we cannot conceive that cursing a public officer is the exercise of religion in any sense of the term'.[84]

Blasphemy finally disappeared from the American legal landscape as the expansion of First Amendment freedoms rendered a blasphemy statute almost totally unconstitutional. For the first half of the twentieth century defendants had offered this defence with growing success. The final act in this was the US Supreme Court's acceptance of this defence in the 1951 Rossellini *The Miracle* case, when the court agreed that a ban on the film was prior restraint upon free speech. In communicating its decision, the court rightly argued that any form of religious censorship would inevitably become a form of favouritism, making the role of such a censor arguably impossible. Justice Clark saw further that First Amendment rights were clearly in danger, through his argument that a test of the 'sacrilegious' would question the guarantee of church–state separation. Most tellingly of all, the judgement concluded that the suppression of attacks upon religious ideas should never be the function of government or its agencies. The appeal confirmed that: 'If there is any fixed star in our constitution . . . it is that no official, high or petty, can prescribe what shall be orthodox in politics, nationalism, religion or other matters of opinion.'[85] These views were effectively reconfirmed in a case which arose in Maryland in 1968. Nonetheless, individual states still retained theoretical powers to at least commence blasphemy

---

[84] *Chaplinsky* v. *New Hampshire*, 315 US 568 (1942).

[85] *Burstyn* v. *Wilson*, 343, US 495 (1952). & In the Matter of Joseph Burstyn, Inc., Appellant, against Lewis A. Wilson, as Commissioner of Education of the state of New York, *et al.*, Respondents. New York Court of Appeals, 1951.

WHAT UNCLE SAM SHOULD DO.

Fig. 16. The separation argument plainly stated.

prosecutions. In the years immediately following the Burstyn case it was possible to find versions of blasphemy statutes in Connecticut, Delaware, Iowa, Maine, Maryland, Massachusetts, and nine other states.[86]

Australia underwent a similar investigation of its inheritance from the English Common Law. The William Lorando Jones case of 1871 (in which an individual declared the Bible to be immoral) allowed the judge to grapple with both English Common Law, and the Hale judgement in the courtroom. Christianity, so it was argued, was part of the Common Law and to attack it was thus to break the law. This view was confirmed when the attorney-general denounced a bill hostile to the Common Law interpretation which had been put before the New South Wales legislative assembly in a reaction to the Jones case. In doing so the attorney-general went further than probably anyone else in associating Christianity with the maintenance of simple morality. Not only did he declare that it was permissable to attack Catholicism, but the ideals of the Anglican

---

[86] The full list is Connecticut, Delaware, Iowa, Maine, Maryland, Massachusetts, Michigan, New Hampshire, New Jersey, North Dakota, Oklahoma, Pennsylvania, Rhode Island, South Dakota, and Vermont.

church, represented by the Thirty Nine Articles, were also not protected from attack. In the Australian context it was suggested that the support of the scriptures for the rule of law was what Common Law had bequeathed to the nation. Atheists, rather than being critics of Christianity, were individuals who attacked morality through their choice of target and not through the way they conducted their attacks. Whilst blasphemy was not, as a result of this debate, removed from the Australian statute book, sufficient vocal opposition had led to a reduction in the sentence served by Jones. When the issue of blasphemy arose again in Australia, as a colonial offshoot of the case against Foote in 1883, government had to adopt newer and wilier tactics. The authorities chose to use other methods against the English freethought immigrant Joseph Symes, since his lecture events, generally organized on a Sunday, were prosecuted under the sabbatarian entertainment legislation.[87]

Whilst this sort of attrition would occur in American law and in the legal systems of former empire territories, the process of reform in England itself moved more slowly. The English Common Law was so intrinsic to many other areas of the law's activities, that undermining it in the manner the Americans had done was not possible. Yet the fallout of the Foote case after 1883 meant those who were politically radical considered the blasphemy laws to be a piece of class-ridden legislation. Despite the fact that individual radical MPs would consider this to be an issue, it never became a party-political one. Therefore, whenever the matter came before parliament it was always in the guise of a private member's bill which government chief whips would invariably do their best to block at every stage. There was, ostensibly, no obvious political advantage for any individual party in adopting the measure of blasphemy-law repeal as its own. The law clearly looked discriminatory, but to take action against the established church would have been courting political disaster. Attempts were made both before and after the First World War, and abolition bills appeared roughly every two years in the 1920s. The greatest chances of success came in 1929 and again in the middle of the 1930s. On each of these occasions government would not support the bill, although successive home secretaries were nonetheless prepared to listen to the arguments of the Society for the Abolition of the Blasphemy Laws. These were augmented by the numerous members of the great and the good it assembled in its defence. Invariably they argued that the law did not work fairly, was partial, and was thus effectively an anachronism.

Although home secretaries expressed varying degrees of sympathy, when such attitudes were publicized around the Home Office itself views were rather harsher than this. Generally speaking, civil servants refused to recognize that the law was a dead letter. The most common attitude was to express concern about just how order was to be kept if religious opinions were to inflame crowds or readers of scurrilous and blasphemous works. Occasionally an individual would

---

[87] P. Coleman, *Obscenity, Blasphemy, Sedition: Censorship in Australia.* (Brisbane, 1966), 86–94.

go further than this, and advance an opinion upon the value of the law and the benevolence of its function. One such individual in 1913 took exception to the arguments that blasphemy was an anachronism, declaring: 'First it is said that the law under which defendants are tried is old and obsolete. This is untrue: the law of blasphemy is on the contrary a striking instance of the Common Law adapting itself to the times and changing in accordance with a general change of view in regard to reigious matters.'[88] This pointed out to the home secretary, and whoever else would listen, that the law was not out of date because it was based on the organic Common Law. The law would thus adapt to circumstances and would display, quite readily, what was acceptable or unacceptable in society at any given time. As far as this civil servant was concerned this was a real strength of the law, and as such it should be protected from those who would weaken it. Opponents of this view argued that because the law existed, its use and its penalties would forever be contemplated by judges, lawyers, and legislators.

For those who believed in free speech, such laws festered on the statute book and were an untimely reminder of past persecution. Their eclipse and apparent unpopularity also meant that the suppression of blasphemous material occurred through other avenues. One primary method of proceeding was to consider the material in question to be obscene rather than blasphemous. This was significant, since this category of material received considerably less legal protection or indeed public sympathy. Ernest Pack was always insistent that blasphemy and obscenity had become synonymous terms, and that the Edwardian prosecutions of himself, Gott, and Stewart had used the association with Malthusian ideas to strengthen this link.[89] Evidence exists that obscenity also became a useful charge in America, where the Charles Moore *Blue Grass Blade* case was also brought under Kentucky's obscenity laws. This was especially important, since obscenity received no protection under the First Amendment.

Sometimes present persecution would highlight the danger of such legal relics in the hands of unscrupulous enemies of free speech and modern civilization. This particular phenomenon was highlighted in 1938, when an MP with far-Right Nordic League connections, Archibald Maule Ramsay, attempted to have the blasphemy laws extended to make it possible to expel Jewish communist freethinkers from Britain. In the agitated political climate of Munich and 1938, numerous MPs on all sides of the house lurched into a panic which led many to support him and his views. Although swift action by the government ensured that there were no real repercussions from this incident, it demonstrated to progressives that laws ought to be useful, beneficial, and a credit to the society that retained them.[90]

---

[88] HO4524619, Copy of Memo in 216120/86 signed HB c.May 1913.

[89] Ernest Pack, *The Trial and Imprisonment of J. W. Gott for Blasphemy* (Freethought Socialist League, Bradford, 1912), 80.

[90] See the memos of civil servants in advising the home secretary, contained in HO4524619/217459/247and HO4524619/217459/274.

Law-making and law reform within this climate led most societies in the West to re-evaluate their approach to religious expression and utterance. It was argued that society was now plural, and morality was no more linked to the maintenance of good order in the way that the medieval or early modern period insisted. This was an overall confidence in the power of tolerance, with religion considered to be a private matter. Such views were utopian, but more importantly they were also Eurocentric and over-optimistic, as we have seen from Chapter 1. But initially, forms of liberalization did occur in the post-war period. We have already seen that the assumption of greater scope within the American First Amendment meant that blasphemy would no longer appear in American courts. In Europe a process of attrition began that would bring blasphemy prosecutions and the whole concept to the brink of extinction.

In France the long-cherished distance between the state and the church had long since removed blasphemy laws and statutes. Meanwhile several European countries made moves to severely limit the scope of the offence. Jurisdictions such as Belgium and Spain (since 1988) and to a lesser extent Germany came to assume that if the informed consent of individuals was sought and could be expected then those accused of blasphemy would not be convicted. This also recognized that modern offences would occur in the context of publication, display, or performance—the encounter with the blasphemer at a distance. The issue of consent became related to public space and the ability of passers-by to give informed consent to visual material. This was important in a Belgian case in which painted portrayals of the stations of the cross displayed in the centre of Ghent showed figures engaged in sexual acts. These were considered to 'offend good morals'; whilst the action protected the unwary, this was also acknowledging the public-order dimension which lurked beneath.[91] Some countries, such as the Republic of Ireland, found their supreme courts arguing that case-law was simply not clear enough to define blasphemy, and this has rendered the issue almost impossible to pursue in court ever since.

Other jurisdications, such as Germany, placed a strong emphasis upon any case of blasphemy having to prove the outright intent of the blasphemer to offend and upset. Echoing Coleridge, issues of manner and content were important, although in practice this distinction could be made to seem very slight. This demonstrated that jurisdictions were preoccupied with making blasphemy law, precise and liable to strict tests for conviction. Even Italy, with a more thriving culture of blasphemy law dismissed objections to Scorsese's *The Last Temptation of Christ* because no evidence existed of malicious intent in making or releasing the film. All of this appeared to insist that blasphemy law should be persuaded to wither away, whilst the job of government was to assist this process through refinement and limitation.

---

[91] Interights and Article 19, *Blasphemy and Film Censorship: Submission to the European Court of Human Rights in Respect of Nigel Wingrove v. The United Kingdom* (1995), 13 and 15.

Erosion also seemed to be firmly under way in Britain, where the Coleridge construction of 'manner' had kept blasphemy away from the courtroom since the 1920s. Evidence that review and modernization were liable to account for the extinction of blasphemy seemed well founded when the statute law (9 & 10 William III c.32) was repealed in the context of the Criminal Justice Act of 1967. This alteration went almost unnoticed, and only became highlighted ten years later when the Common Law offence of blasphemous libel was reactivated, to everyone's surprise. The year of the queen's Silver Jubilee witnessed the English Common Law used to prosecute the editor of *Gay News*. The verdict of the law lords in the appeal, however, took the case-law back to the condition it was in before Coleridge had pronounced upon the importance of the 'manner' of someone's speech or publication. All of these issues about style, intention, context, audience, and manner ceased to be defences in court against the Common Law of blasphemous libel. The prosecuting counsel in *Gay News* argued that these issues of 'tone' and 'spirit' were the test of guilt rather than being the substance of the offence. Henceforth, noble motives, or even straightforwardly honest ones, were not enough. An offended party had merely to prove the fact of publication. Once the issue had come to court, the issue of the 'victim' suffering offence was itself no longer relevant.

This made the laws of England significantly buck the trend being established elsewhere, and the tide of liberalization was seen to have turned in England. Not only was the law more draconian again, but its reconfirmation emphasized that the law protected merely Christianity and, if strictly applied, only the Anglican church. Those who protested would frequently argue that these judgements contravened wider declarations of human rights and other internationally applied standards of justice and morality.

Many commentators invoked such international standards as a measure intended to protect newer rationalist beliefs against the spurious claims of religion and older standards of belief and moral behaviour. The United Nations Declaration signed in 1948 contained precisely such provisions to protect liberty, and many of these had a rationalist libertarian ring to them. Article 26, concerning education, affirmed that it was to be directed 'to the full development of the human personality'. Those of specific libertarian mindsets could quickly have argued that religion, by its nature, could be construed as opposed to this principle. However, the issues raised about equality before the law prompted religious groups and organizations to investigate further the wider meaning of human-rights declarations. Another article of the Declaration (Article 7) stated that: 'All are equal before the law and are entitled without any discrimination to equal protection of the law. All are entitled to equal protection against any discrimination in violation of this Declaration.' The arguments of the religious against such a declaration turned around three material issues. The first was to highlight the inconsistency and discriminatory nature of some laws that have been inherited by modern societies, generally those with previously religious establishments. These only protected one denomination of Christianity, in contravention of the spirit (if not in fact the letter) of the Universal Declaration of Human Rights. The second has been to argue that states which seek to be secular as a species of neutrality are deluding themselves. Such states, by enforcing the removal of religious ideas and discourses from public life, are acting in a manner that discriminates against the religious.

Blasphemy might be allowed to become something of an irrelevance, but the search was on for statutory instruments with which to replace it. These could be found in articles in the German Criminal Code, the Spanish Constitution, and an offence in the Swiss Constitution carrying a penalty of unlimited imprisonment. This change of atmosphere, which happened rapidly during the 1990s, is starkly emphasized by the survey of European jurisdictions offered by the organization Article 19 in 1995 and the Report of the Select Committee of the House of Lords report published in 2003. As we have seen, the House of Lords tried to reconcile the competing claims of various religions. Yet the imperative remained when religiously motivated attacks occurred throughout Europe, public order was at risk, and solutions needed to be explored.

Thus, we have almost come full circle in our search for a history of detecting and punishing blasphemy and its offshoots. Society once more is at the centre of the search for legal answers to problems caused by society's moral and religious makeup. Where medieval society wanted the errant individual to be restored to or excluded from their community in the name of Christian civilization, modern law wishes to mobilize the community to provide inclusive comfort to the temporarily oppressed. Only our middle period, where the individual's rights took centre stage, remains something of a modernist liberal blot upon a landscape of paternalist fears.

6

Responses to Blasphemy: Victims and Communities

Past histories have not always been kind to those who believed they were the victims of blasphemy. Some see their views as anachronistic, whilst free-speech-inspired historians suggested they were merely vocal obstacles to the inevitable arrival of religious toleration. Considering blasphemy's longevity makes the history of this particular area increasingly important, and this history becomes much richer than we had previously supposed. We have already encountered some of blasphemy's theological critics, but we must also explain the array of popular movements that organized themselves to protect Christian society from unwarranted attack. From medieval confraternities, followed by societies for the suppression of vice, and culminating in modern media watchdogs, the popular machinery of scrutinizing religious expression has had a significant and unappreciated history. The thoughts and behaviour of these rational responses remain easier to explore than the simple 'fear' of the blasphemer that stalked a society much more accustomed to the idea of divine intervention in everyday life. Nonetheless, a picture of both is another component of our analysis of blasphemy and its significance.

The medieval church was especially clear about the potential evil that blasphemers could do to society. Augustine, whose own writings so often functioned as a manual for ecclesiastical governance, was in no doubt about blasphemy and blasphemers. In his writings against the Donatist heresy, Augustine saw blasphemers as fundamentally imperilling the welfare of those around them. This was to be a concept with considerable longevity. We have already met the conception of blasphemy as a contagion, but Augustine argued that it had the capacity to damn those influenced by it in the life hereafter.[1] During the course of elaborating upon these opinions, Augustine also reminded the Christian community of its own God's power to intervene in the world. This particular idea had a double influence upon those who heard it. First, such an assertion reminded Christendom of the vengeful God of the Old Testament and the commandments, especially those forbidding blasphemy and the taking of

---

[1] Leonard Levy, *Blasphemy: Verbal Offense Against the Sacred from Moses to Salman Rushdie* (New York, 1993), 47.

his name in vain. Secondly, exposure to this idea introduced an enduring link between earthly blasphemy and the intervention of divine providence. Those who heard, or witnessed, blasphemous utterances were fearful of the immediate consequences of divine wrath.

However, these same people were also conscious of the particular responsibility placed upon those in both secular and ecclesiastical authority. Religious or earthly powers that tolerated blasphemy were considered to have scorned divine protection, adding yet another dimension to contemporary beliefs about God's intervention in a secular world. The French Renaissance monarchy, for example, was regularly reminded by clerical advisors to insist upon the full administration of justice upon blasphemers. Such advice readily constrained the monarch's action, since the arrival of any misfortune could be attributed to the monarch's failure.[2] This added a very strong vein of Christian duty to the role of individuals within society, whichever of the three estates they happened to belong to. This peculiarly sharp incentive fuelled concern and action against blasphemous assaults upon the Christian commonwealth. Augustine further argued for the pursuit and persecution of these individuals and their errors, suggesting that toleration would ensure the damnation of all. A further dimension within this disciplinary code was the belief that blasphemy represented the fracturing of the honour society owed to God.

From this prescription it becomes at least possible to speculate about the thoughts that might have passed through the mind of the medieval victim of blasphemy. First, it is highly unlikely that such individuals had a conception of personal affront to religious feelings. In witnessing an incident of blasphemy, these people would have seen earthly and religious authority challenged, and would have looked on in bewilderment. Sacred beliefs held from childhood would have been, at least temporarily, thrown into turmoil, bringing the expectation that the action of some authority would restore their sacred quality. This pattern would be typical of the passive blasphemy model that talked more of the community's immediate and long-term welfare than the feelings of the individual. However, alongside these responses there would also have been an overwhelming fear of the consequences of hearing blasphemy. Consternation and terror would probably be overwhelming, and as historians we get the clearest sense of this last reaction. Divine retribution was a constant of popular beliefs about how God reacted to blasphemers and the challenges they posed. This was closely linked to theological and popular beliefs about providence, which took on a renewed importance in the early modern era to become an element in blasphemy's history. This importance is highlighted by the fact that populations at large frequently complained that authority did not take seriously enough the threat the blasphemer posed.[3]

---

[2] Alfred Soman, 'Press, Pulpit and Censorship in France before Richelieu', *Proceedings of the American Philosophical Society*, 120:6 (Dec. 1976), 439–63, at 460.
[3] Alain Cabantous, *Blasphemy: Impious Speech in the West* (New York, 2002), 70.

Yet the late medieval and early modern era did not simply leave its populations at large to be hapless victims of the blasphemer's violence. On the contrary, just as the heretic and the infidel provoked Christianity to organize, so the prevalence and danger of blasphemy encouraged popular responses. One of the most widespread of these was the establishment of confraternities to combat the effects of this evil in society's midst. Confraternities were Christian Europe's method of organizing its lay population to undertake God's work within the community. Most of them were intended to provide forms of spiritual and practical help to those who needed it most. Thus, confraternities ministered to the ailing and infirm as well as undertaking the distribution of charity and alms. Nevertheless, the establishment of confraternities to combat blasphemy and heresy tells us much about how medieval Christianity thought about the issue. Like other forms of worldly evil or misfortunate, the community could work to eradicate blasphemy's presence. Persuading individuals within confraternities that this was valuable gave them a role in the existing order. It also created a sense of mission, and probably removed the feeling of powerlessness that we have noted clusters so often around the medieval and early modern audience for blasphemy. These confraternities also exemplify a response to the passive blasphemy model in which a flexible institution representing the community took collective action to both restore spiritual order and prevent blasphemy.

Confraternities had evolved as a legitimate alternative to the crusading vow, and were eventually destined to replace this entirely. By the fifteenth century the function of confraternities had been augmented to assist the Papal Inquisition in its work, and this had been a product of the campaign against Catharism. Typical amongst such bodies was the Company of the Holy Cross, founded in Bologna in 1450, which offered some of the spiritual privileges associated with the crusading vow in return for aid to the Inquisition.[4] The changing role of confraternities can also be seen as part of a wider pattern indicating the eclipse of medieval paternalistic attitudes towards the poor, charity, and acts of medicancy. The evaporation of sympathy for the poor was reflected by the growing tendency to see them as sources of antisocial behaviour. Hence, the later history of confraternities suggests a regime of policing the poor as much as of relieving their suffering. These confraternities would later function as regulatory occupational guilds as well as spiritually reforming organizations. In seventeenth-century France sailors' confraternities saw the regulation of blasphemy as preventing nuisance aboard ship, as well as combating the temptations to try divine providence. Those who offended would often find themselves excluded from these maritime trades. Alain Cabantous also found similar confraternities at work in sixteenth-century Paris, noting one, the Brotherhood of the Holy Name of Jesus, which appointed local upstanding citizens as supervisors of local

---

[4] Norman Housley, 'Politics and Heresy in Italy: Anti-heretical Crusades, Orders and Confraternities, 1200–1500', *Journal of Ecclesiastical History*, 33:2 (1982), 193–208.

urban speech. They were also charged with reporting any profane infringements they happened to uncover. Such organizations were augmented and refounded at regular intervals—Paris subsequently acquiring a Company of the Holy Sacrament in 1629 and a Brotherhood of the Passion by the middle of this same century. Such organizations also existed further afield in France and into the Catholic German lands.[5]

What internalized this fear of blasphemy for most early modern people was a combination of religious teachings specifically about blasphemy and the enduring fear of divine providence intervening in their world. The history of didactic writings against blasphemy and the literature of admonition deserve a more detailed study. In French writing the ideas of Augustine were taken further by writers like Pierre Floriot, who in the 1670s took a dim view of the blasphemy against the Holy Ghost which imputed divine actions to the devil. Such views were also echoed by French jurists like Myard de Vouglans, who also noted that such exclamations questioned God's omnipotence. Later eighteenth-century French works would draw an important distinction between the fact of blasphemy and the intention of those writing or speaking it. This partly describes the emergence of active blasphemy, where notions of temporal harm were already informing the thoughts of theologians. In the wider Spanish world there was a similar body of writings which spoke of the evils perpetrated by blasphemers, and how these attended them whilst gambling. Nicolas De Avila, for example argued in the early sixteenth century that the devil placed blasphemous utterances directly into the mouths of gamblers.[6]

The second issue, providence, as many historians have demonstrated, wielded an enormous influence upon the early modern mind. This concept, in particular, deserves to be closely considered as central to the history of early modern blasphemy, because it had the power to actively invoke retribution from a God readily considered as intervening in the world of his creation. The leading historian of this area, Alex Walsham, examined the widespread availability of providential stories circulating in seventeenth-century England. She concluded that they were 'compelling testimonies to the belief that God was no idle, inactive spectator upon the mechanical workings of the created world, but an assiduous energetic deity who constantly intervened in human affairs'. Walsham uncovered how providentialism was more widespread throughout society than early commentators had admitted; certainly, evidence from Europe-wide attitudes to blasphemy would endorse this conclusion. It was an idea that had a profound influence and could, in Walsham's words, 'console'.

---

[5] Cabantous, *Blasphemy*, 31, 35, and 37–8.
[6] See Françoise Hildesheim, 'La Répression du blasphème au XVIII 'siècle', in J. Delumeau (ed.) *Injures et blasphèmes; Mentalités*, ii (Paris, 1989), 63–82, at 65. Cabantous, *Blasphemy*, 19, and Javier Villa-Flores, 'On Divine Persecution: Blasphemy and Gambling in New Spain', in Susan Schroeder and Stafford Poole (eds.), *Religion and Society in Colonial Mexico* (New Mexico, forthcoming), 129.

Blasphemy thus demonstrated the spectre of immanence and divine retribution. Much of this was exacerbated by the coming of Protestantism, which removed the array of intermediaries between the soul and God. This put the soul far more obviously at the mercy of the benevolence or wrath of the creator. Providence contained within it knowledge and power, since God possessed the knowledge of future events and the power to intervene. Yet this drove individuals to the gaming table as much as it made them fearful of everyday occurrences or exceptional misfortune. Most Protestants believed that God had the power to suspend the natural order and to intervene, delivering either miracles or disaster. Moreover, some aspects of Protestant identity strictly depended upon a providential reading of recent historical events.[7] This issue was communicated through a considerably developed genre of providential writing, which told powerful didactic tales of what became of blasphemers. These were prevalent in England, and there is plenty of evidence that they were similarly popular in Europe and may even have originated there. Cabantous found tales of carters losing control of their load and suffering fatal accidents after uttering blasphemy, as well as of individuals struck by lightning after similar curses.[8] It becomes difficult to underestimate just how carefully early modern audiences were prepared for the belief that God would intervene, most readily through meteorological phenomena. A whole entertainment literature describing remarkable events of this nature was a commonplace in early modern popular culture. For example, until the 1620s the visitation of the plague was seen unequivocally as divine punishment for adultery, drunkenness, pride, blasphemy, and other sins.[9]

A typical example of this literature is William Turner's *Compleat History of the Most Remarkable Providences* of 1697, which was essentially a catalogue of providential happenings showing the readership the profound folly of moral misbehaviour. This book was intended for the clergy and the pious heads of households, supplying a fount of stories with which to inculcate godly and moral behaviour. Turner's one-hundred-and-first chapter was a list of the divine judgements the almighty had passed upon blasphemers. These blasphemers included the exalted as much as common men, and their chronology commenced with the heretical behaviour of the Emperor Eugenius. On marching to war, he had threatened to turn the church in Milan into a horse stable, whereupon divine judgement persuaded his soldiers to turn upon him and kill him. These stories within Turner's *Compleat History* placed a strong emphasis upon ensuring adherence to the true faith. Blasphemers in this instance were those prepared to

[7] Alex Walsham, *Providence in early modern England* (Oxford 1999), 2, 9, 12, and 253.

[8] Ibid. 72. Cabantous, *Blasphemy*, 45.

[9] Walsham, *Providence*, 12–24 and 163. See also John Marshall, *John Locke, Toleration and Early Enlightenment Culture* (Cambridge, 2006), 267–9 and 298–300, for the association between providence and the appearance of 'monsters'. See also L. Daston and K. Park, *Wonders and the Order of Nature* (New York, 1998), for the assertion that the blasphemous became associated with the monstrous as a result of the Reformation.

reject the true faith and to recant it publicly. This action was deemed dangerous folly, and numerous famous and commonplace examples were given. The story of the Norwich heretic Thomas Bilney was here rehashed for another generation, as was the story of Jerome of Prague, whose troubled conscience made him deny his recantation, even though this resulted in his own execution. A flavour of how these stories could speak directly to the reader is provided by the story of Thomas Whittle, whose opinions had provoked Bishop Bonner to use physical violence against him. Eventually Whittle was led into recanting them by the bishop's subsequent kindness. Upon doing this, he instantly regretted how he had been led 'by so slight a means to shake off the cross of Christ'. From here Whittle's anguish becomes plain, as the account degenerates into him wailing and warning all comers: 'Oh! The crafty subtilty [*sic*] of Satan in his Members. Let every man whom God shall deliver into their Hands, take heed of them, and cleave fast to Christ: For they will leave no corner of his Conscience unsearched, but will attempt by all guileful and subtle means to corrupt him, and to cause him to fall from God and his Truth.'

Other stories within Turner, if they are remotely true, give a picture of how an anguished audience supremely sensitized to the idea of divine providence could find the balance of their minds disturbed. A fearful Suffolk couple who had affirmed 'popish ceremonies' fell into 'such Trouble and Horror of Conscience that they were ready wholly to despair', Only God's benevolent intervention prevented the man from committing suicide by his own sword. The presence of knives tempted other repenting blasphemers, whilst still more wasted away, taking no comfort from food, drink, or the ministrations of physicians. Several other tales of the same genre noted that God administers poetic justice, with the limbs implicated in sin struck off or damaged. Those engaged in speech crimes, according to Turner, found their tongues turning black. This poetic justice may also have influenced and perhaps reinforced the visual power of bodily punishment inflicted upon blasphemers, since it appeared to also be divinely providential.[10] The danger of retribution bestowed upon individuals as a result of their blasphemy was also a staple of French didactic writing. The bishop of Alet, Nicolas Pavillon, argued that plague would descend upon those guilty of blasphemy, whilst St Vincent de Paul wrote that an ever-vigilant God could reach down and exact instant punishment if he so wished.[11]

Whilst it is perhaps easy for the historian to conclude that these stories had the desired effect intended by their writers, it is possible to trace the impact of this providentialism within specific instances of blasphemy. These are evident as late as the eighteenth century. If we recall our blasphemous Dutch boatman,

---

[10] William Turner' *Compleat History of the Most Remarkable Providences* (London, 1697), Part II, pp. 10 and 11.

[11] Cabantous, *Blasphemy*, 15 and 43–8. Counter-Reformation France had its direct counterpart to these didactic stories in which those who chose reformed religion suffered torments.

Robert Adriaansz. Van Hoorn actively called upon the almighty to intervene to destroy his boat, provoking the retaliation of his passengers and fellow crew. Similarly, our adolescents in the Paris tavern in 1701 who were scattered by the flash of thunder were seen to encourage each other as a result of the fear of divine retribution they inspired in the innocent individuals present.[12] It is noteworthy that the real possibility of conjuring demons remained a potent belief so close to the French capital so late in the eighteenth century. Similarly, the belief that causing direct offence to God was possible and would elicit divine retribution on the perpetrators was widespread. But this was more than a cautionary tale, since the police believed that divine retribution was still expected to be visited upon those who threatened the moral safety of the community. What also lay behind the considerable attention the police paid to taverns and their customers was a more tangible fear that such places were homes to subcultures that would invert society, religion, and the moral order. Occasional outbursts of impiety, and the fear this generated, regularly provided potent evidence that such subcultures existed and were active amongst the impressionable. Nonetheless, some didactic works offered procedures for combating the temptation to blaspheme. One early eighteenth-century English text recommended the following: 'To express our detestation of a blasphemous interjection we should instantly reject and spue out the Abomination, and not suffer the vile thought to lodge in us. As it is but rising and entring, we must rebuke, suppress, forbid and curse it in the Name of the Lord.'[13]

Providentialism also influenced whole territories and their legal jurisdictions to take blasphemy much more seriously. Venice established its famed Esecutori in the wake of a series of material setbacks for the city and its aspirations. Undignified retreat in the face of the Ottoman Empire's military prowess occurred at the same time as Venice was ravaged by a series of plagues. Evidence from the thoughts of contemporaries suggests that the failure to police blasphemous words had incurred the disfavour of the almighty. Venice also suffered something of an urban crisis as a result of these defeats, and from the inward migration that followed them. Contemporaries record the city as overcrowded, cosmopolitan, and dangerously open to influences and further influxes. What Elizabeth Horodowich termed 'the porous nature of Venetian space' became a source of fear and foreboding for the city's authorities. Often they increasingly reacted to these pressures by enforcing standards of behaviour, including the regulated use of language, as a means of defining citizenship and enforcing this upon the city's new comers. The fear that this phenomenon exerted appears justified, since almost two-thirds of those

---

[12] Quoted in Thomas Brennan, *Public Drinking and Popular Culture in Eighteenth-Century Paris* (Princeton, 1988), 270–1.
[13] Benjamin Colman, *The Case of Satan's fiery Darts in Blasphemous Suggestions and Hellish Annoyances: As they were considered in several Sermons, Heretofore preach'd to the Congregation in Brattle-Street, Boston May 1711, and lately repeated to them May 1743* (Boston, 1744), 30.

indicted for blasphemy were foreigners. The Esecutori effectively functioned as a visible means of acculturating these potential Venetian citizens.[14]

Moreover, the workings of the Esecutori further outlined how providence exerted a strange power, even over legal proceedings. Horodowich notes that indictments and records of specific cases contain minimal references to precise words used by malefactors. This prevented the restatement, and presumably reuse, of the perilous words spoken. Even the French monarchy was not immune to linking divine providence with blasphemy. One historian of this area notes that plagues, bad weather, and famine were often preludes to enhanced action against the evil blasphemers and what they allegedly did to society through dishonouring God. Louis XII even commenced a prosecution campaign against blasphemy in thanksgiving for his military victory in Italy in 1510.[15] As late as 1721 English parliamentarians believed that an anti-blasphemy bill would deliver England from the ravages of the South Sea Bubble episode, which had served as a judgment upon a profane and godless nation.[16] Nine years later the Netherlands believed that over-tolerant attitudes to homosexuality had brought divine displeasure upon the nation and made repression necessary.[17] Such sentiments would also regularly erupt in New England. Many diaries and pamphlets record the fear that God's sending of portents and apparitions was a sign that divine disfavour would be visited upon the colonies. Increase Mather wrote his *Illustrious Providences* in the 1680s, outlining a catalogue of strange occurrences indicating the power of providence to be at the forefront of New England's religious and political culture.[18]

Thus, providence had an important role to play in persuading individuals, both lowly and exalted, that blasphemy and blasphemers fundamentally impinged upon their universe. This providence spoke of an immanent God that was prepared to oversee the whole of his creation and to reserve the prerogative of intervention within the lives of individual men and women. It would be tempting to construct a history solely around the struggles of the philosophes and the Age of Reason to push God as far into the background as conventional philosophy of the late seventeenth and early eighteenth centuries would allow. This history would suggest that the work of physical scientists and deists pushed God away from the immanent position he held within the lives of his creation, so that causality came to be subject to more scientific explanations. This version of events could be justified by the suggestion made by many historians that the early

---

[14] Elizabeth Horodowich, 'Civic Identity and the Control of Blasphemy in Sixteenth Century Venice', *Past Present*, 181 (2003), 3–33, at 18–28.

[15] Elizabeth Belmas, 'La Monteé des blasphèmes', in J. Delumeau (ed.), *Injures et blasphèmes; Mentalités*, ii (Paris, 1989), 14. See also Soman, 'Press, Pulpit and Censorship in France before Richelieu', 443

[16] Tina Isaacs, 'The Anglican Hierarchy and the Reformation of Manners 1688–1738', *Journal of Ecclesiastical History*, 33:3 (July 1982), 391–411, at 404.

[17] See Marshall, *John Locke*, 71.

[18] Stephen Foster, *The Long Argument* (Williamsburg, 1991), 231.

modern period in particular was characterized by high levels of marginality. Thus, misfortune could spell serious trouble for individuals and whole communities. From this it would be tempting to believe that men and women therefore became less fearful of the blasphemous challenge to God's honour, and instead began to see blasphemy law solely as a species of intolerance.

However, such neat transitions to modernity are never as comfortably accomplished. It is perhaps an ironic paradox that in the Christian world the immanence of God's intervention became less of a widespread issue for individuals, whilst its persistence as a narrative told by modern states arguably grew in importance. The issues provoked by this are perhaps best explored through investigating the thoughts of deists who actually believed that blasphemy laws were necessary. The ideas of Zephaniah Swift, who was to become Connecticut's chief justice at the end of the French Revolutionary Wars, exemplified precisely this paradox. Swift was appalled by organized religion and was even actively anticlerical in some of his opinions. Yet he also demonstrated a rather modern-looking viewpoint on the social utility of Christianity as a force for promoting morality. Swift saw Christianity as the most accessible and successful manifestation of natural religion, concluding that it was beneficial and useful even if its practitioners tainted its essentially benevolent character. This almost organic view of how Christianity had evolved into a social and ethical system was also reflected in Swift's attachment to English Common Law's organic solutions to America's legal problems.[19]

Whilst individual states reached maturity and sophistication through the security offered by a national religion, the state's history provides important insights. The transition from the early modern period to the modern marked a realization of the power of the state as it gained and nurtured informed consent for its policies and actions. Government thus became a more immanent and immediate source of power, rivalling God's role in the nature of causality. However, it could only contest this space, and never wholly eclipsed theistic versions of causality. Amongst the many lessons that the Bible taught rulers and ruled were the consequences for those whom God had forsaken. The blessings of the almighty could sometimes appear fleeting and fickle, whilst the sixteenth and seventeenth centuries had spawned religious radicals across Europe who saw rebellion against their rulers as a religious duty. This explains the harsh attitudes in England and America to the challenges to power offered by Dissenters and Quakers at the end of the seventeenth century. Nevertheless, the desire to see God's benevolence reach down to the nation-state survived, and was nurtured by secular rulers from the days of the embryonic modern state onwards.

---

[19] For more on Swift see David F. Gerardi, 'Zephaniah Swift and Connecticut's Standing Order: Skepticism, Conservatism, and Religious Liberty in the Early Republic', *New England Quarterly*, 67:2 (Jan. 1994), 234–56, at 240–2 and 248.

However, the state and its local manifestations also began to see secular discipline as an important adjunct to religiously inspired self-discipline. Fear of divine intervention became a desire to reform the manners of the population and to ensure adherence to principles of moral behaviour. If religion was at least respected, then the powers of government would also be ensured and safeguarded. The period after the Restoration in England saw a systematic growth in societies to police morals, such as the Society for the Promotion of Christian Knowledge and the Society for the Reformation of Manners. The work of these groups ensured that the roles of church and state were again linked, and it was hoped that those brought to heel by the state would then be exposed to religio-moral reform. Many of these societies were located close to the capital, and flourished particularly in the 1690s. They condemned the theatre, bawdy-houses, and excessive alcoholism as threatening the stability and peace of the kingdom.[20]

During this same period these societies were replicated in Ireland, spawning a veritable industry of reporting moral lapses. Once again blasphemers were labelled alongside prostitutes, Sabbath-breakers, infanticidal mothers, and other social threats. Wherever English and Irish society looked it found moral problems requiring desperate remedies, and there was no shortage of manpower to undertake the task. Such sentiments underpinned the blasphemy statute (9 & 10 William III c.32), which was strongly promoted by Archibishop Thomas Tenison.[21] Although clerical proponents wanted the church to eventually restore the jurisdiction and power it had exercised under William Laud, the power of lay interest in the early eighteenth century successfully thwarted this.[22] France would see similar long-term interest in reforming the manners of its subjects, with an especial concern for their spiritual welfare.

The history of blasphemy during this period, in both the wider European and colonial American contexts, was part of the deeper debate about the link between church and state. In the medieval period, combating the heretic through the church–state apparatus was the means of protecting the community and safeguarding its unified nature. As the age of enlightenment dawned, the association of the community with the nation was an important method of justifying mechanisms of detection, policing, and punishment. In England, as we have seen, heresy transformed itself into blasphemy as a response to challenges against the political and moral order towards the end of the seventeenth century.

---

[20] David Hayton, 'Moral Reform and Country Politics in the Late Seventeenth Century House of Commons', *Past & Present*, 128 (Aug. 1990), 48–91, at 53.

[21] T. C. Barnard, 'Reforming Irish Manners: The Religious Societies in Dublin During the 1690s', *Historical Journal*, 35:4 (Dec. 1992), 805–38, at 819. Barnard notes that despite the apparent enthusiasm for the measure the Irish Parliament never enacted a bill reminiscent of 9 & 10 William. This was despite the fears generated by the blasphemies of John Toland and his anti-trinitarianism.

[22] Isaacs, 'The Anglican Hierarchy', 391–3, 403.

The blasphemy statute (9 & 10 William III c.32) protected a precarious regime from internal and external challenges to the authority of religion through the Hale judgement. As late as the nineteenth century (and even into the second quarter of the twentieth), the desire to protect the sacred charge the Empire had given the British people represented a more secularized view of this.[23]

Protecting the French Revolution from its enemies had given Jacobins unshakeable justification and resolve to eradicate opposition in occasionally gruesome fashion. Such resolve was also evident in nations which sought to evade the terrors the revolution had so rapidly unleashed. What became an especial feature of these reactions was the notable way in which governments, private agencies, and individuals would work together to identify and marginalize enemies such as the blasphemer. This was prominent in the work of the Society for the Suppression of Vice. This organization was drawn together from the elite members of English society, concerned about the spread of ideas and attitudes that were manifestly godless.

Just as Quakers and anti-trinitarians had posed a serious threat to the church–state relationship, so there was a similar, albeit muted, challenge from Methodism. These years are peppered with the well-meaning, yet frightened, scribblings of those prepared to stand and defend the constitution. More constitutionally minded radicals, and the evangelical branch of Anglicanism, searched for remedies and panaceas for discontent. Such fear for the welfare of the establishment was a genuine piece of old-style Toryism. It valued community, and reminded individuals of their responsibility and society's duty to conserve stability, amidst economically and socially pressing times. Whilst its more benevolent manifestation was the Tract Society, its message had a harder edge when pressed by the Society for the Suppression of Vice. This unashamedly traded upon loyalism, and was adamant that the protection of church and state was a cornerstone of preserving English civilization.[24]

William Wilberforce, an early enthusiast for detecting vice in low places, unequivocally saw the enemies of church and state as identical. Organizations of dedicated, slightly moneyed, and frightened men and women were a feature of Regency England, where such groups defended property and public morals, often seeing the two as interchangeable. In many respects government welcomed their involvement, since they represented a far more acceptable manifestation of loyalism than the 'Church and King' mobs which could frequently be the enemy of property. The Vice Society set itself the target of reducing and eradicating a cocktail of concerns. In particular, it reflected the deeply conservative cultural

---

[23] Linda Colley, *Britons: Forging the Nation* (London, 1992). J. C. D. Clark, *English Society 1688–1832* (Cambridge, 1985).

[24] M. J. D. Roberts, 'Making Victorian Morals? The Society for the Suppression of Vice and its Critics 1802–1886', *Historical Studies*, 21: 157–3 (1984), 159–60.

concern that 'venerable' customs and opinions were now to be openly insulted. The Society also believed that England had been spared the worst excesses of the continent through the intervention of divine providence. Nonetheless, vigilance was still required, and the Vice Society saw its mission to be the encouragement of the law and the chance to direct the procedures adopted by the new police.[25] This would prevent the 'pestilent swarm of BLASPHEMOUS, LICENTIOUS AND OBSCENE BOOKS AND PRINTS, which are insinuating their way into the recesses of private life, to the destruction of all purity of sentiment, and all correctness of principle'. Although the Society was a group who preached vigilance, it also believed that prevention was an important part of the mission. Rousing concerned England would 'strengthen every separate link, that the great chain of society may be firm, compact, and unyielding'.[26]

As such, the Vice Society's public profile would fuel and assist prosecutions, whilst government watched from a safe distance. The Society was also anxious to harness whatever state apparatus it could to discharge its duties. In particular, it was anxious that society should make the most of the law-enforcement agencies, producing a guide which outlined the role of constables encountering every nuisance from blasphemy to vagrants, hawkers, and disorderly alehouses.[27] As befits their status as Tory philanthropists, the Vice Society focused upon Paine's *Age of Reason* as a text that perniciously robbed the poor of the hope of salvation. This disturbed the peace of the kingdom in ways that resonated outwards in all directions. In later years, when Carlile was not railing against the Society's apparent intolerance to him in particular, he would produce more subtle arguments about how the Society for Suppression of Vice had smothered debate: 'Have you no priests in your Society? Why do you not set them to write a volume of the same size to refute the arguments and assertions of Paine? I will pledge myself to sell it with the other.'[28] Carlile was also clear that, although debate was stifled, prosecution gave infidel views publicity which they would find hard to replicate: 'I can assure the Vice Society that I smile to myself, and have the most agreeable feelings when I reflect how much they have contributed to strengthen my attack on the common fraud of religion. I feel that I am quite another being to what I should have been, had I been left alone and not prosecuted.'[29]

What became an important feature of the organization's stance was the psychological geography that the Society attached to these ideas. Generally

[25] *An address to the public, from the Society for the Suppression of Vice, instituted in London, 1802, part I* (London, 1803), 28–31.

[26] Ibid. 43, 53, 56, and 57.

[27] *The Constable's Assistant: Being a Compendium of the Duties and powers of Constables and Other Peace Officers; Chiefly as they relate to the Apprehednig of Offenders, and the Laying of Informations before Magistrates*, 3rd eds. with additions (London, 1818).

[28] Richard Carlile, *A Letter to the Society for the Suppression of Vice, On their Malignant Efforts to Prevent A Free Enquiry After truth and Reason* (London, 1819), 6.

[29] *The Republican*, 13 Oct. 1820, p. 218.

ignoring any semblance of a native tradition of deism, the Society became systematically convinced that the spread of blasphemy was the direct result of Jacobin opinions and writings. These had arrived from across the Channel and posed a danger to the sanctity and safety of English life. This suggestion that blasphemy was a foreign importation was also to be observed within many modern European instances of panic about the issue. But loyalism set against the blasphemous also had other popular manifestations. The aftermath of Peterloo saw an array of popular addresses of support for the government emanating from provincial England. These linked blasphemy squarely with sedition, restating that a hierarchical society maintained that the Christian religion still functioned as a species of consolation. A meeting in Hereford declared: 'Amongst the means most actively used for these pernicious purposes, we view with horror the widely extended circulation of blasphemous and seditious publications; the former calculated to poison the minds of men, and to deprive them of their greatest source of consolation—religion.' This was contrasted with the security offered by the British Constitution, which a meeting in Dudley promoted as: 'that happy constitution which was framed by the genius and wisdom of our ancestors, and has been proved and confirmed by the experience of ages, which is the glory of this country, and the admiration and imitation of surrounding nations.'[30]

Fear of dangerous outsiders and their blasphemy was not by any means unique to British society, and it is possible to see many such fears at work in America. Those with unorthodox views were deemed capable of unbalancing and damaging local communities. This equation had a further complication in the turbulent relationship that state and local jurisdictions had with federal law. Blasphemy was a recurrent opportunity to discuss the nature of the country's constitution and the scope of its freedoms. In the case of *Updegraph* v. *the Commonwealth*, the opinions of the judiciary suggested the words spoken by the defendant would unerringly lead the impressionable into crime and vice. This was contrasted with the defendant's assertion that the crime of blasphemy had been superseded by the Constitution.[31] The fact that blasphemy came from outside was also evident in other instances within the English-speaking world, where sometimes it could feel like entirely a foreign import. The infamous blasphemy cases of the early 1880s in England contained a significant flavour of imported European anticlericalism. G W. Foote's *Freethinker* produced loud and strident copy which thanked the French anticlerical activist Leo Taxil's *La Bible amusante* for the inspiration it provided. In particular, the use of cartoons as an information and satirical medium had an immediacy that brought something

---

[30] *British Loyalty; or Declarations of Attachment to the Established Constitution, in Church and State, opposed to Blasphemy, Anarchy, Sedition and Innovation. By the Merchants, Bankers, Civil Corporations and Parishes of Great Britain* (London, 1819).

[31] 11 Serg. and Rawle. (Pa.) 394 (1824).

new to a British audience.[32] Foote would regularly lament that England itself had not developed a sufficiently virulent anticlerical culture, but intimated that he would be happy to become its pioneer. Related Australian cases of the 1880s appeared to be almost entirely affairs that dealt with 'foreign' issues. Material imported from England was measured alongside the similarly remote English Common Law.

The concept of blasphemous speech and opinion opened a door for populations to discuss the nature of the sacred and of belief. With increasing access to printed media and to the law, the religious were able to articulate their beliefs, feelings, and fears beyond the prompting of religious institutions. Their sentiments provide a unique opportunity to view the interaction of discourses related to God, monarch, and nation. This was visible in Britain since it had been, in a genuine sense, isolated from European-style anticlericalism and de-Christianization. The potent threat that these two enemies of English culture and civilization represented was more than obvious to the Society for the Suppression of Vice. Their writings and communications were infused with this fear, as well as a forthright zeal to protect society and eradicate the evils within their midst. The Vice Society was instrumental in the string of cases that were conducted against Richard Carlile and his shopmen. Although the use of private agencies to prosecute crimes had been a feature of late eighteenth-century England, this agency linked morality explicitly with politics. Increasingly this also occurred in America, where the debate about the Constitution over time fused attitudes around free speech into political discourses.

America had its own contemporary crusaders against godlessness and immorality during the 1830s. The arguments used by Samuel Parker, prosecuting counsel against Abner Kneeland, demonstrated the marshalling of American society's concerns about radical freethinkers and their agendas. Parker saw blasphemy as a component of a much wider desire for licence and licentiousness, which would lead to communal ownership of both women and property. Kneeland's association with Frances Wright and Robert Dale Owen indicated a campaign to spread contraceptive and immoral information, with the aim of corrupting American youth. Kneeland's headquarters were even alleged to contain discreet beds in which the immorality could be practised.[33] The twentieth century saw Theodore Schroeder's quest to confirm freedom of expression opposed by conservative attitudes in the shape of Anthony Comstock. Under Comstock's guidance, societies for the suppression of vice had proliferated throughout America, with particularly prominent and vocal groups in the north-eastern states and

[32] In one cartoon, 'Jehovah's Day of Rest', Foote's Anglicized version gave the almighty a copy of the *Freethinker* to read. See D. S. Nash, 'Laughing at the Almighty', in Wagner Lawlor (ed.), *The Victorian Comic Spirit* (Aldershot, 2000), 43–66.

[33] Samuel D. Parker, *Report of the Arguments of the Attorney of the Commonwealth at the trials of Abner Kneeland for Blasphemy, in the Municipal and Supreme Courts in Boston, January and May 1834* (Boston, 1834).

New England.[34] Henceforth, on either side of the Atlantic, the defence of the nation's morals became linked to a special kind of social and, gradually, political conservatism.[35]

These organizations and alliances came to resemble secular confraternities empowering individuals to take part in and inform important matters of state. Societies for the defence of morals gave the concerned and frightened a vocabulary of outrage and a means by which lobbying pressure could be brought to bear. Interestingly, although the churches were blamed for having neglected their solemn charge and duty, these groups generally saw their task as the indictment and hounding of government and its agencies. Scrutinizing and overseeing the work of policemen, civil servants, lawyers, and politicians became a staple of their work. In this respect roles had been importantly reversed from the medieval confraternities. These had been recruited by clerical authority to act as handmaidens and supporters of the actions of this authority. Nineteenth-century private agencies saw their job as maintaining independent action against malefactors, ensuring that government agencies came up to the mark and discharged their duty.

Thus, in the pursuit of blasphemy the medieval pious laity had evolved into the embryonic modern citizen. However, it became a feature of this new type of scrutiny that moral guardians were not always discriminating in who they feared or pursued. Although it was commonplace to indict and pursue the vulgar, it is surprising that such attention was focused upon the comparatively polite and unthreatening John Stuart Mill. The mayor of Newcastle, William Armstrong, warned the Home Office about two pernicious lectures delivered by Mill in 1850, and begged for government financial assistance to prosecute. Armstrong claimed that these lectures 'tend greatly to promote infidel and socialist doctrines amongst the people and to the disparagement of true religion and all constituted authority. The public are keenly alive to them, and are upbrading [*sic*] the authorities for not putting them down.'[36]

This willingness to express opinion about the use of blasphemous words became a feature of incidents of blasphemy as the nineteenth century progressed. Cases across the English-speaking world in the 1880s indicated that concerned laymen could be quite articulate about both their own fear of blasphemy and

---

[34] For more on Comstock's crusades see Heywood Broun and Margaret Leech, *Anthony Comstock: Roundsman of the Lord* (New York, 1927); Charles Gallaudet Trumbull, *Anthony Comstock, Fighter* (New York, 1913). For a contemporary hostile view of Comstock see D. R. M. Bennett, *Anthony Comstock: His Career of Cruelty and Crime*, (Da Capo Press Reprint ser. (New York, 1971). See also Martin Henry Blatt, *Free Love and Anarchism: The Biography of Ezra Heywood* (Chicago, 1989), 113–27.

[35] See P. C. Kemeny, 'Power, Ridicule, and the Destruction of Religious Moral Reform Politics in the 1920s', in C. Smith (ed.), *The Secular Revolution: Power Interests, and Conflict in the Secularisation of American Public life* (Berkeley, 2003), 216–68.

[36] HO (Home Office) 45 3537, letter of complaint regarding lectures by J. S. Mill from William Armstrong, Mayor of Newcastle, 9 Jan. 1851.

Fig. 17. Anthony Comstock, the censor and 'Roundsman of the Lord', as seen by his opponents, *c*.1912.

of what it might do to society if left unchecked. When George William Foote began his career at the *Freethinker*, the home secretary, Sir William Harcourt, was bombarded by letters and complaints from members of the public. Reactions to the publication of the infamous Christmas number of 1882 involved an uneasy mechanism whereby public complaints became translated into governmental action. Many of the complaints involved the exposure of blasphemous material to the gaze of the young and impressionable. Typical of these complaints was the letter from W. H. Mason of Croydon written to Gladstone, since he felt 'confident that neither you, nor any of her Majesty's Ministers can be aware that so foul and blasphemous a publications is now issued weekly and sold publicly. . . . Surely we have some law by which so horrible a thing can be at once suppressed.' Another correspondent was deeply concerned that he could 'gain no information how to suppress such an abomination'.[37]

But these occurrences of blasphemy also provoked officials to act. Although this was ostensibly in defence of public morals, there was clearly a range of personal concerns involved. The mayor of London, Sir Thomas Nelson, was enraged by the conspicuously heightened attempt at blasphemy contained within the *Freethinker* Christmas number, considering it obscene. When Sir William Harcourt was informed of this by the under-secretary of state, Lushington, the latter reluctantly accepted that the moral man on the spot would press for local action against the *Freethinker*. Lushington was sceptical about the likely success and long-term value of any prosecution, and wanted the Home Office to exercise restraint. He was to be disappointed, since Harcourt was more prepared to support action against cheap and widely available blasphemy. Quite often this task would fall to the lot of unfortunated civil servants in the burgeoning governmental apparatus of nineteenth-century Europe. Whilst professionals would always argue for a cautious approach, those with a much closer relationship to the feelings of the general public would more readily commit themselves to action. This suggests that blasphemy could become a political issue when it was linked with wider perceptions of moral decline. Although politicians found themselves elected to protect public morals, they were also increasingly asked to defend free speech. This was the dawning of the modern democratic dilemma around blasphemy. Western governments had a duty to defend their nation from untoward influences, yet they were also expected to create so-called 'open societies' that would offer protection to the persecuted.

What became an increasing concern for authorities caught in this bind was the power of individuals on the spot to take action that would unwittingly involve government. Powers of restraint could be used against those who took the law excessively into their own hands. But restraining local forces of law and order was still more fraught with difficulty. A flavour of how these problems presented themselves (and indeed, have endured into our own time) is conveyed by a minor, yet interesting, case which occurred in London's Regent's Park in 1884. A Protestant evangelical missionary named William Browne had made derogatory remarks about the Catholic church, resulting in numerous reprisals against him. The police had no powers in Regent's Park, yet found themselves required to intervene when Browne was accosted and a breach of the peace ensued.

---

[37] Ibid. Letter from W. H. Mason from the Croydon Portrait Studio and Repository of Arts, 89 George Street, to Gladstone 6/1/83 and Letter from Salisbury Square 5/1/83 to Gladstone.

The instant that the police intervened, they appeared to have surrendered their impartiality. No sooner had they done so than they were addressed by a Catholic, who accused them of offering protection to an individual stirring up religious hatred. As the indignant Mr Shea stated: 'how would you like to have your religion run down and ridiculed like that; what would you do if you heard me, or any one else, preaching that the Queen was a whore and that sort of thing?'[38]

More readily, police forces were prepared to take action on their own account, or found themselves with power in situations which demanded their immediate response. This phenomenon inspired both senior policemen to make policy decisions and individual constables to respond to disturbances. Public order and peace were at risk, whilst nuisance and challenges to public morals had also to be clearly addressed and combated. These imperatives informed the action taken against the Edwardian blasphemers Pack, Stewart, and Gott, who had their speeches closely scrutinized and their prosecutions actively prepared by police in Yorkshire, Wolverhampton, and elsewhere. The Leeds chief constable, writing in 1911, demonstrated how many policemen felt pressed into action by highly motivated, quasi-political blasphemers: '. . . I do not see how—writing after the event—they [the prosecutions] could have been avoided for the meetings conducted by these men were becoming a public scandal. Letters were appearing in the papers . . . it appeared to be more dangerous to leave them alone than to take action.'[39]

Such fears for the public peace were also instrumental in police activity in Australia, where occasionally high-handed action would land policing authorities and senior policemen in trouble. This particular phenomenon occurred regularly in the United States, where the comparative autonomy of police jurisdictions led to a dramatically enhanced role of moral legislator for the average policeman. Police testimony had been important in preparing the case against Mockus. Police zealousness has also been responsible for the prosecution and notoriety of some of the more minor infringements of recent years. Policemen have been responsible within the last thirty years for prosecuting speeding motorists for the use of profane language, thereby pointing to one of the enduring paradoxes of American society. A civilization which defends free speech also encourages the quite regular policing of the morals of that society and the language used or images seen within it. In more recent times, the readiness of the police in local jurisdictions to confiscate and seize material, sometimes almost at will, indicates a revivified role as protector of public morality.

Nonetheless, more powerful still over the course of the twentieth century has been the way blasphemy has been revived in societies where the nation-state is in the process of apparent dissolution. In the twentieth century the state was

---

[38] HO 459645A3, Religious Disturbances in Regent's Park 1884.
[39] HO45106652, Letter to Sir Edward Troup at Home Office from Leeds Chief Constable 13/12/11.

LAST JOURNAL IN ENGLAND PROSECUTED FOR BLASPHEMY

DEVOTED TO MENTAL FREEDOM AND SOCIAL PROGRESS

The Truth Seeker

CONDUCTED BY J.W.GOTT. BRADFORD.

ESTABLISHED 1894.   PRICE ONE PENNY.

The British Secular League

Is once more actively engaged in carrying out its Summer Programme of Outdoor Lectures in more than a score of different centres   Lancashire, Yorkshire, and Scotland, are all being worked on a scale never before attempted by any Freethought Organisation.   The 15 lecturers of the League are going to all towns were encouragement is extended to them, and they are also carrying the glad tidings of ' Freethought ' to many other places where it is hoped interest will be aroused.

All Freethinkers are invited to help us in the work by becoming Members of the British Secular League (see next page for particulars), or by sending us a small subscription towards the expenses.   We have already received sufficient support to keep the work in full swing for many weeks.   We want ALL FREETHINKERS to " do their bit " and thus help us to beat our own well-established record as the Freethought Organisation which is responsible for more outdoor lectures on Secularism and Rationalism than all other Societies combined. " Blasphemy," " Profanity," " Obstruction," and " Selling without permission " Prosecutions have all failed to stop our progress.   Now is the time to shew your interest in and to give encouragement to a body of workers who are DOING THINGS in what somebody wisely called "the best of all causes."

J. W. GOTT, *Hon. Sec.*

Fig. 18. The English *Truthseeker* defiantly asks for support.

regularly reached for as a guarantor of protection—not in the name of order and governance, but this time for the individual. Blasphemy, in short, became a place where individuals theorized about the state and what it should do to protect rights by refereeing between offender and offended. At times individuals believed that blasphemy represented a godless challenge to religious nations, and would thus destroy morality within them. In the first half of the twentieth century this belief was very often focused upon the corrosive power of modern communism.

Britain had experienced these issues at the end of the Edwardian period, with the agitation and subsequent prosecution of individuals like Pack, Gott, and Stewart and later Guy Aldred. In particular, the association of these people with the wider world of anarcho-syndicalism clearly linked blasphemous opinions with political violence. In early 1920s America, it was this fear which motivated local jurisdications to act against individuals like Mockus. A decade later the power of concerned groups to use the media to create and manage panic became a reality in Britain. In 1938 the innocuous Freethought Congress held in London was subject to close police scrutiny, and an attempt was made to revise the blasphemy laws to exclude and deport dangerous communist freethinkers. What is of especial interest were the innumerable letters of complaint that were received at the Home Office. These linked fear of moral collapse with the dissolution of sacred indigenous institutions brought down by dangerous foreign interlopers. Seen from another perspective, these sentiments demonstrate how individuals still believed in a moral order, in which the divine and temporal governance were linked and sacred. Moreover, the maintenance of this order also still appeared to be a prerequisite for prosperity and peace. Amidst many comments is one from Worcester displaying sentiments that are clearly untouched from the seventeenth century:

If we sincerely desire the blessing of god to rest on England, and the deliberations of His Majesty's Ministers our belief in the almighty must be proclaimed and maintained at all costs. Gratitude for divine favours, and deep faith in the almighty Goodness. Compel [sic] our nation to refuse any countenance to the proposed insult to the divine majesty already banned by a neighbouring country.[40]

Fear was also a method of redefining the nation to suddenly include those religious individuals who might previously have considered themselves outsiders. The campaign against the 'Godless Congress' in England in 1938 was encouraged by Catholics in both Canada and Australia. Their writings sometimes consciously portrayed them as better Christians and defenders of the king and Empire than their cosmopolitan Anglican compatriots in London and the Home Counties.[41]

The fear of communism also had an influence upon how European societies reacted to the appearance of blasphemy. Certainly, Dutch society found itself suddenly confronted by a 'red menace' and was persuaded to bring its laws into

---

[40] HO4524619, Letters written November 1937.   [41] HO4524619/217459/92

Fig. 19. Twentieth-Century French anticlericalism. The appearance of André Lorulot at the Godless Congress in London during 1938 caused concern at the Home Office.

the twentieth century. These reactions had their counterparts in America and Germany, as we have already seen.[42] Although the Dutch legislation was to prove abortive, it demonstrated how governments were prepared to respond to the sensitivity of public opinion and to move against threats before they could have a demonstrable effect upon society. Some of this same language survived to be spoken with renewed vigour and support by Mary Whitehouse in the infamous Thorsen incident of 1977, which preceded the *Gay News* trial. On this occasion the home secretary was persuaded to deny the Danish film director Jens Jurgen Thorsen entry to the country on the grounds that his proposal to film 'The Sex Life of Christ' in Britain would outrage public morals. The script of Thorsen's film contained a scene in which Christ had homosexual intercourse with St John at the Last Supper, and another sex scene intended to be representative of the resurrection. Mary Whitehouse had been assiduous enough to have the entire script translated from the Danish, and the experience must arguably have prepared her for the *Gay News* case.[43]

In England decolonization coincided with imperatives for integration with Europe, and this reawoke the urge for moral isolationism. Where once Europe threatened established imperial markets for agricultural produce, its new threat to Europeanize morals and standards of tolerance proposed a sweeping-away of the moral order inherent in the British Empire. Within this, Britain's fear of the foreign created and sustained some, often comically bizarre, archetypes. British Muscular Christianity of the Victorian period, still in the twentieth century did battle with foreign spirituality or subversive secularism. This last idea found its way into the arguments of Christian evangelical organizations in Britain, who viewed contact with European systems of law and morals as profoundly suspect. This trend towards isolation was particularly noticeable in the English-speaking world, where activists became loud and empowered voices alongside a media more than intrigued by their message.

The most readily identifiable of these voices in Britain was, as we have seen, that of Mrs Mary Whitehouse, who campaigned tirelessly through her National Viewers' and Listeners' Association to combat profanity and, eventually, the blasphemous. Although the libertarian Left and the artistic community often failed to take her seriously, this has proved to be, in hindsight, a grave error. Those who stood opposite her in the *Gay News* case readily admit themselves to have been wrongfooted by her calmness, mastery of rhetorical argument, and infectious sincerity. In this respect the moral backlash against the permissive society was fortunate to have such a talent at its helm. But Mrs Whitehouse's most important achievement was to persuade all who heard her that she spoke for a fearful yet important majority. Accounts of the *Gay News* trial include her conducting prayer outside court and feeling the nearness of God during certain sections of the proceedings. These episodes had an important impact upon

---

[42] See Ch. 3. [43] Mary Whitehouse, *Quite Contrary* (London, 1988), 43 and 47.

supporters, both in her vicinity and also further afield in the country at large. These sentiments were then conveyed further still through Mrs Whitehouse's own books, that became central texts for those concerned about moral decline. Her episodic autobiography *Quite Contrary* contains regular departures from narrative to reflect upon scriptural texts and their inspiration, which were clearly intended to fortify her readers. To Mrs Whitehouse, God's intervention in the *Gay News* case extended even to placing words in the mouth of the prosecuting counsel Geoffrey Robertson. Although it was an astute observation to suggest that 'there had been more of the gospel preached in court this week, in spite of the motivation of those who preached it, than surely ever before in its history', it was probably far-fetched to argue that: 'All the Gays, secularists, and others who packed that court must have glimpsed something of the wonder and beauty of the Christian faith and God must surely have spoken in many hearts.'[44]

Nonetheless, Mrs Whitehouse remained significantly an outsider from the government and the media, and would only appear in the living-rooms of the British population when invited to do so by the media itself. This was profoundly different from the case of the Moral Majority in America, who were infinitely more successful in persuading members of the Senate to back their broad coalition approach to combating moral challenges. Senator Jesse Helms and others frequently demonstrated such support for Moral Majority causes, and seemed bent upon a crusade against the cosmopolitan influences upon American culture. These closely resembled the English Home Counties, suspicions about Europe, and often played to the same isolationist agendas and political aspirations. Paradoxically, Britain's nationalized, chartered British Broadcasting Corporation was more adept at resisting forms of censorship than a so-called free-enterprise media in the United States. Whilst the 1990s was an era of directives which steered BBC programme-makers away from controversy, by the middle years of the next decade they were prepared to defend programmes like *Jerry Springer: The Opera* with some confidence.[45] In America the Moral Majority ultimately perfected the tactic of undermining public funding for the arts. Advertisers could also be very easily frightened away from networks which courted any form of controversy.

Nonetheless, fear of blasphemy persisted on both sides of the Atlantic and in continental Europe. Many in Britain viewed the immanent arrival of European law with some trepidation, whilst elsewhere the effects of globalization and falling national boundaries have had a similar effect. European-wide law for these groups seemed homogenising and liable to produce a lower agreed standard of morality. During the process that culminated in the incorporation of European Convention law into British law, the Newcastle-based Christian Institute showed its deep concern. In particular, it became convinced that the lowest standard of morality and laws to protect it would prevail in the new European community.

[44] Mary Whitehouse, *Quite Contrary* (London, 1988), 50–1.   [45] See Ch. 1.

Such a permissive approach would allow into Britain a frightening array of challenges to centuries-old morality. In such arguments a federal grouping was seen as obviously secular, whilst the distinct nation-state, evolving through its relationship with Christianity, was considered a superior entity worthy of protection.[46]

When the House of Lords Select Committee on Religious offences heard evidence in 2002, the response of Christian organizations that were invited to submit oral and written evidence confirmed this climate of fear. These organizations also readily noted the historical relationship of church and state in defining the kingdom. Here, most obviously of all, was evidence of a collective belief in pre-modern society's conception of community organized for its own defence against its clearly identified enemies. Medieval kingship in contemporary debate was once more capable of breathing life into nationalism and the nation in the face of alternatives. The correspondent from the Inverness Free Church of Scotland saw no ambiguity whatsoever in simultaneously invoking the 'near' nation of Scotland and the 'far' umbrella nation of Britain: 'Our beloved country has over at least 1,000 years been blessed with a public and national confession of the Christian faith as the basis of our constitution and monarchy. This provision has been our glory and our strength and we must not tamper with our inheritance in these days of confusion and anarchy.'[47]

Such fear of the outside world had also been clear in the evidence heard by the New South Wales Law Commission a decade earlier. The effects of Europeanization and globalization respectively upon the nation-state gave weight to the redefinition of its national characteristics. This reached urgently for laws, such as that of blasphemy, that could reinvigorate traditional state nationhood and provide issues around which such debates could be had anew. These debates increasingly empowered individuals and persuaded the victim of blasphemy to speak and be heard in public. The medieval victims of blasphemy were frequently paralysed by shock and had their psychological equilibrium restored by the actions of government or providence. By the start of the third millennium such victims had become articulate and thoroughly capable of seeking legal redress to restore challenges to their identity.

[46] The Newcastle-based Christian Institute displayed this material upon its website in late 1998 and early 1999. The Christian Institute can be contacted at The Christian Institute, 26 Jesmond Road, Newcastle upon Tyne, NE2 4PQ (email info@christian.org.uk).

[47] Submission of Inverness Free Church of Scotland Select Committee on Religious Offences in England and Wales, HL Paper 95, Vol. III written evidence, p. 46.

7

Last Temptations and Visions of Ecstasy: Blasphemy and Film

THE GOSPELS ON SCREEN

The arrival of cinema as a mass medium propelled blasphemy into an important position in modern culture. This is because the moving image's ability to replicate real life has always possessed enormous cultural power. Theologians and censors have thus always been wary of the medium's influence and its capacity to cause offence to religious minorities. Importantly, as cinema eventually came to coexist with television, moving images of the divine would come to shape how individuals saw the biblical story.

The first five years of popular cinema saw no fewer than six biblical interpretations put on the screen, to be followed by more than one for every year that has passed since. Several reasons explain this popularity. The Bible and the Gospels are irrefutably gripping and powerful narratives, and contain somewhere within them most of the experiences possible for human individuals and civilizations. The Bible and Gospels also contain genres ranging from history, philosophy, rhetoric, and the outpourings of the apocalyptic imagination. The West's Judaeo-Christian past also makes such stories, even now, accessible, and they thus prove attractive to audiences and more mundanely to film financiers. However, this should not blind us to the potential of cinema to elaborate and give meaning to the religious, recognized even by religious authorities themselves. Catholicism's emphasis upon free will, for example, was instrumental in creating a didactic and influential role for the religious film. In France the Augustinian order established the 'Bonne Cinema' to show uplifting and spiritually orthodox films in churches.[1] Some biblical scholars have also proved to be optimistic, noting how properly conducted and subtle religious cinema could benefit Christianity. Borrowing from postmodern ideas, critics such as Larry Kreitzer have argued that the cinematic productions of modern culture could have a positive impact upon how events like the crucifixion of Christ are viewed by the public at large.[2]

---

[1] I. Butler, *Religion in the Cinema* (New York, 1969), 36.
[2] L. Kreitzer, *Gospel Images in Fiction and Film: On Reversing the Hermenutic Flow* (London, 2002). See also Butler, *Religion in the cinema, passim.*

But the potential for blasphemy was never far away, because film allowed the opportunity to interpret the Gospel story. This could now reach beyond the sanctioned doctrines of the mainstream churches to reach millions. In particular, film portrayals of the figure of Christ have proven to be the most problematic. Some films did what they could to portray a factual and comparatively straightforward retelling of the Gospel story. Others emphasized specific incidents from the Gospels or, through their selection of these incidents, reinforced specific religious interpretations. The more adventurous film-makers actively tried to problematize the idea of the Messiah, or questioned his divinity. This involved the use of unscriptural speech, or placing the Christ figure in surreal or commonplace modern situations.

Portraying Christ in such contemporary situations also addressed the perceived evils and immorality of modern life. Bryan Forbes's *Whistle Down the Wind* of 1961 had an escaped criminal persuading young children that he was Jesus incarnate, hoping that they would shelter and aid him. The film itself turned on ideas of truth and childlike innocence, alongside the possibility of miracles in a mechanistic and rational age. This innocence seemed to have passed when Andrew Lloyd Webber's 2006 musical version could only make the story credible by moving it to the American Bible Belt and portraying the central character as an adolescent rather than a child. The 1989 film *Jesus of Montreal* arguably took this approach further, and constituted an attack upon commercialism in culture.[3]

How far Jesus could be updated for modern sensibilities was to be a constant subject of intense debate. A recognizable modern-dress Jesus might be acceptable, but a Christ who was unequivocally a part of the contemporary world asked much more of audiences. Robert Frank's *The Sin of Jesus* (1961) depicted a woman married to an angel, whom she later kills in an act of drunken carelessness. A contemporary Jesus then reproaches her with foul language (for the period), only later asking forgiveness for these actions.[4] This profane Jesus was, however, still some distance from Thorsen's burlesque portrayal of a sexually active bankrobber Christ, or Irving Welsh's later portrayal of a drunken, cursing deity in *The Granton Star Cause*.

Perhaps more questioning, and ultimately disturbing for 1960s audiences, was Dennis Potter's television drama *Son of Man*, a deliberately low-key and naturalistic piece which portrayed Christ with a temper and riddled with enraged self-doubt. Potter's Christ punctuated his ministry with uncertainty over his role and identity. This culminated in anguished cries to God of 'Is it me?' Christ had been made more human and fallible in *Son of Man*, whilst such a portrayal was further endorsed by his colloquially charged diatribes against the materialism

---

[3] P. Fraser, *Images of the Passion: The Sacramental Mode in Film* (Westport, Conn., 1998), 98–106.
[4] Butler, *Religion in the Cinema*, 46.

and vested interests of first-century Judaea. These were deliberately given in a style and idiom resonant with the counter-culture of 1969. Potter's Messiah was by turns worldly, odd, and forgiving—yet could also inspire in ways not wholly clear to the disciples, or indeed the audience. The other protagonists, especially Pilate, Judas, and Caiaphas, were all given a degree of plausibility, sometimes bordering on outright sympathy. The Romans were authority figures concerned about the spiritual revolution Jesus might yet bring to their empire. Meanwhile Judas was portrayed as torn between his respect for the authority of Caiaphas and his own earnest wish to see a Messiah. Although unscriptural, such elements might not offend, but the portrayal of Jesus remained potentially problematic. Although never mocked or derided, this was Christ stripped of divinity and exposed to the searing temptation of doubt. While Unitarians and even some humanists might have accepted this alongside more mainstream Christians, there were those who took exception to a Christ unsure of his mission or identity.[5]

Cinema has also used our belief in the purity of religion and piety as a means of showing how human nature and civilization can debase them. Luis Buñuel's film *Viridiana* (Spain 1961) featured calculated attacks upon bourgeois morality using the medium of religious tableau. A group of vagrants appears in the film being photographed seated in positions resonant of Leonardo Da Vinci's *Last Supper*, and these scenes provoked accusations of blasphemy. However, here it is worth remembering the context that produced such accusations. Buñuel had not been the first, nor would he be the last, to invoke this painting (*Quo Vadis* had done so in 1951, and George Stevens's *The Greatest Story Ever Told* did so in 1953, to be followed by the *Da Vinci Code* in 2006). However, Buñuel's depiction did open discussion about whether religious beliefs or their depictions were the source and target of the parody. In this instance Alan Pavelin suggested, in his book *Fifty Religious Films*, that blasphemy was intrinsically in the eye of the beholder.[6]

Blasphemy in film would really only become an explosive issue when it was associated with mainstream culture. Art-house films would please art-house agnostics, but the real damage to the image of organized religion would occur when public figures embraced anticlericalism or criticism of Christianity. Thus, by examining cinematic episodes that involved the well known and the notable we uncover how powerful was the widespread concern for the future of Christianity. Perhaps especially surprising is a discovery that intentions behind the writing and making of films, however honourable (or indeed dishonourable), would neither protect the 'innocent' nor ensure the punishment of the guilty.

---

[5] D. Potter, *Son of Man* (Harmondsworth, 1971).
[6] A. Pavelin, *Fifty Religious Films* (London, 1990).

MONTY PYTHON'S *LIFE OF BRIAN*

Some of these issues need to be borne in mind when considering the blasphemous potential and intention behind Monty Python's *Life of Brian* (1979). To many critics and viewers, this comedy represented a new departure in film's capacity to offend. It brought cult followings and popular audiences for satire into the arena of outright blasphemous discrediting of the Christian religion. In this respect it would be easy to highlight the inveterate opportunism of the Python team, who were working in the wake of Franco Zeffirelli's *Jesus of Nazareth* (even using some of the same sets), and at a time of distinct cultural challenges to establishment beliefs and norms. The very idea for the film seems to have sprung from an off-the-cuff remark made by Eric Idle when questioned about the Python team's next project. Idle quipped that the next film would be 'Jesus Christ—Lust for Glory'. Although the idea for the film may well have sprung from this inauspicious start, there is at least a case for seeing it as reflecting wider cultural elements. These inspired and interested the Pythons as much as they did the troupe's eager and enthusiastic mass audience.

Certainly many of the obsessions that fuelled the humour of *Life of Brian* had emerged in embryo in the troupe's first film epic, *Monty Python and the Holy Grail*, which juxtaposed the earnestness of a medieval world without technology with satire on the frailty and stupidity of human stereotypes. *Grail* was also a film in which the religious epic became an explicit target for Python humour. The whole film removes the emotional power from a raft of medieval epics, from *El Cid* through to *Ivanhoe*, making the filming of more modern counterparts almost impossible. Certainly, most sword-and-sorcery, quest-orientated cinema has, ever since, seemed odd or contained the quality of camp over-seriousness and ill-placed reverence. But *Holy Grail* also represented a further development of Python's attack upon authority and its spurious claims that the defendants in the *Oz* or *Lady Chatterley* trials would have recognized. The film ends with the medieval quest for the Grail abruptly curtailed by the intervention of the all-too-modern police force, complete with sirens and squad cars. This appeared to be the Python team telling us that medievalism and its crass simplicity had clearly had its day.

Indeed, the Python team had enjoyed playful iconoclasm for some time before they ever thought themselves capable of blasphemy. They had also gained a significant track record of confrontation with broadcasting authorities of various kinds (in both Britain and America), as well as a not-always-appreciated capacity for self-censorship. Experience gleaned from their forays into publishing had acquainted them with the need for caution and to have at least some in the legal profession on their side. When *Grail* was released with an 'A' certificate (instead of the expected 'AA' or even 'X'), the comedy troupe proved itself to have been astute in allowing the British Board of Film Censors a co-operative part in their enterprise.[7]

So it seems likely that the Python team were well aware of what they were undertaking with *Life of Brian*, but also were swayed by inspiration. Eric Idle noted that religion appeared to be an unreasonably protected taboo and that the West's cultural restrictions upon its discussion were both spurs to creativity. The period between the inception of *Life of Brian* and its filming was punctuated by other high-profile instances of blasphemous libel hitting the headlines. Whilst 1976 witnessed the furore against Jens Jorgen Thorsen, the following year saw Mary Whitehouse triumph in the *Gay News* case.[8]

The film's backers, EMI, kept a very watchful eye on the progress of the *Gay News* case, and regularly implored the team to be ready to make scriptural and cinematic provision for cuts and alterations. Eventually the Python's regard for artistic control, which they had trumpeted in the past, resurfaced and they refused to compromise on the script. With a degree of relief, EMI and Lord Delfont withdrew from the film, citing its cost and (in a much lower key) its capacity for both blasphemy and anti-Semitism as reasons for not backing it. An eventual lawsuit by Python against EMI was quietly settled out of court. After a shorter hiatus than expected, Eric Idle's friendship with the ex-Beatle, George Harrison, led to the latter becoming the main backer of the film through what was to become Handmade Films. In agreeing to this, Harrison had taken a decisive step that was to influence subsequent British film-making and inspire its willingness to take more chances than it might otherwise have done. He apparently was prepared to back the Pythons because he wished 'to see the film', and filming duly began in Tunisia, amidst the Zeffirelli set and away from the prying eyes of Christendom.

The resulting film is generally considered to be flawed, if entertaining, and the targets of its satire to be, at least partly, vanquished. If this was all that anyone wanted from the film, then the Pythons were successful. Some British critics damned the work with faint praise, accusing it by turns of being too genteel and not more anticlerical in a recognizably European style. Peter Ackroyd, in the *Spectator*, argued that Python did not have the intellectual clout or menace to be properly blasphemous. In noting its thoroughgoing Englishness, he declared that the film 'consists of being naughty without being interestingly offensive; in being knowing rather than clever; in being obvious rather than imaginative'. Meanwhile, Philip French, in the *Observer*, argued similarly that it was all too

---

[7] The film classification scheme which commenced operation on 1 July 1970 assigned one of four certificates guiding admissions to film performances. These were: *U* Universal admission; *A* Children aged 5 and over admitted unaccompanied but parents are advised that the film may contain material they would prefer the children under 14 not to see; *AA* No admission for children under 14; *X* No admission for children under 18. This system has subsequenctly been revised on three occasions.

[8] G. Perry, *The Life of Python* (London, 1994).

safe: 'The comedy does not have the wry, bruised resignation of Jewish Humour. Nor is there any of that Catholic fascination with the liturgical and the sacerdotal one meets in the anti-clerical joking of Continental film-makers like Fellini, Pasolini and Buñuel.' [9]

The film took a series of calculated swipes at religion. Its main theme was the life of Brian of Nazareth, which paralleled that of Christ, or at least seemed to in the context of this biblical anti-epic. Brian's nativity is attended by the Three Wise Men who, realizing their mistake, take back their gifts and head towards the real event some distance away. Brian himself has a 'ministry' in which he preaches to a small crowd as the means of escaping his Roman pursuers, though he eventually becomes a political prisoner at their hands. Like Jesus, Brian is crucified, although significantly this is the film's end, and no attempt is made to suggest anything resembling a resurrection. The Pythons always believed that only when viewed carelessly did the film appear to be a parody of the life of Christ, but this was nonetheless the view many had of it, especially those who baulked at seeing the film itself. If viewers wanted to they could see the idea of a Messiah and his ability to dispense miracles held up to systematic ridicule. In particular, the climax of the film provoked the greatest range of condemnation. This final scene showed Brian and others crucified in a conclusion which emphatically denied the idea of an afterlife, those on the cross collectively singing 'Always Look on the Bright Side of Life' whilst swaying to the music. At once this appeared to deny Christ's suffering, to deny the notion of redemption through such suffering and, finally, to deny the resurrection and the Christian notion of life after death.

In their defence, the Pythons argued that the film was infinitely more sophisticated than this, and to some extent these arguments hold water. In particular, they specified that their real attacks had been on organized religion and various levels of human stupidity which were bred by it. Ironically, one of the film's fiercest onslaughts was against the Judaic approach to blasphemy. In particular, an unfortunate defendant who repeats his blasphemy (uttering the name of God) in an attempt to defend himself from the accusation is greeted by further charges and a premature attempt to stone him. Indeed, the way stoning in the film is presented as a ritualized Saturday afternoon sport makes important points about the nature of intolerance and its routine assimilation into people's consciousness.

Brian's own 'ministry', such as it is, provides food for thought in suggesting the ease with which the even slightly charismatic can attract quasi-religious followers. It should also be remembered that the realm of politics was not immune from the Pythons' invective in this film. The innumerable splits between the political opposition to Roman occupation ('the People's Front of Judaea' etc.) are relentlessly lampooned, suggesting that a human capacity for misunderstanding and self-seeking is scarcely the monopoly of organized religion. Some have also argued that the Python's portrayal of Jesus himself was even sympathetic. His

[9] *Spectator*, 17 Nov. 1979; *Observer*, 11 Nov. 1979.

first appearance is in the nativity tableau at the start of the film; yet there is still an element of satire here, though more of the religious epic than of the founder of the Christian religion. The other appearance of Jesus in the film is when he is delivering the 'Sermon on the Mount'. In this sequence the Christ figure delivers the sermon in a recognisably orthodox manner, but his words are misheard by those at the back ('Blessed are the cheesemakers . . .'). Again, the Pythons argued that this was part of their suggestion that mankind was inherently capable of being wrong-headed and wilfully ignorant.

However, even in this perhaps laudable intention, the Python team once again astutely operated a form of self-censorship. A sequence which involved a character representative of extreme forms of Zionism eventually was consigned to the cutting-room floor, in the interests of smoothing the way for the film's distribution in America. Viewed alongside their other works, it was also possible to see the Pythons further indulging their cultural obsessions. Eric Idle's wordplay, Cleese's manic officiousness, and Terry Gilliam's obsession with flotsam, filth, and detritus were all tools brought to bear upon the genre of the biblical epic. The Holy Land must have been squalid and it must have contained the awkward, dull, and obnoxious, or so the Pythons were determined to make us believe. If Monty Python's *Life of Brian* did not ultimately shake the foundations of Christianity, it may at least have fostered a distaste for the sanitized, melodramatic biblical-epic versions of it. Although they were scarcely great cultural innovators, the Pythons' very public discovery of Christlike figures as ordinary and flawed made the subsequent reinterpretations of Scorsese and Wingrove possible.

Many believed not only that the Pythons may not have intended to blaspheme against the Christian religion, but that the whole idea of 'intention' was itself a red herring. Far more important than this was the actual effect of the film and its portrayals. As many pointed out, Python had a cult, as well as mainstream, following for its films, records, books, and television programmes. The lawyer and writer John Mortimer was even of the opinion that the sheer popularity of Python might constitute a form of protection from potential prosecution. If the sentiments on view in the film could in any way be construed as widely accepted or even popular, then the likelihood of prosecution would fade rapidly. Whether unwittingly or wittingly, individuals were being led into questioning the very foundation of the Christian religion. Christian commentators could legitimately wonder whether individuals could ever mentally encounter the 'Sermon on the Mount' without mistakes and mishearings. We might here remember how the comic portrayals of the Bible by George William Foote relied on childhood comic mishearing of important words and biblical terms.[10]

Python also drew on the ludicrous and the grotesque in a manner that would have been recognized by a cultural theorist of 'carnival' such as Mikhael Bhaktin.

---

[10] For more on this see the relevant chapter in David Nash, *Blasphemy in Britain* (Aldershot, 1999).

Python never managed to be outrightly anticlerical, but their arguments for freedom of speech and their liberal-humanist swipes against organized religion were arguably more effective in most branches of the English-speaking world. Was Monty Python's cult popularity going to lead its followers into questioning the religious? In a sense this pitted popular culture against undiluted revealed religion in a battle for supremacy. It was perhaps ironic that George Harrison should have backed the film, since it had been his fellow Beatle John Lennon who had first focused this argument with his initially shocking assertion that for some elements of youth the Beatles were 'more popular than Jesus'.

The astute self-censorship of the Pythons meant that significant material relating to the film remained unpublished. Some of this found its way into a book version of the script, with an associated scrapbook containing the omitted material. In a quite ironic reversal of most conceptions of blasphemy, in which the more public the encounter with blasphemous material, the more dangerous it is, the book's Canadian publishers ensured that while the film played to packed houses the book remained under lock and key in the warehouse. Inevitably the shadow of the *Gay News* case loomed over all of this, many legal opinions taking this case to be a barometer of public opinion. Methuen, the book's Canadian publishers, sought the reaction of the country's leading publishing lawyer, Julian Porter, who noted how the approach of the Pythons themselves to the production of *Brian* had woven a path through the implications of the *Gay News* judgement. Citing *R* v. *Hetherington*, which still had legal force in Canada, Porter saw many sections of the book as falling under the rubric of 'scurrilous, offensive and contumelious'. Porter was concerned about the potential reactions of fundamentalists who in Canada, unlike in the United States, could call upon the protection of a blasphemy law.[11] Paradoxically, in this instance the most religiously sensitized society in the world allowed *Life of Brian* and the uncensored version of the book to circulate, theoretically protected by the First Amendment.

Back in England, even the usually optimistic John Mortimer advised judicious care over some sections of the book. In particular, an entire sequence in which a young woman explains to her suitor that she has been fertilized by the Holy Ghost came under scrutiny. Mortimer was fairly confident that this section could be explained away as the girl offering a bizarre and far-fetched excuse for her condition. However, the use of profane and contumelious language in describing miracles unequivocally performed by Jesus was dangerously problematic.[12] Even

---

[11] Quoted in Robert Hewison, *Irreverence, Scurrility, Profanity and Licentious Abuse: Monty Python, The Case Against* (London, 1981), 71–2.

[12] The Scrapbook appeared in the UK as Graham Chapman, John Cleese, Terry Gilliam, Eric Idle, Terry Jones, and Michael Palin, *Monty Python's The Life of Brian* (London, 1979). This contains the 'Holy Ghost sketch', a satire of Brian giving the Sermon on the Mount, and an account of the 'martyrdom of St Brian' in which he describes God as 'a rotten bastard'. These additions perhaps suggest an appreciation of the differing standards of censorship required in the print and film media.

for a libertarian adrift from Christian culture like Mortimer, swearing might
have been one thing but likening such miracles to the work of a conjuror was too
close to the 'Christ as a circus clown' motif which had landed Gott with a prison
sentence in 1922.

Indulging their penchant for free speech, the Pythons decided to publish and
be damned, no doubt soothed by the fact that even the most pessimistic of
legal advice really doubted the likelihood of a prison sentence. This did not,
however, stop the book's printers from consulting John Smyth, the lawyer who
had successfully prosecuted the *Gay News* case. His counsel against printing the
attendant scrapbook meant that hasty alternative arrangements had to be made.

When the film was released the strongest protests against it—as would be the
case with Scorsese's *Last Temptation* occurred in America. The absence of state
protection for religion, or even a nationally enforceable code of film classification,
meant that the country would become the centre of informal protest. Once again
issues of blasphemy would provide a backdrop to the struggle between federal
and state law. In some people's perceptions the rights of the individual against
the claims of big government were what was really at stake.

Perhaps surprisingly, the first complaints emanated from a Jewish group, the
Union of Orthodox Rabbis of the United States and Canada. This group found
Life of Brian, again perhaps surprisingly, sacrilegious and blasphemous rather
than anti-Semitic.[13] The Roman Catholic Office for Film and Broadcasting made
it a sin to see the film, whilst a number of Protestant groups investigated the
possible formation of a rainbow-style coalition to bring a prosecution. Certainly
most of these protests saw in *Brian* a deliberate parody of the scriptures, and were
not impressed by attempts to make them think more widely about the issues
which the Pythons satirized.

But not all objections to the film were straightforward, and the distance between
the gentle English anticlerical humanism the Pythons inherited and some sentiments which fundamentalism had spawned were graphically demonstrated. The
evangelical Roger Fulton, who ran a church in Greenwich Village, expressed
some undiluted and arcane objections to the film. In noting the appropriate-
ness the group's name—he referred mistakenly to as 'Monty Snake'—Fulton
was not surprisingly unimpressed by the colourful language in the film. He
was especially unhappy about the cross-dressing of Terry Jones as Brian's
mother, and the expression of the desire to change sex by one of the characters, which he saw as an unscriptural abomination.[14] Some other areas of
obscenity were mentioned, which together suggested that Python had, for Fulton, offended against a stricter moral climate which was already evolving in
America.

---

[13] Douglas L. McCall, *Monty Python* (London, 1991), 71.
[14] Address of Roger Fulton, 16 Sept. 1979. Reproduced in Hewison, *Irreverence, scurrility,
profanity*, 80.

This climate would increasingly make itself felt through local communities seeking to use their direct pressure to change local minds. However hard the Citizens Against Blasphemy Committee might call for a reinstatement of New York State's blasphemy law, it would be informal action that would prove most effective in America. Thus, a number of local cinema managers were persuaded by community pressure to abandon plans to show *Brian*. Having the film accepted in the more cosmopolitan east and west coasts was one thing, but the issue began to write itself large when the film went on nationwide distribution to midwest and southern states. Throughout the Carolinas, Louisiana, Mississippi, and Florida the film's runs were sometimes curtailed or punctuated by the pressure of local communities and organized religious groups. Surprisingly, some jurisdictions managed to gain extended showings of the film through the use of local ballots. Meanwhile some renowned censorship regimes, such as that in Utah, bizarrely granted a showing without comment. Nonetheless, more serious attempts were made to stop the film by reactivating recently moribund state blasphemy laws. Attempts to do this in Oklahoma and Massachusetts resulted in legal pronouncements that the film would not reinstate such laws.[15]

Whilst some local authorities in Britain banned *Brian*, the attitudes displayed in these local decisions varied enormously, and their effects were sporadic. The film was banned in ten districts in England (predominantly in the West Country and West Yorkshire) and was subject to an 'X' rating in twenty-seven others. This piecemeal pattern was repeated in Scotland, with showings in Edinburgh passing without comment whilst Glasgow witnessed demonstrations. The film found itself effectively proscribed in Ireland, but the action of a crusading priest, Father Brian D'Arcy, resulted in a significant alteration to Ireland's censorship laws. Up to this point these laws had not covered sound recordings in the form of records or cassettes and, in conjunction with the *Irish Independent*, this anomaly was now addressed, giving the Censorship of Publications Board powers to intervene hereafter. This effectively curtailed circulation of the Soundtrack of *Brian*, which had already been withdrawn from sale as a result of numerous threats.[16]

In Britain at least, Mary Whitehouse's Festival of Light appeared to have learned a little composure from its experience in the *Gay News* case. So its opposition to the film was surprisingly measured, in some of its arguments. In a letter sent to its supporters, the organization acknowledged that the failure to prevent the public consumption of films like *Godspell* and *Jesus Christ Superstar* had left Christians in a difficult position. This seemed to argue for a sort of totalitarian position, in which any modernization, or democratization, of the scriptural message for a twentieth-century audience represented both a dilution and a source of error. It also suggested that the sacred should remain taboo

[15] Hewison, *Irreverence, Scurrility, Profanity*, 82–3.
[16] Ibid. 91.

from those trying to render intelligible what was beyond human intelligibility. The letter also represented a gracious, if grudging, acceptance of Mortimer's argument about popularity. Nonetheless, the Festival of Light was still anxious to suggest that *Brian* was a step too far, and claimed they now knew where the boundaries lay. From this point on it was clearly essential that criticism offered around *Brian* should be 'both informed and deserved'. Fearing the consequences of this argument, and the power of the liberal free-speech lobby, the Festival of Light argued for action on the American model, offering lower-key local activity. This was an alternative to taking on an establishment that the organization seems to have increasingly construed as mindlessly liberal and hedonistically libertarian. However, in proffering this response the Festival of Light must have thought deeply about King-Hamilton's suggestion in his summing-up of the *Gay News* case, that Kirkup's poem had been blasphemous 'on its face'. Even the Festival of Light conceded that *Life of Brian* was, according to the strict interpretation of law, not blasphemous, since the distinction between Brian and Jesus had been clearly indicated by the film-makers.

Nonetheless, what was abundantly clear was that the Festival of Light admitted that *Life of Brian* was damaging to Christianity, and further anxious analysis by concerned Christians doubtless pleased the Python team enormously. The organisation's Raymond Johnston acknowledged the inadequacy of strict interpretations of the law in asserting that the film was in poor taste. Yet he maintained that the film would 'tend to discredit the New Testament story of Jesus in semi-pagan minds'—all of which amounted to sentiments that the Python troupe would roundly have endorsed. This echoed the astute arguments of the hostile American Catholic commentator, the Revd Patrick J. Sullivan, who argued that the film was 'blasphemous in its effect, though probably not in intent'.[17]

What all of this showed was that Monty Python's *Life of Brian*, when placed alongside the *Gay News* verdict, had exposed dangerous inconsistencies in the cultural application of the handling of blasphemy. *Gay News* had demonstrated that an unorthodox portrayal of the genuine Christ, no matter how 'innocent' or well intentioned, could be successfully prosecuted, even if this curtailed completely its readership amongst an already obscure audience. Monty Python's *Life of Brian* demonstrated that those with deliberate and calculating satirical intent could carefully word and construct a work of art or entertainment which would evade the law. More than this, it would reach a still wider audience awakened to it by the sporadically successful campaigns of detractors. Moreover, the inertia of authority would not stop religious groups seeing damage and offence caused to a series of cherished and valued beliefs. As the bishop of Southwark, Mervyn Stockwood, would declare on a television debate with members of the Python team, the film would not have been made had Christ not have existed. This, however, was also a way of drawing the Pythons into

17 Quoted in Ibid. 79, 84.

saying that they had mocked the incarnation, something which especially upset Malcolm Muggeridge.[18] Eric Idle would later reply that all that was of value should be capable of surviving humour. This was an attack upon Christianity's claim for immunity and special privileges, which a modern and open society had a clear interest in denying.

In the final analysis, the Python team would certainly have to concede that they were bringing Christianity into disrepute, through attitudes and images that were deliberately mocking and contumelious. The paradox is that they escaped major proceedings against them or significant limitations upon the distribution of their film. This was perhaps because they spoke to an audience potentially outside, or even without, the religious sensibilities they were mocking. Python ultimately asked questions about the nature of the religious, but not necessarily of the divine. Indeed, they could have argued that a major theme of their work was to highlight the unfortunate divide between the two. Audiences were split on Python, with those enthused and those offended allowed to go their separate ways. Much more problematic was the work of those who claimed to come from within the Christian community who were prepared and interested enough to seek inspiration from the Gospels. It was not only ridicule, contumely, and mockery that would produce controversy and accusations of blasphemy.

THE LAST TEMPTATION OF CHRIST

Martin Scorsese's film *The Last Temptation of Christ* was probably the culmination of the desire to produce an experimental and believable Jesus. At least one critic has seen this as the most thought-provoking and original of the film portrayals of Christ.[19] Although some would come to question Scorsese's motivation, there is no evidence that mockery of, or scoffing at, Christianity or its central tenets was ever an intention.

Scorsese always, however, knew that filming Nikos Kazantzakis's novel *The Last Temptation* would be fraught with difficulty. The book had resulted in its author being excommunicated by the Greek Orthodox church, and the book itself was thereafter banned. Scorsese came from a Catholic background and had, at one stage, seriously contemplated the priesthood. It was clear that his upbringing was steeped in the iconography of Catholicism, and he had also, from a particularly early age, wanted to produce an enduring film about the life of Christ.[20] In this he perhaps fits our profile of the film-maker as an honest seeker after images. Just as George Harrison had

[18] *Friday Night–Saturday Morning* (BBC2), 9 Nov. 1979.
[19] Fraser, *Images of the Passion*, 171–6.
[20] Ian Christie and David Thompson (eds.), *Scorsese on Scorsese* (London, 2003), 118.

wanted to see *Life of Brian*, so Scorsese desired to see the products of his own imagination created and realized for others. The initial production company, Paramount, pulled out after consulting with theologians and the intervention of Cardinal Lustiger, the archbishop of Paris, prevented the French government from providing public funding for the film. Only in 1987 did the production commence under Universal Pictures, with a budget cut by more than half.[21]

Scorsese's choice to use the Kazantzakis novel did fundamentally shape the Christ that appeared in *Last Temptation*. But the Jesus created by Scorsese owed much to the ideas and themes he had dealt with in many of his earlier films. Far too many critics for comfort saw the lone Christ as an archetype evident in *Raging Bull* or *Taxi Driver*. This was compounded by Scorsese's continued collaboration with Paul Schrader, the scriptwriter of these two films. This led some to suggest that their work on *Last Temptation* was the completion of a trilogy based around the motif of suffering.[22] Christ's sparring with and dependence upon Judas led one critic (Richard Corliss) to see *Last Temptation* as the 'ultimate buddy movie'.[23] All this suggested real problems in viewing a religious film in an age in which the cinema had become so ubiquitous, with access to film, the ability to view and review it, available as never before.

Moreover, an obsession with suffering and blood-drenched sacrifice was never far from the surface in Scorese's films, periodically exploding onto the screen in *Last Temptation*. Scorsese had even used the motif of crucifixion in an earlier film, *Boxcar Bertha*.[24] The streets of New York were also unfortunately invoked through the use of familiar actors (such as Harvey Keitel and Willem Dafoe), who brought to mind some of the problems encountered earlier by directors hampered with 'Hollywood in Sandals'. In some respects the troubles this film faced highlight the difference between religious belief considered to be a literal truth, and religious ideas as the food for inspiration. It also highlights the problems that the film-maker might encounter through the use of allusion, metaphor, image, and close representation as a means of conveying an idea of the sacred. For Martin Scorsese all these were tools to aid his imaginative representation. For those wishing to project their own idea of Christ and his passion upon the film, they represented the source of error and blasphemy. Scorsese's own disclaimer, shown before all screenings of the film, emphasized its distance from a literal portrayal of the Gospels. However, this arguably served to highlight the personal indulgence that the film-director had allowed himself in making the film. As one commentator

---

[21] Lawrence S. Friedman, *The Cinema of Martin Scorsese* (Oxford, 1997), 152.   [22] Ibid. 63.

[23] See Richard Corliss, 'Body and Blood: An Interview with Martin Scorsese', *Film Comment* (Oct. 1988), 42.

[24] Friedman, *The Cinema of Martin Scorsese*, 49.

suggested in hindsight, Scorsese had transgressed the rules '. . . that regulate the image of a God and mark one group's truth from the brush of another's imagination'.[25]

Scorsese tried, in the course of *Last Temptation*, to create a Middle Eastern ambience through the use of an appropriate soundtrack. In doing so he enlisted the services of the musician Peter Gabriel, an advocate and afficionado of world music. However, very quickly theological critics of the film noted that much of this music was Arabic in origin, and appeared at wholly inappropriate moments. In this Gabriel and Scorsese were asking viewers to view the Gospel story through a multicultural prism in which the sacred was transcendent and could stand as an inclusive phenomenon bringing the essentially religious together.[26] Conservative and fundamentalist critics did not see things this way and held the film up to their own conceptions of the scriptures. Besides noting the general inappropriateness of such liberal use of Arabic music, these critics were deeply concerned by its use in Scorsese's portrayal of the Last Supper. This event takes place juxtaposed with Gabriel's recording of an Islamic call to prayer. This succeeded in upsetting both Christians and Muslims who viewed the film. For Christians, the Muslim denial of the incarnation rendered the use of the call to prayer potentially offensive. For Muslims, the use of their prayer to associate it with the possibility of an incarnation was similarly offensive.

In wanting to display a series of motifs that were important to him Scorsese departed from the Kazantzakis novel as much as he did from the Gospels. In the film Scorsese introduced a scene in which Christ displays his own sacred heart, a highly visceral image dripping with blood. Whilst this was a familiar motif for those brought up in the Catholic tradition, there were other interpretations at work beyond the religious context. Here it was difficult again to forget that Scorsese's work was also viewed as a canon in which blood, mortified flesh, and bodily suffering formed an essential tool for the portrayal of sacrifice. Here again the critic and viewer were made aware of how difficult it was becoming to view a religious film in a vacuum.

Perhaps an even greater difficulty that lay ahead for the filmmaker and their audience was how far cultural theories of interpretation had come since the dawn of the religious film. Such criticism was able to see *Last Temptation* as a series of postmodern appropriations and borrowings of style, genre, and intention. Indeed, in this new climate of cultural criticism Scorsese's 'reading' of the passion story, as well as Kazantzakis's novel, were both potentially seen in this light. Certainly there appeared to be a deliberate postmodern playfulness in some areas

---

[25] Thomas R. Lindlof, 'The Passionate Audience: Community Inscriptions of the *Last Temptation of Christ*', in Daniel A. Stout and Judith Buddenbaum (eds.), *Religion and Mass Media: Audiences and Adaptations* (London, 1996), 148–67, at 165.

[26] See Christie and Thompson (eds.), *Scorsese on Scorsese*, 139–42, which illuminates Scorsese's own admiration for Gabriel's musicianship and a preoccupation with atmosphere and ambience rather than doctrinal orthodoxy.

of the film. Where once the episodic appeared to be in tune with the Gospel narrative, it now rather seemed to be removing a sense of overarching narrative from the story.[27]

Much religiously inspired criticism concentrated upon the film's portrayal of a human and insecure Christ. Many critics have suggested that that this was quite revolutionary, either unaware of, or forgetting, the central theme of Dennis Potter's *Son of Man*. Like Potter's Jesus, Scorsese's Christ was riddled with doubt about his abilities and his mission, and brooded over his capacity to fulfil what might possibly be asked of him. Where Potter's Christ had appeared naturalistic and fresh, Scorsese's carried the baggage of the American anti-hero movie of the 1970s and 1980s, which portrayed the loner in search of equilibrium and redemption.[28] The Jesus in *Last Temptation* was also torn in two, as the anti-hero is, by conflicting calls upon his love; in this case Christ was torn between his love for God the father and his love for men. Nonetheless, the Scorsese Jesus appeared less decisive and engaging than his Judas. Where Scorsese further differed significantly from Potter was in offering a Christ beset by sexual longing and temptation, sufficiently potent and powerful as to constitute the 'Last Temptation' of the title. Early in the film Christ is shown in a voyeuristic scene viewing a naked Mary Magdalene entertaining her clients in a brothel. Although this was arguably gratuitous, as in Thorsen's filmed version of his 'Sex Life of Christ', *Jesus Vender Tilbage* (*Jesus, the Return*, 1992), its portrayal of temptation signified that the director's intentions were very different. The sequence was nonetheless very disconcerting for religious audiences.

However, a human Christ open to, especially, the temptations of the flesh led to a sequence which was condemned almost universally as offensive. Whilst on the cross the Christ figure enters a fantasy in which he is led from the cross by an angelic young girl. This concentrates upon the potential normality of temptation, as Christ fantasizes about marriage to Mary Magdalene and sexual relations with her. After her death he subsequently marries Mary of Bethany and Martha, in the process becoming a father of numerous children. When the angelic presence dissolves into Satan the true nature of temptation is revealed, and Christ is persuaded to resume his place upon the cross, largely at the behest of Judas. For many here the blasphemies present were numerous, but this did not prevent arguments about their degree and severity. Although the portrayal of an sexually active Jesus may have offended taste and deviated from scripture, this could nonetheless be plausibly explained.

Many religious commentators found the scene offensive but were astute enough to realize that the portrayal of the human, sexualized Jesus was a part of the fantasy sequence. But there were also disputes about the nature of the last

---

[27] For a sympathetic counter-interpretation see Michael Bliss, *The Word Made Flesh: Catholicism and Conflict in the Films of Martin Scorsese*, Filmmakers Series, na. 45 (London, 1995), 90–4.
[28] Fraser, *Images of the Passion*, 176.

temptation. Was Scorsese trivializing the passion and the whole realm of existence by suggesting that the last thing to conquer was sexual longing? Others accepted a more palatable explanation, in which the film's tendency to 'normalize' Christ had culminated at this point. This told modern audiences that a normal life, with normal expectations and the passions of mortal man, was the last temptation for a divine, yet mortal, Christ. Others still saw the ultimate blasphemy to be Christ's personalized and introspective consideration of his own desires at the moment of death.[29] For a great many Christians, interpretation of this sacrifice and atonement was not up for discussion, whilst a wholly inappropriate focus upon the world and its trivial temptations was an attack upon the divine. A Christ tempted was scriptural, but a Christ who had not resolved the tension between his humanity and divinity was emphatically not. From this unacceptable idea Christians perhaps asked themselves whether the effect of this film would be to adversely influence the partly religious. Some were in no doubt—the Christ figure's 'discovery' of his divinity at the age of 30 was seen as a didactic challenge to all in the angst-ridden West to discover their own divinity.[30] This was a quasi-New Age Christ, with a message of highly individualized salvation for a therapy culture. To traditional Christians this was a dilution, and arguably missed out what they thought of as the tougher ideas associated with Christianity. Would all this make Jesus far too human and the truly transcendent divine a cultural memory? What would happen if Christ were then to be commercialized? As F. LaGard Smith mused: 'Saatchi and Saatchi [Britain's premier advertising firm] might present Jesus to us with all the excitement of a high performance automobile, but can *awesome* (which might describe a super performer on the motorway) really replace a sense of the divine *awe*?' Perhaps Muslims had retained their sense of the sacred precisely because they insisted upon the facelessness of the Prophet.[31]

For many, these were the central issues present in *The Last Temptation of Christ*, and they ensured that it faced trouble wherever it was screened. Once again the majority of attacks upon it at local level occurred in the United States, and most of them stemmed from the Catholic church. In many respects this was understandable, since *Last Temptation*'s doubting Christ was substantially anti-trinitarian, and the stealthy attack upon the unimpeachably divine was most offensive to Catholic doctrine. Once again local action was the most effective, even if protestors could occasionally find strange allies amongst the film-making community. Franco Zeffirelli was one of the first to condemn the picture, arguing that it presented a particularly shabby view of a sacred subject, one that he himself had sought to glorify for the modern age. Although an

---

[29] F. LaGard Smith, *Blasphemy and the Battle for Faith* (London, 1990), 103.
[30] Scorsese regularly declared that one of his motivations in making the film was to display the struggle of all humanity. See Friedman, *The Cinema of Martin Scorsese*, 152–3.
[31] Ibid. 104 and 107.

attempt was made to use the blasphemy statute of Massachusetts against the film, this was unsuccessful.[32] The matter did eventually come to court using arguments that religious fundamentalists were later to adopt with impunity. The plaintiff, Veda Nyack, argued that the state, in permitting the showing of *Last Temptation*, was in violation of the First Amendment through promoting a thoroughly secular world-view. This, it was argued, denied the rights of freedom of worship and religion. In a 1988 case in France several groups asked the court to ban the showing of *The Last Temptation of Christ*. The court rejected this application, noting that the right to respect for beliefs should not interfere in an unjustified manner with artistic creativity. When Mary Whitehouse tried two years later to prevent the film being shown on terrestrial television, she turned on prominent members of the established churches, accusing them of abdicating their responsibilities in allowing the media to become 'intellectual and humanist'. With profound anger she railed: 'Where were you when they crucified my Lord? Busy counting the collection and signing the latest petition in favour of easier divorce or abortion?'[33]

A NEW AGE OF RETRENCHMENT?

The naive multiculturalism of Scorsese's film gave viewers and critics an insight into how toleration was not universal, nor was it prepared to be entirely indulgent in the name of freedom of expression. Unwittingly, it gave an increased sense of power and mission to moral-retrenchment movements throughout the United States, such as the Moral Majority. These individuals and groups were seen to be taking a stand against creeping attacks upon what were portrayed as sacred ideals which had shaped and protected western society. Film-makers, writers, artists, and the cosmopolitan fringe were people merely experimenting for profit, gain, and amusement with the beliefs that for many underpinned and gave fundamental meaning to actual lives. So frequently this juxtaposition of the fleetingly expressive, against the constant and timelessly cherished, gave power to the latter in the minds of politicians and other censorious and regulatory bodies.

Much of this rhetoric had its counterparts in Europe, and this was to be demonstrated by some high-profile cases. A precedent was set by the Austrian government when it seized a film version of Oskar Panizza's *Das Liebeskonzil*, precipitating the notorious Otto Preminger-Institut case.[34] One especially portentous element in the eventual judgement of the case was that audiences who actively chose to view religiously challenging works realistically had no protection in law. The

---

[32] Robin Riley, *Film, Faith, and Cultural Conflict: The Case of Martin Scorsese's 'The Last Temptation of Christ'* (London, (2003), 30.

[33] Mary Whitehouse, *Quite Contrary* (London, 1993), 72.

[34] *Otto-Preminger-Institut* v. *Austria* (1995), 19 EHRR 34 (Ct.) (1994).

attempt to show the film had constituted what most western countries would recognize as a 'club' showing, with entry restricted to those over 17 years of age. Advertisements for the film were unambiguous, clearly warning potential audiences of the challenging religious content. The European court remained unimpressed and found the film-showing to be a 'public offence' which actively infringed the rights of others guaranteed under Article 10 of the European Convention on Human Rights, even though it conceded that committed Christians were highly unlikely to view the film.[35]

Although this was only one case, the impact of this judgement had potential repercussions throughout Europe. Many European countries, especially in the north, had long argued that individuals were more responsible for what they encountered than the European Court seemed to believe. Clear and coherent warnings about the potentially challenging religious content of a film or publication had offered protection to film-makers and authors as well as the premises where such material would be viewed. Such a stance appeared to constitute a balance between free speech and the protection of sensibilities. This minimized the chances of the religiously committed encountering words or images they found blasphemous. The Otto Preminger judgement placed more power back in the hands of authorities and government, instilling in these two a rejuvenated responsibility for protecting the public good. Citing Article 9 of the European Convention on Human Rights, enshrining the protection of religious feelings, the judgement argued that the right of freedom of expression (Article 10) could not exist in isolation. Moreover, a reading of the whole convention would impel expression to be mindful of religious feelings.[36] The international human-rights group Article 19 had, by this time, begun to interest itself in the whole phenomenon of freedom of expression throughout the world. In noting the progress of the blasphemy laws in international contexts, the organization told the European Court of Human Rights that only in Italy and England were films of a religious nature liable to be prosecuted with any degree of success.[37] This pronouncement was motivated by the court finding itself embroiled in a significant legal case. This was produced by the decision of a British quasi-governmental agency which had denied freedom of expression to an individual. Yet the historical context of how Britain feared what was within its midst, yet also hid from the consequences of applying its laws, needs to be understood.

The late 1980s saw moral retrenchment voiced and utilized by government as almost an instrument of policy. This period saw the effects of free-market policies and their trail of social exclusion spill over into polite society. There began to be manifested a series of dangers, which for modern conservatism became a

---

[35] Report quoted in Select Committee on Religious Offences in England and Wales HL, Paper 95, Vol. III, written evidence, p. 5.

[36] Judgement quoted in ibid., Vol. I, Report, p. 17.

[37] Interights and Article 19, *Blasphemy and Film Censorship: Submission to the European Court of Human Rights in Respect of Nigel Wingrove v. the United Kingdom* (London, 1995).

touchstone for the dangers of social collapse. As in previous periods in Britain, the urge to link these with continental forms of depravity was never far away. The notion of forms of filth and corrupting material 'spreading' through the country reinforced 'little England' mentalities. Pornography was linked in the mind with the continent, and the defence of British ways of life produced and nurtured powerful forms of culturally insular Euroscepticism. The rapid democratization of new media, particularly video, was fuelled by a consumer boom and the collapsing prices of white-good technology. 'Film' and the cosmopolitanism that went with it was now available to all and, as always, the impact of moving pictures and their capacity to corrupt became immeasurably worrying. In some respects it is easy to forget the impact of this revolution upon the culture of censorial anxiety.

Britain's censorship infrastructure was forced to respond quickly to this threat, and middle England assumed it would do its job with considerable gusto. But all was not as it seemed at the British Board of Film Classification. For much of the period the primary protagonist in the formation and discharge of these considerable duties was a closet liberal, James Ferman. For some time Ferman had believed that the legislation in Britain which had governed the regulation of obscene material had been living on borrowed time. It appeared to reflect a siege mentality, in which the country's island status had provided benign and comforting protection from continental European laxity. Like all such siege mentalities, the enemies appeared to be everywhere and to be multiplying. Technological developments in satellite broadcasting threatened to make the control and regulation of published material redundant. Ferman never seemed convinced of the logic or purpose of censorship in its blunt and undiscriminating form, and often appeared caught on the fence. His willingness to operate limits was an affront to some libertarians, but also made those in the 'trade' assume and argue that censorship looked arbitrary. For authoritarians and those scared of public moral corruption, Ferman was the active hand of creeping liberalization. Ferman had refused to move against material that contained consensual sexual activity, but his attitude was somewhat more stringent towards material of a religiously challenging nature. Evidence shows that the British Board of Film Classification would intermittently order cuts from films and videos that came before it. These ranged in scope and degree, and touched both mainstream and arthouse experimental material. In many of these instances, the logic behind the Board's decision was not always clear and seemed a response to a presumption of possible offence, a decision which had not previously been the basis of English blasphemy jurisprudence. Whilst this could be done relatively discreetly there would be no public outcry, but the furore that surrounded the Wingrove film was to expose this action to public gaze.

Nigel Wingrove's film *Visions of Ecstasy* was refused a classification by the British Board of Film Classification and was, as a result, banned from sale or public display in Britain under the Video Recordings Act of 1984. The film depicts the religious and erotic visions of St Theresa of Avila, in which she bestrides and kisses the crucified Christ, mutilates herself, and has a sexual encounter with another female character intended to represent her own alter ego. Attention was closely focused upon the precise role of the Christ figure in the film, and whether he had actively responded sexually to St Theresa's actions. Here, the preoccupation with the recent past and thoughts about the Scorsese film were uppermost in the minds of those who passed judgement on the film. Wingrove himself would always express astonishment at the trouble his film had caused, and might have reasonably thought that his distance from the Gospels themselves, or even a fictional rendering of them, constituted a species of safety. The BBFC was clearly a genuinely concerned body of individuals undertaking sometimes difficult work. As their annual report for 1989 suggested, they regularly had the responsibility to note the distinction 'between manners and morals, offence and harm'. Although this clearly addressed an agenda associated with minimizing harm, their work was sometimes also given a much more positive gloss. In arguing for what the Board described as 'a mannerly society', the protection of individual feelings became a moral issue. The suggestion here was that feelings and emotional attachment to beliefs would most likely be the source of problems. Critics argued that the Board operated as prior restraint in the name of outrage, thus producing an inconsistency of views. In offering evidence around the Wingrove case, James Ferman saw the real offence as contempt for the divinity of Christ, and stated that the Board, if the occasion arose, would take the same action against films contemptuous of Muhammad or Buddha.[38] Such pronouncements offered protection to the mainstream branches of the three religions mentioned, yet denied protection to some minority beliefs, such as the Unitarian denial of Christ's divinity.

Wingrove himself appealed to the European Court of Human Rights, arguing that the BBFC had clearly denied him freedom of expression, and had been heavy-handed in exercising prior restraint. The group Article 19 again highlighted these two objections, and drew the Court's attention to the situation in eleven other countries. Wingrove's submission was that the uncertainty surrounding the law of blasphemy meant that he could not reasonably have predicted the reaction of either the Board, or a hypothetical jury (whose likely decision the Board had to consider). Wingrove's submission was accepted initially by the European Commission on Human Rights. But this was overturned in November 1996 by a decision of the Court considering an appeal by the British government.

Although some suggested that Wingrove's film was little more than quasi-sophisticated soft porn, with episodic religious musings, there were other factors to consider in this. The BBFC had taken the extraordinary step of seeking to ascertain Wingrove's motives in making the film, a process wholly alien to its practices in previous instances. No films of a violent or extreme sexual nature

---

[38] Report quoted in Select Committee . . . , Vol. III, written evidence, p. 8.

had ever been subject to such a test. Yet surprisingly the film was explicitly denied a certificate by the Board, which claimed that Wingrove was simply a pornographer. It was further suggested that *Visions* would fail a test of seriousness which something like Scorsese's *Last Temptation of Christ* would pass. The Board concluded that, if this were the case, *Visions* should be banned on the grounds that the video 'might be blasphemous'. This last assertion was odd, and short-circuited the Common Law offence of blasphemous libel in Britain, which up to this time had maintained supreme confidence that juries were best equipped to decide what was unacceptable in society.

Nonetheless, some of the BBFC's arguments were muddled and apparently circular. Despite the fact that the *Gay News* case had removed the Common Law's emphasis upon manner, the same concept appeared in the Board's considerations. Writing in the relevant annual report, BBFC chairman James Ferman addressed Wingrove: 'The video work submitted by you depicts the mingling of religious ecstasy and sexual passion, a matter which may be a legitimate concern to the artist. It becomes subject to the law of blasphemy, however, if the manner of its presentation is bound to give rise to outrage at the unacceptable treatment of a sacred subject.' Ferman then suggested that Wingrove's cultural crime was his failure 'to explore the meaning of the imagery beyond engaging the viewer in an erotic experience'. The suspicion was that Wingrove's agenda had come more from the genre of soft porn than from the mystic tradition. When his video was once again considered on appeal, by the Video Appeals Committee, attention was drawn to the youthfulness of the actress portraying St Teresa—it was noted that St Theresa had allegedly turned 39 before her revelations began—and similarly the absence of lesbian emotional longing in her writings (in contrast to her depiction in the film) was also a feature of dismissing the appeal. Mistakenly, the Committee still assumed that, under English law, they could upbraid Wingrove for the manner of his portrayal. They compounded this by suggesting he could thus have wholly forseen that his film was blasphemous. The appeal also denied the mitigating claims that the film's portrayal of a dream was different from a rendering of scripture. Nonetheless, Ferman's judgement here was suggesting that some portrayals of religious experience were acceptable, whilst others appeared not to be. A sober, contemplative approach to relationships with the almighty perhaps reflected the post-*Honest to God* world, but other aspects of spirituality had equally left this behind.[39]

Nigel Wingrove argued that the erotic nature of the experience he chose to portray on film was its central point. St Teresa of Avila felt her relationship with the almighty and Christ in particular to have a demonstrably sexual component. Moreover, a more sexually liberated world, which at least might understand this element of *Visions of Ecstasy*, should be allowed to compare this to the

---

[39] BBFC Annual Report. Quoted in evidence to the Select Committee . . . , Vol. III, written evidence, pp. 5–12.

religious ecstasy of previous generations. Certainly such ideas potentially had the power to speak to fringe elements of Christian worship, which had come to terms with their sexuality and sexual identity as aspects of creation. Ferman and the BBFC appeared to have closed the door to some more modern and modernizing versions of Christianity. Almost twenty years after the *Gay News* case, this was a subsequent denial of James Kirkup's wish to portray a Christ with 'the sexual equipment of the rest of us'. Similarly, the denial of the artistic desire to 'dream' also closed off some ways of thinking about the nature of Christ and some potential ways to know and reach revelation. The Christian mystics of an earlier age might not have wholly approved of Wingrove, but they may have been more open to the suggestion he was capable of being misunderstood. Such attitudes also echoed the time-honoured suggestion that class was at the root of blasphemy laws and how they were implemented. Considered, intellectual, and sober reflection was permissible, yet when necessary the inappropriate use of a particular genre, or the track record of a filmmaker (in this case Wingrove's career as a pornographer), would count against an individual film.

The fallout from the Wingrove case, though, came to set important precedents and to influence the views of the concerned judiciary. The verdict of the European Court allowed one judge to pronounce upon the moral decay that was just around the corner. One legal official, Judge Pettiti, saw an instant connection between religion and obscene pornographic images. These in turn were, in his opinion, part of a campaign by video distributors to conceal the circulation of videos designed to be consumed by from paedophiles. This associated Wingrove's film with material distant from it, and made all those involved consider the issue to be about the obscene when it had always been about the blasphemous.[40]

The European Court's eventual decision came as a relief to fundamental Christianity's claims upon British culture. In overturning Wingrove's appeal, Britain's conception of blasphemy could continue to exercise its jurisdiction under the conditions of the so-called 'Margin of Appreciation'. This denied the writ of the European Court in areas that were the culturally distinct business of individual member states. Britain's blasphemy law thus had judicial recognition beyond its shores, and was enshrined as a vital piece of cultural inheritance. The widespread nature of such views in high places was echoed in 1996 by the archbishop of York in a letter to *The Times*.

The group Article 19 was less than impressed, and pointed out Britain's isolation from practice in the rest of Europe. It concluded that such action was incompatible with the guarantees offered by Article 10 of the European Convention on Human Rights. It also protested against the wave of centralizing tendencies that had hung over the law and human rights in the late 1980s and early 1990s.[41] Christian groups in England began to claim that the secular continent of Europe was going to force a lowest common denominator of morality upon

---

[40] Interrights and Article 19, *Blasphemy and Film Censorship.*   [41] Ibid.

an unprepared and largely unsuspecting United Kingdom. Perhaps both film classifiers and Wingrove himself had learned important lessons. Although backers of his films may be more wary, he has gone on to produce more quasi-erotic films with religious over-and undertones. A recent offering, *Sacred Flesh*, is part of the 'nunsploitation' genre which may cause distaste in some quarters, in the manner of Ken Russell's *The Devils*, but has avoided depictions of the divine. The BBFC has also adopted a more restrained approach and allowed screening of such films largely without intervention.

RELIGION, VIDEO, AND ROCK AND ROLL

Whilst the BBFC continues to routinely order cuts in specific films, widespread public condemnation of the content of religious films has been sporadic and unfocused. Irving Welsh's *Granton Star Cause*, with its portrayal of a drunken, abusive God, was the object of one of Mary Whitehouse's last mini-crusades. Although her complaint gained column inches, it only alerted audiences to the film's content. Trepidation may have preceded the television programme *Messiah*, with its picture of a possible Christ returning to earth, but all concern disappeared with the film's clear portrayal of the protagonists as disappointed and deluded by an imposter. Film posters, which can present individuals with a casual encounter with disturbing content, have themselves proved troublesome, especially in France. In England a picture of actor Robbie Coltrane in papal dress, used to advertise the film *The Pope Must Die*, was briefly withdrawn to avoid offence.

More recently the film *Dogma* (Kevin Smith, 1999) lampooned Catholicism far more than the character and incarnation of Christ. This film again suffered from its allusions to other genres—its heroine's quest to stop two wayward angels from re-entering heaven appeared to be the plot for an offbeat road movie. Sections also resembled the chaotic surrealism of Russ Meyer's attacks on over-righteous middle America, whilst some also seemed borrowed from Tarantino-style gangster movies. Ultimately the depiction of God as a woman, and the casting of the rock singer Alanis Morrisette as a hippy God, certainly ploughed interesting theological territory. Morrisette, a mainstream rock star, was a choice which deliberately invoked the singer's own dialogue with her Catholic faith. This was laid bare most notably in her song 'Farewell', which suggests a variety of reasons for individuals attending church without the spiritual being uppermost among them.

This particular piece of casting should alert us to the close proximity of cinema to youth culture and rock music in particular. Moral commentators were always concerned about audiences in seats being exposed to blasphemous material in a confined space, whereas the transient and ephemeral nature of pop and rock music seemed less threatening. Popular music's appeal was most readily confined to specific age-groups. Attitudes fostered by pop music were transient, and lapsed according to the whims of fashion or the wisdom of age. This changed somewhat with the arrival of the music video that brought such displays into the home. The Devil's Music had spawned dangerous material before, but it had never been seen as a lasting threat. Although parents had taken exception to Alice Cooper's gothic style, and the crazed Voodoo blues of Screaming Jay Hawkins, their offspring had eventually survived unscathed. Brushes with the gothic and the sillier side of Satanism, in the shape of Marilyn Manson, could always be dismissed as merely a phase—or the short-lived triumph of style over substance.

Morally aware audiences would now be more worried when mainstream performers once more brought their cultural power to bear upon the religious. Perhaps foremost in this was the video that the singer Madonna produced for her best-selling single 'Like a Prayer' (1989). Madonna, herself the product of a background similar to Scorsese, found herself wanting to explore the Catholic psychological link between passion, redemption, and the spiritual. This link also resurfaced in 2006 with Madonna's re-enactment of the crucifixion on stage. 'Like a Prayer' portrayed sexual longing and gratification as the answer to prayer and a form of redemption in itself. Love, lust, and salvation became wrapped up as one sacrament, with unsophisticated audiences considered incapable of distinguishing these components. All this was reinforced by the use of much Catholic imagery in the video, including crucifixes, amidst dancing of an, at the very least, sensual variety. It is worth remembering that Madonna was already creating a myth and a career around her own various 'transgressions'. She was subsequently described as someone who 'consistently and deliberately teases the presumed lines between art, popular culture, and pornography'.[42] But with censorship debated, and the idea of sexual and religious portrayal being the subject of controversy, it was scarcely surprising that artists of her turn of mind would fuse the two. Madonna's popularity seemed in danger of exposing youth to an association between Catholicism and carnality that they were arguably not ready for. Moreover, because this was a new medium, with the attendant fear of its possibilities, morality seemed under threat. If the Madonna video could be endlessly replayed in the privacy of the home, there might be a danger that its message about the spiritual would become a lasting one. More worrying for the religious, it seemed that praying for a sexually able and potent lover had become as valid as praying to God.

Cinema took hold of religion, the Bible, and the Gospels and found in them a popular and intelligible narrative for audiences. But the logic of writers and directors seeking to explore and interact with the sacred itself produced cultural and legal problems for these individuals. Cinema and the moving image made

---

[42] Marjorie Heins, *Sex, Sin, and Blasphemy: A Guide to America's Censorship Wars* (New York, 1993), 53.

western culture public again, in a way it perhaps had not been since medieval religious spectacle. But this was also a culture which had enfranchised people's opinions and legitimized their private beliefs through a series of rights. It is an irony that, as display and spectacle became more public, this nurtured the development and sophistication of the private thought. This meant that feelings of personal offence and its attendant discourses would become of increased importance to the individual and society. In the search for a relevant Gospel, or a human, or anodyne, or sexually active Christ, film-makers were all capable of offending someone. Similarly ecstasy, particularly female religious ecstasy, could captivate and enthral, if it could also repel and enrage. If conventional religion had retreated from the public sphere, film seemed the most likely way in which it would become mainstream again. Cinema made religious images move, but in their desire to reach audiences films became objects of scrutiny. They also became the site of contests to define the religious and its meaning for consumption by the public at large.

Conclusion

Blasphemy has concerned societies when they have been conscious of widespread upheavals that threatened to undermine their very existence and identity. This emphatically tells historians the reasons for blasphemy's longevity and its continued relevance to a number of very different societies. To so many commentators, over the last 200 years, the idea of prosecuting and punishing individuals for their words and opinions seemed antique, oppressive, and wholly out of keeping with modern views of tolerance. This also transgressed the enlightenment ideals which gave rights to individuals. Blasphemy's survival is also puzzling because there has been little enthusiasm for it as a concept. To authority structures it has been a source of fear of disorder, and eventually of embarrassment. To those scared of its impact upon their lives, it was an event or occurrence to be feared or shunned. Even to those who could be classed as practitioners, its status has often been ambivalent. For those who spoke blasphemy in fear, confusion, anger, or drink, it was an emblem of their foolishness. For those who defied religious authority with contrary religious opinions or with outright scorn, blasphemy was a tactic which furthered their wider causes or beliefs.

But this is a phenomenon that affects not simply societies but communities within societies. Where identity and security, broadly defined, have been threatened, questioned, or in the process of being forged, then blasphemy as concept has flourished. Blasphemy emerged from heresy at the end of the medieval period as a result of local jurisdictions establishing their own authority. The desire to protect the community gave birth to our passive blasphemy model. In this, standards precious to the community were offended and legal apparatus and punishment regimes reflected this emphasis. Since the whole community was involved in the act of proceeding against the blasphemer, the simple knowledge that blasphemous words had been spoken was enough to excite concern and horror. Since individuals came to believe that blasphemy was an ever-present possibility and could excite the intervention of divine displeasure, systems of policing and punishment acted on the community's behalf.

This chronology and model sits reasonably well alongside the transformation suggested by Norbert Elias within his 'civilising process'. The attempt to establish support for the legitimate nature of oaths and promises looks superficially like an attempt to reform manners and behaviour. However, the schema outlined by Elias assumes the historical success of its own propositions. According to European scholars, blasphemy still occurred beyond the early modern period as specific incidents. Similarly, an almost ageless connection with both drink and its attendant cultures poses some problems for the reformed individuals constructed by the 'civilising process'. The stubborn proximity of oaths, profanity, and species of blasphemy to extreme emotion, to charged situations when individuals require luck or are in peril, remains a clear, even fêted, part of popular culture.[1]

The Reformation's transformation of the religious landscape created, in Diarmud Maculloch's words, 'a house divided'. This redefined the nature of how God could be thought about and described. Within the doctrinal hothouses of Geneva, Basle, and beyond there was also a premium upon disciplining populations and limiting the boundaries of dissident thought. Here blasphemy became a component of discipline and a species of thought crime. Whilst the typical blasphemy case from this period was a lower-class offence against restraint, there is much evidence that blasphemy could exist across the social spectrum in early modern Europe and beyond. This pattern was also indicative of the offence into the eighteenth and nineteenth centuries. This would undermine somewhat the authoritarian, class-regulated, chronologically specific 'civilising process' offered by Elias.[2]

Laws which saw the blasphemer as an outsider, and a threat to the community, spawned shame punishments which reinforced the community's cohesion. Thereafter the state had empowered itself to police the ideology of its population. The widespread acceptance of intention through the concept of *mens rea* (in which individuals are deemed to intend the consequences of their actions) in the perpetration of a crime has been an important theme within legal history. Yet this concept only found its way episodically into consideration of the crime of blasphemy.

The late seventeenth century saw a Europe-wide concern to police and control populations against internal strife and external threat. The final third of the seventeenth century saw *ancien régimes* and constitutional monarchies alike enact laws which associated blasphemy with the maintenance of order and the sanctity of government. Within this epoch branches of newly established Christian sects were bound to be treated with suspicion and hostility. When the implications of their

---

[1] Schwerhoff's work exhibits scepticism about blasphemy's relationship to a 'civilising process'. Blasphemous oaths did not decline but were subjected to changes in fashion. Similarly, Schwerhoff found evidence that blasphemy was thrust away by all sections of society and thus could not be equated with a bourgeois modernizing project. Paradoxically this may also have ensured its survival in some forms as species of popular cultural practice with the capacity to shock and enrage.

[2] As we saw with German unification, the Penal Code of 1871 had no hesitation in adopting the provision against blasphemy previously contained in the penal code of the Northern German League. Although many European states liberalized their attitudes to blasphemous occurrences, the stubbornness of some jurisdictions, particularly in America, should also be noted.

doctrines regarding power and governance were investigated, their oppression became utterly inevitable. These newer conceptions of power and governance became transformed into a system which Michel Foucault termed '*surveillance*'. In many European countries this coincided with the late seventeenth century's embrace of statute blasphemy and the discipline it brought. Foucault denied that this was solely a product of centralizing states, suggesting that such surveillance replicated the wider patriarchal structure of policing.[3] This process appeared to coincide with European and North American states starting to view the preservation of public order as a priority. However, it remains impossible to establish that blasphemy was a sufficiently widespread menace to require the exertion of control from a deliberately conscious authoritarian project. Blasphemy may have been a crime that attracted harsh penalties, yet throughout its history these were never uniform, and the attitudes of legal systems and communities themselves were surprisingly varied. Whilst Alain Cabantous's conclusion might follow Foucault in suggesting that petty blasphemy was eradicated, it can clearly be argued that the arrival of a more sophisticated and cost-effective print culture drove it underground and gave it more intellectual aspirations.[4] Paradoxically, where Elias sees liberalism and the apogee of civilization is where the strongest evidence for a controlling authoritarian project emerges. Interestingly, Elias's model flounders when it is applied to blasphemy in England, especially when associated with his creation of a uniquely English 'habitus'. Elias saw strong parliamentary government as an important brake upon violent social relations within the upper tiers of society, and as a moderating influence upon policy and authoritarian action. But as we have discovered, English seventeenth-century blasphemy statutes were contemporary with those in other, more obviously *ancien régime* states in the rest of Europe. Moreover, they were accomplished with the consent and active sponsorship of members of parliament and the bench of bishops. In this England only becomes unique in its widespread and comparatively long-lived consent for such measures. At the end of the eighteenth century concern about blasphemy and morals may well also have been a door through which the middle classes passed in order to aspire to social dominance and governance.[5]

[3] Colin Gordon (ed.), *Michel Foucault: Truth and Power. Power/Knowledge: Selected Interviews and Other Writings 1972–1977* (Brighton, 1980), 121. Michel Foucault, 'Politics and Reason', in Lawrence D. Kritzman (ed.), *Michel Foucault; Politics, Philosophy, Culture Interviews and Other Writings 1977–1984* (London, 1990), 57–85, at 72. Alain Cabantous, *Blasphemy: Impious Speech in the West from the Seventeenth to the Nineteenth Century* (New York, 2002), 51–4.

[4] The work of Robert Darnton and Roger Chartier is especially relevant here. See the former's *The Literary Underground of the Old Regime* (Cambridge, Mass., 1982) and *The Forbidden Best-Sellers of Pre-Revolutionary France* (New York, 1995). See also the latter's *The Cultural Origins of the French Revolution* (Durham, NC, 1990) and *The Cultural Uses of Print in Early Modern France* (Princeton, 1990).

[5] See the outline of the 'English social habitus' in Jonathan Fletcher, *Violence and Civilisation: An Introduction to the work of Norbert Elias* (Cambridge, 1997), 95

The late eighteenth century's tolerance of the blasphemous was also less obviously progressive than had previously been supposed. The Romantic Age and the end of enlightened despotism unleashed criticism of established religion the like of which had never been seen before. This was met with an equally strong desire to police the seditious doctrines that removed salvation from the minds of the populace. This passing of Foucault's era of *surveillance* did nothing to retard or end the perception of blasphemy as a crime. Although the psychological state of the blasphemer was occasionally pathologized, it is impossible to suggest that this was universal and the characteristic of a global change of outlook. Beyond this, Foucault's subsequent new 'age of confinement' failed to break the link between blasphemy, libertineage, immorality, and issues of public order. Coarse, lavatorial, and explicit depictions of God remained the most offensive. Moreover, the perennial proximity of blasphemy to the spread of potentially immoral knowledge about family limitation enshrined cultural guilt by association.[6]

Certainly, the course of blasphemy in nineteenth-century England, and to a lesser extent America, owes its impetus to the ideas generated by the same ideologues who spawned the French Revolution. All of these conclusions and the persistence of this articulate opposition to revealed religion seems scarcely exposed to the long-term effects of the 'civilising process'.[7] Indeed, an especially notable feature of blasphemy is how often it was a manifestation of coarseness and flouting of manners, continuing long after that process's so-called triumph. Moreover, the model of violence offered in Elias concentrated wholly upon the face-to-face encounter with a (generally male) assailant. The 'civilising process' in this instance described what it termed 'decreasing impulsivity' as a component of altered behaviour.[8] Again, this fails to fit with the chronology of blasphemy outlined in this book. Blasphemy as a mode of conducting religious relationships did not disappear, but with its access to new methods of offence it became a model for a specific form of resonating violence. In doing so it regularly qualified the nature of religious tolerance, just as often as it demonstrated to individual societies the limits of this concept. Modern societies have regularly panicked and

---

[6] The *Freethinker* case of 1883 focused on a ribald, arguably lavatorial, portrayal of God, whilst Abner Kneeland, J. W. Gott, and Thomas William Stewart offered advice on family limitation alongside coarse critiques of revealed religion. Jens Jurgen Thorsen covered similar territory in the 1970s. Thorsen was responsible for a mural painted in Copenhagen which depicted Christ with exaggeratedly oversized genitalia, whilst he also spent several decades seeking to film 'The Sex Life of Christ', which finally appeared, as *Jesus Vender Tilbage*, in 1992. Nigel Wingrove's *Visions of Ecstasy*, James Kirkup, and Martin Scorsese all mixed religion, with sexual content.

[7] See Cabantous, *Blasphemy, passim*. See also Elizabeth Horodwich, 'Civic Identity and the Control of Blasphemy in Sixteenth-Century Venice', *Past & Present*, 181 (2003), 3–33, which assumes the work of the Escutori in Venice can be fitted into Elias's arguments about state formation being central to the desire of jurisdictions to wield power over manners and behaviour.

[8] Manuel Eisner, 'Modernization, Self-Control and Lethal Violence: The Long-term Dynamics of European Homicide Rates in Theoretical Perspective *British Journal of Criminology*, 41 (2001), 618–38, at 619.

ransacked their legislative legacies for models from sometimes quite anachronistic legislation to combat religious hate crimes.[9]

The final quarter of the nineteenth century saw fears about mass print culture and its corrupting influence lead to professional censorship regimes and scrutiny of printed, sketched, and painted artefacts. This capacity of print culture to produce premeditated violent offence to be consumed haphazardly suggests that the civilizing ability of the mass media was something of a double-edged sword in the hands of blasphemers. Whilst it enabled its audiences to understand the worlds of others, its power in the wrong hands could also replicate and magnify single acts of violence against individual beliefs.[10] Similarly, the consumption patterns of some of these new media also altered the dynamics of the offence. Pictures, cartoons, and films could all be consumed in a much more leisurely fashion than the expletives of a drunken tavern blasphemer or street demagogue.

Where Monty Python's *Life of Brian* saw humour in the intolerance of biblical Palestine, and the experimental film-maker Nigel Wingrove saw eroticism in St Theresa of Avila's *Visions of Ecstasy*, the consumption of both of these took place in different contexts. In each case individuals gazing upon both films were not in control of the desires, thoughts, and dreams such images inspired. Whether laughter, repulsion, or indifference was the result, the use of the religious seemed to place all the power in the hands of the artist. But it has not simply been artists who have actively produced caricatures of the sacred. Many forms of anticlericalism reached for the cartoon as an expression of contempt. Such practices reached their zenith in the nineteenth century, when liberal secularism pointed to the ridiculousness of biblical stories and episodes. Such images were intended to destabilize the meaning and introduce alternative readings of such episodes, ruining the one-dimensional view of the sacred and its purposes.[11] Those who sought offence could always find it. The newspaper *Le Trombinoscope* speculated in 1874 that French censors would look at cartoons continually until they found something offensive.[12] Certainly, it is possible to see how some

---

[9] Note the enthusiasm of the House of Lords Select Committee on Religious Offences (2002) for the Indian Criminal Code of 1860. In the Netherlands, Theo Van Gogh's murder led to similar calls to apply previously dormant laws against 'scornful blasphemy' (Art. 147 of the Dutch Penal Code).

[10] Eva Österberg, 'Criminality, Social Control, and the Early Modern State: Evidence and Interpretations in Scandanavian Historiography', in Eric A. Johnson and Eric H. Monkkonen (eds.), *The Civilisation of Crime: Violence in Town and Country since the Middle Ages* (Urbana, Ill., 1996), 52.

[11] See David Nash, *Blasphemy in Britain 1789–Present* (Aldershot, 1999) and 'Laughing at the Almighty: Freethinking Lampoon, Satire and Parody in Victorian England', in Jennifer Wagner Lawler (ed.), *The Victorian Comic Spirit* (Aldershot, 2000), 43–66. Tarnishing the long-term power of the sacred is the central argument of Joss Lutz Marsh's ' "Bibliolatry" and "Bible Smashing"': G.W. Foote, George Meredith, and the Heretic Trope of the Book', *Victorian Studies*, 34: 3 1999, pp. 315–36.

[12] Quoted in Robert Justin Goldstein, *Political Censorship of the Arts and the Press in Nineteenth Century Europe* (Basingstoke, 1989), 82.

blasphemous and anticlerical cartoons worked on different levels. Many of the blasphemous cartoons of G. W. Foote displayed their blasphemous intentions on their sleeve. Those which ridiculed Old Testament stories and the life of Jesus were being self-consciously offensive.[13]

Yet there were also images that required deeper reading, and indeed to be 'gazed' at. These were not blasphemous, yet they clearly indicated that an appreciation of artistic devices was an adjunct to appreciating these fully. Then, as now, the consumption of religious images invites the viewer to bring either belief or ridicule to the image they view, inspiring a 'pious gaze', a 'blasphemous gaze', or a secular 'indifferent gaze'. This also can turn importantly upon the context in which such images are viewed. Graham Sutherland's *Christ* was shocking and controversial, yet not offensive, because its intention is accepted implicitly through its location in Coventry Cathedral. However, the believer is on guard in an art gallery even before encountering the images created by Andres Serrano. Religion has thus become a potentially attractive cultural resource with resonance through other raw and visceral emotions. We have already noted the work of Andres Serrano, but the work of the photographer Bettina Reims and her portrayal of the passion in her book *INRI* also courts controversy, whilst Tracey Emin's tapestry equating religious and sexual ecstasy is in a similar vein. As such, they follow in the wake of the earlier Situationist Jens Jurgen Thorsen, who pursued a lasting interest in caricaturing the sacred. Irving Welsh and (arguably) Salman Rushdie have explored religious ideas as constituting a lingering taboo, while others, like Theo Van Gogh and Gurpreet Kaur Bhatti (the author of *Behzti*) have used the exploration of religion as a mirror to awaken controversy about the societies they investigate. This perhaps indicates the potentially ambivalent nature of any 'civilising process', and adds credence to the idea that blasphemy potentially exists as a species of regulated danger. Artists drawing attention to the nature of the sacred regularly encouraged audiences to 'gaze' upon the religious in new contexts without even discussing the idea of belief.

Blasphemy has always been about images, but it has also historically been a public-order problem, where beliefs have suffered harm from the words of others in interpersonal situations far removed from the church, the cinema, or the art gallery. Moreover, the concept of the gaze still contains (in spite of its acknowledgement of Freud) a significant degree of conscious intent from all concerned, especially from the artist's desire to problematize. This is not wholly evident in, for example, Wingrove's *Visions of Ecstasy* nor can we find it definitively in Scorsese's *Last Temptation of Christ*, nor even in Serrano's squalid depictions of the crucified Christ. The picture, whether moving or not, has been the means of providing ideas rather than constituting the ideas themselves. Gazing at images may have been the mechanism of offence, but blasphemous cartoons,

---

[13] See the cartoons 'The Comic Life of Jesus', Figs. 6, 15.

for example, wanted their audiences to think more deeply about the doctrines that lay behind the images—for them the real sources of piety and offence.[14]

The 'civilising process' also did not bring a neat chronological end to the phenomenon of religiously inspired offence or violence. Similarly, it did not produce Elias's hoped-for lessening of difference.[15] On the contrary, all late twentieth-century evidence suggests that combative religion, prepared to refute or indulge in blasphemy, has become a powerful motif of identity. Artists and writers did not align themselves solely with the bourgeois values of the 'civilising process'. Once again, barbed opposition to such assumptions was frequently the order of the day. In challenging such a society, the support given to it by religion, almost in a manner Sir Matthew Hale would recognize, became a legitimate target.[16]

Blasphemy and its implications also sent the modern state into a retreat which Elias and the 'civilising process' would never have predicted. The history of blasphemy has placed the state itself in some anomalous and, to say the least, incoherent situations. The architects of the American Constitution were divided over the respective positions of church and state. The resulting Constitution assumed that individual states would continue to establish religion as they had done when they were colonies. This proved to be the case in New England states (Massachusetts, Connecticut, and New Hampshire) and southern states such as Georgia and South Carolina, which continued the process of evolution, moving from a single to a multiple religious establishment based upon broadly Christian tenets. Yet still others (Rhode Island, Pennsylvania, and Delaware) had no established religion. The situation was further complicated by a number of states where religious tests for public office were retained, and Delaware even restricted toleration to trinitarians. The situation in some states, such as Maryland, which reserved the right to raise taxes for the support of religion, suggests that Christianity was conceived of as a national religion even if the awkward intricacies of establishing one version of it were avoided.[17] These individualized and pluralist approaches led to problems in some states, such as Virginia, where the limits of such multiple establishments excluded some Protestant groups. In some other states multiple establishment collapsed, leading

---

[14] See the American cartoons from the *Truthseeker*, Fig. 21, 22. These anti-religious images were more sophisticated than the more obviously blasphemous ones, to encourage deeper thought and to inspire revulsion. These persuaded the audience to consider religious doctrines and clerical attitudes at length.

[15] See Norbert Elias, *The Civilising Process* (rev. ed.), tr. Edmund Jephcot, ed. Eric Dunning, Johan Gouldsblom, and Stephen Mennell (Oxford, 2005), 7.

[16] As we have seen, the late nineteenth century saw prosecutions for blasphemy against August Strindberg in Sweden, Oscar Panizza in Germany, and Siegfried Sassoon in New Zealand. The early twentieth century saw accusations against works by George Bernard Shaw (UK), Georg Grosz and Wieland Herzfeld (Germany), and Arnulf Øverland (Norway). With the subsequent accusations against Andres Serrano, Tania Kovats, James Kirkup (*Gay News*), and Nigel Wingrove (*Visions of Ecstasy*), it is possible to argue that proceedings against blasphemy have sometimes been purely a form of censorship.

[17] William H. Marnell, *The First Amendment* (New York, 1964), 110.

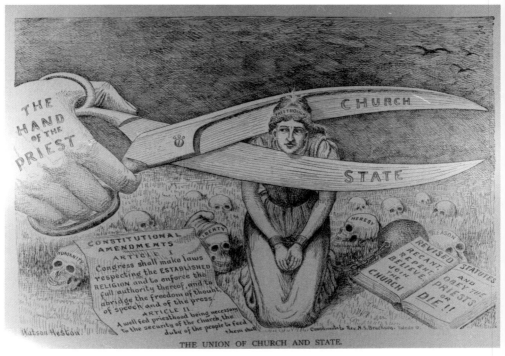

THE UNION OF CHURCH AND STATE.

Fig. 20. American freethinkers could be extremely wary of religious interference in matters of state. Note the parodied constitutional amendments threatening a theocratic future.

to the logic of the First Amendment's removal of government participation in religion.[18] Yet there had also always been dissenting voices that still craved national solutions. Some, like Thomas Jefferson, wanted a theoretical separation of church and state combined with a stringent protection of free speech. In his 1786 Act for Establishing Religious Freedom, he noted the futility of imposing temporal punishments upon religious dissidents. Although Jefferson accepted the Constitution's First Amendment as a national solution, he continued to campaign for secularist positions and against religiously sponsored education.[19] Others, like James Madison, saw taxation in support of religion to be a violation of religious liberty, which should remain a private matter. These latter arguments appeared in the famous *Memorial and Remonstrance* document which prevented the re-establishment of religion in Virginia. Such arguments eventually undid the

---

[18] Jon Butler, *Grant Wacker and Randall Balmer, Religion in American Life: A Short History* (Oxford, 2003), 156–9.

[19] See Leonard Levy, 'Jefferson as a Civil Libertarian', in *Constitutional Opinions: Aspects of the Bill of Rights* (Oxford, 1986), 171–92.

THE SECOND COMING.

For the Lord shall himself descend from heaven with a shout, with the voice of the archangel, and with the trump of God : and the dead in Christ shall rise first.—Thess. iv 16.

Fig. 21. The American *Truthseeker* mocks the Second Coming, *c.*1900.

multiple-establishment approach, moving towards a wider concept of religious, freedom.[20] Madison also outlined arguments that speak more directly to our own time. He suggested that establishment created inertia amongst the religious, and that the enforcement of an unpopular law discredited the legitimacy of governments that would enact it.

In practice, the American judiciary had real doubts about how both the ideals of free speech and separation were to be accomplished, whilst preserving peace and good order. In this respect the nineteenth century displayed the legacy of grappling with this problem. Some legal commentators have suggested that a distinction should be made between disestablishment and full separation of church and state. The first was a significant reality by the end of the nineteenth century, whilst the second was never achievable nor was even an aspiration.[21]

[20] Leonard Levy, 'The Original Meaning of the Establishment Clause', in ibid. 135–61, at 160.
[21] H. Frank Way, 'The Death of the Christian Nation: The Judiciary and Church–State Relations', *Church and State*, 509 (1987), 509–29.

Justice Kent felt he had produced some sort of compromise in adopting the English Common Law as a model. This at least had precedent, and would impose wider standards than individual state law offered. In this it is perhaps surprising how long the ideas of the Hale judgement persisted, if only as unspoken influence. Still more surprising is how far Kent entertained still older attitudes, which saw religion as central to the maintenance of oaths and their apparent sanctity and security.[22] Through this line of thinking religion was instinctively a necessary promise of good and stable order, and provided visible protection for these. As hostile attitudes to the precepts of the First Amendment hardened, the state could no longer be seen at all as an agent of the 'civilising process'. First Amendment rights were to be skirted around or avoided in the name of upholding local standards of morality. For some individual believers, the state was an impediment to civilization and morality, making the push to establish local standards an imperative. Such a situation was replicated in Europe, where local and national standards of morality saw themselves as under threat from supra-national justice. This came in the shape of European human-rights law and jurisprudence, which conservative critics saw as potentially offering a lowest-common-denominator definition of morality. In the course of events these fears were unfounded, particularly after the Otto Preminger Institut judgement. For those concerned by such developments, the state, and the super state, were not conceived of as agents of progress and civilization but as agents of chaos, remote from the interactions and experiences of real life.

The libertarian distrust of the state marked the emergence of the active blasphemy model, in which legal systems began to require proof of actual harm and required individuals to speak about the affront to their religious beliefs and to defend these in court. This development was a logical consequence of the state seeking to surrender its powers in the area of religious prescription and protection. Those inspired to take action to defend beliefs within the active blasphemy model were always reluctant to do so. Often they considered they had been betrayed by government and the consensual attitude of established and denominational churches.

The history of blasphemy also suggests that religious toleration and secularization, both relevant to the 'civilising process', were episodic and conditional episodes rather than sustained changes. The spread of technology and information, as a way of knowing and understanding one's neighbours, in this context also looks significantly overrated. New technology made society both comfortable and provided new diversions for it. But this same process equally produced new media of communication that provoked fear of moral collapse. These concerns evoked governmental and individual reaffirmations of belief in the face of the moral abyss. The actions of the Vice Society against Richard Carlile in the 1820s, the

---

[22] This is alluded to by Sarah Barringer Gordon in 'Blasphemy and the Law of Religious Liberty in Nineteenth Century America', *American Quarterly*, 52: 4 (Dec. 2000), 682–19, at 686.

Fig. 22. Enlightenment rationalism calls to woman. The American *Truthseeker* also covered serious subjects in its cartoons.

fear of blasphemous images in G. W. Foote's new, tabloid-style *Freethinker* in the 1880s (and related Australian prosecutions), and in later years Comstock's actions and the attempts to disrupt and break up large public meetings in the Edwardian period were all reactions to new media and their dangerous possibilities.

Even if religion appeared to be no longer secure upon its earlier institutional base, its meaning to individuals remained significant. Indeed, incidents around blasphemy often reacquainted populations with the legacy of their religious pasts and the legacy of religious beliefs. The weakness of institutional churches when confronted by blasphemy also gave the initiative to concerned members of the laity, who would rail against inaction or ineffectiveness. Although western states had originally been interested in religious conformity and were prepared to convict and punish accordingly, the twentieth century saw government and judicial enthusiasm for this collapse. Blasphemy laws then entered a legal and cultural limbo in which their use was only occasionally contemplated, yet they remained as a reassurance against moral and cultural disintegration.

The gap between the optimistic historical works of the late 1960s upon the subject of blasphemy and those of subsequent generations was a significant one. The tolerance which the post-war world hoped it was ushering in relied upon a balancing act between the ideas of freedom and responsibility, enhanced by a desire to encourage equality. However, by the end of the twentieth century this situation had come to an end. From the 1990s onwards blasphemy frequently appeared as a tool grasped by individuals to defend religion and the legacies of its past. Often the very act of using this tool revitalized religious belief and brought it again into a public sphere that increasingly sought defence for identities founded upon religion and belief. The push for pan-European answers to such problems witnessed a backlash against their attempts to provide homogenous legal solutions across Europe. Laws like that of blasphemy rejuvenated national perceptions of the state and its role in the religious life of its citizens. In the Netherlands, blasphemy provoked an examination of the country's history of tolerance, and asked whether this would in future be sustainable. In America, questions turned around the security of the First Amendment and over quite whether Christianity could be regarded as the country's official religion, even if it could never be its established one. In Britain, an isolationist legal situation became untenable in the face of arguments against religious partiality that came from both minority groups and European human-rights legislation and prescription.

Some of these conclusions concur with the analyses of Daniéle Hervieu-Léger, Callum Brown, and Daniel Duboisson. These writers have reshaped the idea of secularization as a 'process' to see individuals and societies engaged in an evolving and changing relationship with religion.[23] Hervieu-Léger, in kicking against the

---

[23] Daniéle Hervieu-Léger, *Religion as a Chain of Memory*, tr. Simon Lee (Oxford, 2000); Callum Brown, *The Death of Christian Britain* (London, 2001); and Daniel Duboisson, *The Western Construction of Religion: Myths, Knowledge and Ideology*, tr. William Sayers (London, 2003).

Fig. 23. The *Gay News* case twenty-five years on. George Melly and Keith Porteus-Wood protest about the blasphemy law in Britain at an anniversary reading of the Kirkup poem.

modernization models and the postmodern disengagement models of religious change, describes religion as constituting a 'chain' of memory. Within this continuum the apparent symptoms of the secular should be viewed as this elastic relationship stretched to its limits. Duboisson sees Christianity in particular as reliant for its appeal and power upon the establishment of binary opposites (such as 'truth' and 'apostasy'), arguing that orthodoxy is made credible through the justification offered by texts and the individual's relationship to these. From here religion becomes almost consciously a conflict model, what Duboisson calls a 'polygon of controversies'.[24] For our purposes, this view perhaps fleshes out the complaint from blasphemers that the push for religious conformity throughout the ages has actively produced its blasphemous opposite. The related observation from theologians, that establishing orthodox belief will invariably produce a definition of heresy, is also pertinent here.

The theme of orthodoxy and its supposed imposition has also opened up an interesting tributary to blasphemy's history in the numerous sensationalist works claiming that Christianity's real secret history has been hidden by a well-organised conspiracy. Chief amongst these, at least in terms of popular exposure, is Dan Brown's novel *The Da Vinci Code*, which prompted both the Archbishop of Canterbury and the papacy to refute the book's chief allegations. Not only did this revive the notion of 'heresy' within the new millennium, but it strongly confirmed that popular fiction and film were the new powers capable of shaping the sacred and its image amongst believers and non-believers alike.

The West's relationship with the sacred has been substantially defined and partly affirmed through its collision with the blasphemous. The medieval and pre-Reformation periods showed intense concern to preserve the completeness of the Christian community, whilst the blasphemer nullified a society's spiritual and material connection with God. This connection was strengthened through the Christian doctrine of providence, which could become a dangerous popular mandate for gamblers and those involved in other forms of speculation. The devout were occasionally exposed to such speculation and considered such blasphemy to imperil their lives and their eventual salvation. The Reformation in northern Europe saw the devaluation of visual depictions of the sacred, to be replaced with the chance to encounter the almighty primarily through the text. Such a transformation was neither smooth nor complete, and blasphemy could occur along the fault-lines where the older and newer emphases coexisted. Nonetheless, some aspects of popular belief transferred themselves seamlessly into modernized religious belief and practice. The idea of divine influence upon causality persisted, and Hervieu-Léger has argued that this is partly a reason for the persistence of popular attachment to Christianity in the West.[25] Such belief in divine intervention appeared in the actions of gamblers, soldiers, and sailors, as well as in the fear exhibited by those who were unwittingly made the audience for blasphemous utterance.

We can only speculate over whether future developments in the popular media may aid the capacity to offend and bring offence squarely into the homes

---

[24] Duboisson, *Western Construction of Religion*, 190.
[25] See Hervieu-Léger, *Religion as a Chain of Memory*, 72–3.

of the unsuspecting. The capacity for 'casual encounters' with objectionable material will clearly persist, but we must hope that the reaction to it will be proportional to the intention of those causing offence. Religion may feel it can be sophisticated, but so can satire and criticism of religion. Ultimately our ability to communicate adapts to the forms that we use with astonishing rapidity and surprising calmness. Nevertheless, an enduring theme of the history of censorship is suspicion of new communications media. So often restrictions and limitations follow such suspicions, sometimes rather to the detriment of innocent users and consumers.

In the first years of the new millennium it seems evident that the blasphemy industry is poised for significant growth. The door to this innovation has been opened by the assumptions that go with the concept of incitement to religious hatred. Whilst religion remains, at best, crudely defined, the capacity for offence and the feelings of the offended have been extended to new boundaries. If the retention of a blasphemy law placed a premium on the status of the offended, the developing harassment agendas takes this a stage further. This is confirmed by the failure of legislative bodies to remove blasphemy laws, even though incitement laws now exist.

Lastly, we should ponder precisely what the future holds for blasphemy's own relations with the sacred. Religion remains potent as a substitute for ideology, and as a building-block of identity to resist everything from unpopular laws to seemingly unstoppable phenomena like globalization. In this, many religious groups which associate their beliefs with species of identity are rejuvenating the ideal of religious community. This in turn is arguably reviving the passive blasphemy model, which in its earlier phase allowed communities of believers to determine the nature of language and utterance in public space. Events like *Jerry Springer: The Opera* have also rejuvenated the passive blasphemy model at the expense of the more usual actual active encounters of more recent years. The medieval conception of damage to the community through damage to the honour of God has here made a surprising comeback. As religious fundamentalists tore up the agendas of quietism and tolerance, blasphemy regained some of its power. This in part explains the complaints made by the numerous individuals who had not witnessed *Springer*. To know that their God had been lampooned in this way was enough. In some respects these communities also judged world events through the prism of divine providence. Such views have now returned, seeking to police thoughts and the nature of expression. Fundamentalists who claim ultimate protection for their beliefs and wish to see prohibitions upon even the production of challenging material are further reviving the passive model. In this, it becomes a blasphemy that the production of such material is even contemplated, echoing the medieval perception that blasphemous utterances should only be judged at face value. Such a concept of passive blasphemy arguably threatens art and expression which depend on irony, wit, metaphor, and allegory. Yet western society has not retreated from the idea that beliefs are beyond criticism, and this is clearly a culture war that will embroil the West in the near future.

For believers, religion draws upon stories of hope, of adversity, of comfort, and of resistance. But it has also provided the focus for struggle and hatred. This last observation is not explicitly to disparage religion, but to note how individuals and communities have used it. Whilst such attachment exists, the attempt to defend this core of the sacred means that blasphemy and its works will persist and remain part of the landscape. Since the law is now defending the individual within the community, we should also now consider that such individuals are starting to live in a post-tolerant society, as sensitivity and hurt are becoming more highly prized than pragmatism. Perhaps such a society might eventually alienate street and popular culture to such an extent that its subsequent rebellion will scare authority in a manner that Renaissance princes, judges, and burgomasters might recognize. Literary culture may also rediscover and glorify its ability to say the unthinkable—driving itself underground in a way resembling the French pre-Revolutionary philosophes and their trade in clandestine works.

Yet there may still be hope. The rediscovery of communal religious identity cannot simply pretend that the individualization of rights and opinions has not happened. We should thus endorse the words of Robert Ingersoll in arguing for a less contentious future: 'There is a law higher than men can make. The facts as they exist in this poor world—the absolute consequences of certain acts—they are above all. And this higher law is the breath of progress, the very outstretched wings of civilization, under which we enjoy the freedom we have. Keep that in your minds.'

Select Bibliography

ALDRED, G. A., *The Devil's Chaplin: The Story of the Rev. Robert Taylor, M.A. M.R.C.S.* (Glasgow, 1942).

ALPERT, MICHAEL, *Crypto-Judaism and the Spanish Inquisition* (New York, 2001).

An Association of Prayers against Blasphemy, Swearing and the Profanation of Sundays and Festivals, under the Patronage of St. Louis, King of France, Approved by the Archbishop of Tours. Translated from the French by Edward G. Kriwan Browne (London, 1847).

ANDERSON, MARY R., *Art in a Desacralized World: Nineteenth Century France and England* (Lanham, Md., 1984).

Anon., *An address to the public, from the Society for the Suppression of Vice, instituted in London, 1802, part I* (London, 1803).

—— *A Warning to Gamblers and Swearers in the awful death of Richard Parsons whose flesh rotted off his bones, agreeably to his impious wishes, when disputing at a geme of whist. . . . To which is added an affecting narrative of the death of Joseph Shepherd who was struck with a mortal disease in the same such manner* (London, 1814).

—— *The Constable's Assistant: Being a Compendium of the Duties and powers of Constables and Other Peace Officers; Chiefly as they relate to the Apprehending of Offenders, and the Laying of Informations before Magistrates,* 3rd edn with additions (London, 1818).

—— *The Report of the Proceedings of the Court of King's Bench, in the Guildhall, London, on the 12th, 13th, 14th and 15th days of October; Being the Mock Trials of Richard Carlile for Alleged Blasphemous Libels* (London, 1822).

APPIGNANESI L. and S. MAITLAND (eds.), *The Rushdie File* (London,1989).

ASAD, TALAL, 'Ethnography, Literature, and Politics: Some Readings and Uses of Salman Rushdie's *The Satanic Verses*', *Cultural Athropology,* 5:3 (Aug. 1990), 239–69.

—— 'Medieval Heresy: An Anthropological View', *Social History,* 11 (1986), 354–62.

ASTON, M. E., 'Lollardy and Sedition, 1381–1431', *Past & Present,* 17 (1960), 1–44.

ASTON, NIGEL, *Religion and Revolution in France 1780–1804* (Basingstoke, 2000).

BAELDE, M. R., *Studiën over Godslastering* (The Hague, 1935).

BANNER, STEWART, 'When Christianity Was Part of the Common Law', *Law and History Review,* 16:1 (Spring 1998), 27–62.

BARNARD, T. C., 'Reforming Irish Manners: The Religious Societies in Dublin During the 1690s', *Historical Journal,* 35:4 (Dec. 1992), 805–38.

BAUGH, L., *Imaging the Divine: Jesus and Christ-Figures in Film* (Kansas City, 1997).

BELMAS, ÉLIZABETH, 'La Monteé des blasphèmes', in J. Delumeau (ed.), *Injures et blasphèmes; Mentalités,* ii (Paris, 1989).

BENNETT, D. R. M., *Anthony Comstock: His Career of Cruelty and Crime,* Da Capo Press Reprint series (New York, 1971).

BERMAN, HAROLD J., 'The Origins of Historical Jurisprudence: Coke, Selden, Hale', *Yale Law Journal,* 103:7 (May 1994), 1651–738.

BESANT, ANNIE WOOD, *Blasphemy* (London, 1882).

BETTS, C. J., *Early Deism in France* (Kluwer, 1984).

BICKNOLL, ALEXANDER NOWELL EDMOND and G. ELD, *A word against swearers and blasphemers: Shewing the lawfulnesse of an oth, and how great a sinne it is to sweare falsely, vainely or rashly. In this edition purg'd of many faultes committed in former impressions* (London 1609).

BIDDLE, JOHN, *Gods glory vindicated and blasphemy confuted, being a brief and plain answer to that blasphemous book intituled, Twelve arguments against the deity of the Holy Ghost, written by Tho. Bidle, Master of Arts, and now burnt by speciall command from the Parliament on Wednesday the 8 of this present September: . . . wherein the arguments of the said book are set down together with proper answers thereto, and twelve anti-arguments proving the deity of the Holy Ghost* (London, 1647).

BLATT, MARTIN HENRY, *Free Love and Anarchism: The Biography of Ezra Heywood* (Chicago, 1989).

BLISS, MICHAEL, *The Word Made Flesh: Catholicism and Conflict in the Films of Martin Scorsese*, Filmmakers Series no. 45 (London, 1995).

BLOM-COOPER, LOUIS, *Blasphemy: An Ancient Wrong or a Modern Right?* (London, 1981).

BOSSY, JOHN, *Christianity in the West, 1400–1700* (Oxford, 1985).

BRADLAUGH, CHARLES, *Heresy, Its utility and Morality: A Plea and a Justification* (London, 1870).

—— *The Laws Relating to Blasphemy and Heresy* (London, 1878).

BRADLAUGH-BONNER, HYPATIA, *Penalties Upon Opinion, or some Records of the Laws of Heresy and Blasphemy* (London, 1934).

BRADNEY, A., *Religions, Rights and Laws* (London, 1993).

BRENNAN, THOMAS, *Public Drinking and Popular Culture in Eighteenth-Century Paris* (Princeton, 1988).

BROUN, HEYWOOD and MARGARET LEECH, *Anthony Comstock: Roundsman of the Lord* (New York, 1927).

BROWN, CALLUM, *The Death of Christian Britain* (London, 2001).

BROWN, PETER, *The Body and Society: Men, Women and Sexual Renunciation in Early Christianity* (London, 1988).

BROWN, PETER D. G., 'The Continuing Trials of Oskar Panizza: A Century of Artistic 24: Censorship in Germany Austria and Beyond', *German Studies Review*, 3 (Oct. 2001), 533–56.

BURKHOLDER, ROBERT E., 'Emerson, Kneeland, and the Divinity School Address', *American Literature*, 58:1 (Mar. 1986), 1–14.

BURLEIGH, MICHAEL, *Earthly Powers: Religion and Politics from the French Revolution to the Great War* (London, 2005).

BUTLER, I., *Religion in the Cinema* (New York, 1969).

BUTLER, JON, *Grant Wacker and Randall Balmer, Religion in American Life: A Short History* (Oxford, 2003).

BYNUM, C. W., 'Did the Twelfth Century Discover the Individual?', *Journal of Ecclesiastical History*, 31:1 (1980), 1–17.

CABANTOUS, ALAIN, *Blasphemy: Impious Speech in the West from the Seventeenth to the Nineteenth Century* (New York, 1998).

CAIRNS, JOHN W., 'Blackstone, an English Institutist: Legal Literature and the Rise of the Nation State', *Oxford Journal of Legal Studies*, 4:3 (Winter 1984), 318–60.

CALDER-MARSHALL, ARTHUR, *Lewd, Blasphemous and Obscene* (London, 1972).

CAMPBELL, G. A., *Strindberg* (London, 1933).

CARLILE, RICHARD, *A Letter to the Society for the Suppression of Vice, On their Malignant Efforts to Prevent A Free Enquiry After Truth and Reason* (London, 1819).

—— *Blasphemy [a Denial of the Charge of Blasphemy, Brought against Richard Carlile and Others.]* (London, 1821).

CHAPMAN, GRAHAM, JOHN CLEESE, TERRY GILLIAM, ERIC IDLE, TERRY JONES, and MICHAEL PALIN, *Monty Python's The Life of Brian* (London, 1979).

CHRISTIE, IAN, and DAVID THOMPSON (eds.), *Scorsese on Scorsese* (London, 2003).

CHRISTIN, OLIVIER, 'L'Iconoclaste et le blasphémateur au début du xvie siècle', in J. Delumeau (ed.), *Injures et blasphèmes; Mentalités,*ii (Paris, 1989).

CLIFFORD, B., *Blasphemous Reason: The 1797 Trial of Tom Paine's Age of Reason* (Hampton, 1993).

COBB, SANFORD, *The Rise of Religious Liberty in America* (New York 1902; 1968 edn).

COLEMAN, PETER, *Obscenity, Blasphemy Sedition* (Brisbane 1966).

COLMAN, BENJAMIN, *The Case of Satan's fiery Darts in Blasphemous Suggestions and Hellish Annoyances: As they were considered in several Sermons, Heretofore preach'd to the Congregation in Brattle-Street, Boston May 1711, and lately repeated to them May 1743* (Boston, 1744).

COMMAGER, HENRY STEELE, 'The Blasphemy of Abner Kneeland', *New England Quarterly* 8:1 (Mar. 1935), 29–41.

CONNELL, WILLIAM J. and GILES CONSTABLE, 'Sacrilege and Redemption in Renaissance Florence: The Case of Antonio Rinaldeschi', *Journal of the Warburg and Courtauld Institutes*, 61 (1998), 53–92.

COOKE, BILL and the Rationalist Press Association, *The Blasphemy Depot: A Hundred Years of the Rationalist Press Association* (London, 2003).

COWAN, BRIAN WILLIAM, 'Mr. Spectator and the Coffeehouse Public Sphere', *Eighteenth-Century Studies*, 37:3 (Spring 2004), 345–66.

COX, NEVILLE, *Blasphemy and the Law in Ireland, Irish Studies* (Lewiston, NY, 2000).

CRESSY, DAVID, *Agnes Bowker's Cat* (Oxford, 2000).

DALZELL, GEORGE W., *Benefit of Clergy in America* (Winston–Salem, 1955).

DARNTON, ROBERT, *The Corpus of Clandestine Literature in France 1769–1789* (New York, 1995).

—— 'Trade in the Taboo: The Life of a Clandestine Book Dealer in Pre-Revolutionary France', in Paul J. Korshin (ed.), *The Widening Circle: Essays on the Circulation of Literature in Eighteenth-Century Europe* (Philadelphia, 1976).

DASTON, L. and K. PARK, *Wonders and the Order of Nature* (New York, 1998).

DAVIE, GRACE, *Religion in Britain since 1945* (Oxford, 1994).

DEAN, TREVOR, *Crime in Medieval Society* (London, 2001).

DELUMEAU, JEAN, *Sin and Fear: The Emergence of a Western Guilt Culture 13th–18th Centuries* (New York, 1990).

DIEHL, PETER D., 'Overcoming Reluctance to Prosecute Heresy in Thirteenth Century Italy', in Scott L. Waugh and Peter D. Diehl (eds.), *Christendom and its Discontents: Exclusion, Persecution and Rebellion 1000–1500* (Cambridge 1996).

DUBOISSON, DANIEL, *The Western Construction of Religion: Myths, Knowledge and Ideology*, trs. William Sayers (London, 2003).

DUINDAM, JEROEN, *Myths of Power* (Amsterdam, 1995).

DÜLMEN, RICHARD VAN, *Theatre of Horror: Crime and Punishment in Early Modern Germany*, trs. Elisabeth Neu (Cambridge, 1990).

DUNLAP, ANDREW, *A Speech delivered before the Municipal Court of the City of Boston in defence of Abner Kneeland on an Indictment for Blasphemy, January Term 1834* (Boston, 1834).

DWORKIN, RONALD, *A Bill of Rights for Britain: Why British Liberty Needs Protecting* (London, 1990).

EATON, DANIEL ISAAC et al., *Trial of Mr. Daniel Isaac Eaton, for publishing the third and last part of Paine's Age of Reason, before Lord Ellenborough, in the Court of King's Bench, Guildhall, March 6, 1812: containing the whole of his defence, and Mr. Prince Smith's speech in mitigation of punishment* (London, 1812).

EDWARDS, JOHN, 'Religious Faith and Doubt in Late Medieval Spain: Soria circa 1450–1500', *Past & Present*, 120 (1988), 3–25.

EISNER, MANUEL, 'Modernization, Self-control and Lethal Violence: The Long-term Dynamics of European Homicide rates in Theoretical Perspective', *British Journal of Criminology*, 41 (2001), 618–38.

ELIAS, NORBERT, *The Court Society* (Oxford, 1983).

—— *The Civilising Process* (rev. edn), trs. Edmund Jephcott (Oxford, 2005).

EMERSON, ROGER, L., 'Latitudinarianism and the English Deists', in J. A. Leo Lemay (ed.), *Deism, Masonry, and the Enlightenment* (Newark, 1987), 19–48.

EPSTEIN, JAMES, *Radical Expression: Political Language, Ritual, and Symbol in England, 1790–1850* (Oxford, 1994).

ESTES, JAMES M., 'Johannes Brenz and the Problem of Ecclesiastical Discipline', *Church History*, 41:4 (Dec. 1972), 464–79.

EVANS, RICHARD, *Tales From the German Underworld* (New Heaven, 1998).

FABRE-VASSAS, C., *The Singular Beast: Jews, Christians and the Pig* (New York, 1997).

FERNANDES-DIAS, MARIA SUZETTE, 'Les Fées ont Soif: Feminist, Iconoclastic or Blasphemous', unpublished paper, Negotiating the Sacred II: Blasphemy and Sacrilege in the Arts, 3/11/05. Centre for Cross-Cultural Research, Australian National University.

FEBVRE, LUCIEN, *The Problem of Unbelief in the Sixteenth Century: The Religion of Rabelais*, v. Beatrice Gottlieb (Cambridge, 1982).

FERLING, JOHN, *Setting the World Ablaze: Washington, Adams, Jefferson and the American Revolution* (Oxford, 2000).

FLETCHER, JONATHAN, *Violence and Civilisation: An Introduction to the Work of Norbert Elias* (Cambridge, 1997).

FLYNN, MAUREEN, 'Blasphemy and the Play of Anger in Sixteenth Century Spain', *Past & Present*, 149 (1995), 29–56.

—— 'Taming Anger's Daughters: New Treatment for Emotional Problems in Renaissance Spain', *Renaissance Quarterly*, 51:3 (1998), 864–86.

FOOTE, G. W., *Blasphemy No Crime. The Whole Question Treated Historically. Legally, Theologically, and Morally, With Special reference to the Prosecution of the 'Freethinker'* (London, 1882).

—— *Defence of Free Speech: Being a three hours Address to the Jury in the court of Queen's Bench Before Lord Coleridge on April 24ᵗʰ, 1883* (London, 1932 edn.).

—— *Full Report of the Trial of G. W. Foote and W. J. Ramsey for Blasphemy* (London, 1883).

—— *Prisoner for Blasphemy* (London, 1886).

—— *The Flowers of Freethought* (London, 1894).

FOSTER, STEPHEN, *Notes from the Caroline Underground: Alexander Leighton, the Puritan*

Triumvirate and the Laudian Reaction to Nonconformity, Studies in British History and Culture, Vol. 6 (Hamden, Conn., 1978).

—— *The Long Argument* (Williamsburg, 1991).

FOYSTER, ELIZABETH, 'Creating a Veil of Silence? Politeness and Marital Violence in the English Household, *Transactions of the Royal Historical Society*, 12 (2002).

FRASER, P., *Images of the Passion: The Sacramental Mode in Film* (Westport, Conn., 1998).

FRENCH, RODERICK S., 'Liberation from Man and God in Boston: Abner Kneeland's Freethought Campaign, 1830–1839', *American Quarterly*, 32:2 (Summer 1980), 202–21.

FRIEDMAN, LAWRENCE S., *The Cinema of Martin Scorsese* (Oxford, 1997).

FROST, J. WILLIAM, *A Perfect Freedom: Religious Liberty in Pennsylvania* (Cambridge, 1990).

GAILHARD, J., *The Blasphemous Socinian Heresie Disproved and Confuted* (London, 1697).

GASKIN, RICHARD, 'Changes in the Criminal law in 18th Century Connecticut', *American Journal of Legal History*, 25:4 (Oct. 1998), 309–42.

GERARDI, DAVID F., 'Zephaniah Swift and Connecticut's Standing Order: Skepticism, Conservatism, and Religious Liberty in the Early Republic', *New England Quarterly*, 67:2 (Jan. 1994), 234–56.

GINZBERG, LORI D., 'The Hearts of your readers will shudder': Fanny Wright, Infidelity and American Freethought', *American Quarterly*, 46:2 (June 1994), 195–226.

GOLDSTEIN, ROBERT JUSTIN, *Political Censorship of the Arts and the Press in Nineteenth-Century Europe* (Basingstoke, 1989).

GORDON, COLIN (ed.), *Michel Foucault: Truth and Power. Power/Knowledge: Selected Interviews and Other Writings 1972–1977* (Brighton, 1980).

GORDON, SARAH BARRINGER, 'Blasphemy and the Law of Religious Liberty in Nineteenth Century America', *American Quarterly*, 52:4 (Dec. 2000), 682–19.

GRAHAM, RUTH, 'The Revolutionary Bishops and the Philosophes', *Eighteenth Century Studies*, 16:2 (Winter 1982–3), 117–40.

HACKWOOD, F. M., *William Hone: His Life and Times* (London 1912).

HARLING, PHILIP, 'The Law of Libel and the Limits of Repression, 1790–1832', *Historical Journal*, 44:1 (2001), 107–34.

HAYES, DAWN MARIE, *Body and Sacred Place in Medieval Europe, 1100–1398* (London, 2003).

HAYTON, DAVID 'Moral Reform and Country Politics in the Late Seventeenth Century House of Commons', *Past & Present*, 128 (Aug. 1990), 48–91.

HEINS, MARJORIE, *Sex, Sin, and Blasphemy: A Guide to America's Censorship Wars* (New York, 1993).

HERRICK, JAMES A., 'The Rhetorical Career of Thomas Woolston: A Radical Challenges the Rules of Discourse', *Quarterly Journal of Speech*, 78 (1992), 296–316.

HERVIEU-LÉGER, DANIÈLE, *Religion as a Chain of Memory*, tr. Simon Lee (Oxford, 2000).

HERZFELD, MICHAEL, 'The Significance of the Insignificant: Blasphemy as Ideology', *Man*, NS 19:4 (Dec. 1984), 653–64.

HEWISON, ROBERT, *Irreverence, Scurrility, Profanity and Licentious Abuse: Monty Python, the Case Against* (London, 1981).

HILDESHEIM, FRANÇOISE, 'La Répression du blasphème au XVIIIe siècle', in J. Delumeau (ed.), *Injures et blasphèmes; Mentalités*, ii (Paris, 1989), 63–82.

HOLE, ROBERT, *Pulpits, Politics and Public Order in England 1760–1832* (Cambridge, 1989).

HOLLIS, P., *The Pauper Press: A Study of Working Class Radicalism of the 1830s* (Oxford, 1970).

HOLMES, GEOFFREY, 'The Sacheverell Riots: The Crowd and the Church in Early Eighteenth-century London', *Past & Present*, 72 (1976), 55–85.

HOLYOAKE, GEORGE JACOB, *The Last Trial for Alleged Atheism in England: A Fragment of an Autobiography* (London, 1850).

HONE, WILLIAM, *The Third Trial of William Hone on an ex-officio information at Guildhall London December 20, 1817 before Lord Ellenborough and a special Jury, for publishing a parody of the Athanasian Creed*, 3rd edn. (London, 1818).

HORODWICH, ELIZABETH, 'Civic Identity and the Control of Blasphemy in Sixteenth-Century Venice', *Past & Present*, 181 (2003), 3–33.

HOROWITZ, HELEN, *Rereading Sex: Battles Over Sexual Knowledge and Suppression in Nineteenth Century America* (New York, 2003).

HOUSLEY, NORMAN, 'Politics and Heresy in Italy: Anti-heretical Crusades, Orders and Confraternities, 1200–1500', *Journal of Ecclesiastical History*, 33:2 (1982), 193–208.

INGERSOLL, ROBERT GREEN, *The Trial of C. B. Reynolds: Robert G. Ingersoll's Address to the Jury*, American Atheist Press edn. (Austin, Tex., 1986).

Interights and Article 19, *Blasphemy and Film Censorship: Submission to the European Court of Human Rights in Respect of Nigel Wingrove v. The United Kingdom* (1995).

ISAACS, TINA, 'The Anglican Hierarchy and the Reformation of Manners 1688–1738', *Journal of Ecclesiastical History*, 33:3 (July 1982), 391–411.

JELAVICH, PETER, 'The Censorship of Literary Naturalism, 1890–1895: Bavaria', *Central European History*, 18:3/4 1985, 344–59.

JENNER, THOMAS, *Quakerism Anatomised and Confuted* (London, 1670).

JOHNSON, Eric A. and ERIC H. MONKKONEN (eds.), *The Civilisation of Crime: Violence in Town and Country since the Middle Ages* (Urbana, Ill., 1996).

JONES, PETER, 'Blasphemy, Offensiveness and the Law', *British Journal of Political Science*, 10:2 (1980), 129–48.

KARANT-NUNN, SUSAN C., 'Neoclericalism and Anticlericalism in Saxony 1555–1675', *Journal of Interdisciplinary History*, 24:4 (Spring 1994), 615–37.

KELLY, HENRY ANSGAR, 'Inquisition and the Prosecution of Heresy: Misconceptions and Abuses', in *Inquisitions and Other Trials in the Medieval West* (Aldershot, 2001).

KEMENY, P. C., 'Power, Ridicule, and the Destruction of Religious Moral Reform Politics in the 1920s', in C. Smith (ed.), *The Secular Revolution: Power, Interests, and Conflict in the Secularisation of American Public Life* (Berkeley, 2003), 216–68.

KENNY, COURTNEY, 'The Evolution of the Law of Blasphemy', *Cambridge Law Journal*, 1 (1922), 127–42.

KNEELAND, ABNER, *A Review of the Trial, Conviction, And Final imprisonment in the Common Jail of the County of Suffolk of Abner Kneeland for the alleged crime of blasphemy* (Boston, 1838).

—— *Speech of Abner Kneeland: Delivered before the Full Bench of Judges of the Supreme Court, in His Own Defence, for the Alleged Crime of Blasphemy: Law Term, March 8, 1836* (Boston, 1836).

KORS, ALAN CHARLES, *Atheism in France 1650–1729*, Vol. 1: *The Orthodox Sources of Disbelief* (Princeton 1990).

KREITZER, L., *Gospel Images in Fiction and Film: On Reversing the Hermenutic Flow* (London, 2002).

KRIEKEN, ROBERT VAN, *Norbert Elias* (London, 1988).

LAGARD SMITH, F., *Blasphemy and the Battle for Faith* (London, 1990).

LAMBERT, M., *Medieval Heresy: Popular Movements from the Gregorian Reform to the Reformation* (Oxford,1992).

LANSING, CAROL, *Power and Purity: Cathar Heresy in Medieval Italy* (Oxford 1998).

LAWTON, DAVID, *Blasphemy* (London, 1993).

LEAR, FLOYD SEYWARD, 'Blasphemy in the Lex Romana Curiensis', *Speculum*, 6:3 (July 1931), 445–59.

LELAND, JOHN, *A View of Principal Deistical Writers that have appeared in the Last and Present Century and some account of the answers that have been published against them* (London 1754; 1837 edn).

LENNSTRAND, VIKTOR, *The God Idea. A lecture, for delivering which the author was sentenced to six months imprisonment for blasphemy in Sweden*. Translated from the Swedish. With an Introduction by J. M. Wheeler (London, 1890).

LEVY, LEONARD, *Blasphemy in Massachusetts: Freedom of Conscience and the Abner Kneeland Case, A Documentary Record* (New York, 1973).

—— 'Jefferson as a Civil Libertarian', in *Constitutional Opinions: Aspects of the Bill of Rights* (Oxford 1986), 171–92.

—— 'Quaker Blasphemy and Toleration', in *Constitutional Opinions: Aspects of the Bill of Rights* (Oxford, 1986), 40–71.

—— *Blasphemy: Verbal Offense Against the Sacred from Moses to Salman Rushdie* (New York, 1993).

LINDLOF, THOMAS R., 'The Passionate Audience: Community Inscriptions of the *Last Temptation of Christ*', in Daniel A. Stout and Judith Buddenbaum (eds.), *Religion and Mass Media: Audiences and Adaptations* (London, 1996), 148–167.

LINTON, W. J., *James Watson: A Memoir of the Days of the Fight for a Free Press in England and of the Agitation for the People's Charter* (Manchester, 1880).

LOETZ, FRANCISCA, 'How To Do Things With God: Blasphemy in Early Modern Switzerland', in Mary Lindemann (ed.), *Ways of Knowing; Ten Interdisciplinary Essays* (Leiden, 2004), 137–151.

LUDMAN, BARBARA *et al.* (eds.), Limits of Liberty: *Obscenity, Blasphemy and Hate Speech: How Much Can We Tolerate?* (Cape Town 1993).

LYON, EILEEN GROTH, *Politicians in the Pulpit: Christian Radicalism from the Fall of the Bastille to the Disintegration of Chartism* (Aldershot, 1999).

McCALL, DOUGLAS L., *Monty Python* (London, 1991).

McCALMAN, I. D., 'Popular Radicalism and Free-Thought in Early Nineteenth Century England: A Study of Richard Carlile and His Followers, 1815–32' thesis MA, Australian, National University (1975).

—— *Radical Underworld: Prophets, Revolutionaries, and Pornographers in London, 1795–1840* (Oxford, 1993).

—— 'Ultra-Radicalism and Convivial Debating Clubs in London, 1795–1838', *English Historical Review*, 102 (1987), 309–33.

McCalman, I. D., 'Unrespectable Radicalism: Infidels and Pornography in Early Nineteenth Century London Movement', *Past & Present*, 104 (1984), 74–110.

MacCulloch, Diarmaid, *Reformation: Europe's House Divided 1490–1700* (London, 2003).

McGrath, Alistair, *The Twilight of Atheism* (London, 2004).

McLaren, Angus, 'Contraception and the Working Classes: The Social Ideology of the English Birth Control Movement in its Early Years', *Comparative Studies in Society and History*, 18:2 (Apr. 1976), 236–51.

Maher, G., 'Blasphemy in Scots Law', *Scots Law Times* (1977), 260.

Marnell, William H., *The First Amendment* (New York, 1964).

Marsh, Joss Lutz, '"Bibliolatry" and "Bible Smashing": G. W. Foote, George Meredith, and the Heretic Trope of the Book', *Victorian Studies*, 34:3, 315–36.

—— *Word Crimes: Blasphemy, Culture, and Literature in Nineteenth-Century England* (Chicago and London, 1998).

Marshall, John, *John Locke, Toleration and Early Enlightenment Culture* (Cambridge, 2006).

Mennell, Stephen, *Norbert Elias: Civilization and the Human Self Image* (Oxford, 1989).

Merrill, Louise Taylor, 'The Puritan Policeman', *American Sociological Review*, 10:6 (Dec. 1945), 766–76.

Meyer, Michael, *Strindberg* (Oxford, 1987).

Mitchell, Alex F. and John Struthers (eds.), *Minutes of the Westminster Assembly of Divines* (Edinburgh, 1874).

Mockus, Michael X. and Theodore Schroeder, *Constitutional Free Speech Defined and Defended in an Unfinished Argument in a Case of Blasphemy (against Michael X. Mockus)* (New York, 1919).

Moehlman, C. H., *The American Constitution and Religion* (Berne, Ind., 1938).

Moore, R. I., 'Popular Violence and Popular, Heresy in Western Europe, c. 1000–1179', in W. J. Shiels (ed.), *Persecution and Toleration, Studies in Church History*, Vol. 21 (Oxford, 1984), 43–50.

—— *The Birth of Popular Heresy* (London, 1975).

—— *The Formation of a Persecuting Society* (Oxford, 1987).

Mortensen, Reid 'Art, Expression and the Offended Believer', in Rex Ahdar (ed.), *Law and Religion* (Aldershot, 2000), 181–97.

Moss, Jane, 'Les Folles Du Québec: The Theme of Madness in Québec's Women's Theatre', *French Review*, 57:5 (Apr. 1984), 617–24.

Nash, David, *Blasphemy in Modern Britain* (Aldershot, 1999).

—— 'Laughing at the Almighty', in Jennifer Wagner Lawlor (ed.), *The Victorian Comic Spirit* (Aldershot, 2000), 43–66.

—— ' "Look in her face and Lose thy dread of dying": The Ideological Importance of Death to the Secularist Community in Nineteenth Century Britain', *Journal of Religious History*, 19:2 (Dec. 1995), 158–80.

—— *Secularism, Art and Freedom* (London, 1992).

Naylor, James, *A Discovery of the Beast Got into the Seat of the False Prophet . . .* (London, 1655).

Nelson, J., 'Society, Theodicy and the Origins of Heresy: Towards a Reassessment of the Medieval Evidence', in D. Baker (ed.), *Schism, Heresy and Religious Protest* (Cambridge, 1972).

NICHOLLS, DAVID J., 'The Nature of Popular Heresy in France, 1520–1542', *Historical Journal*, 26:2 (June 1983), 261–75.

Nokes, G. D., *A History of the Crime of Blasphemy* (London, 1928).

O'HIGGINS, PAUL, 'Blasphemy in Irish Law', *Modern Law Review*, 23:2 (Mar. 1960), 151–66.

PACK, ERNEST, *The Parson's Doom* (Bradford, Freethought Socialist League, n.d.).

—— *The Trial and Imprisonment of J. W. Gott for Blasphemy* (Bradford, Freethought Socialist League, 1912).

PACKARD GEORGE, 'The Administration of Justice in the Lake Michigan Wilderness', *Michigan Law Review*, 17:5 (Mar. 1919), 382–405.

PALMER, ELIHU, *A Report of the Trial of James Watson: For Having Sold a Copy of Palmer's Principles of Nature, at the Shop of Mr. Carlile, 201, Strand . . . .* (London, 1825).

PALMER, ROBERT R., *Catholics and Unbelievers in Eighteenth Century France* (Princeton, 1939).

PARKER, CHARLES, 'The Moral Agency and Moral Autonomy of Church Folk in the Dutch Reformed Church of Delft 1580–1620', *Journal of Ecclesiastical History*, 48:1 (1997), 44–70.

PARKER, SAMUEL D., *Report of the Arguments of the Attorney of the Commonwealth at the Trials of Abner Kneeland for Blasphemy, in the Municipal and Supreme Courts in Boston, January and May 1834* (Boston, 1834).

PAVELIN, A., *Fifty Religious Films* (London, 1990).

PERRY, G., *The Life of Python* (London, 1994).

PESTANA, CARLA GARDINA, 'The Social World of Salem: William King's 1681 Blasphemy Trial', *American Quarterly*, 41:2 (June 1989), 308–27.

PFEFFER, LEO, *Church, State and Freedom* (Boston, 1967 edn.).

PICKWORTH, HENRY, *A Charge of Error, Heresy etc . . . and offered to be proved against the most noted leaders &c of the People called Quakers* (London, 1716).

POPKIN, RICHARD, *The History of Scepticism from Erasmus to Descartes* (Assen, 1964).

POSTLES, DAVID, 'Penance and the Market Place: A Reformation Dialogue with the Medieval Church (c.1250–1600)', *Journal of Ecclesiastical History*, 54:3 (2003), 441–68.

POTTER, DENNIS, *Son of Man* (Harmondsworth, 1971).

RADZINOWICZ, L., *Sir James Fitzjames Stephen 1829–1894* (London, 1957).

REITH, GERDA, *The Age of Chance: Gambling in Western Culture* (London, 1999).

ROBIN RILEY, *Film, Faith, and Cultural Conflict: 'The Case of Martin Scorsese's The Last Temptation of Christ'* (London, 2003).

RIVERS, A. J., *Blasphemy Law in the Secular State, Cambridge Papers Towards a Biblical Mind*, 1:4 (Stapleford, 1992).

ROACHE, ANDREW P., *The Devil's World: Heresy and Society 1100–1300* (Harlow, 2005).

ROBERTS, M. J. D., 'Making Victorian Morals? The Society for the Suppression of Vice and its Critics 1802–1886', *Historical Studies*, 21:157–73 (1984).

ROBERTSON, GEOFFREY, *The Justice Game* (London, 1999).

ROBILLIARD, ST JOHN A. *Religion and the Law: Religious Liberty in Modern English Law* (Manchester, 1984).

E. J. DE, ROO, *Godslastering* (Deventer, 1970).

ROOYEN, J. C. W. VAN *Censorship in South Africa* (Cape Town, 1987).

ROYLE, EDWARD *Victorian Infidels* (Manchester, 1974).

ROYLE, E., *Radicals, Secularists and Republicans: Popular Freethought in Britain, 1866–1915* (Manchester, 1980).

RUTHVEN, M., *A Satanic Affair: Salman Rushdie and the Wrath of Islam* (London, 1990).

SAUER, EBERHARD, *The Archaeology of Religious Hatred in the Roman and Early Medieval World* (Stroud, 2003).

SAWYER, JEFFREY K., ' "Benefit of clergy" in Maryland and Virginia', *American Journal of Legal History*, 34:1 (Jan. 1990), 49–6.

SCHLEGEL, DOROTHY B., *Shaftesbury and the French Deists* (Chapel Hill, Nebr., 1956).

SCHROEDER, THEODORE, *Constitutional Free Speech Defined and Defended in an Unfinished argument in a case of Blasphemy* (New York, Free Speech League, 1919; De Capo Press edn, 1970).

—— *Law of Blasphemy: The Modern View Exhibited in Model Instructions to a Jury* (New York, Free Speech League, 1919).

SCHULMAN, FRANK, *'Blasphemous and Wicked' The Unitarian Struggle for Equality 1813–1844.* (Oxford, 1997).

SCHWERHOFF, GERD, *Zungen wie Schwerter: Blasphemie in alteuropäischen Gesellschaften 1200–1650* (Konstanz, 2005).

SEARS, Hal D., *The Sex Radicals: Free Love in High Victorian America* (Kansas City, 1977).

SLAUGHTER, M. M., 'The Salman Rushdie Affair: Apostasy, Honor, and Freedom of Speech', *Virginia Law Review*, 79:1 (Feb. 1993), 153–204.

SMART, BARRY, *Michel Foucault* (London, 1985).

SMITH, OLIVIA, *The Politics of Language, 1791–1819* (Oxford, 1984).

SOMAN, ALFRED, 'Press, Pulpit and Censorship in France Before Richelieu', *Proceedings of the American Philosophical Society*, 120:6 (Dec. 1976), 439–463.

SPRIGGE, ELIZABETH, *The Strange Life of August Strindberg* (London, 1949).

STARK, GARY, 'The Censorship of Literary Naturalism, 1885–1895: Prussia and Saxony', *Central European History*, 18:3 1989 326–43.

—— 'Trials and Tribulations: Authors' Responses to Censorship in Imperial Germany, 1885–1914', *German Studies Review*, 12:3 (Oct. 1989), 447–68.

STEPHENS, JOHN N., 'Heresy in Medieval and Renaissance Florence', *Past & Present*, 54 (1972), 25–60.

STOYANOV, YURI, The *Hidden Tradition in Europe: The Secret History of Medieval Christian Heresy* (Harmondsworth, 1994).

SUTHERLAND, N. M., 'Persecution and Toleration in Reformation Europe', in W. J. Shiels (ed.), *Persecution and Toleration: Studies in Church History*, Vol. 21 (Oxford, 1984), 153–62.

SWANCARA, FRANK, *Obstruction of Justice By Religion* (Denver, Colo., 1936).

SWEET, WILLIAM, WARREN *Religion in Colonial America* (New York, 1943).

TAYLOR, ROBERT, *The Devil's Pulpit* (London, 1831).

THOMAS, DONALD, *A Long Time Burning: The History of Literary Censorship in England* (London, 1969)

TIPTON, BAIRD, 'A Dark Side of Seventeenth-Century English Protestantism: The Sin Against the Holy Ghost', *Harvard Theological Review*, 77:3/4 (July–Oct. 1984).

—— *Piety and the Professions: Sir John Taylor Coleridge and His Sons* (New York, 1987).

TRAVIS, ALAN, *Bound and Gagged: A Secret History of Obscenity* (London, 2000).

TRUMBULL, CHARLES GALLAUDET, *Anthony Comstock, Fighter* (New York, 1913).

TURNER, WILLIAM, *Compleat History of the Most Remarkable Providences* (London, 1697), Part II.

VILLA-FLORES, JAVIER, 'On Divine Persecution: Blasphemy and Gambling in New Spain,' in Susan Schroeder and Stafford Poole (eds.), *Religion and Society in Colonial Mexico* (New Mexico, forthcoming).

WADE, IRA, *The Clandestine Organisation and Diffusion of Philosophic Ideas in France from 1700 to 1750* (Princeton, 1938).

WALKER, JONATHAN, 'Gambling and Venetian Noblemen c1500–1700', *Past & Present*, 162 (1999), 28–69.

WALSHAM, ALEX, *Providence in early modern England* (Oxford, 1999).

WALTERS, KERRY S., *Rational Infidels: The American Deists* (Durango, Colo., 1992).

WATT, JEFFREY R., 'The Reception of the Reformation in Valangin, Switzerland, 1547–1588', *Sixteenth Century Journal*, 20:1 (Spring 1989), 89–104.

WAY, H. FRANK 'The Death of the Christian Nation: The Judiciary and Church–State Relations', *Church and State*, 509 (1987), 509–29.

WEBSTER, RICHARD, *A Brief History of Blasphemy: Liberalism, Censorship and 'The Satanic Verses'* (Southwold, 1990).

WEIS, RENÉ, *The Yellow Cross: The Story of the Last Cathars* (Harmondsworth, 2000).

WICKWAR, W. H., *The Struggle for the Freedom of the Press, 1819–32.* (London, 1928).

—— *The War of the Unstamped* (Ithaca, NY, 1969).

WIENER, JOEL, *Radicalism and Freethought in Nineteenth-Century Britain: The Life of Richard Carlile* (Westport, Conn., 1983).

WHITEHOUSE, MARY, *Quite Contrary* (London, 1988).

WHITELOCKE, BULSTRODE, *The Charge to the Grand-Jury, And other juries of the County of Middlesex at the General Quarter Session of the Peace, held, April 21st at Westminster Hall.* (London, 1718).

—— *The Second Charge to the Grand-Jury, And other juries of the County of Middlesex at the General Quarter Session of the Peace, held, April 21st at Westminster Hall* (London, 1718).

WOLKOVICH, WILLIAM, *Bay State 'Blue' Laws and Bimba* (Brockton, 1975).

WOODWARD, JOSIAH, *A Disswasive from Gaming* (London, 1707).

BLAIR, WORDEN, 'Toleration and the English Protectorate', in W. J. Shiels (ed.), *Persecution and Toleration: Studies in Church History*, Vol. 21, (Oxford, 1984), 199–233.

WRIGHT, SUSANNAH, RICHARD CARLILE, and Society for the Suppression of Vice, *Report of the Trial of Mrs. Susannah Wright, for Publishing, in His Shop, the Writings and Correspondences of R. Carlile: Before Chief Justice Abbott, and a Special Jury, in the Court of King's Bench, Guildhall, London, on Monday, July 8, 1822. Indictment at the Instance of the Society for the Suppression of Vice* (London 1822).

Index